Enterprise Architecture
and
New Generation Information Systems

Enterprise Architecture
—— and ——
New Generation Information Systems

Dimitris N. Chorafas

ST. LUCIE PRESS

A CRC Press Company

Boca Raton London New York Washington, D.C.

Library of Congress Cataloging-in-Publication Data

Chorafas, Dimitris N.
   Enterprise architecture and new generation information systems / Dimitris N. Chorafas.
      p. cm.
   Includes bibliographical references and index.
   ISBN 1-57444-317-8 (alk. paper)
   1. Management information systems. 2. System design. I. Title.

T58.6 .C45 2001
658.4′038′011—dc21   2001048503
                                                              CIP
         Catalog record is available from the Library of Congress

Visit the CRC Press Web site at www.crcpress.com

© 2002 by CRC Press LLC
St. Lucie Press is an imprint of CRC Press LLC

No claim to original U.S. Government works
International Standard Book Number 1-57444-317-8
Library of Congress Card Number 2001048503
Printed in the United States of America   2 3 4 5 6 7 8 9 0
Printed on acid-free paper

PREFACE

Written for trained professionals in business, industry, government, and education, as well as for graduate students and researchers, this book approaches the subject of *enterprise architecture* and the best applications of current technology from many viewpoints. Producers, consumers, designers, and end users are considered, as is practical everyday implementation of advanced technology from both entrepreneurial and academic perspectives.

Designing the proper network and using it to integrate the computers and communications resources of our enterprise is a demanding task. It means, first and foremost, having an architectural concept. It also calls for becoming familiar with hundreds of suppliers of hardware and software, including network switching, transmission, management, and maintenance gear, as well as of methods and techniques for system integration.

The primary role of an *enterprise architecture* is to tie together all components into one aggregate; define the functions to be supported, including their tolerances, their resource requirements and their timing; answer enduser needs with precision, but also in the most cost effective manner. The enterprise architecture incorporates the protocols under which the different components must operate, as well as the interfaces — including user interfaces. On the whole, this must follow open architectural principles, providing compatibility between systems and devices procured from different vendors but working together seamlessly.

This text helps to understand the issues and interpret the significance of changes underway so that interpretation can become a liaison agent. Both policy and technical issues are considered. The 16 chapters present what needs to be known about effective use of technological resources currently at our disposal or available in the next couple of years.

A practical, hands-on approach has been chosen because, as leaders of industry know, the market is always forcing us to look at the best way to stay close to state of the art, if not somewhat ahead of it. This permits us to serve our customers and respond to their needs in the best possible way. We should also appreciate, however, that to provide the best products and services at competitive prices, we have to organize our company in a way that is customer-oriented rather than simply product-based.

Customer-oriented developments must be technologically supported through open standards and must be architectured. This is the message of Section I, which concentrates on "next generation" information systems technology. Years ago, when systems architectures were designed, they were made to serve hierarchical computer networks supported by a vendor's own software. This is a concept which now belongs to the Paleolithic age. A modern enterprise architecture is primarily designed by the user organization to serve its particular environment cost-effectively.

Chapters 1 to 6 present new developments in enterprise architecture. They outline the methodology, systems, and materials that will dominate the future. They also make the point that technology helps the company to reposition and reinvent itself in the market, but only when it is properly used. Therefore, the enterprise architecture we design should have the broad perspective of our business operations. It should cover the needs of senior managers and professionals; it should not be limited to transactions, as many current projects tend to be.

The theme of Section II is that of future breakthroughs, which start their systems impact today. Chapters 7 to 11 review some of the most promising projects, the methods and tools which they use, and their projected deliverables. Also, what can be achieved through new systems designs and an improved methodology, such as intelligent location-independent computing and concurrent engineering, are addressed.

There are reasons why Section III asks, "Is the Internet the 21st century's answer to an enterprise architecture?" In recent years, the need to follow a customer-based strategy has been amplified by the Internet economy and its rapid growth. What this means to the user, plus the need for security, is the message conveyed by Chapters 12 to 16.

The World Wide Web entered the business-to-consumer (B2C) relationship in 1993, and became the most diffused any-to-any network in history. Five years down the line, a study by the University of Texas found that, in 1998, the Internet economy in the U.S. generated over $300 billion in revenue and was responsible for more than 1.2 million jobs. Since then there has been another major leap forward. In less than a decade, the Internet economy already rivals the size of century-old sectors such as autos, energy, and communications. Milestones that took ages to achieve in the aftermath of the Industrial Revolution are now reached at a staggering pace, which most companies find difficult to follow.

One of the peculiarities of the Internet is that it emphasizes the need for cooperation while working in a business-to-business (B2B) environment even between companies that compete with each other. No company really knows the virtual market space deeply and inclusively enough; therefore, synergy is necessary to set the new economy's perspectives. This has dire consequences in engineering, manufacturing, merchandising, and finance.

A premise of the new economy is that we have not yet seen the biggest changes at all. On this basis, Chapter 1 presents benefits and challenges expected from a modern enterprise architecture. It explains why the market rewards companies that have a cogent enterprise strategy, reviews developing business opportunities, explains why rapid innovation requires frequent reviews of strategic decisions, and suggests that, while technology costs are dropping, technology risks are increasing.

The mission of Chapter 2 is to define the right enterprise architecture and to assure that its technical features answer the company's business needs. It also makes a case for open architectural standards. Chapter 3 offers reasons why technology repositions the organization in a competitive market. It does so at three levels of reference: policy formation, command and control, and infrastructural base.

What should the information technology strategy of the organization be? Chapter 4 answers this query by examining information technology (IT) policies which have paid dividends. It also provides a case study on how a company can reinvent itself through innovative solutions. Chapter 5 follows up on this by suggesting ways and means for revamping the technological infrastructure of a modern industrial enterprise. It also explains why this is necessary and how to go about such a demanding mission.

Chapter 6 completes Section I by discussing some of the leading-edge projects in IT; for instance, the drive for better client focus, the not-yet-successful effort to cut down the paper jungle misjudgments about third-generation mobile telephony licenses (to the tune of more than a quarter of a trillion dollars), and research on nanoscale engineering which might take more than a decade to be realized. Whether they succeed or fail, all these projects have an impact on enterprise architecture.

Chapter 7 presents MIT's Intelligent Environment Project (Project Oxygen). This example includes the tools and the background needed to promote imaginative new departures in man–machine communication. Even the most advanced solutions, however, must fit within a business architecture permitting integration of new technology with existing applications, and making it possible to get the most out of competitive and legacy software. To this subject, Chapter 8 adds the flavor of practical implementation by addressing applications using an intelligent environ-ment advantageously.

Issues relating to the use of knowledge artifacts within the realm of nomadic computing, filtering, and patterning are addressed by Chapter 9, which also explains the need for using agents to support Internet com-merce. This chapter also includes a methodology for observing time-critical constraints through knowledge engineering tools, as well as making a case for fuzzy engineering.

As a practical example on enterprise data storage, Chapter 10 treats the twin subjects of rapidly growing storage requirements for information systems and state-of-the-art solutions addressing a corporate memory facility. Imaginative approaches go beyond traditional datamining and into patterning, as shown by case studies.

Another prerequisite for growth and survival is flexible organization and structure as shown in Chapter 11 through examples from engineering and manufacturing. This discussion broadens the implementation horizon of technology through the contributions of modeling and experimentation, practical cases in concurrent engineering, and possible benefits from fast time-to-market.

The last five chapters of this book underline the need for getting ready to face shifts in market power. These go well beyond the more classical supply–chain relationships because they involve agency costs and call for integrated solutions. The broader perspective is given by Chapter 12, which focuses on the information economy at large and, more specifically, the role played by the Internet as merchandising agent.

Another contribution to this subject is made by Chapter 13, which explains the notion of Internet time and its impact on our daily business. This chapter deals with the extended policies required by Internet time for effective implementation, the necessary cultural change, and the requirements of personal accountability which go beyond what is seen as a "must" so far.

Because innovative applications and the new culture correlate, the theme of Chapter 14 is on working end-to-end with the Internet. The text addresses the motivations of companies, the ways and means they are using, issues associated to open networks, and wing-to-wing coverage as defined by General Electric. Chapter 15 extends this discussion to intranets and extranets, explaining why they are more efficient solutions than the expensive private networks designed and implemented in the early- to mid-1990s.

On-line solutions can be instrumental in restructuring the supply chain, but they will fail if we do not pay a great amount of attention to security. Chapter 16 presents the reasons why this is true, by emphasizing my personal experience in security assurance, as well as absence of appropriate security measures. It also shows how some companies capitalize on new technology such as biometrics to improve security. These new applications horizons, however, are not free from challenges and pitfalls, as this text will demonstrate.

The text generally takes practical examples from pacesetting entities of today, although tomorrow they could either become part of mainstream business or disappear from the market. The survival of companies using advanced technology is by no means assured; new challengers will show up to take the place of current leaders. What is more or less sure is that failure to capitalize on an advanced enterprise architecture can be lethal.

Experts envision the 21st century as empowering people through imaginative solutions — any time, at any place, for any product. New technology is a means permitting knowledge and information to flow seamlessly through businesses, offices, and homes. But are we taking advantage of it? The means are available to implement flawless Internet-commerce operations for a wide range of products and services; however, only the best managed organizations capitalize on what is currently available.

I am indebted to a long list of knowledgeable people and organizations for their contributions to the research which made this book feasible. I am also grateful to several senior executives and experts for constructive criticism during the preparation of the manuscript, particularly Dr. Heinrich Steinmann and Dr. Derek Duerden. The complete list of the 136 senior executives and 78 organizations who participated in this research is shown in the Acknowledgements.

Let me take this opportunity to thank Drew Gierman for suggesting this project and seeing it to publication and Judith Simon Kamin and Maureen Kurowsky for the editing. To Eva-Maria Binder goes the credit for compiling the research results, typing the text, and creating the camera-ready artwork and index.

Dimitris N. Chorafas

THE AUTHOR

Dimitris N. Chorafas has been advisor to financial institutions and industrial corporations in strategic planning, risk management, computers and communications systems, and internal controls since 1961. He is a graduate of the University of California at Los Angeles, the University of Paris, and the Technical University of Athens. Dr. Chorafas was a Fulbright scholar.

Dr. Chorafas has advised such financial institutions as the Union Bank of Switzerland, Bank Vontobel, CEDEL, the Bank of Scotland, Credit Agricole, Österreichische Länderbank (Bank Austria), First Austrian Bank, Commerzbank, Dresdner Bank, Mid-Med Bank, Demir Bank, Banca Nazionale dell'Agricoltura, Istituto Bancario Italiano, Credito Commerciale, and Banca Provinciale Lombarda. He has worked as consultant to top management for multinational corporations including General Electric–Bull, Univac, Honeywell, Digital Equipment Corporation, Olivetti, Nestlé, Omega, Italcementi, Italmobiliare, AEG–Telefunken, Olympia, Osram, Antar, Pechiney, the American Management Association, and a host of other client firms in Europe and the U.S.

Dr. Chorafas has served on the faculty of the Catholic University of America and as visiting professor at Washington State University, George Washington University, the University of Vermont, University of Florida, and Georgia Institute of Technology in the U.S. Abroad, he has been a visiting professor at the University of Alberta, Ecole d'Etudes Industrielles de l'Université de Genève, and the Technical University of Karlsruhe.

Dr. Chorafas is the author of 120 books, some of which have been translated into 16 languages. His seminars in the U.S., England, Germany, other European countries, Asia, and Latin America have been attended by more than 6000 banking, industrial, and government executives.

CONTENTS

SECTION II: PRESENT BEST APPLICATIONS AND FUTURE DEVELOPMENTS IN TECHNOLOGY

SECTION III: IS THE INTERNET THE 21ST CENTURY'S ANSWER TO AN ENTERPRISE ARCHITECTURE?

I

NEXT GENERATION INFORMATION SYSTEMS TECHNOLOGY

1

BENEFITS AND CHALLENGES EXPECTED FROM AN ENTERPRISE ARCHITECTURE

INTRODUCTION

A successful company identifies needed technologies, introduces them quickly, and then commercializes them. The company that cannot do so will be absorbed by a competitor who is ahead of the curve, or simply slide downhill to oblivion. Thus, senior management demands that its technologists develop and implement a first class enterprise architecture to give the firm an upper hand over its competitors.

One of the principal roles of an enterprise architecture is to align the implementation of technology to the company's business strategy. This can be effectively done when technology investments target state-of-the-art solutions. Another key objective is to make technology serve innovation economics. Astute architectural approaches and dynamic planning help to transform the enterprise. Companies with experience suggest this means two things: 1. ability to define and keep on redefining the enterprise architecture in a business environment in full evolution, while 2. providing life cycle management of technology and all other investments which target the ability to stay competitive.

The implementation of an enterprise architecture is usually done at one of two levels. The more common but less exciting is that of a tactical instrument able to handle transactions. This addresses the lower half of the information environment shown in Figure 1.1. Its objective is to operate within a structured information environment, as well as assist middle-to-lower management and other personnel in improving their productivity.

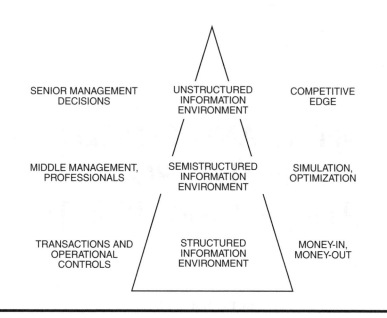

Figure 1.1 A core function of the enterprise architecture is to assure a competitive edge.

The reason for this limited view is largely historical. Years ago when systems architectures were developed, the focal point was transactions. Even at this lower level of complexity, however, the study, implementation, and maintenance of an enterprise architecture requires clearly stating the company's current and projected business objectives:

- Is the company a product manufacturer or on the sales front?
- What is the company's value-added advantage?
- How does the company bring its products to the market?
- How does the company personalize its products for its customers?

These are core issues to design of the enterprise architecture, even if it addresses only the structured part of the information pyramid in Figure 1.1. The technological side of answers to these queries will be derived from a factual and documented response to where the company is in the value chain. Is it at the front-end of rapid innovation? Is its strength special products? If the answers are yes, then its interests lie in more complex architectural requirements.

This value chain is shown in the diagram in Figure 1.2. Front end needs are highly market sensitive. Therefore they belong to a fairly unstructured context. Alternatively, the company may be at the backend of the supply chain, where products are sold out of stock. Here the architectural requirements are simpler; however, huge issues of scalability and reliability exist.

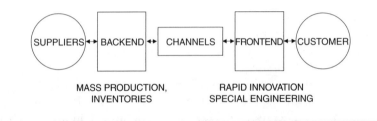

Figure 1.2 To properly project an enterprise architecture, it is important to first define location in the value chain.

Reliability, scalability, and dependability are issues present with every enterprise architecture; their importance increases with a solution which addresses the information environment depicted in the top half of Figure 1.1. Because business prerequisites dominate, some companies call such structures business architectures (see Chapter 2), though a more appropriate label would be *strategic information technology* (IT).

No two companies have exactly the same strategic IT solution, but these solutions share certain general characteristics. Real-time information is a common example because it is critical in obtaining synergy from the different channels supported and promoted by the company. Another critical factor often found in strategic level architectures is seamless integration of channels. Also, adopted solutions must be customer-oriented because customers today have more clout than ever before.

THE MARKET REWARDS COMPANIES THAT HAVE A COGENT ENTERPRISE STRATEGY

Nobody in any business should believe that, in a global business environment, the road ahead is hazard-free. The principle of uncertainty in corporate policies and business transactions evidently applies all the way from client to supplier partnerships. Some companies think supply chain management, coupled with world-class engineering and the latest production technology, can make anything possible. This still remains to be proven but, as an aim, it requires a first class enterprise architecture. Otherwise, it will not be realized.

The services provided by the architectural choices to be made must resolve several contradictions prevailing in today's environment, for instance, getting a meaningful sense of direction out of the plethora of easily available information. Data, figures, opinions, and projections are presented without sufficient time to absorb them, unless a system is in place for organizing and distilling information.

The type of company that an organization is presents advantages and challenges. For instance, pure Internet companies do not seem to have the ability to fulfill their goals efficiently, while traditional brick-and-mortar companies lack flexibility and have difficulty defining the services an enterprise architecture should provide or in using the Internet to become a *brick-and-click* company.

The stock market crash of "pure" Internet companies in 2000 showed that there are advantages in merging the means used by traditional and virtual enterprises because, ultimately, a company's fulfillment capability is the critical element in how well its strategy will work. One of the least discussed characteristics of the enterprise architecture is that the services which it provides must go well beyond better communications to the technical aspects of an architectural solution. These are usually seen as irreducible core characteristics including not only technology, but also bulletproof security (see Chapter 16), cost, and pricing of services. In this domain lie some of the key decisions a company must make; therefore, the search to find the best technology provider is critical. This domain, however, is subservient to that of strategic choices.

Because organizations consist of people, and their structure is usually layered (see Figure 1.3), the enterprise architecture can be viewed as consisting of at least two major layers. One is concerned with management decisions, the other with technical choices regarding its design, implementation, maintenance, and future development. The lower layer addresses technology choices and their details and the upper layer, or metalayer, outlines the prerequisites posed by the business environment.

These prerequisites define the services the company requires to support its product and market efforts. Neither layer offers freedom to make all of the choices; today's decisions must be frequently reviewed and reevaluated because both technology and the business environment change. One of the choices regarding the technical layer, for example, may be that of open standards (see also Chapter 2). But which open standards?

In the late 1960s, in the manufacturing industry, the standard was the manufacturing automation protocol (MAP) by General Motors (GM).

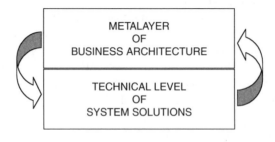

Figure 1.3   An enterprise architecture involves decisions at two levels of reference.

Eventually it faded. In 1978 the open system interconnection (OSI) by the International Standards Organizations (ISO) was considered to be *the* open standard, but its life cycle did not reach two decades. The open standard version of electronic document interchange (EDI), developed by the United Nations, has not been successful. Today some minor miracles are expected from extended hypertext markup language (XML) as the lower level protocol of end-to-end interconnection. XML is a modernized version of the Web's original protocol and its adoption sounds reasonable. It remains to be seen how successful this may be.

Important design issues such as technical standards, technical criteria, and the choice of "bread and butter" components correlate. Technical standards depend to a significant extent on business choices; and some of them have far reaching effects. For instance, to decide whether the company's basic infrastructure should be wired or wireless, it is necessary to determine which option would allow local independence in the most cost-effective and secure way.

Choices are not necessarily clear-cut. A great deal depends on the specific industry and its requirements. In banking, for example, the general notion is of permanent connection; because steady handholding with the clients is very important. No major player in the finance industry can afford not to be accessible to its business partners at any time, wherever the institution operates.

Neither can solutions concerning security be taken for granted. More confidential information and real-time execution of transactions have increased the security threshold even for unsophisticated types of business. Because higher security cannot be taken for granted and, if available, costs more money, a properly studied enterprise architecture should provide the option of security level on demand.

This brings this discussion to return on investment (ROI), which should characterize the study of any technological solution. ROI is a prerequisite to the authorization of spending money. Everything must be priced out and every benefit proven. Expected returns from successful implementation should be quantified and a price should be put on delays, design changes downstream, and outright failure.

An enterprise architecture should also be examined from a competitive perspective. What would happen if a competitor had a first class architectural solution linking on-line its business clients and suppliers and one could not compete in terms of cost-effectiveness? This question brings back the issue of strategic IT. Board members and senior executives should be aware — and indeed they are becoming increasingly convinced — that their decisions about technology have much to do with opportunities, challenges, and pitfalls encountered along the company's way.

THE INTRODUCTION OF OPPORTUNITY COSTS CHANGES THE RULES OF THE GAME

A cogent enterprise architecture requires that guidelines be established and choices made at top management levels which means that decision-making about technical issues, particularly the more pace-setting, has moved from IT shops to executive committees and people in charge of lines of business. Such decisions become more pragmatic and bring with them the notion of opportunity costs, thus changing the rules of the game.

The criteria used by senior management in strategic IT decisions tend to enlarge their horizon. They introduce issues which, in all likelihood, would have been left in the background or at least disconnected from the operational viewpoint. Even if modern technology both impacts and is affected by deregulation, globalization, and innovation, some people fail to see that these issues are interrelated with the company's product evolution line and daily business activities.

As Figure 1.4 suggests, at the intersection of four major forces affecting the modern enterprise can be found better business opportunities and a greater amount of risk. Therefore, senior management needs a governance model provided by the enterprise architecture, and also must continuously evaluate whether present solutions respond effectively to anticipated requirements. Factors determining a company's present and future clout are:

- A continuing ability to innovate
- Content and design features that appeal to clients
- Fast timetables for deliverables
- Lean production and distribution capabilities
- High quality compared to that of competitors

When the nuclear scientists of the Manhattan Project presented General George Marshall with some statistics on the destructive power of the weapon in the making, the U.S. Chief of Staff asked them how many atomic bombs per month the $2 billion project would deliver. The scientists had not thought of their project in these terms. The power of the military rests in its continuing ability to deliver, Marshall advised them. Quite similarly, the power of the modern corporation rests in its continuing ability to innovate.

Business success is also dependent on the company's capability to compress time and cost. Observing strict timetables for deliverables is a relatively new concept, particularly in IT. The enterprise architecture to be designed and implemented must act as a facilitator in keeping to strict timetables. It must also contribute to high quality and lean production —

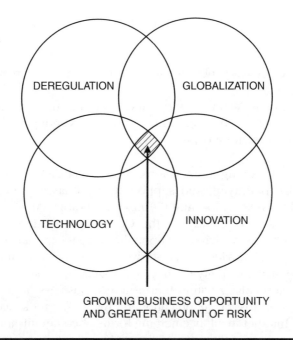

Figure 1.4 The main forces propelling rapid growth of business opportunity in the financial and other industrial sectors.

two issues that correlate with and assist one another. That is why technology audits must be steady and performed by qualified, independent auditors.

Technology audits are a relatively new concept in IT and nowhere are they more explicitly needed than in connection to enterprise architecture and the services it supports. They should serve as the means of assessing the nature and level of sophistication of technology used to run the business, the costs involved, and the returns obtained. Technology audits consist of:

- Evaluating the cost-effectiveness of current solutions
- Looking into deliverables and their timetables
- Assuring software and hardware are ahead of the curve
- Controlling the quality of technology personnel
- Proposing intensive training and other remedies

Technology audits require a supporting methodology like General Electric's Six Sigma (see Chapter 5). Their execution should be shielded from the political pressures that invariably exist in every organization. They should take place within a basic notion of modern business: that of creating value. No innovation, technology, new product or new market is worthwhile if it does not create value. Critical concerns are:

- How to develop new technology in a way that creates value for customers
- How to link technology to markets and business partners
- How to use technology to keep people working for the organization up-to-date and productive

One way of looking at an enterprise architecture is as a fundamental framework for portraying and supporting the phases of entrepreneurial activity, and for help in locating the *next* technology. Most interesting are the results of a recent study by the Geneva Association, the insurance industry's think tank, which drew upon the current experience of insurance intermediaries worldwide. This study confirmed that knowledge and advice, more than the ability to effect a transaction, are key to the changing role of the intermediary within the insurance business or, for that matter, in any business. Insurance practitioners' responses took account of the fact that the Internet in all its emerging forms of communication, including digital wireless technology, is transforming the way a wide range of services are produced, intermediated, and consumed.

Some of the participants in the study suggested knowledge-based services as the critical concept of the 21st century,* emphasizing that the production and consumption of many services increasingly requires an advanced base of knowledge, skills, and on-line access to business partners. Real-time access is a vital part of the theme of intermediation, including the associated process of disintermediation, in which new intermediaries are spawned by new technology.

An enterprise architecture can be the pivotal point in reintermediation. On-line services over the Internet, particularly for business-to-business applications (see Chapters 12 and 13), are restructuring industries from within as well as breaking down long-standing boundaries between industrial sectors. Companies are reinventing themselves internally, taking advantage of intelligent network architectures and software for advanced business applications.

Banks must go through similar chores to those of insurance companies because of emerging financial intermediaries and developing forms of money. Service industries are not the only ones profiting from this major transition. In the mechanical and electrical industries, too, the old manufacturing and services dichotomy has broken down and traditional

---

* See also the discussion on agents in Chapters 7 and 9, and on mobile agents in Chapter 14.

manufacturers, from GM to IBM, are reinventing themselves as service companies.

How is managing in the new economy different from managing in the old economy? Globalization, innovation, and technology aside, management in the new and old economies has many of the same characteristics: financial discipline, the bottomline, handholding with customers, answering market needs, and building a first class management team. Also, it is necessary to be ready to exploit business opportunities as they develop and even to create them using a first class enterprise architecture.

REENGINEERING MEANS BEING READY TO EXPLOIT BUSINESS OPPORTUNITIES

Alfred P. Sloan gives an excellent example of the need to be ready and react quickly when he describes how GM avoided the aftermath of the Great Depression suffered by other companies: "No more than anyone else did we see the depression coming... We had simply learned how to react quickly. This was perhaps the greatest payoff of our system of financial and operating controls."[2] (See other references to Sloan's business viewpoints in Chapter 12.)

Sloan's dictum on quick response is an excellent example of the mission the enterprise architecture should accomplish at the metalevel (outlined in Figure 1.3). Senior management decisions are never made in the abstract; they are based on financial and marketing information and their execution is controlled through internal feedback. This, too, must be properly supported by the architectural solution chosen by the company, whose functional alignment at three different management levels is shown in Figure 1.5.

At the senior management level the goal of IT support is factual decisions and competitive edge (as shown in Figure 1.1). Remember that this is an unstructured information environment to be covered by the enterprise architecture in the most flexible manner, supported through sophisticated software, and designed in a way always open to innovation. Senior management's responsibility is to provide future vision, which should be adequately supported through IT. To do so, one must organize the firm for coming market challenges, which means that data flows and models must be in place not only for projecting the market's evolution but also for positioning the company against the forces of the future — a top management job.

At the middle management level, including the professional level, simulation, experimentation, and optimization are the common ground of design objectives. Experimental approaches came into industrial practice in the 1950s with operations research,[3] in the 1960s with simulation

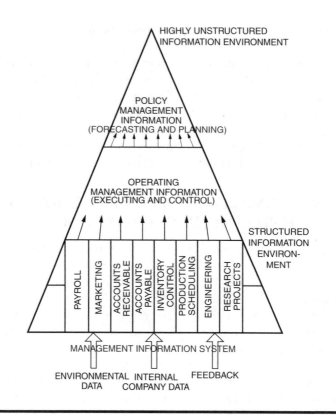

Figure 1.5 An information environment ranges from unstructured to structured, depending on functions performed.

studies,[4] in the 1970s with decision support systems (DSSs) and management information systems (MISs), in the 1980s with expert systems,[5] and in the 1990s with agents.[6] During the past five years, the two most productive tools for middle management and professionals have been enterprise resource planning (ERP) and customer relationship management (CRM). Support along this line of reference, too, is a domain which should be covered by the enterprise architecture.

At the lowest layer (Figure 1.5) are transactions and operating controls and the structured environment. These are the most common areas to which an enterprise architecture addresses itself. Although necessary, this is not enough. Technology's architectural information environment should be extended toward the upper two layers.

Because it takes an integrative view of the three layers, the functional graph in Figure 1.5 offers a global perspective to modern enterprise. Not long ago, business processes in the marketing area were viewed as a natural extension of those on the factory floor. Optimizing for worker efficiency created an industrial paradigm of sales work based on task specialization and repetition in which workers were often viewed as interchangeable parts. But in the 1990s, the introduction of enterprise networking and concurrent engineering software (see Chapter 11) obliged the command-and-control hierarchy to change prevailing industrial organization structures. Business process reengineering is the challenge of readiness. It calls upon boards and chief executives to view their business processes as strategic assets and renovate outmoded practices. It also brings senior management attention to the critical importance of processes involving collaborative teams, where productivity cannot be measured solely in piecework terms.

It is this cultural change which makes an enterprise architecture mandatory at the senior management level. Unlike factory floor operational processes, typically seen as costs to be reduced, senior management decisions involve complex and changing collaborative processes that are largely market-oriented. They are also closely connected to revenue growth and so their relative importance increases.

Through the advantage of an enterprise architecture, these changes can assist the company in formulating its business policy and technological strategy. Only top-tier organizations appreciate that business and technology are intimately connected . Implementation of this strategy has enabled the leaders of industry and finance to break ranks with the majority of their competitors and put themselves in the forefront of new developments.

Exceptional individuals move fast and see their policies through. After salvaging Turkey from disintegration, Mustafa Kemal Atatürk favored replacing Arabic with Latin script. He applied steady pressure at all levels of society, visiting towns and villages and talking to the common man. Once engaged, reform was carried through within 6 months.[7]

This, however, is not the way the average executive operates. Organizations are made up of people and people are often slow in making decisions — even more so in putting them into effect. Therefore, the metalayer of an enterprise architecture should act as a catalyst for rapid motion, providing management with the ability to spot opportunities instantly, but always keeping in mind that business opportunities are often a by-product of mismatched, short-lived conditions.

The company must have a fast reaction time because mismatched conditions, which create opportunities, tend to reach equilibrium quickly and then disappear. The enterprise architecture must enable testing new products on a trial basis, modifying them as the market requires, and readiness to transform them into a volume operation to keep up with expanding demand when they succeed.

At the same time, as Sloan aptly suggested, accurate and timely financial information should be available. This is vital because the company must always be prepared to withdraw if its product does not meet with market acceptance, or risk and return are not as projected. The company must also be able to cope with a multiplicity of financial risks. The market's rapid pace and global nature require constant attention to position risks, credit risks, and liquidity risks.

Figure 1.6 is a chart for interactive reporting of exposure based on a real-life implementation with a major financial institution.[8] A thoroughly studied and well implemented enterprise architecture is very important because the construction of a technological environment which multiplies the effectiveness of the company's resources cannot be achieved using past traditional data processing approaches. The beaten path in IT usually involves large development teams, which can lead to inertia and bureaucracy; long development times, which can result in slow reaction and response; and large up-front investments, which can affect profit figures without providing corresponding benefits.

Though each well-managed company will follow its own architectural design characteristics, in general terms, the goal of an enterprise architecture should be to help develop an environment which makes product creation and delivery possible in accordance with the market's pace and requirements. Examples of objectives by tier-1 companies are: new products on demand implemented quickly and economically, direct business partner access anywhere in the world, for any product, at any time, and

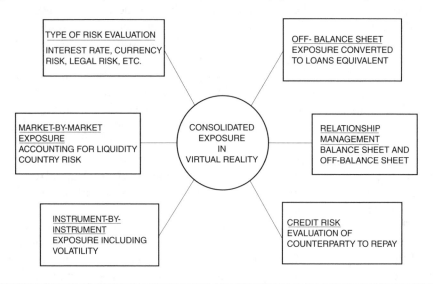

Figure 1.6 Component parts of a risk management structure designed for off-balance-sheet operations.

global reach because customers can be anywhere in a market more competitive than ever.

AN ENTERPRISE ARCHITECTURE MUST CARE PARTICULARLY FOR THE CUSTOMER

Alert businessmen appreciate that market pressures come not only from competitors but also from customers, whether companies or individuals. This sort of market pressure worries many enterprises because deregulation, globalization, and technology have made it possible for diverse businesses to take a share of their turf, as well as lowering the barriers to customer exit. The old concept of customer loyalty exists no more.

Companies must act fast to safeguard their customer bases, and technology serves in implementing a sound market-oriented policy. This is not possible when the technology that the company uses is wanting. Particularly hard hit is the notion that signing up a client means a long-standing deal, and all that is needed is be nice, answer the phone, and bring up the new contract for signature. Industry does not work this way anymore. To keep up our market leadership, it is necessary to continue being competitive, keep on innovating, and drive down costs on a steady basis — not just once every five years.

Another "must" in the 21st century is to keep up the speed of everything happening, as the previous section suggested. Speed of deliverables is necessary in order to face customer requests and confront current competitors, and to position the firm against challenges posed by new entrants. This presents a number of problems to be overcome. Banks, for example, have to continue promoting on-line delivery of financial products, even if Internet banking has not been successful so far.

Concomitant to the requirements of higher speed and lower cost is the adoption of new standards as they evolve, as well as the use of Web software for all functions for which it is available (see Chapter 15). The Web's potential for low-cost replacement of current, proprietary information technology solutions has not reached its limits and will not do so in the foreseeable future, even if technology's "earthquake" in late 2000 and early 2001 makes future prospects for Internet companies look rather bleak.

It seems likely that the market will rebound as soon as some of the excesses of the 1990s are out of the way. Growth in information technology spending slowed to 9% in 2001, down from 12% in 2000, but competition has increased. The $750 million corporate portal market already has over 50 competitors. Established portal companies, like Yahoo, must somehow extend their consumer brand in a way that inspires big businesses to fork over payments for Web software and services.

Today more and more competition is extending its influence in all industry sectors. The greater the competition, the better is the choice and the lower are the prices.

Another requirement for any company faced with transition to an enterprise architecture, is cultural change, which is important not only on the organization's side, but also on the client and supplier side. Much of this challenge is not a technological debate, even if technology acts as both catalyst and accelerator. Cultural change is primarily a management issue whose importance is magnified by market forces, competitive drive, and the aftermath of technology.

The notion of what is good and bad in a cultural and organizational sense changes with time. In the 1950s, 1960s, and part of the 1970s, mainframes saw to it that the aftermath of information technology was a centripetal force. In the legacy model, information was pushed from the periphery to the center, from the small to the large, from a personal preoccupation to the prerogative of the centralized "ivory tower" of IT.

In the 1980s and, most particularly, the 1990s, these ideas have changed. The influence of new technology, deregulation, and globalization during the tail-end of the 20th century has resulted in business systems driven by a centrifugal force, pushing power out from the center to the edge: the customer's end of the deal. The bottom line is the concept of market forces.

Historians will one day write that the switch in technology, though not yet in systems architecture, started with the development of the personal computer at the end of the 1970s. The client-server style of computing in the late 1980s put networked processing power on people's desks and did away with the ivory tower of IT.[9] Involving end users freed them from the centralized straightjacket and allowed them to use their own initiative.

The dispersal of control to customers of IT resources — the end users who reside on the network's edge — cut out whole layers of middle managers who had shuffled questions and answers between bosses and staff. This is the single most important factor leading to the productivity boom that America enjoyed in the 1990s, placing the customer at the center of the product development cycle.

Using technology in the best manner they could, companies struggled to please the customer. Toyota offered to produce and deliver a car made to customer specifications in $3\frac{1}{2}$ days. Other companies went into a soul-searching process of reinventing themselves, this time putting market wishes and customer demands at the center of their value systems. This had an important impact on the enterprise architectures these companies had developed and used.

The telephone industry is a good example of this. One of the most visible centrifugal forces at work today is that of remaking the telephone system in the image of the Internet. Nothing compares with the complexity of the telephone system's vast, centrally controlled, multitier hierarchy of switching centers still dominated by 19th century technology. But forces are at work to change that through wireless communications and voice-over Internet protocols.

Out of necessity, telephone carriers are adopting the packet-switching techniques that made the Internet user-friendly and innovative. The individual intelligent phone, which helps to propel this revolution, takes control for setting up the phone services that a customer may need. It moves the line of authority out of the hands of the central office and places it firmly in those of the end user.

Some industry specialists see this as a bigger technological innovation, with associated disruption of past practices, than all previous breakthroughs in technology. It is also, most likely, a greater market opportunity than the emergence of the personal computer. Because of technology made available at an acceptable price, the customer is in command of a process which has been centralized for more than a century.

It surely is a challenging time that carries with it some major risks, of which one is product liability. It is as well a time in which companies can end up owing vast sums of money. At the dawn of the 21st century, the bifurcation based on product liability will be, in all likelihood, the single most common pitfall created by lawsuits concerning antitrust, intelligent property, employee conduct, contractual failure, shareholder actions, and antitrust violations.

In 2000, Sotheby's, an international auction house, and UST, a chewing-tobacco firm, saw their credit downgraded because of publicized antitrust violations. Beverly Enterprises was hit for violating America's complex Medicare billing practices; American Home Products was downgraded following a $12.3 billion settlement stemming from its production of a diet drug that cleared federal safety hurdles but was later found to be dangerous.[10] A better known product liability case is that of asbestos. These are examples of operational risks.[11]

In conclusion, as the centrifugal force accelerates, companies may find themselves at the litigation end of events not quite of their own doing. Some industries will be more severely affected than others, but all need a first class customer-oriented enterprise architecture able to bring good and bad news in real-time to senior management, so that corrective action can be taken and damage control can be exercised in a timely manner.

REVAMPING BUSINESS STRATEGY AFTER 10 YEARS OF TECHNOLOGICAL INNOVATION

The old computer age, often referred to as electronic data processing (EDP), was linear. By contrast, the modern information technology age is about exponential innovation in man-made devices and systems, derivative financial instruments, analytical approaches, and increasing-return economics. Companies that do not take seriously the need to steadily adapt to the ongoing business evolution and reinvent themselves do not survive. Although this has always been true, it has become particularly pronounced since the last decade because of the accelerated pace of development.

There is nothing new about the mortality of industrial enterprises. Like people, products, and factories, companies fail. Look at the roster of the 100 largest U.S. firms at the beginning of the 1990s. Only 16 are still worth talking about. To a degree, the wave of change started in the 1950s, but in the mid 20th century change was gradual; it has accelerated in the last decade. Consider *Fortune* magazine's first list of America's 500 biggest companies, published in 1956. Only 29 of its top 100 firms could still be found in the top 100 by 1992 because of mergers, acquisitions, and business failures.

One might wonder how it is possible that so many supposedly wealthy, well-managed, successful firms fail. Evidently something happened to make them unfit for their business environment. At the risk of repetition, note again that globalization, deregulation, innovation, and technology changed the rules (though not everything is due to these factors). Quite potent negative factors to the individual company have included:

■ Slow-moving management
■ Falling behind the state of the art, therefore making the force of technology disruptive
■ Misusing of technology, making it difficult to reinvent the firm and/or capitalize on changes in the market

A financial analysis by Merrill Lynch reveals what the capable use of technology can provide: "One of the real luxuries at GE is the wealth of management and systems which they can apply to a problem."[12] The analyst who wrote this document then considers General Electric's acquisition of Honeywell, and how deeply GE is examining and preparing to fix Honeywell. Corrective action includes improvements in management, focused cost controls, visibility of earnings, facilities rationalization, better utilization of shared services, optimization of sales and distribution assets, and revamping to get more cash earnings.

Another financial analysis by the same investment house indicates that an enterprise architecture and financial innovation correlate. It highlights financial innovation within Cisco, taking as one of the better examples the virtual close and saying that the company is using its advanced enterprise systems to drive financial performance.[13] For example, Cisco management has the ability to track revenue, discounts, and product margins on an hourly basis. Other variables such as expenses, head count, and market share are tracked on a weekly, monthly, or quarterly basis. The financial analyst at Merrill Lynch underlines also that, of these metrics, revenue growth appears to be the most important to Cisco's top management, at this point.

A good question linking this discussion to the central theme of this book is: what kind of enterprise network does the leader of network gear envision? According to Merrill Lynch, Cisco believes the future is in an integrated optical network and Internet protocol (IP), with each used for its strengths. Optical will be employed to rapidly expand the bandwidth for a low cost per bit; IP will be helpful in managing, expanding, and linking the network in an integrative way.

An enterprise architecture with the optical core vision will be able to rapidly move multimedia information between points of presence (POP). From POP to the desktop, mobile device, home, etc., fiber will work alongside other electronic media, for instance, cable, direct subscriber line (DSL), Ethernet, dial up, and third generation (3G) wireless services (see Chapter 6).

At current state of the art, key industry factors such as quality of service (QoS) are worked in all-optical networks. Another design parameter is that approximately 80% of traffic should be between the user and a cached POP, with IP playing a key role in managing this traffic. For this reason top-tier vendors are continuously seeking to expand the reach of IP. Cisco believes that the wireless IP market is clearly at an inflection point, soon to show tornado-like growth. Therefore, the company is participating in 13 out of 15 IP-based wireless networks built in Europe.

According to Merrill Lynch, part of Cisco's wireless IP strategy has been based on building relationships with the leading radio and wireless device manufacturers. This looks quite normal for a high tech vendor. Less evident, but just as normal, is the fact that it should also be the policy of user organizations that are eager to:

- Link technology and business strategy so that they effectively support one another
- Capture the value of technological innovation to enhance their market presence
- Optimize product and process development time, in order to be ahead of their competitors

■ Assure synergy between their technical capabilities and market needs, for more cost-effective response

Consider investment banking as an example. Some of the key terms heard in the investment banking business are *placement power* and *distribution network*. If one is in the business of originating loans, underwriting or placing securities, and performing other investment banking activities, one must have a distribution network capable of turning over assets at a competitive pace by selling them to investors wherever they might be located. This distribution network must be characterized by certain key attributes embedded into the enterprise architecture:

■ Accounts for fluidity and shifting patterns of worldwide political and economic situations
■ Reaches every corner of operations, and every potential investor, to deliver the desired financial service
■ Addresses the risk of major losses if reaction time is too slow

The preceding three points are valid in revamping business strategy, and also in managing the professional work force in day-to-day activities as well as in large, complex, global projects. This last reference suggests the wisdom of customizing the enterprise architecture because business processes evolve over time, as do their automation requirements. Whether in manufacturing or in banking, real-world processes span a continuum of conceptual and structural elements including an amalgamation of activities whose natures change as one adapts to the market's evolution.

TECHNOLOGY COSTS ARE DROPPING, BUT TECHNOLOGY RISKS ARE INCREASING

The costs of communications and computing are falling rapidly (see Chapter 3 on Moore's law and the law of the photon). This has been technology's contribution to innovation and globalization, resulting in the fall of the natural barriers of time and space that, over centuries, separated national markets. For example, the cost of a 3-minute telephone call between New York and London has fallen from $300 (in current dollars) in 1930, to $1 today (see the trend curve in Chapter 6).

Although cost-cutting in classical channels has slowed down, the sharp drop in prices is expected to resume with increased use of optical fibers and satellite communications. Over the past couple of decades, the cost of computer power shrank by an average of 30% a year in real terms, as Moore's law predicted.

But there is a slowdown, too, in these cost cuts. Experts expect the curve of computer-related prices to flatten in the coming years unless new technologies come along. Precisely because computing costs will not continue dropping so dramatically forever, during the past 5 years top-tier companies have focused their efforts on better organization. Smarter use of available technology can make the difference in competitiveness in the post-PC era.

In hardware or software terms, new devices costing $100 with agents and object-centric new architectures will steal the show. Small agents with business logic will most likely dominate the future applications landscape. These will assist goal-seeking activities with execution capabilities like interactive logistics. But, as Figure 1.7 suggests, the emphasis will be in organizational solutions that address business goals and interactive logistics and are better in their conception and execution than those of competitors.

That is how senior management should look at investing in this new world of location-independent distributed computing (for a discussion of

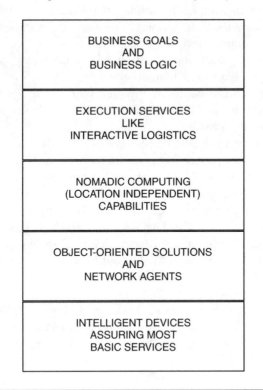

Figure 1.7   A functional view of an enterprise architecture includes several layers, each with a different level of sophistication.

nomadic computing, see Chapter 9). Many companies are preparing themselves for this new environment. Ford, for instance, will pay for all employees to have access to the Internet — a move expected to bring cultural changes to every Ford employee and his or her children.

The preceding issues underline the role of superior organization and add to the importance of projecting, implementing, and maintaining a highly competitive enterprise architecture, because the network is the market. One less appreciated aftermath of this rapid evolution is that the forthcoming organization and cultural change will lead to exposed pricing because everyone can see everyone else's bids, and bring along many associated risks.

Consider a couple of examples of man-made unreliability to better explain technical failures and their likelihood because of lack of attention to quality management. In 2000, problems with Japan's famed *shinkansen* bullet trains threatened passengers' lives. Among other happenings, large slabs of concrete peeled off tunnel walls and slammed into passenger compartments of passing bullet trains. Investigation revealed that tunnel concrete was made using improperly desalinated beach sand, rather than more expensive quarry sand. With age, such concrete becomes brittle and is easily shaken loose by the vibration of a train racing past at 250 k/h (155 mph). Japan Railways blamed the contractors for sloppiness, but experts suggest that the company lowered its own design and inspection standards in order to save money after it was privatized in the 1980s and lost its government subsidy.

Another case of unreliability concerns nuclear plants. In 2000, chain reaction at a uranium-processing plant in Tokaimura, Japan, exposed three workers to lethal doses of radiation and irradiated hundreds more with smaller amounts. This event was the world's worst nuclear disaster since Chernobyl. Investigation revealed that the company had hired unskilled laborers for specialized technical jobs and provided little training. Also, the factory workers who unknowingly dumped six times more uranium oxide into a mixing tank than they should have were under instructions to break safety rules to save time and money.[14] Outdated equipment was used in sensitive jobs as well.

Part of the background reasons for these failures is lack of ethics, but most of these and many other recent mishaps around the world reveal a great deal of mismanagement. Planning, organizing, staffing, directing, and controlling have taken leave; cost-cutting is used as a cheap excuse to explain why people fail in their accountabilities.

People and companies can be ahead of the curve in organizational goals if they are able to help themselves acquire know-how by:

■ Elaborating the requirements needed to support their objectives

- Providing justification and explanation of what a job requires in a time-sensitive sense
- Detecting and resolving conflicts that arise from multiple viewpoints
- Giving proof that they are in charge of their responsibilities.

For instance, design conflicts may arise if two or more requirements cannot be supported by the projected enterprise architecture.

If the problem is portability, then portability can be improved through a layered approach, usually at some cost to performance. When the requirements of portability and performance conflict, tradeoffs in hardware components, software supports, and process strategies must be examined. Potential conflicts among quality attributes must be identified, and then options to resolve conflicts early in the life cycle of the enterprise architecture should be suggested. Interaction conflicts may result if the satisfaction of one managerial or technical requirement impairs that of another.

The best solution is to conduct an independent technical audit that makes pairwise comparisons across all specifications, targeting conflict resolution. Such an audit must also provide guidance for better control over conflicting goals (see the third section on technology audits).

Design conflicts and interaction conflicts, as well as rapid obsolescence of huge investments are technology risks. Both end users and system designers should appreciate the practical limitations of theoretical approaches, which usually leave a number of loose ends. This is particularly important in connection to risky operational environments to be served by systems not designed for them.

In conclusion, able solutions require broader and deeper knowledge about the job which we are doing. In system design, for example, particular attention should be paid to interfaces. Users and operators of the resulting architecture also need to appreciate certain fundamentals concerning operational risks and countermeasures. No design is foolproof.

Because technology advances so fast, the knowledge of designers, end users, and operational personnel must increase dramatically over time, to reflect such rapid evolution. Although fundamentals do not change as quickly as the solution of the day, "God is in the detail," as Mies van der Rohe once said. The devil is in the fact that it is not always possible to mask complexity and people do not always care about its risks. In theory, system complexity can be hidden from view, but in practice, inadequate understanding of new and exceptional cases can result in disasters.

New risks associated with system design arise steadily, largely because of lack of understanding of the idiosyncrasies of architectural solutions, mechanisms, human interfaces, use of technology, and the surrounding administrative chores. Yet, all the elements are part of the overall system solution. While many of the elements underpinning a new enterprise architecture have real merits, they also further complicate implementing, maintaining, and using systems. Chapter 2 addresses this subject.

REFERENCES

1. Chorafas, D.N., *Integrating ERP, Supply Chain Management and Smart Materials*, Auerbach/CRC Press, New York, 2001.
2. Sloan, A.P., *My Years with General Motors*, Pan Books, London, 1963.
3. Chorafas, D.N., *Operations Research for Industrial Management*, Reinhold, New York, 1958.
4. Chorafas, D.N., *Systems and Simulation*, Academic Press, New York, 1965.
5. Chorafas, D.N. and Steinmann, H., *Expert Systems in Banking*, Macmillan, London, 1991.
6. Chorafas, D.N., *Agent Technology Handbook*, McGraw-Hill, New York, 1998.
7. Mango, A., *Atatürk*, The Overlook Press, New York, 2000.
8. Steinmann, H. and Chorafas, D.N., Risk management with derivative financial products, *Risk Manage.*, New York, July, 1994.
9. Chorafas, D.N., *Designing and Implementing Local Area Networks*, McGraw-Hill, New York, 1984.
10. *The Economist*, March 24, 2001.
11. Chorafas, D.N., *Managing Operational Risk. Risk Reduction Strategies for Investment Banks and Commercial Banks*, Euromoney, London, 2001.
12. General Electric Co., Merrill Lynch, New York, December 12, 2000.
13. Cisco Systems, Merrill Lynch, New York, December 6, 2000.
14. *The Economist*, March 4, 2000.

2

DEFINING THE RIGHT ENTERPRISE ARCHITECTURE FOR THE COMPANY

INTRODUCTION

It is far easier to create or adopt a bad enterprise architecture than to correct it later. This concept is known in political science as "the tyranny of the status quo." It is not difficult to design a good architecture capable of answering the business and technical requirements of the company, provided these requirements are defined in a factual and documented manner.

Some companies resist changing their enterprise architecture because "the better is the enemy of the good." This is true only if the "good" is good enough; usually, it is not. A challenging aspect of architectural design of computer and communications systems is the rate at which it changes. The intellectual foundation on which a good solution rests appears to shift every 10 to 15 years; however, in the Internet age this pace has accelerated as a new wave of concepts dominates the business environment.

Architecturing complex communications and computer systems, like any other sophisticated trade, takes time to learn. One of the challenging aspects of a good enterprise architecture is its ability to support flexibility and efficiency in operation because sometimes these two requirements contradict one another. Operations must be able to evolve to meet an innovative, market-driven solution. This is necessary to remain competitive in the fast changing product landscape. Major thrusts include the capability to 1. roll out new and evolving services with short-cycle times, 2. respond to customers' demands globally in an individualized, tailored manner, 3. ensure that customers can be serviced at first point of contact, and

4. support the company's internal cross-departmental functional and geographic pattern.

A valid architectural design should ensure that technology at the company's disposal is effectively used, regardless of existing and potential customers' points of contact, such as factories, service centers, or sales branches. To achieve this goal in a cost-effective manner the enterprise architecture must pay attention to the operational infrastructure, which is always one of the basic design prerequisites.

Though the nuts and bolts of the enterprise architecture primarily address the technologists' domain, the board and CEO must appreciate that technology strategy depends significantly upon business strategy. An effective distributed computing and communications environment must support global R&D, production, and delivery, integrating rich multifunctional workstations that access diverse platforms and servers. The solution adopted should promote applications able to lower costs of production and distribution, while improving the quality of products and services.

Apart from its overall design, in its fundamentals the enterprise architecture should address routing management of work to appropriate service representations based on functionality, availability, and other decision factors. It should interface with customers on-line, and aim to answer high performance, reliability, and security requirements.

Finally, the enterprise architecture designed must capably answer the characteristics of the new economy (see Chapter 12) and therefore of the upcoming decade. Open, increasingly competitive markets, demand for sophisticated services, and toughening competition in every field of operations are such characteristics and national barriers and other artificial obstacles no longer provide protection.

Solutions must emphasize human capital, whose importance has increased significantly thanks to technology; at the same time, they must be flexible enough to account for rapid maturation and decay of products and services in a market more competitive than ever. This is a tremendous challenge for architectural design.

THE DIFFERENCE BETWEEN AN ENTERPRISE ARCHITECTURE AND A SYSTEMS ARCHITECTURE

Many companies, and even some experts, confuse *enterprise architecture* with *system architecture* (see the next section). For the majority, the enterprise architecture of their computers and communications network is whatever resulted from years of haphazard growth, while the system architecture is usually an inflexible, decaying structure bought from a favorite vendor in the 1970s or 1980s. As a result, many of the existing computer and communications networks lack flexibility to support new, evolving applications and ability to cope with unforeseen demands, or impeding the company's ability to deploy products and services quickly.

The good news is that several companies and many experts realize that change is necessary. With the convergence of data, voice, and video to a single backbone, a multiservice network is needed to support the entire enterprise. Therefore, a modern company-wide, business-oriented architecture becomes crucial. Solutions must be flexible and able to address ad hoc situations. They must also provide effective support to the company's evolving client base, the information technology strategy established by the board, and the most recent developments on which to capitalize, for instance, the Internet (see Part III).

While traditional architectures are driven by cause-and-effect linear thinking that works in a simpler, slower moving world, the Internet is causing linear relationships to give way to nonlinear, complex adaptive systems. As technology becomes more sophisticated and competition intensifies, first class architectural solutions are required for companies to successfully implement business strategies. Organizations that succeed will be those that are first to exploit business opportunities.

This is the kernel of the difference between systems architecture and enterprise architecture. The concept of systems architecture was established in the 1970s with IBM's system network architecture, or SNA. (The concept of a system architecture is explained in the next section.) SNA was hierarchical, mainframe-based, and inflexible, but at the time it was a welcome advancement. Today, a systems architecture must be layered, distributed, and flexible.

The first model to follow this grand design was the open system interconnection (OSI) of the International Standards Organization (ISO). The ISO's OSI model was released in the late 1970s, but for a long time vendors did not follow it, even though its characteristics were basically technical. As Figure 2.1 demonstrates, many technical issues must be

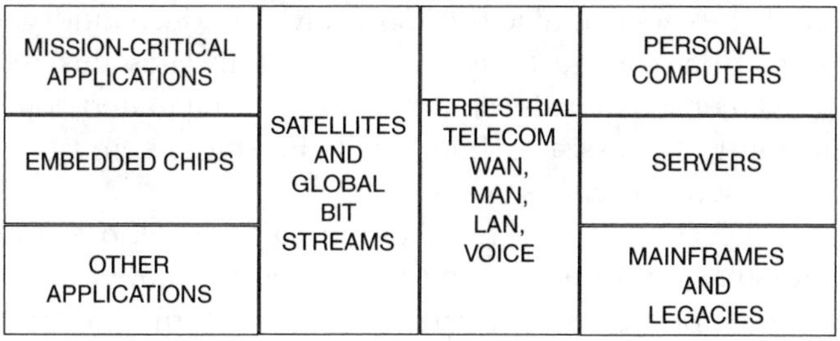

MISSION-CRITICAL APPLICATIONS	SATELLITES AND GLOBAL BIT STREAMS	TERRESTRIAL TELECOM WAN, MAN, LAN, VOICE	PERSONAL COMPUTERS
EMBEDDED CHIPS			SERVERS
OTHER APPLICATIONS			MAINFRAMES AND LEGACIES

Figure 2.1   The layered architecture of current computer and communications solutions.

solved in a layered architectural manner. This is not the goal of an enterprise architecture, whose core issue is business intelligence.

In business as in war, material only wins hands down when the intelligence and morale of the side possessing it are at least fairly comparable with that of the opponents. Otherwise, Byzantium with its "Greek fire" would have ruled the world.[1] A top-notch system architecture might be compared to a weapon: it must be available, but it will not win the war unless many other conditions are present.

To a considerable extent, business intelligence is provided by marketing. Marketing in the post-industrial economy gives customers more power than they had in the industrial age. The marketing metaphor has changed over time from hunting to gardening, implying that customers are now to be cultivated rather than captured.

The old customer lock-in, coercive approach that worked in the past is hard, if not impossible, to practice in a world of Internet standards — thus, the need for the enterprise architecture. Companies have another major incentive in creating a first class business-oriented architecture. They have to invest considerable money in infrastructure in order to shift from general-purpose to adaptive special-purpose solutions. This requires the flexibility to ensure that the infrastructure converges as devices diverge while, at the same time, providing greater intelligence at network edges. The result is an evolutionary approach to architectural design.

Because the enterprise architecture and the infrastructural base (see Chapter 1) work in synergy, the solution adopted must be able to ensure timely service from employees and effective commercialization of goods and services to meet the firm's market objectives. There is an iterative process between architecture and structure because they both require knowing the company and its competition, and steady analysis of the industry, in order to set technology directions in a business context.

One of the prerequisites in updating the enterprise architecture is to give the product units a better focus on market needs. Using Internet-based technologies to manufacture innovative products and get them to market faster is one of the tools. Figure 2.2 translates this requirement into a three-dimensional axis of reference for integrated logistics. The architecture must also assist to build skills inventories and create imaginative development programs.

This way, the company and its key workers develop the know-how they need for the future. For all the reasons just outlined, the enterprise architecture must be flexible and adaptable, as information requirements are expected to change as fast as business and technology do. Adaptation is a never-ending business; as many firms now appreciate, if they cannot incorporate a new technology within three months or less, they will be left behind.

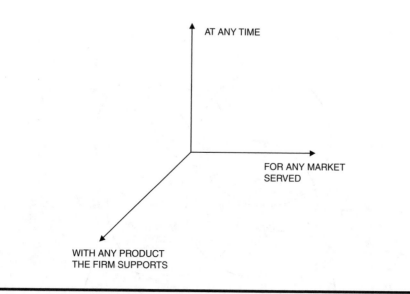

AT ANY TIME

FOR ANY MARKET
SERVED

WITH ANY PRODUCT
THE FIRM SUPPORTS

Figure 2.2   The solution space for integrated logistics can be served only through high-performance computing power.

By the same token, increasingly visible time constraints are forcing corporate treasurers and money managers to reassess existing banking and other relationships. Sophisticated customers want to trade any security or currency, on any exchange, anywhere in the world, at any time of day. A business strategy that only pays lip service to real-time response requirements, or forgets about them altogether, will fail because it cannot guarantee the company's competitive advantage.

One of the participants in the research project which led to writing this book stressed that the enterprise architecture must help different interconnected departments provide the annual 30 to 40% price and performance that are the norm in information technology. No two companies are exactly the same and therefore each organization has its own strategy to reach this goal. Many critical factors come into play in defining the best solution for the company; an example is given in Figure 2.3. Notice, however, that at the kernel is the company strategy defined by the board and CEO.

Furthermore, the enterprise architecture created must be able to march at Internet time (see Chapter 13). Because of globalization and technology, with Internet time moves much faster than most people expect. Response is practically instantaneous, not only with e-mail but also with complex transactions, messages, and cooperative action. "I wasted time, and now doth time waste me," Shakespeare wrote in *Richard V.* "I can give you anything but time," Napoleon told one of his lieutenants.

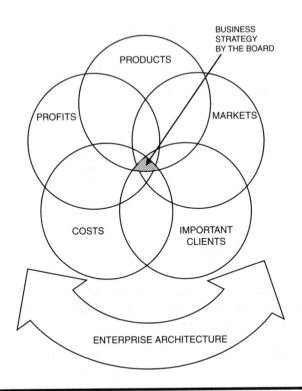

Figure 2.3 Many critical factors come into play in defining the best business architecture for the company.

FUNCTIONS THAT THE SYSTEMS ARCHITECTURE IS EXPECTED TO PERFORM

To understand better the concept of systems architecture, it is necessary to start with what a system is. Dictionaries define a system as a world or universe; an arrangement of things so related or connected as to form a unity, an organic whole. A system is also a set of rules, principles, and facts which are classified or interlinked in a regular form.

This very broad definition includes organizational perspectives, but this is not exactly the way in which systems are treated when the technological side of computers and communications is considered. In engineering the word *system* is used to identify an aggregate of assemblies and components working together to perform a specific function. A systems architecture does this as well.

While a method or plan of classification is a system and so is an orderly way of doing something, the engineering definition focuses primarily on technology and the underlying architectural perspectives. Based on these notions, an outline of a system architecture would show that it 1. provides a stable basis for planning, 2. gives common direction in distributed computers and communications aggregates, 3. makes it possible to integrate software and hardware vendors seamlessly, and 4. ensures that technology will be made to work the way people work and machines operate.

The reference to the way machines operate includes, among other critical subjects, latency control, bandwidth allocation, traffic prioritization, interfacing, and other important technical criteria. Methods and techniques along this line of reference are needed to deliver quality of service and they must be considered on an end-to-end basis. As Figure 2.4 suggests, on that basis the systems architecture significantly extends the capabilities of any single machine attached to it.

At the systems level of reference (the infrastructure), the solution provided by the systems architecture should enable developers to work out applications that are consistent, easy to use, and structured to access all attached resources. Supported facilities must assure that application users become more productive through agile, friendly, and fairly uniform interfaces that help them work faster in a comprehensive manner.

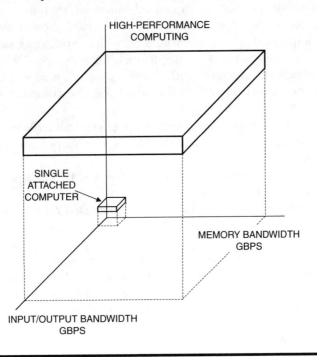

Figure 2.4 A reference framework for expected performance of a systems architecture.

One of the better examples of a successful implementation of a solution at the intersection of an enterprise architecture and a system architecture was implemented by General William G. Pagonis and served greatly during the 1990–1991 Gulf war. As head of the U.S. Army's Central Support Command in Saudi Arabia, Pagonis made sure that the 350,000 U.S. soldiers fighting the ground war had what they needed to win, in terms of logistics. "Good logistics is combat power," the general said.

Pagonis' ad hoc solution was made to fit the requirements of a desert war. Starting from scratch, he built a distribution network of 50,000 workers and 100,000 trucks, with massive open-air warehouses and operating expenses approaching $1 billion. Putting together this systems solution required the kind of skill that would test the capabilities of a seasoned executive, and was accomplished by adopting centralized command but decentralized execution. Like any strong CEO, Pagonis delegated almost everything but the big decisions, which he made on his own. To do that effectively, he developed a system and a methodology for obtaining essential information without bogging down in extraneous detail. He had to provide masses of men and women with logistics whose accuracy of execution could make or break the war effort.

Similar situations exist in globalized business. Therefore, an architectured approach should make possible a seasoned growth into the new scenario demanded by the environment, while capitalizing on both new and existing investments. In order to make that happen, it is important to have a well documented and clearly communicated system solution supported by skilled people. In the aggregate, the company needs:

■ Controlled system cooperation via effective interfaces
■ Separation but also collaboration between applications and infrastructure
■ A logically flat (horizontal) network served by efficient communication facilities
■ An infrastructure that leverages an increased proportion of bought software

Within the perspectives provided by this approach, the systems solution chosen should permit integration of smaller cooperating units, down to atomic units, and their ad hoc recombination. It must allow the company to structure applications services around business objects; use message-based, looser coupling between applications wherever possible, and employ standards to facilitate development of new application components.

To meet these objectives, system development tools may need to be updated, policies changed to allow for more reuse of components, and a controlled migration to new environments made feasible without rewriting all applications. Because the process of meeting these goals is fairly demanding, the credibility of vendor architectures decreases, pushing major users to in-house development. This, too, helps to differentiate between enterprise architectures designed by user organizations and systems architectures developed and sold by vendors.

Business-oriented architectures and systems architectures correlate in that the former elaborate business vision and goals to be reached by technology investments with the purposes of customer value and end-to-end service. By contrast, the latter address the nuts and bolts of the hardware and software aggregates that make up the infrastructure.

To interface the two architectures, designers need to understand that few processes in business and technology truly create and deliver value to the customer, unless the value is present at the drafting board. Interfacing is the precursor to the effective shift to a new applications environment across the enterprise. Establishing flexible architectural processes creates the blueprints for business models, and defines the framework for technology-related work. It also generates core capabilities that help to establish specifications of highly configurable and tailorable service elements, thus ensuring that costs for creating products and services are kept down, and operational risks are reduced over time by integrating newer, more effective technologies and work-flow processes.

Whether at enterprise or systems level, no architectural solution will be satisfactory if it does not pay due attention to the need of ensuring overall coherence between various basic processes looking after operational effectiveness. In essence, the architectural perspective discussed here and in Chapter 1 is a process-driven approach which should allow the company to leverage its technology as a corporate asset on a global basis, and to do so in a manner coordinated with business objectives.

WORKING WITHIN THE CONFINES OF AN ARCHITECTURED SOLUTION

Users of an enterprise architecture are rarely aware that they are not interacting with the computer but with the designers of the software programs and hardware components supported through this architecture. In terms of effectiveness this has an interesting aftermath inasmuch as most programmers have much more experience in information processing than in business operations, and are trained to work in situations where tasks are sequential rather than simultaneous, as in commerce.

Some of the experts participating in the research project that prompted this book suggested that a great deal of designer bias, along with many new technical challenges, is, consciously or unconsciously, built into the system because of the programmer bifurcation identified in the previous paragraph. They also said that it is important to change this frame of mind of designers and programmers by following the coordinated approach described in Figure 2.5.

To understand why some integrated information handling systems are more useful than others, it is useful to examine the design of their architecture, which essentially means the underlying concepts. These design concepts directly affect the suitability of a technological solution within the unique environment of the organization.

Friendly end user interfaces are an example. The principle is that the end user should be able to concentrate upon desired results affecting his or her work, rather than be concerned with mechanics of input–output or with intricate system operations. In other words, when interacting with a computer and communications aggregate, the end user must concentrate on the task which he is paid to accomplish, and do it well. Complexities of the machine should not distract him from how this task will fare.

Sometimes this approach goes contrary to embedded culture because, in programming circles, it is a matter of pride to use different computer languages and procedures in a way that is not transparent to the user. By contrast, a successfully integrated operation will communicate with the end user in the most empathetic of human language terms, always employing signs and rules in the same way, and acting through the same command and control interfaces.

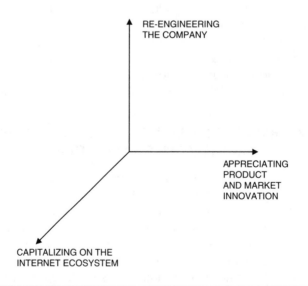

Figure 2.5 Able solution for growth and survival during the next decade can only be found in this coordinated approach.

Technical requirements fall under the systems architecture. Well-designed systems provide full internal compatibility between operations on an end-to-end basis. Although few companies have the will and know-how to capitalize on this principle, appropriate technologies are available to meet the growing range of friendly interfacing requirements. Also, many companies do not possess the necessary methodology for creation of the metalayer: the enterprise-wide business architecture which uses a high level of consistency in its interfaces.

Consistency is important for man–machine interfaces as well as for other critical factors of architectural design. There should be design consistency even if functional diversity exists. More technical criteria must also be brought into perspective. A basic criterion is control of stress. Each solution adopted stands a chance to be subjected to stress conditions. Load, for example, is the quantity of messages entering the technological system within each unit of time. Stress load helps to reveal the degree to which successive sets of messages can be effectively handled by the system as it approaches saturation.

To study the effect of differential loading of several traffic lines in the architectured system, the degree and timing of the stresses imposed on the entire communications network are varied. The desired pattern, which might not be supported by the adopted solution, is one of regularity in functionality under different kinds of demands imposed from the operating environment.

Also desirable is coherence, the degree to which the demands imposed by different users of system resources are compatible with the design principles which characterized the architecture. Because a crisis will probably occur, it should be defined in terms of message streams entering the communication network and the demands placed upon it by consumers of its resources.

Quality of operations is often defined by 1. the sequences in which limiting factors occur, 2. their specific kinds, duration, and aftermath, and 3. their overall composition and manner of easement. All three factors constitute what designers view as crisis conditions. Once these elements are specified, their kind, duration, and magnitude can be controlled. A computer-based simulation can do more than simply provide experimental observations; documented operational effects can help in making extrapolations. In testing and experimenting, as well as in real-life situations, some observations are direct, or first order, while others may be considered second order.

Second-order observations consist of a combination of direct recording and computer interpretation by means of data analysis designed by the experimenters. Among first order data that generally are directly recorded, is information relating to performance of the technological system. Critical factors, for instance, are:

- Elapsed time of messages through the system, by category of messages
- Order of messages entering the system vs. order leaving, a priority filtering discipline
- Times when overload conditions occur and the type or occasion of overload
- Utilization and underutilization of available system transport capacity
- Degree to which imposed demands are satisfied by the aggregate; also nature and timing of imbalances.

Chapter 1 stressed the need to distinguish between requirements posed by the top and mid layers served by the enterprise architecture, and those of the lower layer, whose functions are largely transactional. All of the five critical factors address each of these layers, as do first- and second-order characteristics.

Volatility in a first order recording program of multimedia streams is not unexpected when one thinks that an enterprise architecture is used to serve multiple objectives. All interactions in a fully automated environment take place over computer and communications lines and nodes tailored to specific needs of each atomic unit attached to the system. However, thousands of different atomic units can operate simultaneously, and each may have its own pattern of behavior which the chosen architecture should satisfy.

BENCHMARKING THE FUNCTIONALITY SUPPORTED BY THE ENTERPRISE ARCHITECTURE

There are some developments in technology that, in a positive way, are a threat to the existing order. Some people call these developments *disruptive technologies* because they disrupt the 50-year "legacy" of how computers are programmed and used, as well as how networks work. When systems architectures were first developed, they were designed to serve mainframes and maxi computers, not a fully distributed environment. Users of computer resources were expected to be satisfied with what the information technologists wanted to give them. They were not believed capable of posing their own requirements and then standing by them.

The advent of an enterprise architecture changed that prevailing mentality. Therefore, the enterprise architecture is a disruptive technology, but this disruption is positive. Extending the legacy software's life brings stagnation and loss of competitiveness to the firm. Two other technologies can also be considered disruptive: 1. open source software (OSS, commodity, or off-the-shelf software), and 2. extensive use of information appliances beyond the now classical distributed computing.

Web software is an example of OSS (see Chapter 15). The most obvious benefit of open source software is that it can provide significant cost savings to users. Indeed, commodity software has changed the pricing of programming products over the longer term, while in the short term it has provided users with the ability to test and benchmark rather than to accept and employ something that does not fit their needs.

The cultural change accompanying what has just been described is significant. While infrastructure software has become mostly open source, big chunks of applied programming have remained parochial. This is changing, however, and thus frees manpower for other duties such as sophisticated developments, benchmarking software functionality, and the implementation of novel architectural characteristics. Figure 2.6 presents in a block diagram an approach to be used in benchmarking a business-oriented architecture and its component parts. This procedure addresses main objectives, functions to be supported in order to reach these objectives, and costs associated with the support of these functions, as well as technical characteristics and their functionality.

Whether one is primarily concerned about business objectives or technical objectives of architectured facilities, it is advisable to experiment on projected solutions, then analyze and interpret simulated results. The recommended benchmarking program is not a conventional statistical program, but is able to provide, under stress conditions, information on sensitivity to loads in the technical part of the system, quality of results at both business and technical levels, and issues relating to the reliability and security of the control system. The goal of experimentation should be that of upgrading functionality while downsizing the cost of technological supports. Although the need for upgrading is self-evident, often people who talk of downsizing the cost factor have a major misconception of the issue.

Downsizing targets costs, which, when left unchecked, may run wild. By contrast, the functionality of services provided should be in an upswing. This twin aim of downsizing and upgrading is attainable through ingenious system design that capitalizes on high technology. To reach this double goal, however, one must use imagination to avoid repeating past errors at an even more complex level of implementation. One must also guard against dependence on promises rather than accomplishments.

It is not possible to build any long term structure — city, building, network, business division, or sales network — without a master blueprint that includes the goals and the tests. Neither can a long term information

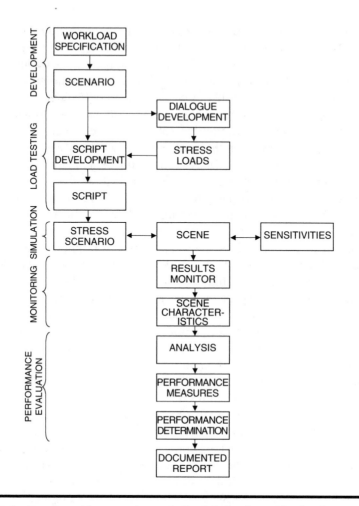

Figure 2.6 Benchmarking a system solution's behavior under load.

technology structure be developed without using blueprints to define basic component parts and supported facilities.

Before they are finalized, blueprints must be benchmarked, particularly if they are used to set the longer term technological infrastructure. Benchmarks must assist in accomplishing selection of hardware, operating systems, and other technical details and enabling functions. Properly conducted, benchmarks ease the burden of application development and allow for better coordination of all parts composing the system. They also permit knowledge of the functionality of what is purchased off the shelf or built by third parties, and identification of whether bought utilities are up to standard and can deliver under stress.

Benchmarks cannot be attempted independently of the enterprise architecture. The objective of a business-oriented architectural solution is to provide a master plan, just as that of a data architecture is to make data understandable and available to all authorized users in a secure way. The existence of a valid enterprise architecture significantly simplifies testing new applications, provided it can truly deliver what is needed. Hence, the service provided by benchmarks must ensure that technology is able to serve specific business goals, and define evolving information requirements within the business framework.

After the most essential goals, other objectives may be added because of the fiercely competitive nature of markets such as:

- Effective support for shorter lead time in systems development
- Better focused product cycles
- Lower development and production costs
- Ability to offer global products over heterogeneous platforms
- Increased need for knowledge-based systems

The architectural solution chosen must help to meet business requirements within the boundaries of what is technologically feasible; benchmarking should assure that this is the case. For this purpose, attention must be paid both to the grand design, with its broader perspective and overall impact, and to the details, whether the main theme is a product, a market, or risks.

THE CONCEPTUAL MODEL SHOULD BE BASED ON OPEN ARCHITECTURAL PRINCIPLES

A critical reference point for rethinking the company's requirements for an architectural solution revolves around the need to implement open systems. Open systems use commodity software, that is, wares which are no specific vendor's property. This makes it feasible to switch among hardware vendor platforms without reprogramming, therefore, it leads to an open vendor policy, which addresses all the layers shown in Figure 2.7.

Open systems and an open vendor policy should be a strategic decision reached by top management. Open systems are more important in dynamic business environments. Experience with networked solutions tends to improve if these support an open architecture in software and hardware. The market today is wiser and will not be coerced by a vendor. But many approaches advertising themselves as open are not.

Once an open vendor policy decision has been made by the board, the definition of an open system architecture implies a whole range of

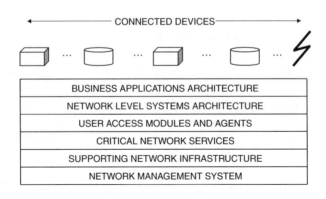

Figure 2.7 An open vendor policy leads to an enterprise architecture which employs commodity software in all layers of the organization.

decisions in regard to devices, services, and protocols. Therefore, a comprehensive policy needs to be elaborated in terms of physical and logical facilities. In turn, this requires functional definitions regarding, among other factors, transport utility, nodes and gateways, transactions and messaging, application-to-application communications, data storage and access mechanisms, and system management services.

Transport utility provides interconnections between a number of networking protocols and systems platforms which may be heterogeneous. A corporate backbone network transport utility will assure transparent access across disparate networks. Enough bandwidth must be provided to support high performance, cost-effective usage of transmission facilities, as well as prerequisites regarding transport management.

Gateways are necessary at every node because they ensure interconnection between dissimilar systems. Gateways are designated points of entry to the global network that enable users to gain a certain level of functionality within the service boundary of the enterprise architecture. Gateways may also provide data for network monitoring and control service, offer assistance in appropriate authentication and authorization, and ensure directory services as part of the core network directory service.

Gateways should be designed and managed efficiently in the context of a global solution. Both functionality and security assurance should be chosen in a manner that enhances running operational requirements of end-to-end applications. Integrity controls should be exercised over all proprietary domains, including routing in a declarative and dynamic sense while observing functional prerequisites, identification and authentication of communications and database services, and mapping all privilege and control attributes for privacy and security (see Chapter 16).

A subsystem dedicated to handling transactions and messaging may provide storage and forwarding services between external and internal networks including format conversion (see Chapter 15 for discussion on intranets and extranets). Directory facilities are a value-added characteristic of network management systems on disparate technologies for address and object name mapping and network configuration management.

Application-to-application communications over an open system should be independent of the underlying mechanisms by which the business-oriented architecture provides the required level of service. The solution adopted should ensure that peer-to-peer communications among applications are as easy as interprocess communication within a single system.

Data access services have several objectives. The ability of applications to access data contained in databases provided by different vendors, as well as in a heterogeneous network environment, is key to the realization of global service offerings. Heterogeneous data access should be seamless to the user; the architecture must facilitate the connectivity between applications and information elements.

Networks, databases, and applications should be managed within a consistent and comprehensive framework. Network management services provide facilities and protocols for the exchange of information and commands between subsystem management entities. This includes fault and event handling, reconfiguration assistance, performance evaluation, time accounting and usage tracking, resource distribution, and service allocation.

Time services are important for a widely distributed computing environment because they provide a common view of dating over the entire network and its component parts. Several functional services can make effective use of the time service, for example, order events for network management. The time service should have the necessary software able to synchronize all subsystems and components within the network, thereby providing a consistent view of the time.

The life cycle of the solution developed is also important since it indicates how costs will be amortized. In the context of the Internet, time-to-live (TTL) is a new metric advertised by some information providers who tell the customer what is expected TTL. However, because of rapid growth in requested new developments, solutions recently adopted cannot always live with original premises made at the time an off-the-shelf package was bought.

A present day paradox is that companies who reengineered themselves very effectively are now worried about how to keep up with fast evolving parameters impacting their solutions' life cycle. This is one reason why they develop technology acquisition strategies (see the next section).

Strategic relationships help in upkeep; the downside is that business partners who are used for technology transfer do not necessarily face the same problems as the company, and their approach leaves much to be desired.

The system solution adopted by the enterprise architecture should support any-to-any linking, cross referencing any product to any product, accessing the files of any client or supplier anywhere in the world, and interconnecting any location to any location, including after-hours networks for sales and trading. The described functionality should rest on one logical network, able to promote a growing range of on-line services — which is, after all, the goal of any well designed enterprise architecture.

A FINANCIAL SERVICES ARCHITECTURE AND EXAMPLE OF A SUCCESSFUL IMPLEMENTATION

Conceived in 1990 by Bankers Trust,* the financial services application (FSA) architecture targeted the construction of a solution which follows the principles outlined in previous sections. This solution was ahead of its time; many of the principles on which it rests have not yet been implemented by the average company. FSA is an open enterprise architecture that allows the bank and its business partners to exchange information in a uniform manner regardless of location, platform, or data structure.

Financial services data exchange (FSDX), the infrastructural custom-made utility of FSA, has been in use on a number of platforms: IBM/CICS, DEC/VMS, DOS/DESQView, MS/Windows, DEC/Ultrix, OSF/1, AIX, and NT. This service system brings together in a seamless manner all of the institution's independent applications and information-sharing requirements. At the core of FSDX design is its ability to permit owners of information to publish their multimedia streams by means of an easy-to-use record broadcast mechanism. Cross-system facilities permit multiple subscribers to receive the published multimedia streams in real-time, if they are currently listening, or through the utility's store and forward subsystem.

The publisher of data is differentiated by descriptive tags which make it feasible for subscribers to reference any or all information elements through the use of the FSDX remapping capability. This allows publishers to add or move data within their publication domain without adversely affecting subscribers, since subscribers reference the virtual data tags rather than the physical data record.

---

* In the late 1990s, Bankers Trust merged with Deutsche Bank.

Only those subscribers interested in the newly published information need modify their applications to receive it. The system also provides control over subscription to the information source, giving publishers the ability to preauthorize who can access information, down to the individual record level.

These are examples of checks and balances by which any communications-related utility must abide in order to be implemented successfully in a dynamic, evolving, and diverse business environment. Such utility must be platform-, location-, data-, and time-independent and also highly flexible in terms of allowing for changing information requirements while providing a consistent user interface.

The FSA architecture ensures that publishers, who need to communicate their information only once, no longer need to maintain multiple, customized data links to various applications that need such information. This helps to reduce the expense of maintenance programmers and related technology. It also assists in avoiding errors; yet, surprisingly enough, this feature is found only in some applications environments.

Furthermore, applications' communication with each other using a common utility makes it possible to apply advancements in communications technology to a single set of software, rather than requiring each individual system to implement modifications separately. This again helps to decrease the cost of long term maintenance and to exercise greater control over technology investments.

The flexibility and functionality of the FSDX utility has enabled Bankers Trust to develop, among other key applications, a comprehensive global risk management application (RMA), which came on-line in 1994. RMA receives information real-time from trading systems around the world, supporting an environment that can provide credit risk and market risk exposures and making them interactively available to top management trade by trade, across all business lines, and anywhere in the world, in connection to any counterparty.

FSDX has also been chosen as the underlying transport mechanism of the bank's global asset application architecture. For this purpose, the FSDX mechanism has been extended from purely interapplication data exchange to customer interfacing — in other words, down to the user on the workstation (through the Excel interface).

The example just presented helps in documenting the polyvalence of solutions based on a well designed architecture and its supported services. Goals and facilities described in previous sections are there to permit the construction of interactively supported information services at different levels of the organization's hierarchy, including higher layers that target specific applications areas such as risk management.

Today, an architectural methodology which follows FSA principles should be enriched with knowledge artifacts (see Chapter 9 on the use of agents). Two different design approaches are possible: bottom-up, which starts by building a knowledge-intense infrastructure along the FSA example, and top-down, which targets applications first. The choice will dictate the kinds of agents to be developed and used and the structure of the enterprise architecture.

Designers of a knowledge-enriched architectural methodology should carefully review the lessons learned by top-tier companies that have become more competitive by exploiting new horizons in supported facilities, including the contributions of agents. A sound methodology will pay special attention to architectural semantics, on-line assistance through knowledge robots, and experimentation through simulation.

To develop a simulator, one must decide what to target, which databases to use, which results to achieve, and the mathematics to be employed. Architectural semantics describing the exact behavior of each component part in the broader description of wanted services must also be added. These may include, for example, the conditions under which data are placed in the pipeline of each facility, and the stages of transformation undergone by a product or process to be tracked in the market.

Architectural semantics assist in the effective integration of modules which should constitute the infrastructure and the application's building blocks. To be successful, it is necessary to analyze state-of-the-art practices worldwide, including those of business partners, and identify opportunities presented by the availability of intranets and extranets (see Chapter 15). Risks involved in the solution should also be assessed.

In conclusion, emphasis must also be placed on value-added services supported through knowledge engineering, since use of intelligent networks[2] is discussed. The enterprise architecture cannot forego the benefits of high technology and still claim to be successful; neither should one neglect to identify and properly train its users. Real-time information can only be adequately conveyed to trained receivers.

REFERENCES

1. Williams–Ellis, C. and Williams–Ellis, A., *The Tank Corps*, George Newnes, London, 1919.
2. Chorafas, D.N. and Steinmann, H., *Intelligent Networks. Telecommunications Solutions for the 1990s*, CRC Press, Boca Raton, FL, 1990.

3

TECHNOLOGY AND ORGANIZATION REPOSITION THE COMPANY IN A COMPETITIVE MARKET

INTRODUCTION

Three major waves of technology have influenced the way we worked and, to a significant extent, the way we lived, during the last 50 years. The first came in the 1950s with computers and high-compression engines, the second in the 1970s with microprocessors (see the next section) and distributed information systems, the third in the 1990s with any-to-any telecommunications networks, through the Internet and wide-area broadband solutions.

Roughly 20 years separated any two of these three waves, each of which promoted the introduction of new, more sophisticated applications, enlarged the size of the market, but also led to a bifurcation. At one side there was a concentration of power among bigger organizations, at the other, a proliferation of small, innovative companies which extended the frontiers of knowledge. Deregulation and globalization also had an effect, e.g., the redefinition of critical mass and financial staying power.

Among the bigger companies, superior organization is the major force transforming the way they work, communicate, collaborate, and trade. Every technological breakthrough calls for new, more advanced organizational practices. General management principles were developed in the mid- to late 19th century with the industrial revolution; time and motion study was born in the early 20th century, with the advent of line production; staff and line began in the 1920s with the evolution of large industrial structures. Today emphasis is placed on policy formation and command and control (see the third through sixth sections).

To a significant extent, technology and organization decide whether an entity succeed or fails; they are tough judges. The Internet has not only enlarged the communications horizon but also increasingly impacts the way in which products are designed, marketed, and serviced (see Section III). This is what some companies today call the *i-fication* (or *e-fication*) of business — a term denoting concentration on Internet-based business transformation, on-line client service, and advanced computer applications.

Internet or no Internet, the products designed and marketed are for the product users. The prime objective is not the intellectual satisfaction of their developers, though this too is present, but profits and cash flow derived from the sale of products and services, so that the company making them can grow and survive in a market more competitive and demanding than ever.

As new products and services become routine, the contributions the cutting edge of technology made when they were still in the laboratory are forgotten. Sometimes, new solutions are introduced as a step function. The passenger vehicle engine compression ratio moved almost linearly from 6.0 in 1935 to 7.3 in 1954. Then it took off exponentially, reaching 9.5 in 1958.

The story of microprocessors and microelectronics in general, as well as their most significant contributions to business and industry, is too well known to be retold. Its best expression is Moore's law (see the next section) which has ruled the change in computer power. The fact that power doubles every 18 months at practically stable prices has effected a revolution. Like high-compression engines, microprocessors have had a great impact, well beyond what was originally foreseen. During the last three decades microelectronics and computers outstripped the industry's overall growth by a significant margin.

The impact of microprocessors and the phenomenal growth of microelectronics have had a major effect on the way that the enterprise architecture is designed and implemented; therefore, this chapter is a necessary supplement to Chapters 1 and 2. To make a rather accurate estimate of what lies ahead with new developments and their practical applications, one needs to understand the role of trigger technologies. By creating an environment that opens business opportunities, breakthroughs, which at first sight seem to be unrelated, work in synergy, thus entering a large variety of products and creating a snowball effect.

Trigger technologies shape the direction of industrial development and alter the perspective of whole sectors of the economy. Therefore, understanding them and their impact helps in assessing the potential of a new industry and the architectural solution necessary to serve it, for example, what happens today and may happen tomorrow with the Internet.

THE AFTERMATH OF MOORE'S LAW AND THE LAW OF THE PHOTON

Industrial planners working along the road of prognostication develop the ability to project relationships and assess potential synergies between new technologies and the behavior of markets. But to shape knowledge and understanding of how technologies combine to create value, it is necessary first to focus on how they affect the organization and alter its information structure. This is the focus chapter, and the best way to start is with two laws which have reshaped the industrial landscape.

Moore's Law has been correctly predicting for decades that densities of transistor technology would at least double every 18 months. This "law" was coined by Intel's founder, Gordon Moore, who described the phenomenon of higher density parts and improvements in their cost structure:

- New product innovations such as denser memories or faster microprocessors are designed and sold at high initial prices.
- As the volume of production grows, the amortization of equipment becomes smaller for each unit and yields increase; therefore, unit costs decrease.

Typically, intense competition ensures that the cheaper the part is to manufacture over time, the lower the price the manufacturer can charge. Market elasticity causes volumes to go up even more. At some point, new design rules are developed to increase the packing density. With this, a shrink is implemented to decrease the die size, which improves yield and makes the part even cheaper to manufacture.

Based on elasticity of demand, the declining prices the customer sees promote usage of the part. This happens just about when demand becomes inelastic and stable prices will not stimulate demand anymore. Then, a next generation part becomes available again, as Moore's law suggests. From the mid 1970s to the late 1990s, this cycle has driven down the cost of computer power quite sharply, as seen in Figure 3.1.

Although Moore's prognostication regarding microprocessors has become a classic, the validity of its calculation is expected to continue for only a few more years. Eventually the steeply rising curve will taper off, hence the interest in nanotechnologies discussed in Chapter 6. Moore has frequently warned that physical limits will be reached in crucial factors such as feature sizes, manufacturing techniques, and integration of semiconductors.

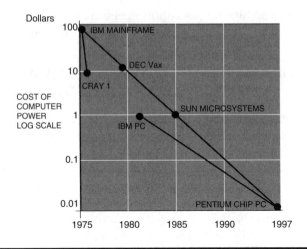

Figure 3.1 Cost of computer power in dollars per instruction per second (1975 = 100).

It is not clear how to make faster components with today's dominant technology CMOS, though many companies try to break perceived limits. The current estimate is that significant barriers will be reached by 2010 or thereafter. On the other hand, technology has frequently shown an uncanny ability to overcome projected limits.

Experts believe that another postulate by Gene Amdahl may also be reaching its critical barrier. This hypothosis states that a program can run no faster than the time required to execute its sequential sections. Algorithms are typically cast in the form of an equation that accounts for the time spent in the parallel, or vectorizable, and sequential parts of the code. Amdahl's postulate is that:

■ If a program can be parallelized at 80% and 20% must be executed sequentially
■ Then, the maximum reduction in execution time is by a factor of five

Also known as Amdahl's Law, this rule was thought to provide a practical limit to the number of processors that could be used profitably in a parallel computer. But this approach did not account for the fact that, as the size of the problem increases, for many scientific applications the sequential fraction of the computation tends to decrease. In a parallel system the speed and memory of the processors enable a user to tackle bigger problems.

A lesson to be derived from the downgrading of Amdahl's postulate is that significant advances in both hardware and software technology make old rules obsolete. There is, as well, a change of emphasis on what constitutes the focal point of an epoch. In a very dynamic industry, yesterday's critical subject is not the same as that of today's and tomorrow's.

A salient present and future problem is bandwidth for multimedia telecommunications (see Chapter 6). The any-to-any network infrastructure is going to be driven by the low cost of optical solutions and universal mobile telecommunications in the core, and by high-speed Internet access technologies like cable modems and asymmetrical digital subscriber lines (ADSL). The concept underpinning this infrastructure, which can be seen as analogous to that of semiconductors in the computer industry, is becoming the basic building block of bandwidth in telecommunications channels. The best available estimates suggest that core bandwidth will increase by a factor of 2 or more every 9 months, while cost is held constant. The problem that has not yet been properly studied is how this capacity can be used so that companies and consumers are willing to pay the costs.

On the technology side, the industry statistics just mentioned underpin the law of the photon. This rapid rise in bandwidth characterizing telecommunications speed dramatizes the likelihood that high speed Internet access interconnecting all offices and homes will be a reality that supports voice, data, graphics, and image. Contrarians, however, suggest that, in business terms, the law of the photon has backfired because it has led many companies, particularly the carriers, to the wrong conclusions. In terms of business opportunity, the challenge is not to establish the channel but to fill the channel. This has a parallel in commercial aviation where the challenge is not in flying an airplane, but in filling the seats before it takes off.

A fact behind the law of the photon is that the late 1990s has seen an acceleration in speeds connected to optical data transmission, largely related to dense wave division multiplexing (DWDM). One should also keep in perspective that, while optical data transmission is now doubling every 12 months, this is surpassed by advances in wireless communications connected to spread spectrum. Experts think that more impressive technological developments are still to come and will have a very significant impact. For example, the cost of bandwidth may be falling ten times faster than the cost of computing (Gilder's postulate), and the value of a network will increase with the square of its participants (Metcalfe's postulate).

Metcalfe's postulate and the growth in PCs correlate. The essence of Metcalfe's prognostication is that the value of a network tends to equal the square of the number of nodes attached to it. This is an important statistic for peer-to-peer computers and communications systems. Bob Metcalfe did not specify, however, how many peripherals could or should be attached to a networked personal computer to fulfill prerequisites of his "square rule." A device attached to the network may have many microprocessors.

The continuing growth in PCs, in defiance of what many experts suggest about putting one's own information on servers at Web sites, stems from the fact that the personal computer is no longer a small island. A wild guess is that some 400 million of today's estimated 500 million to 600 million PCs are connected at one time or another (or at least can have access) to the Internet — forming a big digital universe.

This impacts in an important way enterprise architectures. As Intel's Craig R. Barrett says, "...if you look at the center of that digital universe, the focal point for the big bang is the core of the PC."[1] One can appreciate that this duality greatly influences the way architecture enterprise solutions are architectured. The more PCs are attached to the network, the network's power increases, not linearly but by its square rule. The more the network's power expands in an exponential way, the more PCs, hand-held devices, and other end user gear will be attached to it.

The practical aftermath of such prognostications should be given appropriate weight. If Metcalfe's postulate is true (and there are good chances that this will be the case), then the number of internetworked clients of a financial or industrial organization will take on new significance. In fact, some companies are already betting on that likelihood. For instance, Citicorp will target 1 billion account holders by 2010, the large majority of them interconnected.

There is as well Romer's postulate of increasing marginal returns. It states that there are spillover effects as the same technology cross-fertilizes different areas of industry and the economy. Value is migrating to software, says Paul Romer, an economist who talks in terms of wealth creation in the coming years. His theme is that software is the vital catalyst.

If technology's bust in 2001 is any guide, and if forecasts about 2002 are valid, then software has given proof of its resiliency in a falling market. What about value embedded in the information which becomes available to the organization and its clients?

WEALTH CREATION, SPAN OF ATTENTION, AND SPAN OF CONTROL

"The effective executive," advises Peter Drucker, "focuses on contribution: what can I contribute that will significantly affect the performance and the results of the institution I serve? His stress is on responsibility."[2] After explaining that the effective executive holds himself accountable on performance, Drucker asks the provocative question, "And what do you do that justifies your being on the payroll?" He then says the typical answers one gets is that "I have 850 people working for me," "I am in charge of sales," "I run the accounting department." Only a few say: "It's my job to give our managers the information they need to make the right decision" — yet this is what is truly important.

There is nothing abstract in the sense of making effective, focused decisions which serve organizational purposes. The right type of information is crucial in concentrating on a few major issues where outstanding results can be produced. Superior performance is a prerequisite to the creation of wealth, and invariably it feeds on strengths of the decision-maker.

Information, particularly timely and accurate information, has been a scarce commodity for a long time. Today, in terms of processor capacity and channel bandwidth, Moore's law and the law of the photon see to it that technical limits become elastic. What is scarce is the ability to provide the end user with personalized, filtered information which serves him or her in the best possible way. A manager's and a professional's jobs (see Chapter 3) need timely and accurate information presented in a way that sustains a competitive edge, flexible structures, plural communications, and an increase in one's span of attention.

In his aforementioned book, Drucker explains span of attention through an example. One of the company presidents to whom he was consultant always scheduled their meetings for an hour and a half. When Drucker asked him why always an hour and a half, the bank's president answered that he had found out that his span of attention was about that long.

What the company president really meant was that was the amount of time he could really focus on his energies, with a clear mind, concentrating on a specific subject. If he worked longer on any one topic in an uninterrupted manner, he lost attention or repeated himself. At the same time, the man said that he had learned from experience that nothing of importance can really be tackled in a shorter period of time.

An executive's span of attention and the span of control featured by a company's organization and structure correlate. Management theory has long taught the importance of span of control, which deals with how many subordinates an executive can effectively manage. In the 1970s and 1980s, many office automation projects, for instance Citibank's Project Paradise, sought to enlarge the span of control from an average of 5 to an average of 8 subordinates by eliminating the time spent on trivia. The larger the span of control is, the less the intermediate management level. This significantly increases efficiency and cuts administrative costs.

A study done by Bankers Trust in 1989 demonstrated that the average executive spends about two thirds of his time on trivia and administrative duties, which so often are considered "inescapable." As shown in Figure 3.2, based on this finding, the 1990 to 1995 information technology strategy by Bankers Trust set as a goal to reduce this wasted time by half, which would essentially double the executive's time dedicated to productive activities.

One of the problems with the implementation of information technology during the last 50 years has been that, in general, little attention has been paid to the span of control. Significant gains in span of control and the reduction of trivia, like those targeted by Citibank and Bankers Trust, will not happen by their own will. However, when such milestones are properly planned, they spell the end of the monolithic information systems like those of most companies.

It is more or less self-evident that making the manager's and professional's spans of attention as well as the organization's span of control focal points in the design of a modern enterprise architecture and its applications systems is a strategy leading to the creation of wealth. At the same time, it is a major switch in current policies and practices requiring a deep cultural change so that the users of information can become the motors of this evolution.

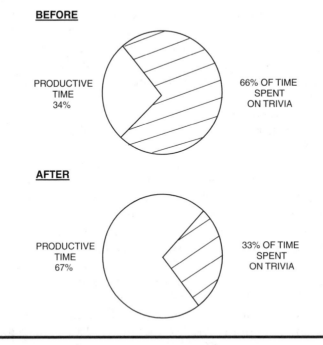

Figure 3.2 A basic goal of information technology is to reduce the time spent on trivia as far as state of the art allows.

The previous section showed, through practical examples supported by the most recent laws or postulates of applied science, that technology permitting realization of the best-ever applications of computers and communications is on hand. What is missing is cultural change and organizational reengineering — the Chorafas postulate. Technological performance ratios are impressive and document that bandwidth has replaced transistors as the driving technology. But they say nothing about how well or how badly these technological achievements will be put into practice for the ultimate client.

Culture and organization make up a metasphere of accomplishment in wealth creation, where only the best-managed companies pay due attention (see Chapter 4). A well-managed company is one that demands return on investment (ROI) from information technology before spending more money on computers, communications, and software. ROI is a cultural and an organizational prerequisite: top management should see to it that the lion's share of IT investments goes to projects that make the future, rather than repeating yesterday. For its part, information technology management must assure that every breakthrough in applied science is used to improve return on investment by means of tangible results.

A rapidly advancing technology ensures that solutions are not linear. There is a long list of pitfalls on the road to implementation of advanced IT into which companies fall time and again. One of the more common in connection to new information technology developments is that, while mainframe computers have reached their limits, companies keep adding mainframes. Another trap is that the majority of computer operations keep running three or more different operating systems, none of which is current.

While a list of pitfalls in IT can be long, it is necessary to examine only one more critical factor: generally, systems personnel are *not* up to date on technology. At the heart of this problem is the fact that information technology management is usually more preoccupied with maintenance and trivial enhancements to existing applications than with new solutions. Yet, as Figure 3.3 shows, a survey done by MIT documented that the topmost requirement today is to match IT investments and solutions with strategic corporate requirements. This is the right approach but it cannot be done through patched-up technology.

An advanced enterprise architecture, knowledge-enriched applications, fast deliverables, and attention to ROI constitute best possible use of technological capabilities because they are synonymous with the creation of wealth to be employed for further investments. Saying that experts think that bandwidth is coming into an exponential gross abundance should simultaneously imply that new, effective organizational solutions will revolve around this breakthrough.

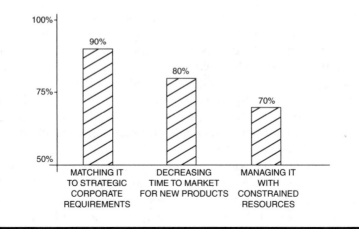

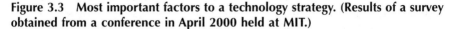

Figure 3.3 Most important factors to a technology strategy. (Results of a survey obtained from a conference in April 2000 held at MIT.)

Failure to account for this second leg of organizational performance leads to white elephants like UMTS licenses in Europe. In 2000 and 2001, telecoms hard-pressed for cash overleveraged themselves with bank loans to build a UMTS factory whose down payment was $130 billion for airwaves alone (see Chapter 6), but which had no clear plans about products or their pricing.[3] A good way to test if ROI is what is really meant is to ask: what has been and will be obtained from:

- Transistors shrinking by half, twice every 18 months?
- Photonics doubling work speed every 9 months?
- Wireless tripling its speed every year?
- Internet traffic doubling every 4 months?

Also, this rapid pace in technological development creates imbalances which must be addressed through rigorous organizational studies and restructuring the company's information system. This is a salient problem for the board of directors and the chief executive officer, and vital to the profession of information technologists.

Based on these facts, what should be the guidelines of the new grand design of the enterprise architecture? As Bob Metcalfe correctly points out, the value of a network can grow exponentially: the real growth of information networks is not in time but in users, and it is polynomial or exponential. If the network is growing in the square of the number of its users, then this should be the focal point of the architecture's design and implementation strategy.

Polynomial growth is faster than linear growth, and exponential growth is even faster. The bottom line with the oncoming wave of multimedia communications is that the future is already here, but it is unevenly distributed because of huge cultural and organizational differences. Only people with conceptual skills and companies with superior organization can really take advantage of the sophisticated technology currently at their disposition.

RETHINKING INFORMATION TECHNOLOGY ALONG LINES OF CULTURAL CHANGE

Effective decisions are usually judgmental. They are based on personal opinions rather than on consensus, though the sense of a meeting can play a key role in understanding the decision. Differences of opinion are inevitable because, while everyone may have the same or similar information, each perceives, understands, and interprets it differently. Background and experience play a key role in the decision being made, and the way this decision is spelled out conditions its impact during the weeks, months, and years to come.

What I just stated can be inverted and it still remains valid. Effectiveness is a complex of practices, but to be up-to-date, decisions must feed on information which is accurate and timely as well as assisted by prognostication of the aftermath of choices made. What should be the grand design of an enterprise architecture which serves these purposes by capitalizing on half a century of experience in the IT domain?

This is a legitimate query, which must be served through a factual and documented answer. This chapter keeps to the fundamentals, while Chapter 4 covers the information technology strategy of leading organizations and Chapter 5 outlines the new technological infrastructure, Section II elaborates on some of the best applications and Section III addresses the broader perspective of the Internet economy. The central theme these references have in common is how to organize the future to compete with the present, and how to go from here to there at a pace ahead of the curve.

The type of organization of concern to this book is any industrial or financial organization composed of more than 100 people that produces a product or renders a service. The focus of references is the recurring and, whenever possible, defining characteristics that make the organization challenging and yet difficult to study in terms of information requirements, e.g., its complexity.

Unlike small groups where members meet face to face to conduct their business, larger groups necessarily depend upon a structure of departmentalization. Therefore, they need organized information moved forward, and also require feedback. Larger groups operate, so to speak, through intermediaries. The whole sense of an organizational hierarchy is embedded in this preceding sentence (see also the third section on span of control). Organizational structure is built level upon level; the enterprise architecture consists of multiple subsystems.

The underlying structural approach has classically been hierarchical, with the many intermediate levels ensuring an element of anonymity or facelessness. It makes little difference to the group who decides "this" or "that," or answers specific queries critical to the work in process. What is important is that activity messaging gets accomplished, and transactions can take place.

A hierarchical organization typically entails formalized standard routines, whether operating procedures or communications channels. Sometimes these channels operate inefficiently; therefore, larger groups tend to develop subcollectivities or units within which they operate face to face as if they were smaller groups. This leads to the growth of informal structures which sometimes become more powerful and effective than formal structures.

A fact appreciated only by tier-1 organizations is that Moore's law and the law of the photon significantly change organizational relationships. From a strategic planning perspective, it is important to understand the new organizational dimensions associated with Moore's Law and what these mean for the enterprise. Consider innovation and marketing as an example.

To dominate the market that evolved around the Internet, a company must be more innovative than its competitors, developing or licensing leading-edge products and services, and racing to stay ahead. This strategy is necessary to keep up with spiraling demand as hundreds of millions of people, much more than ever before, use the Web from diverse devices.

Each company has its own perception of what Moore's law, the law of the photon, Metcalfe's and other postulates mean to its business, and how it can exploit them for product innovation and marketing reasons. The strategy of Sun Microsystems provides a reference. This company is working on two tracks: 1. massive computing and data storage boxes with plenty of microprocessors which will be used as networked servers, and 2. distributed computing solutions permitting the load to be divided between smaller machines linked by high-speed networks.

Sun Microsystems is also betting it can leapfrog its competitors by giving customers the essential Internet wares they need to run their electronic businesses in one package. This is supposed to attract companies facing a blizzard of offerings. The result of diversity in platforms is that it costs a fortune to make them work together. Sun microsystems, therefore, aims to provide seamless integrative solutions.

Chip manufacturers, on the other hand, are on a different track. Their goal is to accelerate power at a rate between 10 and 100 times faster than

Moore's law, which holds that chips double in speed every 18 months. This way, they will catch up with the law of the photon, which leaves progress in computing as defined by Moore's law well behind.

By all evidence, the product planning and marketing strategies of Sun Microsystems and chip manufacturers diverge but, in terms of their contribution to the growth of organization and structure among user organizations, they converge. This should be seen under the perspective of an intelligent environment (see MIT's Project Oxygen presented in Chapters 7 and 8). The utilization of steadily increased computer power, agents, and distributed massive data storage promotes new solutions in organization and structure. Before they can be formalized, these new organizational approaches will be reconfigured to meet rapidly evolving market drives and product innovation.

Within the context of organizational restructuring, which has practically no time limit, attention should be paid to another critical element of larger industrial, financial, and social systems: their tendency to specialize. This leads to proliferation of functions. It also separates the lines of formal authority from those of technical competence. An aftermath is power-skill interdependencies.

Still, another element particularly intrinsic to a hierarchical organization is the tendency by different departments and their managers to withhold information because information means power. Like knowledge and status, information conveys more power to its holder, and those who have it think they are ahead of their colleagues. On a personal level this is an absurd idea, yet it is widely practiced. It is really disastrous at the company level, however, because it starves the organization of information.

Early network solutions of the 1970s, for instance the system network architecture (SNA), followed a vertical, hierarchical approach. Therefore, such networks permitted (and in some cases facilitated) a continuation of hierarchical management practices. By contrast, modern enterprise architectures are horizontal; they work peer to peer. This is already a cultural change of some magnitude.

One of the cultural changes whose time has come is a result of the level of sophistication of the desired solution. Taking the year 2000 as a starting point, it is proper to consider the state of the art of organizational and technology issues as low when compared to what is expected to be available by 2010. As Figure 3.4 shows, every projection suggests that the level of organization and technology will grow rapidly during the coming years among tier-1 financial institutions and industrial companies. The sophistication of organizational solutions and tools at end users' disposal will, in all likelihood, move faster than technology. This is necessary in order to catch up with the cultural and organizational lag of the past decades, and also to remain competitive in a highly demanding market.

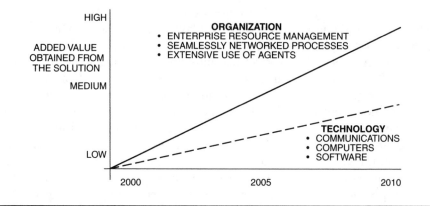

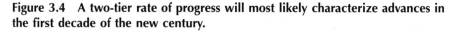

Figure 3.4 A two-tier rate of progress will most likely characterize advances in the first decade of the new century.

The preceding considerations merit attention because they bear importantly on strategic planning, policy formation, and the management of change, as well as information flow and language of communication. Every one of the factors outlined enters into the conceptual model of an enterprise architecture and the organizational transformation it brings along. This conceptual schema must then be translated into a working model permitting study and experimentation on the approach that will best serve the company's requirements for greater effectiveness.

POLICY FORMATION, COMMAND AND CONTROL, AND INFRASTRUCTURAL BASE

Most board members, senior executives, and their immediate assistants treat the implementation of high technology as a technical problem rather than as a means to win business. This turns the issue on its head because the latter is much more important than the former. The nature of the cultural change necessary to use IT in a way to win new business should be evident: get off the beaten path. Perhaps somewhat less evident is the role of information technology in policy formation and command and control.

Because the extent of cultural change is not always appreciated, it takes senior management much more than usually imagined to come to terms with its investments in information technology so as to derive benefits from them. The needed cultural change requires clear objectives and a determined effort to learn from the leaders (see Chapter 4). The leaders in IT implementation have found that, in the end, companies confident of their skills and their decision can develop state-of-the-art enterprise architectures, while laggards throw money at the problem, lose their position and their market, and find it increasingly difficult to survive.

Consider a practical example. The most effective structure is one characterized by wide span of control, and thus few layers; Figure 3.5 retains only four layers. The top two, CEO and executive vice presidents form the strategic and policy system. The next level is that of command and control (see Chapters 7 and 8 on the revamping of this layer through an intelligent environment). The bottom layer constitutes the organization's infrastructural base.

A knowledge-enriched enterprise architecture would expand the span of control, permitting a flat organization. It is necessary, however, to appreciate that even a flat organization observes a hierarchy. Through strategic choices and policy formation, senior management provides the controllers with directives and standards. Policy makers establish the plans and controllers determine what should be done at which time; together they prescribe criteria in terms of accomplishments that can be evaluated.

Typically, in a manufacturing company the infrastructural base is a technological system into which labor, raw materials, and raw data are poured, and through which materials are processed into a final product or service. Interestingly enough, with a few changes, a similar model characterizes banking. In a general sense, materials may be professional know-how, manual work, messages, iron ore, automotive parts, customers orders, or transactions. The infrastructural base suggests the basic productive work of the organization, which is rendering the services the firm provides to its clients.

Over this infrastructural base, Figure 3.5 postulates a metalevel group which constitutes the command and control system whose services are absolutely vital to any worthwhile operation. The elements in command and control are implementers; they schedule, direct, and manipulate the way the infrastructural base delivers services, by interpreting decisions and policies developed at and ratified from the top.

Command and control monitors the criteria of accomplishment for the entire organization. Each individual in this control system has a finite domain of power where his or her authority is commensurate with his or her responsibility. Both are reflected into the infrastructural base. Typically, he or she receives feedback information concerning performance and problems primarily within restricted area of accountability.

Based on a current forward-looking technological project by MIT, Chapter 7 presents an excellent example on how this command and control system can benefit from state-of-the-art solutions, namely, any-to-any broadband networks and agents.[4] Specialized, knowledge-enriched artifacts help in restructuring time-honored concepts of what a control system should do when assisted by computer, software, and communications channels. While reading Chapters 7 and 8, contrast the revolutionary aspects of Project Oxygen with the more evolutionary

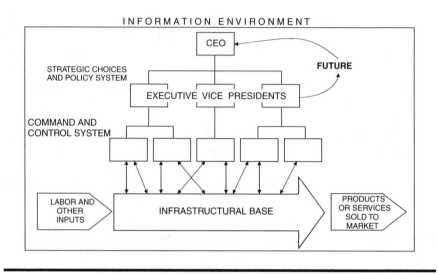

Figure 3.5   The information environment envelops and serves the three management layers as well as the infrastructural base whose job is production.

approaches on how the infrastructural base can be improved step by step followed in engineering, manufacturing, and logistics.

Both evolutionary and revolutionary approaches have a role in industry because each addresses a different time horizon in terms of deliverables. While the controllers attempt to schedule and track inputs to the infrastructural base, policy makers have the duty to anticipate demands placed on the entire organization by the market. Such anticipation helps in providing a relatively stable environment for the controllers so that they know what they ought to do, and what they ought to achieve.

Policy makers and controllers face two connected internal operational problems. The former must devise strategies that position the organization against the forces of the future and that individual controllers can understand and execute. The latter must devise tactics which follow these strategies, and at the same time they must know how to make the infrastructural system tick. This dual synergy is needed to enable the infrastructure to contribute to accomplishing results required by the governing organizational layers.

Another problem confronting the upper layers of organization and structure is to predict the performance of the entity, given knowledge of what it takes to execute established strategies and appreciation of what the entity as a whole is able to deliver. Even the best studied strategic plan is void of substance if the organization that should execute it is not able to follow it.

To meet the goals of an ambitious strategic plan, the best solution is to grow resources. But if the plan has been made in a way disconnected from existing human capital, product base (including R&D), marketing skills, and financial staying power, then growing resources and repositioning the organization and moving it forward may not be an option.

The enterprise architecture enters into this discussion from a dual perspective: providing information on status and resources, and ensuring an open line to feedback, for example, on results obtained through repositioning and tactics employed by individual controllers. This should be seen within the perspective of a threefold conceptual schema of policy, control, and infrastructure. In larger organizations, each of these reference layers is a complex maze in its own right. Each level of reference contains elements of executive command, managerial planning and control, and technical skill. Furthermore, within each level there is significant diversity in the exercise of policy formation and control functions. Appearances and official statements often are at variance with real distributions of power, making the restructuring of information channels and their successful operation on a day-to-day basis much more difficult.

This said, for purposes of clarification and exposition it is useful to consider larger organizations as consisting primarily of a limited number of clear and distinct levels, assuming that certain key notions concerning organizational relationships and structural problems can be formulated so that their investigation is effectively undertaken. One of the key issues requiring attention is interrelation between policy formation and managerial control, examined in the next section.

To better appreciate how an enterprise architecture should reflect on the notions presented in the preceding paragraphs, consider a quick paradigm of an atomic unit of reference which can help in the decomposition of any system at any level of functionality. As shown in Figure 3.6, stimuli enter this atomic unit and activate it. The result is a transform function changing the input into output, or response, but also producing an error signal. In real life, at any level of reference, the stimuli and the environment are constantly changing; new demands and challenges continually confront the atomic unit, which must therefore adjust itself accordingly.

These notions are behind the fact that a dynamic organization is constantly altering its goals as well as the criteria of performance in view of anticipated future events. The "red blood cells" of this atomic unit are information that must always be accurate and timely. The objective of restructuring the company's information system is to maintain and enhance this flow of red blood cells. It is important to keep this in mind when designing an enterprise architecture.

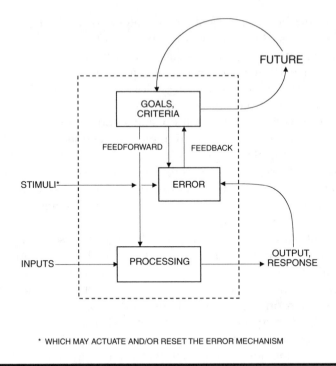

* WHICH MAY ACTUATE AND/OR RESET THE ERROR MECHANISM

Figure 3.6 The atomic unit of communications into which feedforward and feedback mechanisms integrate.

TECHNOLOGY HELPS IN POLICY FORMATION *AND* IN COMMAND AND CONTROL

New knowledge is needed to better understand the work being done. Such understanding helps in the quality of work. Starting in the 1920s, new knowledge, and the way it is applied, have been increasingly based on scientific methods, as evidenced by the attention paid in the pre- and post-World War II eras to scientific management or, more precisely, the scientific methodology helping management to do a more focused job. All six functions of management — forecasting, planning, organizing, staffing, directing, and controlling — can benefit from the application of scientific tools and the technology that comes with them. The directing and controlling activities are close to day-to-day problems.

The opposite is true of the metalayer (higher level) of policy formation, which includes forecasting and planning. Command and control are, almost entirely, activities addressing themselves to present challenges or to the immediately foreseeable future. The control system is almost wholly preoccupied with the inner, domestic issues of a given organization: its operationally ongoing demands and processes. By contrast, policy formation must look far in terms of markets, products, and processes and their financing. It should also actively search for ways and means through which the company can prosper and survive.

It follows logically that policy formation has longer range prerequisites. The need to be ahead of the curve in product innovation is present; decisions about costs, quality, and prices also must be made in timely manner. Quality and prices correlate. In classical economics, prices are typically established based of one's own cost of production and distribution. Today this process has been inverted. Prices must be established while considering future events which are uncertain, and integrating into pricing decisions the risks to be assumed.

As a result, pricing increasingly resembles the nonlinear process employed in insurance. In the global market, the old industrial model of a demand–supply equilibrium does not hold. While a big company may spend billions of dollars in R&D, challenging products may come out of the brains of youngsters working in a garage; lower cost products might come from anywhere in the global economy. The most critical factor in this nonlinearity is uncertainty of an outcome.

Uncertainty has become a cornerstone notion of the service economy. In today's interconnected environment, business risks are exploding. This tends to make the simple feedback mechanism obsolete. That is why, in Figure 3.6, the atomic unit is connected to a feedforward loop, which is enriching established goals with prognostication about likely outcomes.

Notice that the channels of feedforward and feedback are crucial at any layer of the organization, from policy formation to command and control and the infrastructural system (see the previous section). Without them no atomic unit would be able to achieve commendable results, or effects deserving careful monitoring because of their contribution to the final goal.

In its fundamentals the concept behind the block diagram in Figure 3.4 is valid at every layer of an organizational structure, but the exact mechanics of its functionality vary with the mission each layer must perform. At the level of control, for instance, the functionality of atomic units is tuned to the role of a watchdog that follows accepted, set plans and specified prescribed goals. When this happens, the atomic unit tends to view the external environment as no more than a means to its organizational objectives, and views the organization as a closed system, an immediate environment that remains relatively stable through time.

In contrast, at the top layer of policy formation, the preoccupation is with future events and their uncertainty. This brings into the picture more complex issues. Not only is the future contingent, but policymakers also must deal with possible options and alternatives, as well as with their likelihood. Policymakers must concern themselves with the possible consequences of any given alternative, which is what prognostication is all about. The options they examine might even be mutually contradictory and incoherent, yet they are the bricks with which long-range plans are made.

The members of the board and the CEO find themselves in the paradox that, although they live in the present, it is the future which dictates their complex decisions, and it does so right now. Rooted to the past and present, corporate plans are nonetheless directed toward something that is not yet a real thing and, when it becomes real, it might be different from what the decision-makers have imagined.

There are situations wherein a set of enacted consequences are hard to reverse. On other occasions, an opportunity has been lost, or time passed without action. As every senior executive worth his salt will appreciate, to be competitive and to sustain his competitiveness, one must steadily evaluate himself, the organization, its products and services, and the customer's response.

One of the main weaknesses of information technology as practiced today is that, in the large majority of financial institutions and industrial organizations, there is a horde of conceptual weaknesses. Also, there is resistance to tuning the system to requirements existing at top management level. Instead, huge investment occurs at the bottom of the pyramid of functions while the top is starved for information.

Figure 3.7 dramatizes this reference. Current allocation of funds generally ensures that top management gets, drop-by-drop, the information

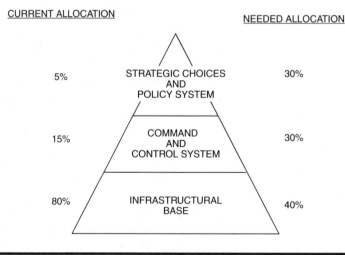

Figure 3.7 The actual allocation of funds for information technology does not correspond to real needs for the company's growth and survival.

it needs. However, top-of-the-line institutions have moved away from this very bad practice toward an allocation of IT funds that, first and foremost, benefit senior management and the professionals. That is what is meant by needed allocation in Figure 3.7.

Only when this happens can technology help in policy formation and in command and control. "Technology" does not mean only computers and communications but also agents, expert systems, mathematical models, experimental design, and advanced statistical tests. Classical software (the billions of lines of Cobol code, which costs a fortune to write and maintain) is nothing more than old accounting machines emulated to run on computers. It hardly merits the brainpower, time, and cost of developing and using an enterprise architecture.

REFERENCES

1. *Electronic Design*, February 19, 2001.
2. Drucker, P.F., *The Effective Executive*, Heinemann, London, 1967.
3. Chorafas, D.N., *Liabilities, Liquidity and Cash Management. Balancing Financial Risk*, John Wiley & Sons, New York, 2002.
4. Chorafas, D.N., *Agent Technology Handbook*, McGraw-Hill, New York, 1998.

4

INFORMATIONTECHNOLOGY STRATEGIES BY LEADING ORGANIZATIONS

INTRODUCTION

"On the Internet every company is the same size — the size of the screen," says Richard Gordon. Adds James J. Dorr, "We are much more concerned on what Internet would mean to us and our business than whether the supplier will be IBM, Compaq, or Sun." The aftermath of an information technology strategy is indeed one of the top preoccupations of all well-tuned firms. As executive vice president for information technology at Boston's State Street Bank, Dorr knows what he is talking about. Gordon, Dorr, and thousands of knowledgeable executives today appreciate that the pace of technological change is not only creating new opportunities and leading to new industries almost overnight, but it is also redefining the company's competitive edge and playing a strong role in cost displacement, therefore in competitive performance.

No large company in any country, in any sector of the economy, anywhere in the world could match the pace of innovation characterizing the many little companies of the Internet. Matching newcomers and oldtimers entails doing away with the latter's past policies, business habits, and operating practices. Old economy companies able to gain leadership in the new economy are those from which everybody should be eager to learn.

Instead of showing leadership, however, many entities fall under the vendors' spell and use catchwords instead of cutting-edge strategies. What catchwords? Management information bases (MIBs), for example, is one;

storage-area networks (SANs) is another, and user-centered design (UCD) is another still. While not everything falling under an acronym is void of benefits, a new term or anagram does not make the difference, but, rather, the substance that goes into preparatory work and goals.

Leaders in information technology have been careful to ensure that their IT culture looks toward the future, not back at the past, and does not stifle innovation and initiative, therefore leading to gross inefficiencies. The leaders appreciate that technology is changing almost daily and even an enterprise ahead of its competitors can become tomorrow's laggard.

Another useful guideline is that, when designed and implemented, an enterprise architecture has dramatic impact on management communications, product renewal, inventory turnover, work methods, market impact, capital gains, and return on invested capital. The services the architecture supports should help the business become more efficient, increase marketing reach without incumbent labor costs, make administrative tasks more productive, thus freeing up labor, and allow greater sourcing power than the solution it replaces.

Companies with experience in building successful enterprise architectures suggest that their reality test is what they contribute to customer service. What exactly do customers want from their suppliers when alternative sourcing possibilities are richer than they have ever been? *Communications International*[1] asked respondents to rank measures of customer service from their telecom vendor. Here is the result, in order of importance:

- Offering new solutions to the client
- Responding at the frequency at which problems occur
- Speeding up service provisions
- Employing people who understand their client's business
- Being proactive, not reactive
- Getting it right the first time

It is not enough to respond to the client's problems; this is only part of the challenge. Customer service is also not an overt route to increasing customer spending. What customers want is an ongoing conversation that the vendor's enterprise network supports in an effective manner because problems can occur at any time, even in the best-run operation.

SOFTWARE IS THE HIGH GROUND OF AN ENTERPRISE ARCHITECTURE

Companies with a recognized leadership position in their implementation of information technology find time and again that their approach to upgrading software is wanting. It also leads to interruptions which affect their ability to compete successfully.

All companies face this problem. The difference is that those at the forefront of technology understand the challenge, while others do not. Theoretically, an enterprise architecture does not solve problems connected to software upgrading; practically, it does, however, because it should include policies and procedures which establish system reliability standards and regulate the implementation of new software releases.

For man-made systems, classical reliability metrics are mean time between failures (MTBF), mean time to repair (MTTR), and availability.[2] Mean time between system interrupts (MTBSI), and mean time of system interrupts (MTOSI) should be used with complex aggregates involving many hardware and software components.

The statistics on MTBSI in Figure 4.1 are based on a project on computers and communications systems reliability undertaken with a major financial institution. The time series covered 26 months. In this practical example software is much more reliable than hardware, but there is a sharp reduction in MTBSI with new releases. Hardware dependability has been improved through redundancy, but addition of new components bends the hardware MTBSI.

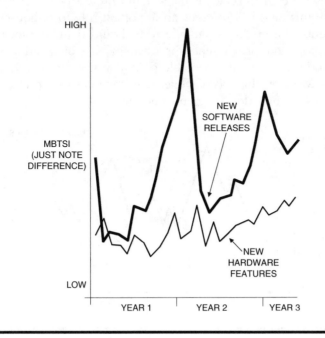

Figure 4.1 Mean time between system interrupts of a large-scale computer and communications system.

One of the most important factors influencing mean time of system interrupt is the programming skills available to bring the system back to life. Lack of highly skilled system programmers magnifies the software's impact in interrupts. MTOSI is also influenced by the quality of software documentation, including its functional completeness, regular update, ability to pinpoint failure causes, and precision in describing necessary corrective action. Typically, the introduction of new applications leads to an increase in MTOSI because of inexperience with specific failures which are part and parcel of its usage, as Figure 4.2 suggests. Therefore, high quality documentation must include: types of possible failures, ways and means to take care of them in a rapid manner, and necessities for training applications and systems programmers in trouble shooting. These references should also be an integral part of the rules governing the enterprise architecture.

Rules embedded into the enterprise architecture should regulate the way in which applications are developed and tested, as well as the very crucial write or buy decisions concerning applications routines. With first class Web software available off the shelf at an unbeatable price when compared to in-house developments, a reasonable ratio between write and buy is one quarter or less for write and three quarters or more for buy. The "write" quarter should be primarily reserved to top-of-the-line, highly competitive applications targeted to senior managers and professionals.

Because this ratio still reserves an important role to in-house software developments, the enterprise architecture should definitely include rules and regulations on programmer productivity, a policy on prototyping methods and tools, and an inviolable policy on fast deliverables. Top-tier companies work on this basis, while their competitors are forced to add extra months to their development schedules.

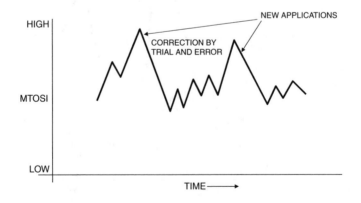

Figure 4.2 Introduction of a new application causes an increase in MTOSI that is not always addressed.

For corporate developers, shortening of the application development cycle is becoming a business-critical issue. Study after study demonstrates that, in the large majority of cases, the development cycle routinely eclipses the business opportunity it is intended to support, sometimes taking twice as long. One need be no genius to understand that this is wrong. A basic reason is overdesign: the ultimate end user, the recipient of these applications, employs in general only about 20% of all the features developed.

Top management should understand that at a time when so much in senior management support depends on computers and communications, the ability to produce deliverables fast is most crucial to business competitiveness. A similar statement is valid about software maintenance chores which, figuratively speaking, are still in the Paleolithic era. This is evident because, depending on the way the job is organized, within many organizations the maintenance of software consumes between 65 and 85% of programming resources and contributes to development cycle deceleration.

Those companies that do not let themselves be pulled into maintaining 20- and 30-year-old unsustainable software hold the high ground in IT. They create a new business paradigm driven by the benefits available through the best technology of the day; they make the most out of opportunities present in their operating environments. They have also been able to significantly reduce systems downtime along the line of reference shown in Figure 4.3.

As computer and communications systems become more interwoven into every phase of a company's business, hardware and software reliability affects every operation of the firm. The same is true of flexibility. The goal should be to make all software components easy to move from one place to another, so that the maximum possible flexibility is attained.

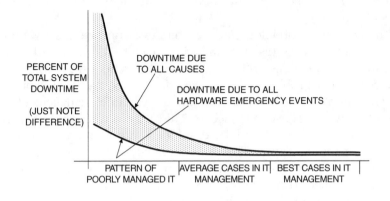

Figure 4.3   On average, 50% of all downtime includes only 12% hardware failures.

Today, one of the major problems with software is that it is not readily movable. Most programming products appear to be designed on the assumption that only one machine will ever be utilized in any given company to do a given job. No established policy exists on moving libraries from one platform to another; maintaining duplicate libraries is extremely difficult and costly in most current environments.

Principles characterizing the enterprise architecture should ensure that software design permits applications routines to be fully and easily movable between machines so that any program normally runs on most, if not all, platforms available. This is doable with Web software and therefore should become a policy characterizing all in-house developments.

ESTABLISHING AND MAINTAINING A NEW SOFTWARE METHODOLOGY

Based on policies and practices followed by the best managed companies, the previous section reviewed a range of reasons why software is the high ground of an enterprise architecture. The factors range from competitive advantages in the market to reliability and uptime. In real-life situations, the concepts underpinning this discussion have provided plenty of documentation why proactive software policies and a new software methodology are most important to growth and survival in a market more demanding than ever.

The board, CEO, and senior management should never be satisfied by oral assurances that strategy and tactics concerning their company's software development, purchase, usage, and sustenance are under control. They should demand hard proof that this is indeed so, examining practical evidence on the methodology used, its state of the art, and its steady update.

The chosen methodology must account for concurrent software engineering requirements (as explained in Chapter 11) in regard to other concurrent engineering projects. It must also reflect that large projects may pose major problems. Beyond a certain point, the burden of project administration and diffuse responsibility in personnel management seems to work actively against their success. This negatively affects an enterprise architecture because it cannot be developed without a cooperative effort involving many specialists. Therefore, a methodology must be in place to use talents and abilities of different people without creating a top-heavy structure doomed to self-destruction.

Experience with many software projects proves that it is unwise to place a large group of analysts and programmers in one single location because they are decoupled from end users' problems. A better way to build applications software is to locate the core competencies of the project near the end users, outlining specific contributions and leading to discussions and clarifications when necessary.

The task of advanced software development becomes so much more efficient if the programming team is small and well-integrated with end users. This greatly improves accuracy of acquired data, helps to control the quality of processes, and generally supplements the skills of analysts and designers with those of end users. It also assists in promoting innovation-driven software development, which is instrumental in return on investment. The principal arguments supporting this approach call for fast software development, high design quality, and extended software functions.

Software development can be significantly accelerated through proto-typing tools and a methodology that breaks with the beaten path of programming. This path is the so-called waterfall method shown in Figure 4.4a. By contrast, Figure 4.4b shows the progressive development method, which presents significant advantages along all eight axes of reference of the radar chart.

One of the reasons some companies became leaders in technology is that they have been able to reduce their software development cycle from years to months, and from months to weeks. By dramatically cutting development time, they significantly improve time-to-market and reduce costs several times over. Consequently, greater resources are available to create new state-of-the-art applications and determine better ways of solving existing and future business problems.

An equally important criterion of success among industry leaders is that they made IT subservient to their strategic planning. Their dictum has been that what you innovate is what you sell, as opposed to their competitors' standard that emphasizes yesterday's technology, years to deliverables and, at the end, a questionable quality of results.

Senior management in these leading companies has seen to it that information technology is aligned with business needs, not vice versa. The monolithic nature of yesterday's software, for example, constricts IT's ability to address the users' fast changing business challenges. Conversely, new policies adopted permit the company to keep flexible by anticipating business requirements and associated IT support and developing new applications within the window of business opportunity.

This in essence amounts to a philosophical and technical framework for the development efforts behind a firm's operating environment that is open and extensible at all levels: end users are able to add value to applications thereby enlarging the development environment. This also creates the opportunity to incorporate best-of-breed, plug-and-play capa-bilities, for instance, the rich inventory of Internet software.

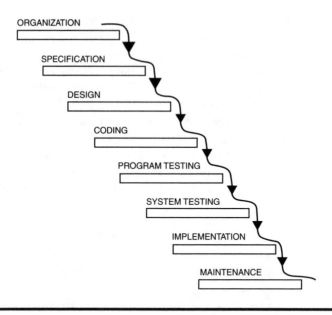

Figure 4.4a The old approach to software development was like a waterfall from one independent step to the next in line.

Another significant move is to sharply increase availability of networked software, bringing over the threshold a wider range of usability (as discussed in the previous section). Companies who have been able to do so have freed themselves from the growing inability of vendor architectures to differentiate and add value to the user organization's products and processes (see also Chapter 5).

Since these policies are not secret, but generally known to business and industry, why do the large majority of companies not manage to give a boost to their information technology? In other words, why do organizations fall behind advanced technology? There are six answers to this query, most of them applicable to nearly every company:

1. Top management is not driven by a competitive environment.
2. Top management is illiterate in technology terms.
3. Information technology is not considered core business.
4. The company fails to steadily train its IT and end user personnel.
5. Routine has the upper hand over innovation.
6. There is no R&D budget in information technology.

To remedy these weaknesses, top management ought to establish a strategic framework for the introduction and effective implementation of new technology. Every company should study the criteria of software

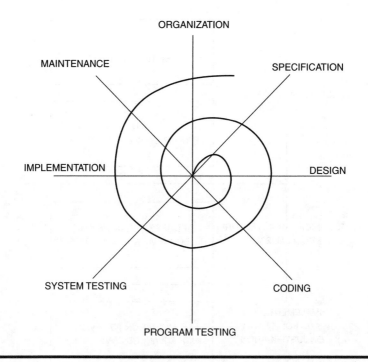

ORGANIZATION

MAINTENANCE

SPECIFICATION

IMPLEMENTATION

DESIGN

SYSTEM TESTING

CODING

PROGRAM TESTING

Figure 4.4b   The new methodology of software development capitalizes on the synergy existing in a progressive approach.

competitiveness best applicable to its products, markets, and future plans. There are no blueprints good for everybody in general, though some guidelines can help. Figure 4.5 presents one model.

It takes clear-eyed management to appreciate that information technology is no longer the great novelty that was permitted to become a bottomless pit for company funds. Today IT is like any other function competing for a place in the budget, and it should be judged by its contribution to the fulfillment of corporate strategy, return-on-investment criteria, and the bottom line.

There is no contribution to the bottom line when deliverables are too late or of a noncompetitive nature. In a recent banking meeting it was stated that there was a time when the window of opportunity in securities dealing was open for 24 hours or more. But with futures, options, and warrants arbitrage the window of opportunity is only open for a few minutes — and sometimes only for seconds.

This is just as true of other fields of activity where the contribution of advanced IT solutions to time compression is a critical competitive advantage. In the cut-throat automobile industry, for example, Toyota strives to

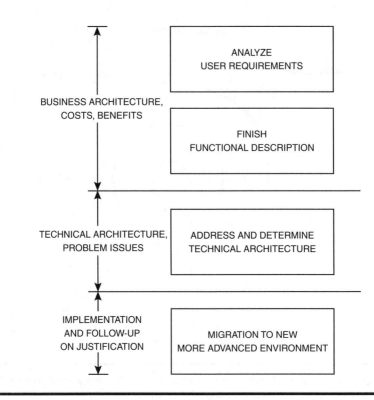

Figure 4.5 A strategic framework for the introduction of new technology and follow-up on its implementation.

maintain market leadership by holding the time-to-delivery at $3\frac{1}{2}$ days from the moment the customer signs the purchasing order.

Using technology, other carmakers are trying to switch to a more sophisticated retail *pull* model rather than one that relies on production *push*. McKinsey calculates that a system of making and supplying cars to the customer's specification could double the rate at which the American car industry turns over its stocks.[3] This means that there is a great deal of emphasis on IT, supply chain restructuring, and thoroughly revamped internal inventory management models.

Plans made just prior to the tech industry's crash in 2000 in terms of Internet supply chain procurement would have taken $25 billion of cash out of the car manufacturing system and given customers the car they wanted, with the options they wanted, at rapid a pace and lower price. If the same approach is applied worldwide, the cost of supplying cars would fall by $50 billion — an impressive reference to what can be achieved through properly applied high technology.

SEARCH FOR INCREASED EFFECTIVENESS THROUGH INFORMATION TECHNOLOGY

In the new economy every industry is faced with its own set of challenges. For instance, rapid technological innovation and the changed behavioral patterns of market participants have considerably increased interest in positions taken in financial markets, but also boosted the risks associated with different instruments. Networks have seen to it that trading and settlement systems have speeded up transactions and reduced their costs.

Better organization and more sophisticated software lead to information that is available earlier and in greater detail, but also in properly filtered form. Also, it is translated into market transactions more quickly with the effect that people and entities are working faster through the price-setting system. However, unless they are supported through high technology, they are not able to confront the multitude of risks resulting from rapid transactions.

Sophisticated software used by the banking industry has worked both in the direction of greater opportunities and amplified risk-taking. It did so because it paved the way for emergence of different types of future markets (although the financial market did not suddenly become efficient). This change has been exploited by institutional players who are able to use technology better than their competitors.

The net result of technology in banking and finance has been to apply considerable resources to the procurement, processing, and distribution of information, converting even minor changes in expectations about market trends into a visual pattern. With the progress made in financial market research and the spread of new instruments, the aftermath is a more complex market behavior replacing the simpler one, but requiring that, like Alice in Wonderland, banks run faster in IT in order merely to stay in the same place.

The enterprise architecture envelops this transformation and finds itself in its core. Figure 4.6 presents the pillars on which rest this evolution. Basic to the able implementation of such a scheme is recognition of fundamental limitations even when the best tools are used. These limitations come from omnipresent, inherent variation in all processes; they become much more pronounced and visible when lower rather than higher technology is employed.

Tier-1 institutions have responded to this challenge starting with thorough reorganization studies and the rationalization of their information technology resources. One of the first significant moves started in the late 1980s has been Citibank's integration of 46 different physical networks into one virtual network, which employed over 200 T1 leased lines and 35,000 other telephone lines. It did so through the able use of knowledge

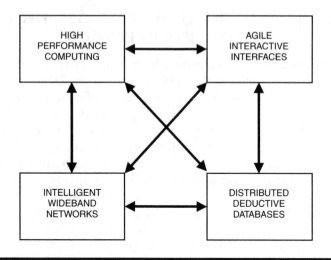

Figure 4.6 Responsible solutions for an enterprise architecture rest on four pillars characterized by a layered approach.

engineering. From design to operation, the chosen solution has significantly reduced overall telecommunications costs.

Innovative as these moves might have been at the time when they were made, nearly 15 years down the line they no longer constitute advanced solutions. Instead, because of dramatic changes taking place in technology and in their business, financial institutions, manufacturing companies, and merchandising firms now face three major technology-related challenges:

1. Knowledge of how to navigate successfully through the unprecedented changes and inevitable complexities building up in the technology market
2. Redefinition of the work their technologists must do in partnership with the company's business channels, as both groups have to respond to dynamic market opportunities
3. Experience on how to migrate effectively to future schemata from the entity's existing installed base of applications, business processes, and technological solutions

To meet these challenges, top-tier financial institutions and industrial companies are establishing an integrated discipline leading to a new overall process structure. They are also setting new directions for corporate-sponsored projects. Great care is taken to specify individual procedures and responsibilities for each key process and the executives responsible for it. This strategy is successfully followed by those organizations that have a vision of the future. Such companies are attempting to find the best way to do things, and then to do them quicker and better than their competitors. The solution space sought by the foremost entities is shown in the three-dimensional diagram in Figure 4.7. The effort by companies ahead of the curve involves a broad range of initiatives covering every aspect of organization and information systems: technology strategy, enterprise architecture, systems architecture, networks, software development, and human resources.

Typically, the foremost companies already have behind them the general technology directions envisioned for the decade of the 1990s, such as distributed computing, client-servers, Web-based applications, knowledge engineering, and object-orientation. The urgent institutional change they are now seeking revolves around a long term technology direction able to serve their business model in the best manner, with the intelligent network providing the infrastructure.

Following the specifications set by the enterprise architecture, the system should be in a position to supply its users with a wide variety of features, including some ahead of current state of the art. A common goal of advanced features is that end users will increasingly transact their business electronically, connecting to the network through a broad array of information devices which are reliable and easy to use.

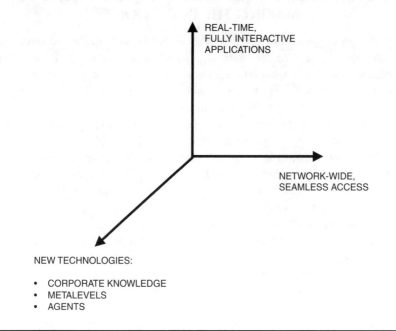

Figure 4.7   Solution space for a new and more efficient IT environment.

A senior technologist of a New York institution underlined that, to his judgment, the businesses of the future will communicate to a significant extent through intelligent software objects, which focus on creating and delivering value to the customer. They will use the common infrastructure created by the enterprise architecture, giving the different channels of the financial business unprecedented levels of flexibility.

All of this technology will sit upon platforms that have to integrate together seamlessly, providing their users with the capabilities they are looking for. Whether the customer is at the office, home, or traveling, he or she should receive intelligence-enriched services delivered through optical media or satellite-supported channels at an affordable cost.

In all likelihood, this intelligent network will be instrumental in transforming the company into a virtual enterprise which puts to profitable use the capabilities of other companies in order to realize the kind of customer services just described. However, implementing this model requires a global view of business and new ways of looking at policy formation, as well as at command and control operations. This is, by all evidence, one of the foremost contributions a properly planned and executed enterprise architecture can deliver.

FORMULATING ALTERNATIVES IS PREREQUISITE TO MAKING THE BEST CHOICE

What the previous section described will not be accomplished overnight. It is part of a longer range planning, which is a creative process. Senior managers must be, to a certain degree, inventors. They do not merely solve problems but also create conditions which permit reaching for solutions able to counteract competitors' moves.

Much of what is suggested here relates to factual, analytical support for decision-making. To perform their duties in an able manner, senior managers must not simply adapt to change, but also anticipate and initiate change by examining their alternatives and experimenting on them. This is one of the goals whose fulfillment should be facilitated by the enterprise architecture and the services it offers.

Some of these services will be analytical. Others will assure the seamless integration of platforms serving managerial objectives (see also Chapter 1). Two user populations are concerned by this reference: 1. the very imaginative executives who project a strange universe, whose perceived needs they want to satisfy, and 2. policymakers who do not live in an exalted world, but still must appraise and screen proposals.

These proposals may originate from within the organizational sector under the manager's authority or from outside — i.e., from business partners, including regular or accidental encounters, or other lines of feedback. Experts in management policy advise that one should view top-level decision-making as a double form of inventiveness or creativity: 1. formulation of alternatives and 2. documented choice from alternatives.

Failure to imagine "still another possible choice" can be truly disastrous. For example, chief executives who, in the mid 1990s, were able to foresee that, by the early 21st century, Internet commerce might represent a large chunk of transactions (if not of value) steered their organizations to capitalize on this trend. By contrast, chief executives who lacked the imagination failed to plan their companies' Internet presence, thereby condeming their organizations to the old economy.

As another example, those software company boards who estimated that Web-compatible software would likely be 50% of the value of all packages sold capitalized on a trend which leaves other software companies in the dust. In telecommunications, too, the most successful companies are those who, some years ago, appreciated that mobile telephony would integrate with the Internet for voice and data and also, that by 2005, data traffic would represent about 500% of voice traffic. This reversed statistics that had dominated policy decisions by telephone companies since the end of World War II.

Quite similarly, in terms of advanced solutions in computing, the most successful service providers are those who appreciate that global standards will develop for modeling and that, in some institutions, modeling will represent 30 to 40% of computing requirements.

The statement "global standards for modeling" might be puzzling. Therefore, consider a couple of examples. Value at Risk (VAR) is a concept which, in the sense of bank regulation, was introduced in January 1996 by the Basle Committee on Banking Supervision.[4] Within less than five years VAR models became a standard dominating the financial industry, as more and more banks and other institutions used this approach to "guestimate" their daily exposure. (On the downside, VAR can handle only a third of exposures confronting an institution, although few appreciate this limitation.) The Black–Scholes algorithm for option pricing was first published in a seminal paper by its authors in 1972. Today it is, quite likely, the most widely used financial model.*

When extreme choices in terms of models and systems solutions were made by top-tier organizations, they were largely based on hypothetical situations. As a professor taught his graduate students at UCLA in 1953, medium to longer range plans are similar to an artistic creation. They imply carving a set of finite options from a tree of nearly infinite possibilities. But

---

* In 1994, Dr. Fischer Black received the Chorafas prize from the Swiss Academies of Sciences. A couple of years later, Dr. Scholes and Dr. Merton were awarded the Nobel prize by the Swedish Academy of Sciences.

these must be live. In its roots, the executive, creative decision process is neither irrational nor spotty. Problems conceived and plans made must be real-life, and there should be genuine possibilities.

Genuine possibilities are those that might really take place, those which could reasonably be anticipated or can honestly be realized. That is why the executive planner should be endowed with imagination, and should be provided with information which makes experimentation on different courses of action feasible. Part of this information is the constraints of relevance: future plans must respond to demands of the present and coming business environment, and a significant amount of relevant information should be conveyed by the enterprise architecture.

Only the best support is good enough because, to be creative in his function as corporate planner, the CEO must be time free and space free. When inventing alternatives, his region is one of pure possibilities. However live his future plans and policies may be and however anchored to the real world of today, these live plans are still in the nonexistent future — therefore, hypothetical, conditional, uncertain, and in need of experimentation to partly confirm their pragmatism.

When top-level decision makers are formulating new alternatives, they cannot live in a universe restricted by a two-valued logic of true and false, the way the command and control system operates. In their roots, executive decisions are neither good nor bad when they are made. They turn that way as a result of subsequent events. Basically, the world of policy formation encompasses degrees of truth and reality like tonalities of gray. The most successful chief executives do not treat exclusively with what exists, can be pointed to, or is recognized as concretely on hand. They go beyond the already realized and existent because they know that policy, once made, does not remain statically fixed.

The ways and means put in place by the enterprise architecture to facilitate executive action must account for the fact that business policy is a continuing engagement with a dynamic environment full of novel possibilities. Hence there is a need to project the future of an organization into its developing business relations. Policymakers' choices shape the environment into which the organization fits and plans to fit in the years to come.

A steady, timely, and accurate information flow is so vital because it provides the necessary bridge among the past, present, and future. Furthermore, once a finite set of possible alternative goals, contingencies, and plans has been elaborated, the question of optimization arises. Optimization typically calls for a subsequent paring down and leads to significant requirements for experimentation and simulation.

In conclusion, the members of the board, the CEO, and his immediate assistants must steadily make choices from alternatives, each with strengths and weaknesses. This is a job of arbitration and deliberately discarding options and, therefore, a rejection of affirmation, denial, and compromise. An enterprise architecture which does not provide timely and accurate information for such decisions possibly deprives the organization of its best business opportunities.

PROVIDING SOPHISTICATED SERVICES TO THE PROFESSIONAL WORKER

The message conveyed by the previous section is that companies are ahead of the curve when they act with urgency and discipline in a coordinated manner to support their business initiatives, and they do so through the right enterprise architecture. To provide direction for this effort, they have identified several key technologies to help them achieve their goals and position themselves for success in the first decade of the 21st century. To a significant extent, these goals revolve around requirements of senior managers and professionals, and can be met only through a disciplined approach to improvement of ongoing processes.

Wise CEOs know that there are no silver bullets. Therefore their vision for technology and customer service is an urgent call for change toward an interactive environment which responds to both present and future requirements. This message has critical implications not only for information technology specialists but also for every individual employee of the firm.

For instance, to keep pace with a rapidly changing financial environment, including the expansion of derivatives instruments, risks associated to off-balance sheet products, and the growing emphasis placed at the liabilities side of the balance sheet,[5] financial institutions need to further develop, both individually and collectively, systems and procedures that enable them to manage their exposure capably. This requires significant strengthening of management and professional skills, involves committing financial resources to the development of risk monitoring systems, and calls for an enterprise architecture which serves core applications in a most efficient manner (see the next section for a real-life example).

Part and parcel of an able solution is revamping present systems and procedures and automating backoffice, accounting, and auditing functions through knowledge artifacts (see Chapter 9).[6] Also important is the steady development of an increasingly sophisticated infrastructural support through the reallocation of IT money in order to help the professional worker (see also Chapter 3).

This statement is as valid for an executive whose main job is policy formation as it is for design engineers, traders, salesmen, and other professionals, including accountants and auditors. Increasingly, regulators require the board of directors to play an active role in targeting and monitoring the institution's internal control, which can be effectively done through advanced IT applications. Activist shareholders, too, would like to see board-level policies result in high multiple value creation and significant competitive advantages.

Board members can benefit from radar charts similar to the one in Figure 4.8 to gain a snapshot appreciation of progress made in planning, implementing, and using information technology. This radar chart shows the result of three consecutive audits of IT along a frame of reference resting on six critical variables retained by the board of the company for which the chart was built.

Taking the statistics in this radar chart at face value, one can observe that, in year 1 every critical variable underperformed. Year 2 showed significant improvement across the board, while in year 3, five out of six performance criteria had fairly improved. Some members of the board did not find this satisfactory because, to their judgment, sophistication of use at the professional's desk did not improve, even if the return on investment (ROI) target seemed to have been met. What these directors questioned was the ability to continue improving ROI without giving professionals a steadily more efficient IT support. The point made in a board meeting was that effectiveness of professional workers is what makes or breaks the firm. By contrast, static quality of IT support at the professional's desk level meant that either ROI was misjudged, or the data underpinning the radar chart presentation were somewhat manipulated, since end user satisfaction and ROI correlate.

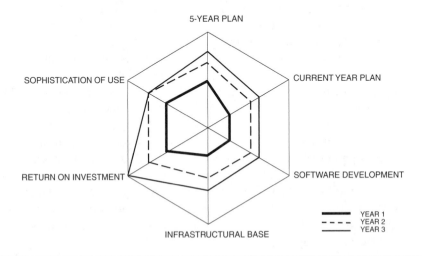

Figure 4.8 A radar chart which maps accomplishments in six key variables during 3 consecutive years.

As this example demonstrates, visualization is a great help. The problem is that many boards are not populated with efficiency experts, internal control specialists, or technology value-savvy directors. Therefore, board members often cannot fulfill the requirements and responsibilities the new perspectives in board accountability thrust upon them.

Tier-1 organizations see to it that clear targets are in place to guide their boards and shed light on what is done, right or wrong, in connection to IT supports and professionals' performance. Targets should also, indicate what needs to be done next to set management planning and control perspective affecting the direction of the company's technology.

Companies that have chosen this strategy steadily re-examine relationships between the board and the specialist departments of the institution, which invest in technology, manage innovation and, most particularly, control exposure. In a nutshell, they see to it that information is managed as a product and adopted solutions are evaluated on the basis of ROI.

The role to be contributed by a properly designed enterprise architecture is further underlined by the fact that, among financial institutions and industrial organizations, for the most part, information is not managed. It is available in overabundance or not at all. To make matters worse from a competitive viewpoint, the information provided to professional workers is seldom timely and complete and has a cost that cannot be readily determined.

The reason for these failures is that, with the exception of some leading entities, a company's approach to information management today is based on yesterday's concept and technologies. The image of what can be done with present-day media dates back three or four decades; it has not been properly updated to take advantage of what is now available in technology.

This is unacceptable because technology progresses so fast that every 6 months something very significant happens that changes the way one looks at the workplace. Best projections indicate that this will continue over the next 10 years. It is therefore urgent to learn from the best applications currently available. For this reason a number of case studies have been included in this book; the next section contains one of them.

LESSONS LEARNED FROM AN ENTERPRISE ARCHITECTURE DESIGN AT NATIONAL MANUFACTURING

National Manufacturing is a fictitious company name, but the facts included in this case study are real. They come from two different implementations of newly designed enterprise architectures: one in an electrical company and the other for a mechanical engineering manufacturing company. Both entities requested that a complete applications environment be designed, able to meet the needs of users who want to achieve the most out of throughput power of networked workstation platforms.

What is rather unusual with this case is that in the early 1990s the board (or, more precisely, each board in the two companies in the background) recognized that much can be gained from the raw computing power of new hardware and software products. Therefore, it asked the IT department to harness that power in handling complex on-line transactions and for concurrent computer aided design (CAD) reasons (see also Chapter 11). Developed from the outset as a real-time solution, this enterprise architecture is supporting hundreds of workstations using databases distributed over local and wide-area networks for concurrent engineering, and processing thousands of complex transactions per hour on a global scale. The adopted solution is entirely scalable, making it possible for thousands of users to query and update database contents pertaining to a number of applications, ranging from CAD to manufacturing, sales, and financial transactions with customers and suppliers.

The designers of the enterprise architecture provided it with a unified development environment which allows programming, compiling, and testing complex applications at each workstation. Object-oriented programming and if-then-else rules, as well as real-time compilation, reduced the amount of code required to produce a fairly sophisticated software. The chosen solution benefited from a novel methodology.

What distinguishes this enterprise architecture from many others is the fact that special attention has been paid to the nature of the processes handled. This encouraged rapid development, implementation, and testing of new product ideas without interference from routines still retained from elder technology. Greater productivity has been achieved through evolutionary prototyping, which permits concepts to be readily implemented and tested, and experts and end users to actually see results through interactive visualization.

In observance of principles outlined in the two previous sections, the designers of the enterprise architecture provided themselves with rich possibilities for selection among alternatives. Experimental tools have been incorporated which ensure that, whenever users opt for one alternative tool over another, they benefit from the services of knowledge artifacts which outline the tool's strengths for the job on hand.

In this as in other applications, the system provides information at a rapid pace, permitting exploitation of available opportunities. For some applications, software is available to offer suggestions about limits, as well as make those limits apparent. Limits may exist in terms of market reach, prices that can be charged, value differentiation, delivery channels, costs, profit margins, and so on.

Cost information has been requested by some board members who wanted everybody's accountability for results strengthened, including the understanding of prevailing cost patterns in the global Internet economy. To a certain extent, this has been a modern application of value analysis — practiced by industry leaders in the 1960s, but then more or less forgotten.

One of the strengths of this enterprise architecture has been the experimental design and powerful statistical analysis features readily accessible to its users. The executive vice president of engineering, for instance, requested software able to support what he called *conceptual specifications*, with the requirement that:

- Engineering specifications and their tolerances must be executable, and therefore complete.
- Technical applications must treat processes and data as if they were from the same piece of cloth.
- A systematic methodology must be put in place for conceptualization, supported by tools to maintain conceptual integrity.

Other senior executives pressed the need to reuse, rather than reinvent, and therefore required IT support able to identify reusability of components. Another principle was that prototypes should evolve and databases be seamlessly available to all users. The overall policy concerning this enterprise architecture has been characterized by a number of design rules that can be highlighted as follows:

- Identify interactively all data abstractions
- Apply inheritance, where appropriate
- Establish flexible relationships between objects
- Clarify attributes of and communications between objects
- Set functionality and limits of operations for each abstraction
- Implement the operations and test each design with scenarios

Perhaps there is no better example of how these principles can be applied than the development of artifacts able to judge the dependability of other software. The technological part of the dependability challenge is an old problem, whose origins lie in fault tolerance. Like reliability, dependability of an artifact depends on the absence of significantly weak links. However, software systems today are riddled with weak links, even if they are supposedly dependable programs. They have embedded bugs which escaped testing, and there are misuses that exceed the coverage of fault tolerance.

Procedural weaknesses can completely undermine the intended robustness. The human part of the equation is always perplexing because anticipating all possible human behavior is very difficult, and expectations vary from one individual to the next. A case in point is basic cognitive functions. In engineering design, abstraction determines our reality: what objects there are and how one perceives them. A similar statement is valid in finance. Typically, concepts apply to objects, but the same concept can apply to many objects. Objects are instances of concepts, but an object can have many concepts that apply.

The designers of the architecture tried to solve a problem associated with the cognitive reference of unwanted complexity. For instance, the C++ draft standard is more than 700 pages and is revised three times a year. Nobody can keep track of these changes in a dependable manner, but failing to do so means off-standard behavior during C++ program development, testing, and operations.

With software, as with every other man-made system, one of the important challenges is to be able to develop and certify dependable aggregates out of less dependable components, especially when the solutions must rely on the behavior of people whose dependability is not certain in terms of abstraction, specification, and employment of deliverables.

In the case of National Manufacturing Company, the board insisted that the enterprise architecture include methods and tools permitting tolerances on interpretation issues. The executive vice president (EVP) of engineering suggested that properly designed agents could make a significant contribution to software dependability by the assistance provided to updating programming standards, formal testing, and other analytical techniques applied in run time.

This approach, the EVP said, was most critical to the effort of detecting vulnerabilities that cannot otherwise be localized. As software increases in complexity, it is becoming impossible to analyze its dependability without structural and functional analysis performed at run time – a job to be performed by the agents. Therefore, the design of the enterprise architecture, and support of its functionality, should make full use of knowledge artifacts (see also Chapter 9).

REFERENCES

1. *Commn. Int.*, November, 1999.
2. Chorafas, D.N., *Statistical Processes and Reliability Engineering*, D. Van Nostrand Co., Princeton, NJ, 1960.
3. *The Economist*, May 22, 1999.

4. Chorafas, D.N., *The 1996 Market Risk Amendment. Understanding the Marking-to-Model and Value-at-Risk*, McGraw-Hill, Burr Ridge, IL, 1998.
5. Chorafas, D.N., *Liabilities, Liquidity and Cash Management. Balancing Financial Risk*, John Wiley & Sons, New York, 2002.
6. Chorafas, D.N., *Integrating ERP, Supply Chain Management and Smart Materials*, Auerbach/CRC Press, New York, 2001.

5

REVAMPING THE TECHNOLOGICAL INFRASTRUCTURE OF A MODERN INDUSTRIAL COMPANY

INTRODUCTION

Every enterprise architecture must pay a great deal of attention to infrastructural issues. As has been apparent since Chapter 1, the role of a technological infrastructure is to help in efficiently supporting all other activities, from policy formation, to command and control, to daily operations. This should be done not only in a dependable way but also at much lower cost than that of rival companies. Only then can technology be used as a strategic weapon against competitors.

Chapter 4 brought attention to the importance of an information technology strategy. One way to judge the effectiveness of the means employed to reach goals is to ask, "Does a shift of any one current function to a new, more modern solution make a noticeable difference in the ability to cope with imposed market demands and internal loads?" Is such shift significantly reducing the cost-effectiveness of operations and, if so, by how much?

Organizations ahead of the curve have developed a torrent of focused questions to judge a new infrastructural solution before they commit to it. Are there large and repeated differences in the way the organization senses, comprehends, and responds to new conditions? Reacts and adjusts to them? Tracks their continuance and consistency? Detects their relaxation? Adjusts to their change?

Preceding chapters paid much attention to this process of adjustment as well as to flexibility. The concept behind the enterprise architecture must be flexible and adjust to changing conditions; steady evolution of the specific infrastructural solution adopted must also be possible.

As far as infrastructural designs are concerned, the most important role is played by a factual and documented evaluation rather than by prognostication. After all, who is truly able to forecast the technological future? In 1968, at IBM's advanced computing systems division, a senior engineer was overheard commenting on the microchip: "But what is it good for?"[1] In 1981 Bill Gates reportedly said, "640k ought to be enough for everybody."

On the contrary, commitments made about precise ongoing enterprise architectures and infrastructural projects, including quality assurance and cost control targets (third and fourth sections), are verifiable. Therefore, one can hold the executive or technical expert making them to his word. The same is true about the infrastructure's flexibility for system adjustments that can be tested. In this connection, a crucial question concerns what the internal patterns of adjustment to changing conditions are.

In an organizational sense, most internal adjustments are extra-formal patterns of authority, involving two-way communications and interactions. Are adjustment patterns upsetting the chosen infrastructure? Can their effects be simulated prior to real-life implementation? Are there large and repeated aftermaths peculiar to specific structures or organizational functions of the firm? Clear answers to such queries are important because, as senior management should appreciate, all current planning is tentative.

When the answers given to these and similar queries are rigorous and when analysis and response succeeds in coinvolving the senior management level, then there is evidence that a cultural change has occurred within the company making flexibility and adaptability feasible. The approach suggested in the following sections helps in simplifying complex situations, assists in innovation, and can be instrumental in cutting personnel and other costs in the production and distribution of goods and services.

THE CHANGING NATURE OF THE INFRASTRUCTURE AS A RESULT OF TECHNOLOGY

The aim of this chapter is to outline some of the benefits reaped by companies that know how to capitalize on state-of-the-art developments and their impacts on the infrastructure. Management awareness of what can be achieved through a modern infrastructural solution is fundamental in maintaining a competitive edge. People and companies are forced to expand their (often narrow) areas of expertise as new technologies develop and job responsibilities change. In many cases, they need to become types of instant experts in new fields.

This steady evolution of one's expertise is underlined because it affects personal careers and companies. Remaining competitive means running fast to catch up with new developments. This is a basic aspect of the fact that any financial expert, scientist, or engineer who has been out of school for at least 5 years has already started to become obsolete. He or she is bound to work with instruments and systems that were not even conceptualized at graduation time.

Professional survival requires new skills, and this means learning details of new and upcoming technologies (see Chapter 6). Professional magazines now provide in-depth design articles to further enhance knowledge of how new technologies can solve different challenges as well as the opposite: how different challenges can only be faced through new technologies.

Coupled with faster time-to-market demands, the rapid pace of technological development requires intensive life-long education to keep abreast of the latest knowledge and techniques. This is not a one-tantum event but a personal challenge; all indications are that it will be amplified in the years to come. Exactly the same principle applies to keeping up the infrastructure on which the company depends for its survival. The infrastructure provides, so to speak, an educational layer to the firm.

Keeping up both personal skills and the facilities supported by the company's infrastructure is much more a cultural issue than a technical one. To better appreciate this statement, back to basics. The term *infrastructure* stands for all facilities, equipment, software, services, and supporting installations needed for the effective functioning of an organization. A utilities infrastructure, for example, consists of transportation systems, communications systems, water networks, and power lines.

The aftermath of the changing nature of an infrastructure can be better visualized if cost-effectiveness is examined as an example. In principle, the lowest-cost method of moving bulk goods is by water. Therefore, throughout history nations put a high priority upon developing a system of navigable rivers and canals. But while water-borne freight was cheap, it was too slow for the Industrial Revolution.

In the late 19th century practically all governments promoted the development of a nationwide system of railroads to move goods. Railroads proved to be more costly than water channels, but were superior in speed and able to bring goods to areas where there was no water transport grid. The railroads provided development corridors for vast stretches of land for nearly a century. However, railroad systems are no longer competitive: passenger traffic channeled itself to airplanes and auto transport, and trucks and airplanes increasingly took over transport of goods.

The result of change in transport infrastructure from rails to autos is a steady shrinkage of railroad mileage per 1000 households. Some people say that, while the road and airfreight systems are essential, they cannot replace water and rail. Also, trucks are getting bigger and heavier, and overloading deteriorating roads and bridges. This is true; a change in infrastructure brings with it new challenges.

In the case of air and auto vs. rail and water, a fundamental argument is that the infrastructure built for the physical economy has become less essential for the virtual economy. Let's add to this the fact that by now the No. 1 requirement for transport is any-to-any broadband networks. The Internet, intranets, and extranets (see Section III) really replace the late 19th century railroads, thus exemplifying a new basic principle: communicate, do not commute.

In the context of financial institutions and industrial companies, one way to visualize what has just been explained in infrastructural terms is by looking at the block diagram in Figure 5.1. Functions performed by senior management in any organization are concentrated at the top two layers and are supported through an infrastructure made of computers, phone lines, software, interfaces, other gadgets, as well as rules regulating the behavior of

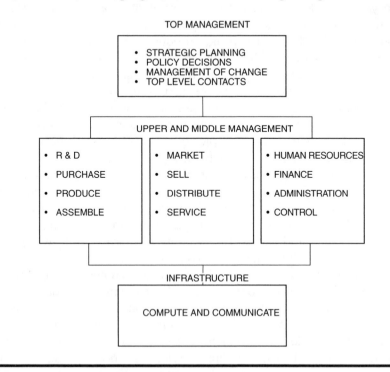

Figure 5.1 The pentomic organization.

the system. Support is also provided by the users of this infrastructure, who are at management layers, and all other employees of the company, as well as (in a growing number of cases) clients and suppliers.

As the examples in the preceding chapters document, companies invest in information technology infrastructure to meet their current and future needs. For reasons of efficiency and cost, this infrastructure reflects the evolution of support requirements, from simpler to more complex solutions. A greater degree of sophistication increases the efficiency of the infrastructure's operators, but also poses stringent technical, managerial, and investment prerequisites.

The enterprise architecture characterizing the coming 5 years will provide plenty of examples of sophisticated infrastructures that grow more complex as they penetrate into many aspects of private and business life for an increasing number of people and companies. Technology is enriching but it is also producing systems of such complexity that they create new dependencies, and introduce several unknowns which represent risks.

The year 2000 (Y2K) problem was an example of these dependencies and their associated risks. It dramatized the fact that infrastructural interdependence is a particularly important element of modern business and industry. Yet, with few exceptions, it was not an issue of primary attention for system designers, and (curiously enough) even less so for system operators.

Today the issue of infrastructural dependence leads many experts to think that one-sided emphasis on "more" and "bigger" is misplaced because it is not counterbalanced through fundamental study of systems, components, and their reliability. A golden horde of examples documents that infrastructural interdependencies are critical in all domains, but most particularly in the domains of computers, telecommunications, and electric power.

These three domains depend greatly on each other because one constitutes the other's infrastructure. Telecommunications equipment uses computer facilities and requires electrical power. The operation of electrical power systems depends on distributed control facilities that rest on computers. The coupling is so tight that major failure in any one of these three systems might bring down a *tsunami* upon users and society at large.

The opposite is also true. When everything goes well the tight coupling is beneficial to every stakeholder, the more so as all three of these aggregates benefit from the same basic technology. This being the case, one of the biggest challenges facing a designer in the next millennium will be initially to define the enterprise architecture, its components with the system to be integrated, and the appropriate infrastructural blueprint.

Figure 5.2 presents in a nutshell how can this be effectively done from a planning and scheduling viewpoint. This is a real-life case with seven different facilities contributing to the enterprise architecture for which an infrastructural solution has been designed. The whole project, whose study

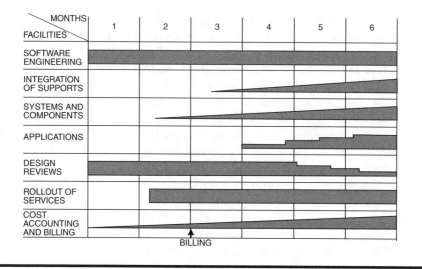

Figure 5.2 Implementation schedule of distributed information infrastructure.

and implementation were customized, was performed at record time. As each component part progressed, its designers had to provide cross-disciplinary functionality. The years of practical experience following the introduction of this infrastructure prove that it was a project well done.

GENERAL ELECTRIC REVAMPS ITS INFRASTRUCTURE FOR BETTER COST CONTROL

In corporate America today cost reduction is not an event, it is a policy and a process. Top-tier industries appreciate that they must restructure their infrastructure periodically to bring their costs and operations in line with business opportunities. This should happen within a framework which benefits shareholders, who are increasingly active in watching over the shoulder of the board, the CEO, and senior management. Investments in IT, and therefore in an enterprise architecture, are no longer secretive issues as they were 30, 20, or even 10 years ago. Today, the key words are *transparency* and *visibility*. The stakeholders want to know: do these investments pay their costs and leave a profit?

Greater shareholder vigilance comes at an opportune moment because intensified competition in business and industry, due to innovation, technology, globalization, and deregulation, has created a new frame of reference for judging corporate performance. The changing dimensions of this growing framework are shown in Figure 5.3. Market response is active rather than passive, different markets are heterogeneous, and many unknowns impact end results.

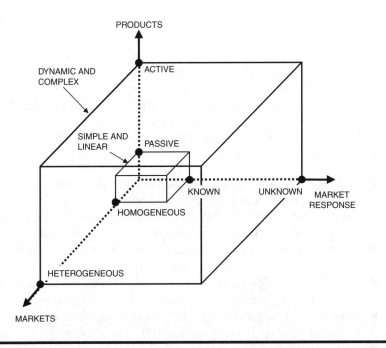

Figure 5.3 Intensified competition in business and industry has created a new, more complex frame of reference.

Within the business perspective established by the preceding paragraphs, companies are embracing Internet commerce as a major way to further improve market appeal and cost control (see Chapter 12). General Electric (GE) commented that I-commerce allows it to address both cost problems and quality challenges, providing its management with insight as to the profitability of every customer and every product. This calls for high-power tools. GE's Six Sigma has been the answer. For starters, Six Sigma addresses every product and every process that touches GE and its customers: defining, measuring, analyzing, improving, and controlling.

Six Sigma targets quality, costs, and market and product leadership. The rationale is that, in a globalized economy, a company cannot afford to field anything but teams of "AAA" players. The cultural change associated with Six Sigma is vast because the target is behavior that demolishes all barriers of rank, function, geography, and bureaucracy.

This message does not go over well with other companies, but at GE all levels of management have been able to adapt to rigorous Six Sigma requirements. Revamping quality, costs, and market and product leadership is a prerequisite to benefiting from the fact that I-commerce technology makes it possible for companies to construct a new business model by exploring key franchises, getting closer to their customer base, outsourcing functions performed less efficiently, and using advanced tools which make possible a neat job.

GE's Six Sigma is an example of using advanced tools to do a neat job. The most important element in its success has been the fact that Dr. John Welsh, the company's CEO, has been the chief evangelist and ultimate authority of this solution. Next in line of importance is the methodology Six Sigma has brought along.[2] The third pillar is the advanced statistical analysis and other tools Six Sigma makes available, which can be briefly described in the following terms:

- Statistical process control methods analyze data, study and monitor process quality, and track performance.
- Other control charts monitor variance in a process over time, and provide alert on unexpected variances which may cause defects.
- A defect measurement method accounts for the number or frequency of defects that hit product or service quality.
- Chi-square testing evaluates the variance between two different samples, detecting statistical differences in case of variation.
- Experimental design permits methodologically carrying out t, z and χ^2 tests regarding two populations (H_0, H_1).
- Process mapping illustrates how things get done by visualizing entire processes, their strengths, and weaknesses.
- A tree diagram graphs goals broken into levels of detailed actions, thus encouraging creative solutions.
- The dashboard maps progress towards customer satisfaction, including fill rate, billing accuracy, and percent defective.
- A Pareto diagram exhibits relative frequency in cause and effect: 20% of the sources usually cause 80% of any problems.
- Root cause analysis targets basic (original) reasons for nonconformance to specifications, aiming at their elimination.

Are the themes presented by these ten bullets really relevant to the enterprise architecture, which is the subject of this book? Surely they are. These are some of the most important tools and processes to bring to life within the enterprise architecture. Without them, the architecture will be another fancy label — and an empty shell.

Furthermore, the able implementation of these tools and success in Internet commerce correlate — if for no other reason than because costs, innovation, and quality matter so much. GE is not the only example of a company which forces itself to be steadily innovative. Dell says that it now derives more than 40% of its revenue over the Internet within the U.S. and about 30% abroad. The Net also helps Dell reinvent itself. Like GE, Dell is radically changing its profile, from a firm that essentially assembles hardware to one selling consumers its products various components, accessories, and services.

As Section III will demonstrate through practical examples, Internet Commerce creates the opportunity to take the just-in-time (JIT) model to a new height of cost efficiency. This leads to better valuation for a variety of reasons, creating the worst of times for companies who are unprepared, but the best of times for those who did their homework satisfactorily. Section III will also show that companies moving fast to embrace I-commerce do so because they expect to reap some juicy business opportunities, including advantages which come from globalization, accelerating revenue growth, and containing costs. Cognizant executives who participated in the research that led to this book also pressed the point that I-commerce makes it feasible to keep suppliers in control. After all, a new supplier could be just a double-click away.

At the same time, entities that focus on customer service and personalize the products they offer, are able not only to get more business from a customer but also to build loyalty. There are significant competitive advantages being the lowest-cost producer in all areas of competition, including reengineering internal processes. High technology is also used to differentiate products. But is the company ready for it?

AN ENTERPRISE ARCHITECTURE FOR ALLIANCES AND SUPPLY CHAIN SOLUTIONS

Companies able to readily consolidate information about clients design more sophisticated goods and services than their competitors. Also, they use technological capabilities in more efficient ways, powering their marketing effort while bettering service quality. Though it may not be self-evident at first glance, at a time of operational alliances and supply chain solutions a rigorous methodology similar to the one developed by GE has become a "must" for every self-respecting organization. One of the indispensable parts of such methodology, not covered in the previous section, is that of ways and means for making factual strategic decisions on build or buy, and choosing partners in an open system defined by the enterprise architecture of choice.

Analytical services leading to factual and documented results should be present to support senior management in "build or buy." Decisions and performance along this frame of reference have a great deal to do with policies and procedures associated with knowledge and information regarding the supply chain. The IT solution adopted must reach all the way into the company's information system and significantly coinvolve the IT of business partners.

General Motors (GM), for example, is in the process of implementing a radical change in its assembly operations that brings suppliers onto the factory floor and cuts production costs by a very significant margin. Ford and Volkswagen use a similar concept of modular assembly at plants in Brazil. Ford is also using this process in building its Focus mid-size car in Europe. These end-to-end IT approaches are laudable, but they cannot be supported in the long run without an appropriate infrastructural solution. The handholding behind such support should be an integral and important part of the enterprise architecture of each business partner entering into the alliance.

At a tactical level, the new techniques developed employ suppliers in novel roles. In the auto industry, for instance, suppliers install complete component subsystems, such as suspension and brake, instead of the classical way of simply relying on outside firms to provide individual parts, like brake shoes and shock absorbers. Motor companies project many benefits beyond the production floor from this approach, for instance, reducing warranty costs, increasing output with fewer employees, and responding faster to market forces.

Another beneficiary is research and development. GM officials suggest that this process could cut the cost of creating a new vehicle from $1 billion to $360 million — king-size savings. But there are prerequisites. While the decision on operational alliances is one of policy formation, its implementation deeply involves command and control and the infrastructural base.

This reference is valid throughout the spectrum of research, development, and implementation (R, D, & I). It is present as well in the many feedback loops within the enterprise. This system is shown in a nutshell in Figure 5.4. Each of the blocks in this diagram can be expanded to further detail and each one can (and should) produce feedback to those preceding it.

The design of a flexible approach to infrastructural implementation is effectively assisted through the atomic unit, whose concept was introduced in Chapter 3. An atomic unit constitutes the building block of a technological solution. Business partners working on the production floor interface through atomic units that they employ. The more similar these units are in terms of basic design characteristics and the way they work, the simpler and more efficient will be their interfacing. At a time when the cutting edge of technology obliges firms to run fast just to stay in the same place, simple but efficient interfaces hold significant advantages in a competitive sense, provided business and technical prerequisites are observed.

Why business prerequisites? Because few companies pay enough attention to the fact that there can be many problems with alliances. Some of the pitfalls result from cultural differences, others from widely different

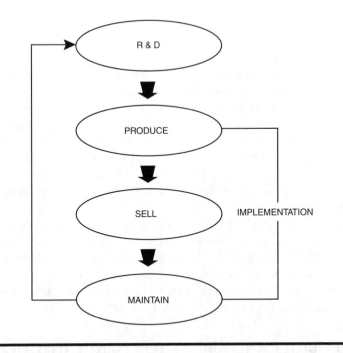

Figure 5.4   The key word in any industry is research, development, and implementation (R, D, and I).

standards, and still others from disparities in organizational size, particularly in technology companies. Misalignments in resources or values may mean that one of the partners will be absorbed by "big brother" or fail to exploit the bigger company's multiple capabilities.

Even alliances made among equals to solve a specific problem are not assured of smooth sailing. One of the earliest efforts among equals in the telecommunications sector was been that of joining forces in creating a common network. In the late 1980s, five Wall Street firms did so to share costs and benefits from a global network: Morgan Stanley, Goldman Sachs, Salomon Brothers, First Boston, and Drexel Burnham Lambert. The five institutions agreed to choose a supplier from among 30 U.S. and foreign contenders.

That such cutthroat Wall Street competitors chose to cooperate in their telecommunications was a first, but the result was not an outstanding success. Drexel dropped out by going bankrupt, and the other four entities had second thoughts. Confidentiality of data is topmost in investment banking, and a common network did not last long as a good concept (see also Chapter 16 on security).

Hot subjects in finance and technology come and go, and what seems great at first may show its ugly face down the line. An entity or group of companies can avoid the downside of risks, if they are clear about the types of necessary or wanted alliances and understand the risks associated with such a move on the business and the technical side.

This is true with strategic alliances and the more common type of operational alliances. Strategic alliances are typically undertaken by companies seeking to enter new industry sectors, or trying to gain a more dominant position in their current field by accumulating a critical intellectual or marketing mass. In contrast, operational alliances are those that target incremental improvement in the performance of an existing business. They do so by filling gaps in a product line, covering a specific weakness in technology, adding a critical feature, or opening a new marketing area.

The goal of each of these examples is to improve business performance at operational rather than strategic levels. Development, production, and distribution alliances, or deals combining production capabilities of one firm with the distribution capabilities of another can expand one's market. In all these cases, much will be gained because of the strengths of the enterprise architecture or lost as a result of its weaknesses.

FLEXIBILITY AND ABILITY TO CHANGE THROUGH INNOVATIVE APPLICATIONS

Oil is now cheaper to find and retrieve thanks to new exploration and production technologies such as directional drilling, which uses telecommunications, models, and computers to exploit in real time the results of seismic and other geological studies. This replaces the old ineffectual method in which data collected from seismic study and drilling stayed in a data warehouse to be exploited "later on," while exploration blindly proceeded.

Whether in oil exploration, in finance, or anywhere else, real-time exploitation of data streams assures a flexible and effective decision environment. Its underlying technology is shown in Figure 5.5. While this block diagram comes from a financial study, specifically, the interactive use of the Black–Scholes pricing algorithm for options, it has a general domain of application and should be one of the subsystems supported by the enterprise architecture.

There are plenty of other examples, besides seismic analysis and options pricing, in which simulation and verification on a real-time basis provide tangible benefits. For instance, the steady monitoring of a product's adherence to design specifications, from initial requirements through final implementation, can significantly reduce quality problems and shorten time-to-market. The challenge is how to do this when a design has been partitioned into hardware and software modules assigned to

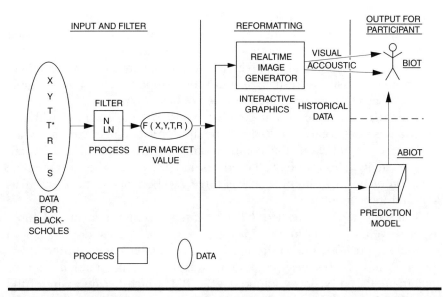

Figure 5.5   Input, filtering, reformatting, prediction, and visualization for the Black–Scholes option pricing model.

different teams, and teams tend to focus on the minute problems of their own assignment rather than on the global view.

The answer is in the institution of a concurrent engineering methodology (see Chapter 11) that starts with definition of the system and component requirements that can be used to build functional entities and then proceeds with simulation of software and hardware components. Simulated components can be exercised to verify that they satisfy their own and the system's functional requirements. When the actual components are developed, they will be substituted for simulated modules and tested to assure they comply to cross-functional specifications.

The visualization (next section) of output of such modules can be derived in an able manner from target applications that represent different types of devices and their use within defined job streams. Test scripts can be developed through a scripting language to define the inputs and compare actual outputs with expected outputs. Such methodology is well established in feedback theory, but is not used by everybody because designers are not trained how to employ it.

The use of graphical interfaces that permit observation and control of software operations, even in abstract terms, helps to keep pace with the growing complexity of applications (see also the next section on virtual reality). If the job becomes bigger, the tools and techniques must become better and more sophisticated in order to maintain a balance between means and needs and assure flexibility.

Experts increasingly believe that, in the future, sustainable competitive advantage will come from innovative firms which know how to put their store of knowledge and technology immediately to their advantage. Innovation really goes beyond creativity because creativity alone will not help in obtaining business results. It must be supported through tangible services that the enterprise architecture is able to offer.

The basic principle is that creativity must be implemented within a precise business context and should be appropriately marketed to create an income stream. Both the company and its customers should benefit from creativity. This is true of all products and processes. The most credible equation of business innovation has three components: technology, market, and implementation.

Time and again, so-called *killer products* typically manage all three aspects well. In fact, in the majority of cases, profits do not go to technology creators, but to the most capable implementers. In the 1950s the innovator in business computers was Univac; the implementer of mainframe-based business solutions was IBM, which became king of the computer business for two decades.

Wireless access in telecommunications presents another good example. More than three quarters of companies addressed through a recent study (whose detailed results are still confidential) do not have clearly defined strategies or goals for the use of mobile telephony, let alone mobile electronic commerce (me-commerce). Many, however, appreciate the benefits it could bring and want to implement "some solutions," which are often poorly defined. The challenge is one of identifying the solutions, screening and evaluating them, and choosing among possible alternatives.

Where may better opportunities lie? Answers to this query are scarce. Projected applications of nomadic computing (mobile access, or location independent computing) seem to favor sales, information technology, and general management — in that order. The histogram in Figure 5.6 classifies eight areas of applications on a "just note difference" basis. (See Chapter 9 on nomadic computing and the intelligent infrastructure it requires.)

Puzzling in the projections in Figure 5.6 is the use of nomadic computing by general management, as well as by IT. It is understandable that marketing and sales would be top users. Theoretically at least, the next in line should be operations, and then finance.

Market studies on nomadic computing are wanting. Projections concerning the use of nomadic computing by industry sectors are most important. For instance, on-line commerce, media, and tourism could be expected to top the list in terms of usage, followed by financial services, device makers, network operators, and aggregators of content.

In all these cases, what is and is not supported by the enterprise architecture plays a critical role in extracting value from the mobile

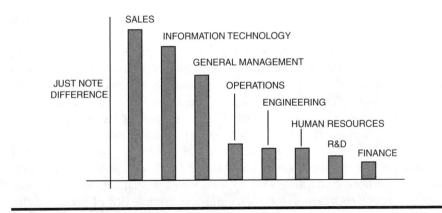

Figure 5.6   Applications domains and level of interest in nomadic computing.

platforms. This is a good example of a strategy that should be followed in all business opportunity analyses. The focal issue is that of looking carefully at the problem, defining its crucial variables, getting a factual market response, and experimenting on the best solution that really works.

The reason why so many of today's computers, operating systems, networking products, and engineering tools are not business successes (or highly reliable) is that they have not examined from this viewpoint. As a result, they lag in human engineering, are difficult to use, and are not incorporated into flexible, integrative solutions. Instead, they are poorly blended amalgams of loosely associated technologies. When designing, investing, or dealing one should always think of short term solutions and long term effects.

INTERACTIVE REAL-TIME VISUALIZATION IS PART OF THE ENTERPRISE ARCHITECTURE

It is often forgotten that Alexander Graham Bell was laboring to translate words into images for his wife, who was deaf, when he discovered the telephone. Vision is the most important of the human senses. A greater part of the brain's activity is devoted to processing visual information than to all of the other senses combined. No design of an enterprise architecture can forget this and still succeed.

Visualization is the translation of data into images. A professor at UCLA, in 1953, taught his students that a manager presented with tables full of numbers tries to convert them mentally into histograms and curves. Therefore, why not give him or her graphics in the first place? I would add that the skills to analyze visual images, picking out complete shapes, and bringing structure to a complex fuzzy environment, is crucial to every person, all the way from visual perception to dealing with complex abstractions.

In business and industry, visual information plays a prominent role; this speaks volumes about the interest now allotted to multimedia solutions and, most particularly, to graphical presentation. Whether one needs to see the whole picture or the details, depends on visual, multimedia information in subtle ways, including interpretation of facial expressions.

The problem is that for 45 long years information technology was not well suited to handling visual information. Available software, channel capacity, and computer power have simply not been able to cope with the vast quantity of data needed to represent a visual image. Also, there was a lack of techniques for managing the complexity of some of the applications requiring real-time update of visualization. This changed in the second half of the 1990s; much technology has been restructured to handling visual information in a relatively concise way. First class visualization is not yet common, however; it represents only a small proportion of total IT applications at the present time.

This deficiency is present particularly at the side of management information systems and decision support processes. The failure in visualization is, to a large part, due to what may be called a computer bureaucracy which fails to appreciate the concept of added value relative to IT. In the absence of an improvement in visualization, the organization is forced to underperform in a competitive and demanding environment. Backward approaches prevent the organization from competing, leaving only a small window with which to view the products and the marketplace.

The designers of the enterprise architecture, as well as the operators, should recognize such fundamental limitations and improve current conditions significantly. A lack of awareness of potent tools does not permit improvements, makes the results of information technology deficient, and is tantamount to the production of tons of paper of nonsense.

Top-tier companies ensure that an infrastructure is built based on high performance computing, optical and high-density magnetic storage, wideband communications, and knowledge-enriched software, with growing emphasis on graphics and visualization. The evolving applications should be facilitating the emergence of new integrative processes. For instance, engineering focuses on integrating computer-aided design and computer-aided manufacturing to marketing and after sales service. Such integration depends on broadband multimedia capabilities, interactive, real-time solutions, and the ability to steadily extend the range of concepts and data on materials that can be captured on computer systems.

The merger of broadband multimedia supports, interactive real-time solutions and concepts underpinning simulation studies has brought to the foreground implementations of virtual reality.[3] In the mid- to late 1990s virtual reality applications were distinguishing companies ahead of the curve from those staying behind. Today every self-respecting firm should be a user of real-time simulation and the enterprise architecture must make virtual reality solutions and tools available.

This is true from engineering to sales, finance, and general management. As an example, Figure 5.7 presents in a nutshell a practical implementation of virtual reality in the construction business. This application comes from Japan and concerns a solution developed by Fujita. Through remote multimedia input–output, the operator in the control room manipulates heavy machinery at a loading site. A whole infrastructure is necessary to support this and similar types of applications. The system involves a relay station, fiber optics, stereoscopic cameras, and supersonic sensors.

Here is another example on remotely accessible facilities, which concerns a new project undertaken at MIT's artificial intelligence laboratory. The goal is that of creating a prototype of remotely accessible multidisciplinary laboratory facilities, with chemistry as central application. Care is taken that the project's software and systems modules can adapt to other domains. The environment contains robotic machinery programmable over the Web. The system remotely conducts and monitors a variety of processes now done by lab technicians.

The semiautonomous robots to be used in this application form a class of integrated, cooperative machinery able to perform lab tests and other processes remotely. They replicate tests to confirm findings and do many routines around the clock to speed the gathering of reliable laboratory results with minimal human intervention. Cornerstone to this effort is the creation of a virtual environment with an Internet extension that makes it feasible to manipulate robotics remotely.

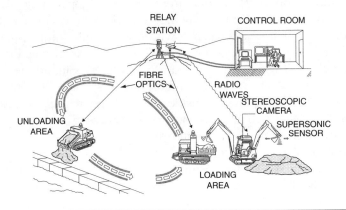

Figure 5.7 A practical implementation of virtual reality in the construction business.

This MIT project employs virtual reality modeling language (VRML), which allows developers to create programs for users to interact with a 3-D environment.[4] Programmed by VRML, generic sensors are combined with robotic machinery to manipulate materials. While performing their programmed tasks, these machines signal when they are malfunctioning or need routine maintenance. Real-time simulation is an integral part of modern IT solutions and the enterprise architecture of every company should take advantage of it.

GLOBAL SOLUTIONS WILL UPSET MANY CURRENT NOTIONS ABOUT THE ARCHITECTURE

Global solutions is a term that can have more than one interpretation. Geographic globality is best exemplified by the globalization of products, services, and marketing reach of many enterprises. When this happens, the technological infrastructure must be extended accordingly to serve clients, link to suppliers, and make feasible efficient operations of the company wherever it has a presence.

Global solutions may be needed not only in space but also in time. Longer term research in science and technology provides for greater prosperity to enterprises and society as a whole — particularly for the nations that fund it. Results, however, presuppose continuity of effort over time. Research partnerships have resulted in the Internet, the Human Genome Project, and global positioning systems (GPS).

A global solution, on the other hand, may be focused only on infra-structural facilities, along the lines of the example in the second section of this chapter. A good way of looking at the aftermath of radically changed infrastructural supports is through an analogy to city planning. Today city planners are convinced that, whether the domain of their activity is metropolitan or that of a smaller town, its economic future rests on the information and communications technologies that the installed infrastructure can deliver. This approach has a business viewpoint and leads to the notion that the quality of telecommunications is one of the three most important factors companies consider in deciding where to locate their business. The other two are ease of access to markets and transport links external to the company's own infrastructure.

Since quality and breadth of telecom facilities are so important for a city to be chosen as a post-industrial base, three dozen major metropolitan areas (worldwide) are now lining up to be listed as advanced wired societies. The question, however, remains: given that each of these projects involves hundreds of millions of dollars for infrastructure and services, is there a financial payback?

The answer to this query does not come easily because, in the general case, city administrators have little information on how much investment and employment is attracted by a first class telecommunications infrastructure. Yet, a factual answer is important, given the large costs. In brief, there is not yet available enough factual and documented information on whether networks have attracted really new companies and promoted employment, even if it is clear that they have encouraged a multiplicity of operators and the establishment of multimedia-based business.

Some analysts are of the opinion that the lack of data from older projects can be explained by their origins as social rather than economic investments. Wired cities started as public information society projects, not as means to attract new business. Therefore, these analysts say, it is only normal for them not to behave in a reliable way in response to current criteria.

Beyond this, in an infrastructural sense, comes the subject of what is really meant by a "wired city." Is coaxial cable enough? Should it be optical fibers? Is broadband access necessary for every subscriber? Should radio links be broadband? At what cost (see Chapter 6)? Is the real competitive advantage two-way multimedia? What about seamless hook-up to global satellite systems to provide end-to-end connectivity from one wired city to another or from any place to any place around the globe?

Looking at these issues from a technical viewpoint, it must be admitted that getting global mobile satellite systems into commercial operation has proved much more difficult than was originally anticipated. At the same time investments are so large, and budget overruns are so high, that several experts are of the opinion failure is not an option; it can lead straight to bankruptcy (more on this in Chapter 6).

But is the likelihood of success documented or is it mainly a hope? In 1985 when Motorola started with the low earth orbit (LEO) concept, an impressive number of experts said that this might be the "ultimate solution." Two years later, in 1987, Motorola started research on the Iridium model,[5] and 3 years down the line Iridium was officially announced. From then on, Iridium encountered many challenges, the euphoria bend, and clouds that burdened its initially rosy business opportunity.

Launched in December 1991, the same month the Iridium company was established, the first commercial GSM network was immediately seen as a serious business threat to the LEOs. A little over 3 years later, in January 1995, the Federal Communications Commission (FCC) granted the Iridium system an operating license for the 1.616 GHz to 1.626 GHz band. In 1995 nobody seemed to doubt that a global wireless system would be a good service to business.

After Globalstar received its final FCC authorization, many investors thought that the "next Microsoft" might be in the sky — and at a bargain price since Motorola had (unwisely) put a low $2.3 billion tag on Iridium.

Few people noted that the system's market appeal, and therefore its cash flow, were not yet proven. In fact, targets and the way to reach them were wanting. The Iridium Project could not stand a serious analytical examination.

In May 1997 the first five Iridium satellites made news, but the system was redimensioned to cut expenses. By the end of 1998 Iridium had cost about $5.7 billion, and this tally gave all signs of growing further. For instance, a cool $1.5 billion was required to cover operational costs. The demise of Iridium in 1999 is by now history; its bankruptcy was the result of financial and marketing blunders as well as technical facts.

Any infrastructural project can fail, whether its target is that of a global telecommunications solution, or a more limited one within the confines of a single firm. What is unaltered, however, is the fact that, whether it succeeds or fails, an infrastructural project will impact the way one looks at the enterprise architecture. The notion that technological dynamics deserve the most careful attention, monitoring, and databasing of results is beyond doubt. But is anybody listening?

REFERENCES

1. *Electronic. Design*, January 11, 1999.
2. Chorafas, D.N., *Integrating ERP, Supply Chain Management and Smart Materials*, Auerbach/CRC Press, New York, 2001.
3. Chorafas, D.N. and Steinmann, H., *Virtual Reality — Practical Applications in Business and Industry*, Prentice-Hall, Englewood Cliffs, NJ, 1995.
4. Chorafas, D.N., *Visual Programming Technology*, McGraw-Hill, New York, 1996.
5. Chorafas, D.N., *Network Computers Versus High Performance Computers: New Directions and Future Applications*, Cassell, London, 1997.

6

LEADING EDGE AND BLEEDING EDGE IN INFORMATIONTECHNOLOGY PROJECTS

INTRODUCTION

On paper, developing the right concept of an enterprise architecture for the company, as well as selecting and using the best hardware and software components and tools for projects undertaken, should not be difficult. There is a plethora of choices. In practice, however, a number of difficulties, constraints, and caveats, which become the bleeding edge of systems design, exists.

Enterprise architecture environments from multiple vendors and for multiple platforms are almost unavoidable. Heterogeneity is as common as operating systems and run-time applications routines. The problem is that many choices are made without proper study and experimentation. Some of the challenges subsequently found are not only due to technical reasons, but also to agency costs (internal frictions), lack of support to business lines, and political plots. A caveat might be an irrational restriction on how a platform is employed, thus limiting its usefulness or the sort of functionality which becomes part of the solution only at a much higher cost.

Artificial constraints concern developers of enterprise architectures and their customers because they have a greater impact on the ability to design and use a fully integrated system with visible return on investment (ROI). Very few products or solutions are created in isolation from one another and they usually depend on each other's functionality in order to perform.

Catchwords often interfere with personal goals and those for deliverables of systems design. Telecommuting was once thought to be the employment of choice of most businesses. At the dawn of the 21st century, however, it has lost much of its luster with U.S. employers. The number of companies allowing current employees to telecommute is shrinking, as management says that the practice never delivered its potential benefits. Today, less than 5% of U.S. workers work from home; and that number is expected to decrease unless something changes in the way telecommuting works.

Because companies are made of people, they are often influenced in their judgment by a general trend whose aftermath might be obscure or uneven when it comes to the individual firm. When results are not visible, telecommuters are not likely to receive promotions. One of the problems, experts say, is that supervisors never get to know what employees are really worth because they do not see them in action.

Quite often, labels can be misleading. A good example is the subject of productivity which often means different things to different people, though in its fundamentals it is indeed a legitimate preoccupation. Productivity gains permit U.S. workers to produce a pair of shoes in 24 minutes, vs. 3 hours in China. That shrinks the cost per pair of shoes to $4 in the U.S. against $1.30 in China,[1] but still leaves China as the supplier of three out of four shoes sold in the U.S. market.

Sometimes mistakes in system design can be very costly because they lead to investments based on high leverage but disappointing results. In 2000 and 2001, this was the case with third generation (3G) mobile telephony services and the colossal sums of money paid for airwave licenses by telecom operators (see third through fifth sections). The worst burned of these operators are those who did not know or did not care to compute ROI or to document their projections.

Also to be considered in gaining insight from what other people are doing is the "new, new thing" that often raises hopes beyond a level of sustainability. Air drums in the 1950s, Josephson junction semiconductors in the 1960s, System Application Architecture (SAA) and OS/2 in the 1980s, copper chips, in the 1990s, and molecule-based logic gates today (see the sixth section), are examples of this. With luck, molecular logic might lead to breakthroughs as silicon technology approaches its limits, But this is not a foregone conclusion.

A PROJECT THAT FAILED: CUTTING DOWN THE PAPER JUNGLE

To be competitive, a company must capture and exploit business opportunities as they unfold. Today one of the better business opportunities is in the focused and rational organization of enterprises and their business activities. The senior management of many companies has for years agonized as the number of employees grew faster than the revenues increased; and few companies have been able to come up with a valid solution.

This has been senior managers' and board members' own faults. As a large majority are computer illiterate, they have failed to realize that, as business challenges grow, the sophistication of computers, networks, databases, and software must also increase significantly. Failure to do so has created the huge gap shown in Figure 6.1. Throwing money at the problem is the result of a near-sighted policy of relying on masses of men and women, plus huge budgets, to face ongoing challenges. This is tantamount to vesting one's hopes on quantity rather than on quality; as experience demonstrates, it leads to deceptions. It has never been a good solution.

Of course some companies can show that they have been able to gain the utmost from technology, but this has been the exception rather than the rule. The rule is that, despite billions of dollars' worth of investment in information technology, most companies have failed to boost their bottom lines or overtake their rivals. Much of the money put into communications, computers, and software has been the business world's equivalent of an arms race.

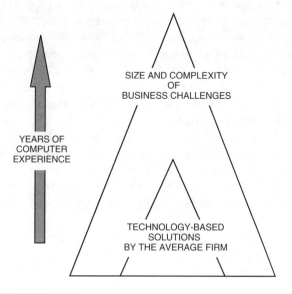

Figure 6.1 The gap between size of business challenges and sophistication of technological solutions increases over time.

Management has generally shown no skill in creating a technology-based industry revolution, and thereby acquiring a competitive edge. Of course cases exist which do not fit this statement, for example, Microsoft, Oracle, and SAP in software, and Sun Microsystems and Cisco in hardware. Notwithstanding these exceptions, business vision has been in short supply. Nobody should confuse the exceptions with the rule.

Neither are there universal solutions for every entity to follow. Every industry and every company has its own problems to address. For instance, nowhere in the financial community is this need for better focused technological solutions more clear than in front desk and back office integration. Computer-integrated banking operations can be instrumental in cutting costs, gaining market advantage, and controlling risk. In the bottom line, these are the goals an enterprise architecture should fulfill.

In the early 1990s, prior to its downfall because of the huge exposure it had assumed as a result of leverage, Tokyo-based Sanyo Securities was one of the world leaders in IT implementation, particularly in integrated banking systems and in knowledge engineering. Because of an effective frontdesk–backoffice integration through a proprietary enterprise architecture at Sanyo there were 0.6 back office employees per front desk executive. At that time, at Merrill Lynch there were 2.5 back office people per front desk.*

This sort of organizational breakthrough and the aftermath on personal productivity are important because companies have plenty of incentive to figure out how to use their staffs more efficiently. Cisco Systems says that it saved nearly $2 billion over the 1997 to 2000 timeframe by implementing Internet-based ordering, manufacturing, human resources, and finance systems. This action cut the need for a lot of "live" bodies and yielded Cisco juicy revenues of about $700,000 per worker. It also ensured that Cisco has a 60% higher productivity figure than the average Standard & Poor's 500-stock index companies.[2]

As should be expected, moves by the leaders of industry have been vastly more effective than the majority of all other of the cases. Because "average" companies failed to reach their computerization goals, set by the overall objectives of the 1980s and 1990s, like the paperless office. These are even more distant today than they were when originally proposed.

Despite the popularity of personal digital assistants, mobile computing, and office automation software, along with improvements in screen technology, paper usage in Group of Ten countries continues to increase. In the U.S., the percent of paper used for printing and writing grew

---

* Data provided by senior executives at Sanyo Securities during a working meeting at its Tokyo headquarters.

significantly from 1970 to 2000, while more than 90% of all business information is still recorded on paper.

There has been no lack of people projecting the end of the paper age, but events have proved them wrong. In 1986, Roger Smith, then chairman of General Motors, said, "By the turn of the century, we will live in a paperless society."[3] Smith had in mind the 20th century, and by now one knows the accuracy of his projection.

Figure 6.2 demonstrates an example from a major financial institution. Over a five-year period, back office work grew fast in proportion to expanding business opportunity, but the paper jungle increased even faster in spite of big money spent on computers and software. This pattern is no alien to business and industry. According to a survey by Wang Laboratory, based on statistical samples of American companies, an estimated 2.4 billion new sheets are placed in paper file folders each day. An average of 600 million office documents is produced each day in the U.S., amounting to nearly three documents for every person living in the country, the Gartner Group suggests.

This pattern of paper usage may be very difficult to change. Factors contributing to the increased employment of printers on-line to personal computers have overtaken those associated to copiers. This has shifted information distribution, but not the habits of people receiving the information. In the U.S. and Europe, studies found that nearly two out of three people interviewed prefer to annotate or underline documents as they read them. The use of paper and pencil is still the preferred option.

Electronics-based reading of documents is possible, of course, but so far it has not changed the user culture. Therefore, those who plan to

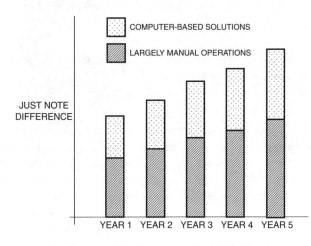

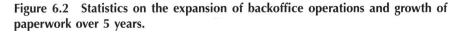

Figure 6.2 Statistics on the expansion of backoffice operations and growth of paperwork over 5 years.

excel in client focus and reach significant paperwork reduction at the same time will be deceived. For nearly 50 years, companies tried to kill paper using computers, yet much more paper is around today than ever before. This is still a paper-based society, after all.

THE QUESTIONABLE IMMEDIATE FUTURE: BREAKING EVEN WITH THE PIE IN THE SKY

Mobile computing is typically location-independent (also called nomadic computing; see Chapter 9). The services which it can provide are evidently of interest to every enterprise architecture, as well as to studies concerning integration. Until quite recently, the Internet and mobile phones have remained separate entities, even though, in several Group of Ten countries, both have become commonplace accessories. In all likelihood the two will merge during the coming years. But on what grounds?

Experts project that a major breakthrough in their integration will quite likely come from Web-enabled wireless portable phones which may be used in Internet commerce. To power these portable engines, Intel and Advanced Micro Devices, among other semiconductor companies, are racing to bring to the market the first 1-GHz chip for desktops and mobiles. Just prior to NASDAQ's meltdown, cellular projects promised to deliver information to people anytime, anywhere, and on any device.

In order to achieve this goal, companies count on partnerships between computer makers, software firms, and mobile telephone network operators. The aim has been to develop a new breed of wireless-enabled communicators. In itself, such strategy has not been wrong, but manufacturing companies, as well as their clients, the telecoms, failed to ask the all-important questions:

- Do I know *my* strengths and weaknesses?
- Do I know *my* business direction?
- Do I have a plan to reach *my* objectives?

A factual and documented approach is imperative because what lies ahead promises to revolutionize the way one looks at communications solutions. Answers to these three queries will change, to a substantial extent, the nature of services offered to clients of telecommunications systems and the grand design of their enterprise architecture.

These questions should be answered in a factual manner by all so-called broadband wireless access (BWA) service providers and should be followed up by analytical evidence on how the different wireless providers will support the "last mile" and "last foot" solutions to their clients.

Otherwise the statement that "the new technology will dominate the next 10 years" is not convincing.

A thoroughly studied business plan is necessary not only in connection to the European Union's new product, Universal Mobile Telecommunications System (UMTS), but also regarding the interfaces of third generation (3G) networks to the existing telecom system. The reasons for 3G are no secret. As traffic continues to increase, the drive to multimedia takes on speed and wireless providers offer faster mobile Internet access. Telecom operators need to significantly improve their installed back-haul networks in terms of channel capacity and systems reliability.

3G is the follow-up to first generation (1G) and second generation (2G) solutions, which are briefly explained in Chapter 7 in connection to Project Oxygen. There is also the so-called 2 ½G for which was designed the Wireless Application Protocol (WAP) as a sort of stopgap. Many people, and some companies, look at the WAP and UMTS as if they were alternatives. This is wrong because WAP is a (not so successful) 2G-based development, the EU's UMTS is 3G, and Japan's DoCoMo is also 3G.

"WAP and DoCoMo are getting closer," said one expert. The answer to the question, "What about UMTS and DoCoMo?" was not forthcoming. Other experts suggested the two would work together as a subset of one another, but most likely at reduced quality levels. Add to this the fact that WAP has been a major success and confusion reigns.

The incompatibility between UMTS and DoCoMo's i-mode is of greater concern. Unfortunately, mobile computing protocols compete for 3G. UMTS and i-mode belong to WCDMA, the same basic protocol developed jointly in Europe and Japan as a spin-off of the code division multiple access (CDMA) protocol (the W in WCDMA stands for wideband). CDMA was originally designed by Qualcomm in the U.S. and has been adopted by a number of companies, including Lucent and Nortel. Today, CDMA 2000 is the North American 3G protocol of choice; it has also been adopted in Latin America. CDMA and WCDMA are rather heterogeneous in spite of what the International Telecommunication Union (ITU) says, and within WCDMA different versions exist.

The major difference between UMTS and the i-mode is not often discussed. To avoid taking uncontrollable risks with too many unknowns, the i-mode has been deliberately restricted in its functionality. For its part, UMTS is a beast with two heads, one of which is an evolutionary step from GSM. It was designed that way deliberately in an effort to capture the market of more than 500 million GSM users, while also parading as 3G.

Modern technology allows one to do business just about anywhere. Therefore it is not acceptable for countries to have different "national standards." Globalization has not yet done away with the "not invented here" syndrome. Cognizant executives opine that the failures of European telecoms are not limited to business opportunity but also involve technical subjects. At top of the list is the question, "Which standard for 3G?" This is a tough question indeed. The EU promotes UMTS; the Japanese promote DoCoMo (by NTT). The difference between the two is relatively small, but modulation is incompatible. Eventually it will be something like PAL and Secam, which split European TV transmission and reception in half. In the longer run, this may make the transition to 4G difficult as Figure 6.3 suggests.

European critics of DoCoMo say that its i-mode is a closed protocol, not an interoperated one, because in Japan NTT has a monopoly and has been able to establish a *de facto* standard which will not sell elsewhere. American experts, however, suggest that lots of U.S. companies are interested in DoCoMo and work to make it an open protocol. As such, it might conquer the American market.

It is too early yet to say which network might control this market, but it is probable that the commercial battle will be won in the American market. What the U.S. networks will pick and promote will carry the day, even if today the U.S. is behind in mobile compared to Europe and Japan. *De facto* standards are nothing new in the computer and communications market.

For all companies that want to deal globally, international standards are essential for developing products and systems that can be used from one continent to another. A century and a half ago this was evident for telegraph communications, sparking the birth in 1865 of the Consultative Committee of International Telephone and Telegraph (CCITT) — the

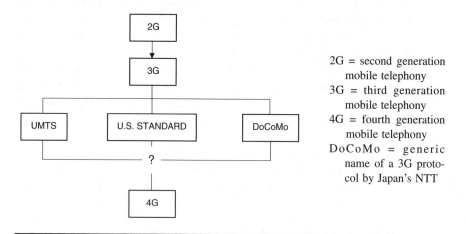

2G = second generation mobile telephony
3G = third generation mobile telephony
4G = fourth generation mobile telephony
DoCoMo = generic name of a 3G protocol by Japan's NTT

Figure 6.3   Standardization of a protocol expected to have wide global application was left on the back burner.

predecessor to the International Telecommunication Union (ITU), which is now developing standards for the industry.

Nowadays, in a manner quite similar to telegraph's case, successful 3G implementation requires everyone to agree upon the use of a common code; in telegraphy's case, this was Morse code. Also, a global agreement is needed on equipment that would guarantee interconnection. A universal standard is the only way to assure global interoperability, any to any and end to end (see Chapter 14). The World Trade Organization (WTO), International Electrical Commission (IEC), ITU, and other agencies should collaborate in establishing a unique 3G standard.

Down to basics, this is not only a technical challenge. It is technical and political — and it is urgent. Many of the devices now coming to the market, particularly in Europe and Japan, combine the features of mobile phones, pagers, and handheld computers. Users can send and receive e-mail, check weather forecasts, consult transport timetables, trade shares, and carry out banking transactions if they desire — and if they are willing to pay for such services.

Normalization is urgently required because a major challenge today is financial; this alters past perspectives significantly. For most of the approximately 140 years of the telephone's history, the big issue has been one of access, particularly in terms of coverage and only secondarily in terms of cost. Now cost holds the upper ground. Theoretically, the cost of cellular coverage is affordable, but by whom and for what sort of services?

In Europe, consumers have shown themselves willing to pay a premium for phone services perceived to be significantly superior to fixed-line communications — the plain old telephone service (POTS) — provided this premium is low and tends to disappear over time. The result of betting on this hypothesis has been that mobile telephony in Europe is becoming a consumer commodity. The trick is that consumer commodities must be kept to a cost appealing to a large population, even with upgrade in functionality; at the same time, operators must receive a good enough market potential to permit recovering their investment and making a profit.

These two conflicting requirements might have been satisfied if the existing GSM networks, which allow mobile phones to be used across borders in Europe, were upgraded to general packet radio service (GPRS) technology. Such change would allow data to be sent at 3 times the current speed, rising to 12 times within a year or two.

But telecom operators saw big, without counting risk and return. They thought the major breakthrough in terms of mobile data was due with the introduction of third-generation networks that use a different type of wireless technology. These would be capable of handling 2 megabits per second (MBPS), much faster than the fastest computer modems today.

The false calculation started with the premise that annual revenues from wireless devices "should be" expected to rise to $130 billion by the middle of this decade in Europe's market alone. For its part, in 1999 the ITU predicted that, by 2001, the number of cellular subscribers would have jumped to more than 650 million, reaching 1 billion in 2002 and resulting in more phones on this planet than TV sets.

With these attractive, but undocumented, prognostications, the big telecommunications operators felt that they could "have their cake and eat it, too." British Telecom, Deutsche Telekom, France Telecom, Telefonica, Sonera, and others violated every rule in investments entering into this airwaves competition.

One step in mismanagement is usually followed by another: the same cash-stripped telecom operators who rushed to take loans from banks to buy the airwaves (see the next section) committed another capital sin in the investment world. They precipitated themselves into foreign acquisitions, partly to become global and partly to talk up their shares and their supposed "customer value."

Big loans were thrown at the problem as if banks just gave money away. As the monthly bulletin of the European Central Bank (ECB) suggested, "Particularly in the autumn of 2000, the financing of UMTS licenses by telecommunications companies seemed to be an important source of the increase in the annual rate of growth of loans granted to nonfinancial corporations." This view is confirmed by the observation that, after very significant monthly growth in August and September 2000 related to the UMTS auction in Germany, short-run dynamics of loans to the private sector became much more moderate.[4]

These *"la folie des grandeurs"* decisions took place while everybody knew that the general trend in pricing telephone services was down and competition was cut-throat. Figure 6.4 shows, in order of magnitude, the cost of a 3-minute telephone call from New York to London. All evidence indicates that this flat cost curve would not bend upward, no matter what sort of goodies the telecoms put on the line.

UMTS LICENSES: THE BLEEDING EDGE OF A TELECOMMUNICATIONS ARCHITECTURE

Eventually, business organizations and the people running them find it necessary to descend from the stratospheric level of their runaway imaginations to solid facts. This is the challenge now facing the majority of overleveraged telephone operators in Europe.

In its origins, the financial precipice of the Universal Mobile Telecommunications System (UMTS) started in Brussels. The bureaucrats of the European Union had the brilliant idea that, since some of the EU countries

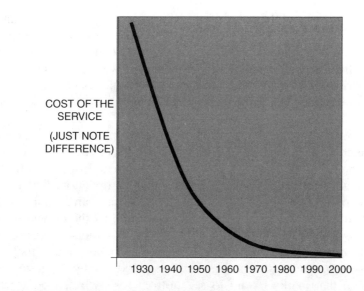

Figure 6.4 The shrinking cost of a 3-minute telephone call from New York to London over a 70-year timeframe.

were ahead in wireless communications, the new generation gadgets and their airwaves were the ideal technology to beat the Americans. The still hazy notion of Internet mobile was their idea, and it had to be put in place very fast.

In 1998, the European Commission decided that all UMTS licenses had to be given by 2001 and the first implementation of 3G mobile communications had to take place in 2002. This decision was made without examining whether such a timeplan was technically possible, and whether it was financially advantageous or disastrous. "Brussels," says Elie Cohen, "incited the [European] governments to launch themselves in a process without visibility."[5]

The different European governments did not examine the current technical feasibility of 3G mobile infrastructure or the strict deadlines and economic soundness of the whole enterprise. Instead, they were happy to keep within Brussels' rapid timetable of 3G deployment, once they discovered that they could make big money by selling UMTS licenses to the telecoms that they partly owned. The British government was the first to benefit from the cash flow, pocketing £25 billion ($35 billion). The Germans exceeded the British intake with a windfall of DM 100 billion (about $50 billion). The French lost out because, by the time they sold the UMTS licenses, the treasury of telecoms was dry. They collected "only" FF 65 billion ($9 billion).

In all, Ministries of Finance of the different European governments brought home nearly $130 billion paid by telecoms who failed to examine whether this UMTS operation had even a remote likelihood of profitability, if it did, whether profitability could be achieved within a timetable permitting servicing the loans and repaying the capital. Banks lending the money seem neither to have asked, nor to have answered, these crucial questions.

Only postmortem did banks and the investment community at large show an increasing reluctance to fund telecom infrastructure projects. With no more money thrown at the problem, as happened over a period of about 2 years (mid-1999 to early 2001), telecom operators had to put network expansion plans on hold until the financial climate improved.

"The market has deteriorated slowly so no one saw the downturn, but it's here now," said one knowledgeable executive. Others suggested that the market never really encouraged operators to build widely first, then wait for sales to catch up. The best business model, they suggested, has always been that markets want to see upfront results based on services and customer demand.

Telecoms, their boards and their CEOs awoke to discover that customer demand for broadband frills promised by UMTS was simply not there. Even more classical broadband access by households proved to be far below what telecom operators hoped. Statistics indicate that, in 2001, access stands under 1% of households, on average, in Europe. It is 2.3% in Scandinavia, but the nordic region is too sparsely populated to weigh on the EU average. Access is at 0.9% in Germany, 0.6% in France, 0.3% in the U.K., and below 0.2% in Spain and Italy.

All this suggests that there is scarcely a window of opportunity for household cable-based broadband, let alone for the optimism of the UMTS. Some experts say there was once an opportunity but it has closed, locking out newcomers in telecoms and any of the established carriers without a fully funded business plan.

To appreciate this argument, keep in mind that 3G mobile will require totally new hardware and software, which will cost a very large amount of money. As for technology, it is a useful reminder that the foremost hardware and software vendors are in the U.S.; this is in addition to the big consumer market. American consumers are usually faster to see the benefits of a new solution. If no U.S. market exists, there may be no immediate need for broadband mobile technology.

None of the references just made should be interpreted as implying that UMTS is dead; however, there is no visible need for it today. At this moment, who really needs broadband multimedia mobile? No factual, documented answer exists in the sense of any massive market. By contrast, 3G demands very large investments to cover Europe in an any-to-any manner but nobody really has the money for such investments or the studies proving they might be profitable.

For any practical purpose, the European governments who pocketed the money of the licenses killed the UMTS project. They did not study how much more capital would be needed to make the system work. The telecoms did not examine the billions they had to put on the table to exploit the licenses they bought, nor did they do their homework on the services to be offered and the cash flow expected from those services. The soul-searching questions should have been:

■ Which new services can we support with UMTS?
■ Will these services be able to carry the market?
■ How much money will these services bring to the company?

There is no evidence that the European telecoms silultaneously examined the three sides of the issue: financial, marketing, and technical. UMTS offers more dense networks. In infrastructural terms, that is a plus, but it is watered down by top-heavy costs and, most importantly, by not bringing the sort of benefits consumers are inclined to buy. Product-wise, the deliverables are simply not there.

A vague idea exists that consumer services will consist of meteorological bulletins, traffic congestion information, stock market prices, and music; nothing is exciting in all that. Nobody seems to have had a clear notion whether UMTS was worth the trouble. Postmortem, what was said about the bottom line was false. No telecom operator investigated risk and return with the UMTS licences by asking questions such as:

■ How many new clients are likely to be acquired?
■ How much more will existing clients spend with UMTS?
■ Why will people opt for paying services when much contained in the UMTS plans is already available gratis?

Again, postmortem, independent research outfits tested the market's response and the likely price structure. They then revealed that, by 2005, on average, money paid by wireless consumers would drop by 15% rather than increasing by 200% as the telecom operators had thought! Markets can always expand if products and targets are available. But there are no new products for the four currently targeted markets: handheld devices, Web applications, Internet access through handheld devices, and interactive digital television (idTV).

Apart from the fact that clear ideas about specific new products are still missing and the whole concept of value-added services is misty, failure to plan ahead has always been a prescription for disaster. For now, the UMTS enterprise is like a company which has spent $130 billion for licenses to build a factory that will manufacture an unspecified product, whose clients are not yet known, and whose market price may vary considerably.

THE DEBACLE OF THE TELECOMS' 3G MOBILE WILL IMPACT ENTERPRISE SOLUTIONS

What the mismanaged telecoms have failed to appreciate is that only business customers can afford high technology offered above minimal cost, and will do so only if they see benefits that exceed the money to be paid and permit them to gain against the competition. This concept is neither new nor unheard of, but it is very often forgotten. The argument advanced by the people who sank the telephone industry into a sea of red ink has been that, as today's teenagers grow up, fixed-line voice will quietly wither away. For them a phone that cannot be carried by multimedia is not a phone at all. This is a far-fetched concept and is followed by another undocumented hypothesis: as they turn into tomorrow's businessmen these teenagers are going to expect and demand the same or better levels of mobility and service with which they grew up.

The telcos living in this dream world forgot that timing is very important. Today's teenagers will become senior businessmen with decision power in 2020 or later, but the $130 billion for licenses was paid in 2000 and 2001. Even if wireless accounts for an ever increasing share of the voice, data, image, and Internet markets before 2020, investments made in 2000 cannot be left hanging.

Investments must produce profits. If they do not, they are not investments, only thrown-away money. Telephone operators projected that the introduction of higher speed mobile networks would allow handheld devices to display full-color, high-resolution video. But they failed to explain what, exactly, the use of it would be and who would pay the bill.

Before the debacle of the telecom industry, that is, as long as the euphoria lasted, even costs were not appropriately studied. Therefore, it was not surprising to find after the 2001 meltdown that the difference in cost between deploying 3G mobile services in Europe and putting fiber into every European home has been a close call.

The way financial analysts looked at this issue in London, with the same expense that British Telecom (BT) has put into the 3G auctions, it could have installed fiber into every home in the U.K. BT paid $6.4 billion for a 10 MHz license in the U.K. radio auctions — to get nothing but spectrum. BT is not even the most heavily committed future 3G builder.

Germany's six 3G license winners paid an average $7.8 billion each for their rights to own mobile data systems. While fiber and 3G are not alternatives, here again analysts are making cost comparisons as projections on 3G rollout costs emerge. The results make unhappy reading for companies who invested money without regard for ROI and for the banks who made the loans. Some analysts suggest that comparing 3G to fiber purely on a cost basis is a flawed proposition because fiber has the advantage of limitless capacity and radio transmission has the cachet of mobility. Those who would rather have seen this huge investment of $130 billion go for fiber — or, more precisely, double that money if one counts the need to equip the spectrum and make a channel out of it — make the point that 3G telephony will almost certainly not drive the techno-revolution as the industry once thought.

Slowly the notion sets in that capacity on 3G handsets in a normal environment is going to be dramatically lower than people and companies expected. Even the most optimistic estimates speak no more of 2 megabits per second, or 30 times the speed of an average dialup Internet connection at home, but of half MBPS instead. Other questions surround the efficiency of 3G deployment, including the need to streamline the currently complex systems architecture shown in Figure 6.5.

Planners and designers should learn from the European UMTS debacle never to go for eye-catching gimmicks. It is unhealthy to be uncoupled from reality, just as one should never follow the beaten path. There is no alternative to thorough study and experimentation, including evaluation of what state of the art really means, costs, ROI, and orderly transition to the new solution.

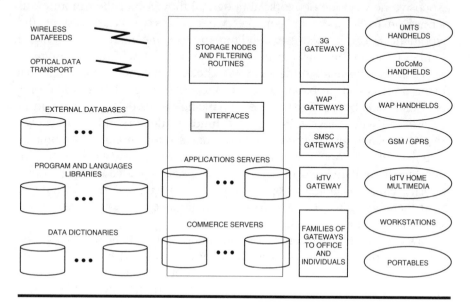

Figure 6.5   The complex systems architecture of 2G and 3G solutions.

For instance, in the case of 3G, because the new technology works over different frequencies from today's mobile telephones, all existing transmitter stations will need to be retrofitted or replaced. There are 20,000 of them in Germany and maybe four times as many in the whole European Union. That is a very expensive undertaking.

Even assuming that every European over the age of 10 buys a 3G mobile phone and runs up more than a four-digit bill in annual user charges, many financial analysts suggest that telecoms will find it difficult to break even before 2010. This has led serious observers to cast doubt on the telecoms' calculations, and the stock prices of such firms have gone into a tailspin.

According to a Forrester Research study, building 3G will be so expensive that mobile operators' earnings will nose downward in 2003 and go negative in 2007. This fact is enough to document that the famous UMTS license auctions are turning out to be one of Europe's biggest public policy blunders, as well as a business misjudgment.

The Sonera–Telefonica consortium in Germany, for example, illustrates what it means to get deeply into trouble: it faces $7.7 billion in license payments and at least another $8 billion in network investments. With all this money irrevocably committed, it will be able to address just 13% of Germany's 3G market, or a population of 10 to 11 million people — the size of Greece's population.

The "victors" face heavy debt and an obligation to build a hugely expensive new phone network, although all they got for their money was permission to compete in a market where the payoffs are distant and hypothetical. The immense expenditures for an uncertain UMTS come at a time of ruthless acquisition battles in the international telecommunications market. This leads some analysts to believe that the next international financial crisis will probably not have a regional trigger but a global one. Its center will be located where financing activities have been most intense and where investors provided funds to debtors indiscriminately.

The telecommunications sector now has second thoughts. Arguments arise that telecom operators should sue the governments (who partly own them) for the inflated cost of 3G mobile licenses. One idea floating around industry circles is that the operators should attempt to demonstrate in court that the license fee is a form of illegitimate taxation, a tax levied on possible future services.

Lawyers are not yet certain of a winning case, but nearly everybody agrees that the British and German governments erred by using the 3G auctions as a huge up-front tax on a nascent industry. Curiously, both governments are socialistic and supposedly care for the public good. These governments actions left the telcos with a ridiculous choice: drowning in debt now to possibly survive later.

If a court action based on illicit taxation does not fly because taxation is a complex aspect of the law, what then? Some analysts suggest that to contest the UMTS license costs the telcos should claim that the governments involved fell foul of the European Union's 1997 licensing directive. This directive made two points: 1. licenses should be awarded on the basis that they only cover administrative costs, and 2. for scarce resources such as spectrum, payment structures should encourage efficient use. From this comes the argument that, by reserving the best license for the party with the deepest pocket, the EU governments were clearly allocating spectrum on a discriminatory basis. By putting the price at billions of dollars the same governments attempted to cover more than just administrative costs.

In conclusion, UMTS is a case study on a failure whose magnitude is not seen every day. Case studies on failures are very important to the designers of an enterprise architecture because they can then avoid "reinventing the wheel," repeating others' mistakes. Success, a proverb says, is what happens when preparation meets opportunity. Every self-respecting company should ask, "Are we prepared to benefit from opportunities that technology presents without incurring huge losses?"

THE EXTENDED FUTURE: NANOSCALE ENGINEERING PROJECTS

Nanoscale engineering, or *nanotechnology*, is a science whose works and explorations begin at the scale of a micron (a millionth of a meter) and move beyond the level of a nanometer (a billionth of a meter). The object of these studies is wide. It currently includes many "nanos:" nanomaterials, nanomanufacturing, nanorobotics; as well as quantum (or molecular) computing and quantum chemistry. Practical results are expected far into the future, offering the synergies of biology, engineering, and materials chemistry.

Nanotechnology is of special interest to the design of an enterprise architecture because, at least theoretically, it could result in much faster, denser, more compact, and cheaper-to-build devices, even if the deliverables are far away. Nanotechnology and molecular logic gates correlate. While still at the research stage, molecular switches are expected to enable creation of smaller, more powerful devices than might be possible with silicon.

Many experts believe that eventually biomaterials will play a critical role in science and technology. The work done in this area to synthesize materials as well as to control their structure and properties can have far reaching consequences. By all evidence, it will influence a wide range of applications such as: tissue engineering, implant devices, delivery of new drugs, health monitoring, and computing gear.

Some experts think this research may merge with projects concentrating on materials at nanomechanical and nanostructural levels. This will most likely permit materials at scales that have not yet been studied, as well as relate a material's properties to molecular, atomic, or grain structure. The way to bet is that nanolevel studies will reveal a world of which we are currently aware only in the most general terms, and that the technological impact might be immense, with microphotonics already spoken of as the next "killer technology," to be followed by nanophotonics.

This is the good news, but they will be delivered tomorrow. There are many challenges to which answers still do not exist. Although one may make quantum switches, how can one access and read the information in them? How can one take data out of an individual molecule when it changes state? Answers to these types of queries are not forthcoming.

Some experts think that to get meaningful answers to this sort of challenging technical issues will take another 10 years, if it is feasible at all. Big companies with well-financed laboratories and foremost universities are working to find the answers. Inventions from a young team working in a garage are possible, but they are not likely because of the necessary huge capital investments.

Nanoscale projects are also not the "ultimate" in R&D. Already many scientists have their eyes on pico-level projects, targeting a thousandth of a micro. The interest underpinning such infinitesimal scales rests on the fact that such technology in the making presents the possibility of building storage, logic, and routing structures comprising a few atomic elements.

Historically, one of the first nanotechnology breakthroughs came to the public eye in mid 1999 when a joint research team of scientists from UCLA and Hewlett-Packard demonstrated molecular-based logic gates. Evidence was provided that these molecules are capable of results equal to or surpassing those of typical silicon, with the added advantage that the molecular circuitry can be defect-tolerant. In parallel to this project, scientists at MIT and the U.S. Department of Energy's Los Alamos National Laboratory have demonstrated that nanoscale semiconductor particles, or nanocrystal quantum dots (see the next section) offer needed performance for efficient emission of laser light. This enables the development of new optical and optoelectronic devices, such as tunable lasers and optical amplifiers.

In conclusion, gates, amplifiers, and other devices basic to computing circuitry are in evolution, but it is too early to tell what will be of practical importance. Potentially, but only potentially, these gates might lead to molecular computers which, by all evidence, would be smaller, faster, and much less expensive than current solutions. They would also consume less power, while offering a large amount of storage allowing data to be hardwired directly into the machine. More about what can be done with, or at least expected from, quantum mechanics, follows.

WHAT CAN BE EXPECTED FROM QUANTUM MECHANICS?

Quantum mechanics may be irrelevant to most computer engineers and telecommunications specialists, but a team at Lucent's Bell Laboratories reckons that an esoteric quantum effect could play a vital role in future microelectromechanical systems.[6] As the previous section showed, before biological circuits become practical, scientists must develop practical ways to access real information in molecular switches. They must also come up with efficient and scalable ways to fabricate long sequences of DNA.

Another major challenge is to bind the molecular sequences in a desired circuit. If this is achieved, biological switching devices might fill biochemical needs at cellular levels, rather than replacing electronic circuits. The future will tell. For the time being, in early 2001, researchers at Cellicon Biotechnologies, Boston, MA, constructed a genetic flip-flop and clock. This is the first building block of a biological state machine. The architecture is rather simple: two DNA elements and their regular genes are arranged in *E. coli* samples. Each gene inhibits the synthesis of the other, and though either gene can be produced at a given time, both cannot be synthesized simultaneously.

Basically, the function of this genetic flip-flop is analogous to that of an electronic circuit. The genetic clock consists of three regulator genes and their associated DNA elements arranged sequentially in a negative-feedback loop in the *E. coli* bacterium.[7] Experts think that molecular computers would most likely be 100 times more efficient than current Pentiums, in terms of energy needed for calculation. The computer's architecture would consist of a set of wires arranged in one direction, a layer of rotaxanes (a class of molecules), and a second set of wires arranged in the opposite direction. Wires and switches would be configured electronically to fabricate logic gates. Molecular switches and wires would be linked together, and the logic circuit would be flexible and reconfigured as necessary.

Speed and novelty aside, this perceived flexibility attracts many scientists and industrialists to molecular computing. Advanced technological products stand a far better chance to succeed if they can be flexibly configured to fit different markets and their applications requirements. Boeing's 700 product line and the Concorde were not only different planes but also followed two quite different design philosophies: the 700 product line was flexible; it could shrink into a city jet or expand toward the jumbo. By contrast, the Concorde was a one-tantum product that could not develop to fit the market's whims.

The fact that there might be a good business future in molecular computing has not escaped the attention of major companies. IBM announced a development which might ultimately pack the power of a supercomputer into a device so small that it could be woven into garments powered by body heat. The concept behind the use of nanotechnology is that eventually machines are built atom by atom, to practical purposes. If they materialize, Quantum computers will be devices that store and process information at atomic scale. They will perform computations in novel ways that conventional computers cannot explore, and will most likely attain very high speed, exploiting memory space at the limits set by the laws of physics.

This potential ensures that interest in nanotechnology and associated advances is growing at a remarkable pace in fields like logic design, circuit manufacturing, computation, robotics, lithography, optical switching, control systems, combustion, imaging, microsurgery, biology, and energy production. Breakthroughs in nanoscale engineering have important implications for many industrial and scientific areas, but it would take another decade or two of intensive R&D to get some tangible results.

Some scientists and technologists expect some intermediate deliverables, which will make the promises of nanotechnology believable. For instance, IBM's February 2000 announcement of an atomic scale inquiry points toward a quantum mirage where information can travel through solid substances without the need for wires, eventually rendering modern electronic circuitry obsolete. If this lab development becomes a practical proposition, it could lead to a complete rethinking of what computers are.

Researchers have found that, by placing an atom at one of two focal points in an ellipse of cobalt atoms, which acts like a mirror, a mirage of the inner atom appears at the other focal point with some properties of the original. This, scientists believe, could lead to transferring information at molecular level without heat. If and when this becomes practical, it will constitute a breakthrough in miniaturization.

But even if the physical side is mastered, systems challenges will be enormous. Replacing the microprocessors of today with nanotechnology would require a complete rethinking of what computers are and for which functions they should be used because new devices could be made almost infinitely small yet equally powerful. Network design will also radically change, requiring new concepts that will dominate an enterprise architecture and radically alter our appreciation of what an enterprise solution is and is not.

One of the most interesting projects whose impact ranges from computation to communications and sensor technology is quantum dots, or artificial atoms. Developments in nanolithography have permitted the construction of quantum dots as nanoscale structures in which electronics can be confined to two-dimensional regions in a semiconductor. These artificial atoms are exhibiting a behavior evaluating natural atoms together with new phenomena of their own.

The application of quantum dots can range from biology to optics. Semiconductor particles in nanometer size show quantum effects in their electronic and optical properties that might be harnessed in a variety of ways. These particles might be manipulated as if they were large organic molecules, incorporated into different environments, and coupled to a variety of molecular entities.

As silicon chips become smaller and features such as wire traces continue to shrink, production may become cost-prohibitive and performance unstable. Nanolithography is important in circuit manufacture, planar processing, communications, and other domains because nanotechnology has the virtues of long-range spatial-phase coherence and high placement accuracy. An important challenge for nanotechnology, perhaps through lithographically created templates, is to find a way to bridge the gap between spatial resolution, and the size of macromolecules.

At current theoretical levels, some laboratory advances in molecular computing hold promise of extending the technology from ROM to RAM, potentially increasing storage for individual systems and components. As more RAM is packed into subsystems, it could reduce the requirements for various forms of distributed network-based storage.

Another branch of nanotechnology, microbial engineering, has the potential to impact not only biology but also computation and control systems. This branch aims to explore the fact that living cells, which possess intricate but efficient nanoscale dynamics, can be modified to address engineering goals like computing and networking. Digital command of biological processes promises a range of implementations from nanofabrication to biological control of architectural constructs, with an evident aftermath for enterprise solutions.

It is too early yet to say if all or only some of the new technology discussed in this chapter will find its way into practical applications. The likelihood is that 3G will be the first to do so after its promoters create a market for it. Many nanoscale projects will see the light, but it is not sure that quantum computing will carry the day. But, as Albert Einstein once said, "There is not the slightest indication that nuclear energy will ever be attainable. It would mean that the atom would have to be shattered at will."[8]

REFERENCES

1. *BusinessWeek,* March 5, 2001.
2. *BusinessWeek*, March 20, 2000.
3. *Commn. ACM*, March, 2001.
4. ECB, Monthly Bulletin, March, 2001.
5. *Canard Enchainé*, March 28, 2001.
6. *FibreSystems Europe*, April, 2001.
7. *Electronic. Design*, April 2, 2001.
8. *Commn. ACM*, March, 2001.

II

PRESENT BEST APPLICATIONS AND FUTURE DEVELOPMENTS IN TECHNOLOGY

7

A LOOK INTO THE FUTURE: THE INTELLIGENT ENVIRONMENT PROJECT AT MIT

INTRODUCTION

In the evolution of command and control systems, first-generation computer-based solutions were the semiautomatic air-to-ground equipment (SAGE) of the late 1950s. This was a military project to protect the airspace of North America from Soviet missiles, but it had commercial fallouts. Its aftermath has opened up a whole generation of technological approaches which used SAGE concepts in their design, as well as some of its hardware.

While the then high speed memory boxes of SAGE were designed to serve the U.S. military, IBM eventually marketed them for commercial usage. More importantly, at the time, computer applications were just beginning and any contribution which went beyond accounting-machine mentality was significant. One of the better known pieces of software that came out of SAGE was been IMS, the hierarchical database management system (DBMS) released by IBM in 1967. Though today IMS is obsolete, it was a first — a beefed-up functionality of file management routines.

These historical references are raised in order to press the point that breakthroughs connected to projects designed for military applications not only find their way into civilian usage but also stand a good chance to be heralded as a new line of products with potential in business and industry. Some of these products are so advanced in comparison to their predecessors that they reshape the use of computers and communications.

DBMSs have developed enormously since SAGE from hierarchical into owner–member (CODASYL, networking), entity relationship, and relational and object-oriented.[1] But to begin a line of evolution one has to start with something. In a similar manner, the Intelligent Room Project sponsored in the late 1990s by the Defense Advanced Research Projects Agency (DARPA) at MIT is probably the first of a generation of command and control systems which will shape the advanced enterprise architectures for the next 20 years.

As companies divide their operations into independent business units and restructure themselves into federations of semiautonomous businesses, they do so around an increasingly intelligent enterprise architecture and the services it provides. Chapter 1 explained that, because the business environment is so competitive, modern management needs knowledge-enriched, real-time command and control enabling telecommuting executives, factories, branch offices, suppliers, and customers to be tied together.

This is presently the major contribution of the Internet, intranets, and extranets discussed in Section III. Today's solutions, however, will not be competitive tomorrow. The MIT project reviewed in this chapter and in Chapter 8 is one of the first to bring the concept of an intelligent enterprise architecture to a logical implementation conclusion. The way to bet is that its knowledge artifacts, or agents,[2] will ensure that entire layers of middle management disappear, and the way one looks at functions of management will be thoroughly revamped.

One should look at the case study in this chapter from both a short term and a long term perspective because this approach helps to better appreciate the results sought from the research and development activities referenced. In 1999 the original Intelligent Room Project was restructured as the Oxygen Project, targeting a 300% improvement in personal productivity. Its core system is composed of three parts: intelligent room (E21) handheld devices (H21), and embedded devices and wireless communications (N21).

The Oxygen Project is sponsored by industry and the U.S. government. Industry sponsors include Hewlett-Packard, Nokia, and NTT. Some 200 people currently work on it, and its budget stands between $50 to $60 million. A working prototype is expected prior to 2005, but intermediate results tell a lot about Oxygen's direction.

BACKGROUND AND FOREGROUND NEEDED TO PROMOTE IMAGINATIVE NEW DEPARTURES

Other authors[3] have treated notions such as invisible or ubiquitous computing, as well as how to go about making computers "as easy to use as breathing," or what human-centered machines can do "for us." The deliberate choice here is to concentrate on the goals of the Oxygen Project and its expected deliverables. Then this text will bring attention to the status of early work in the MIT's Intelligent Room. This is done to understand an advanced subject better by returning to its origins.

The target stated by Oxygen Project is to produce portable, light, low-cost solutions which can be quickly adapted to applications and eventually marketed off the shelf. Projected deliverables aim to help people work together across space and time within the framework established by an enterprise architecture. One of the goals is to interact with computers through speech, vision, and perception. Other objectives include recon-figurability, the use of a low-level communications protocol, and trans-ducers which will be intelligent enough to be human-aware. Along this frame of reference, the Oxygen Project has set the following aims:

- Location of resources by Internet, a totally new goal in computing
- Nomadic (location-independent) software that can be updated on the fly
- Ambient interfaces permitting objects to preserve their physical existence
- Person-centric security, rather than device-centric (which is a novel concept)
- Cross-network integration: local, building-wide, terrestrial, and satellite

Researchers working at Project Oxygen see as one of their contributions that of increasing productivity by a factor of 3, by making machines much easier to use. To do so, they capitalize on interfaces and also on the fact that, in the coming years, bandwidth and processing power will be within easy reach and at low cost, thus making practical new ways of computation and communication.

Future perspectives of an enterprise architecture and its design char-acteristics will depend on a horde of devices: handheld, embedded, and others, practically all of them intelligent. Experts think that change riding on knowledge-enriched system solutions will be much greater and more profound than the one experienced from mainframes to minis, maxis, workstations, and PCs.

Solutions sought by the project will aim to integrate the notion of context. They will (most likely) be able to locate things by intent, while the intelligent software will be endowed with functionality which could assure reconfigurability.

This and other advanced systems projects suggest that location-inde-pendence (nomadic computing) will probably be only one of the axes of reference of the advanced solutions which might characterize 2010 and beyond. A more complete frame of reference is the one that Figure 7.1

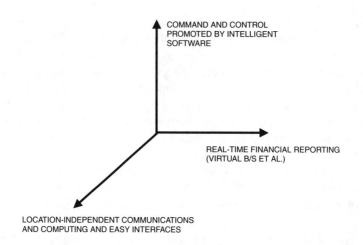

Figure 7.1   Frame of reference of the new enterprise architecture that may result from projects such as the Oxygen Project.

shows, which integrates command and control, communications disciplines, and vital real-time applications such as the virtual balance sheets entering the blood stream of tier-1 business organizations.

In this enterprise architecture in the making, knowledge-enriched devices will be in both the foreground and the background, while one of the criteria for system choices will be the ability to support a low-power solution. Integration within the intelligent room and the broader intelligent environment will be at a premium, involving personal area network, building wide networks, local and metropolitan networks, and wide area networks.

Links will be both terrestrial (largely optical) and satellite-based (see Chapter 6 on 3G). The whole concept of speech and vision — the two main modes of interaction — might be revamped. Today's speech-understanding systems are domain-specific. Project Oxygen targets an interdomain solution. As an example, one of the project's aims is to use vision to augment speech understanding. This might be realized by recognizing facial expression and lip movements. To become a practical proposition, such an approach requires development of portable, light, low-cost speech and vision systems which can be quickly adapted to applications. This is another of the Oxygen Project's goals.

Knowledge-enriched artifacts will be used to deduce relationships between accesses to find appropriate information. The solution sought aims to develop means for semantically driven knowledge access. Some people think that new modes of communication might eventually evolve that will affect both on-line interaction and off-line integration.

Attention is also paid to costs, and rightly so. One of the basic aims is to develop commercially available off-the-shelf systems and components at an affordable price. High-cost solutions might be museum pieces but they would become white elephants in a marketing sense. Cost matters.

Not all of these goals are, of course, novel or will necessarily be attained. To better appreciate the effort behind Project Oxygen, one has to look at the expected deliverables of the system as a whole rather than of each one of its components. In all fairness to other advanced technological projects, it is proper to say that scientists at the Palo Alto Research Center (PARC) of Xerox have also been working on some of the above stated goals, as are researchers at Bell Labs, Microsoft, IBM, Sun Microsystems, Carnegie Mellon University, and other centers of excellence.

Some of these projects address what they call ambient computing; others target pervasive computing and still others ubiquitous or invisible computing. All these terms are just different expressions for the same or similar background concepts. The central theme is that of new, more flexible and more effective ways of communicating among humans, their machines, and the man-made intelligent environment. User friendliness has many aspects. For instance, no person in an intelligent room will need to carry any gear, and it will not be necessary to use a keyboard or mouse.

Sensors are the intelligent room's business. To get the intelligent room's attention, the user says the word *Computer*, and the room immediately responds with an audible, quiet signal (see the next section on the status of the Intelligent Room project).

Another important aspect of these advanced projects is system adjustments. Science and technology rarely go by big leaps, though there are exceptions like the pioneering work of Newton, Einstein, and other giants of science. The usual way is by means of small but consistent steps. In line with this notion is MIT's contribution, starting with the original concept of the intelligent room.

MAJOR COMPONENTS OF THE OXYGEN PROJECT

Nicknamed the Intelligent Room Project, the advanced technology project which started in the late 1990s at MIT addresses one of the key components of the command and control posts of the future. Originally funded by the Pentagon's Defense Advanced Research Projects Agency (DARPA), this is precompetitive research and therefore not classified.

The artificial intelligence (AI) laboratory of the department of electrical engineering and computer science at MIT is directly responsible for research and development connected to the Intelligent Room. This project has benefited many other labs as well as gained from several contributions fundamental to MIT's current research culture, for instance, work done at the media lab, rapid autonomous machining laboratory (RAML), Arbeloff laboratory for information systems and technology, and the lab for information and decision systems (LIDS).

The best way to appreciate the experimental development underway is to look at it not as stand-alone but as part of a network of advanced research efforts within the context of Project Oxygen, whose goals were explained previously. At current state of the art, it is wise to look at the Intelligent Room Project (and at Project Oxygen) as advanced research efforts, not off-the-shelf deliverables. Any inference on the exact nature of the deliverables when they come is premature.

To better explain the overall framework, consider a brief description of the background of some of MIT's other applied research and development efforts. These are instrumental in bringing forward the most recent breakthroughs which promote Project Oxygen. The media lab, for example, was started by former MIT president Jerome Weisner, who wanted to do away with boundaries between basic and applied research, and create an institution where academia and industry interacted freely.

The result of this policy has been that most of the media lab's funding comes from a population of 170 corporate sponsors. The majority of associated industrial firms from the U.S., Europe, and Asia elect to be consortium sponsors. Each pays around $200,000 per year. This is roughly the overall annual cost of hiring one researcher. Currently, these sponsors are organized into three broad consortia: news in the future, digital life, and things that think.

The media lab spends a lot of time putting on practical demonstrations for its sponsors. This is a wise strategy because it helps bring attention from sponsors and sponsors-to-be to work in progress; real-life demonstrations are convincing because they are down-to-earth. Such policy contrasts with the more classical procedure followed by scientific labs that fund their research by writing grant proposals and issuing difficult-to-document interim reports.

Demos are a good policy. Another secret of the success of MIT laboratories is that they reinvent themselves often enough to be ahead of the curve. An example is offered by the rapid autonomous machining laboratory, which not long ago developed a procedure that enables a human user to touch virtual environments with full three-dimensional realism. This advance brings the promise of virtual reality (real-time simulation and visualization)[4] one step closer to representing the intricate aspects of physical world fully.

This R&D effort at RAML concerns a civilian project. In a collaboration with engineers at Suzuki Motor, MIT's researchers are designing the system to promote advanced CAD/CAM applications (see Chapter 11). Combined with a haptic (touch-sensitive) device, the software creates a virtual world of touch with an added dimension that has not been feasible so far. The haptic interface influences a user's action through the sense of touch and monitors provide an interactive visual display to stimulate the sense of sight.

One of the project's contributions is a method that allows haptic systems to work with arbitrary three-dimensional probes, not just a point. In the past, software has approximated the probe of a haptic interface, making available points for a computer to handle, but ignoring full geometry of the tool. Because of this, much of the realism was lost. By contrast, the methodology developed by the MIT team enables full three-dimensional modeling in haptic environments. This is a tangible example of what could filter into the Oxygen Project.

Also in the past, a computer's virtual world was restricted to control of a single point with which users could poke at the objects in the virtual environment. When this facility came about, it was quite a feat because, even point by point, the user was able to touch and feel various surfaces. The new development extends the capabilities of haptic interfaces by simulating the interaction between fully 3-D bodies within the virtual environment. As a result, the user's presence is no longer restricted to single-point control.

Another MIT project relevant to the goal of creating and sustaining an intelligent environment is one targeting a single identification number that would allow global roaming on networks, with the Internet a primary target. The sought-out solution is complex for technical and political reasons; for instance, different countries allocate different frequency spectra for wireless communications, and some countries like to keep control of the content of information flows in airwaves.

There are other challenges as well. To appreciate the effort to deliver a single identification number that customers can use anywhere in the world, including in high bandwidth communications, it is necessary to take a quick look at the evolution of wireless systems, retracing the work done at MIT's Arbeloff lab for information systems and technology. Introduced in the 1980s, the first generation (1G) wireless systems were analog. But in the 1990s, with the second generation (2G), digital approaches became available (see Chapter 6 for discussion on the 3G mobile (UMTS). Second generation systems have been designed (and used) primarily for voice, and they can only support baseband, i.e., low-speed data transmission, around 10 kilobits per second (KBPS).

Because network designers appreciate that big volume wireless transmission in the future will be based on data, the majority of projects today focuses on data requirements. This is important inasmuch as data has a different behavior than voice. It is bursty and sometimes difficult to characterize by voice-oriented tools and methods which dominated our thinking for over a century.

Designers must also overcome current systems' limited functionality, which allows users to send short messages and faxes connecting to the Internet at low speeds through the public switched telephone network. Broadband would change this condition, but it flourishes only if it can deliver at low cost. Cost matters in the success of any wireless solution, indeed, of any product or system.

In this and similar projects, MIT researchers also look at quality of service guarantees, as well as downward compatibility that would allow 2G and 3G systems to work together. They also examine how fourth generation (4G) wireless solutions should be characterized by a single identification number for any customer, anywhere in the world. The target of this 4G research is to allow trillions of objects to be tracked instantaneously, which would become a first in global system solutions. For this purpose, researchers are currently working on HTML/XML types of software and developing an object linking service similar to the Internet's domain name service.

These and similar projects currently under way will converge with the MIT AI lab's Intelligent Room into a landscape of any-to-any multimedia, broadband intelligent environment. This is, after all, the further-out goal of Project Oxygen. The likely path of such convergence is shown in Figure 7.2.

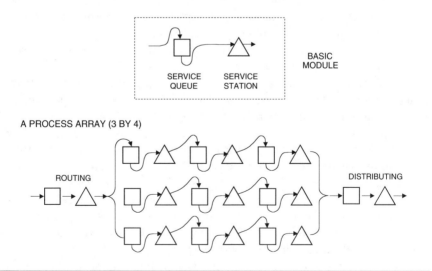

Figure 7.2 Know-how from today's distinct projects will merge in cross-disciplinary applications.

As a whole, an intelligent environment should allow computers to participate in activities that have never before involved computation, as well as permit people and machines (therefore, other animate and inanimate components) to interact with computational systems. Ideally people should work with man-made systems the way they would with other people. Whether such a feat is achievable in the next decade or so remains to be seen.

Within this broader view should be examined the artificial intelligence lab's project. The Intelligent Room Project (explained in the fourth and fifth sections) is essentially a research platform for exploring the design of larger, more polyvalent intelligent environments. Although this project started with DARPA financing and targeted a new command and control solution for the military, the basic concepts underpinning it are just as applicable in industry and banking.

GOALS OF AN INTELLIGENT ENVIRONMENT

When asked if he saw any use for MIT's Intelligent Room Project in bank regulation and commercial banking, a Central European banker responded, "The answer depends on the areas the background computer covers, and on its software. Can the system check if a decision is compatible with the rules? Can it give guidance and advice?" These queries were posed to one of the designers of the intelligent room. Prior to pondering the answer, however, consider what this project is and is not.

One of the first goals of the Intelligent Room Project is to make fully transparent the user interface which, since the 1950s, has been the most cumbersome and least user-friendly part of a computer-based system. Contrary to virtual reality, which embeds the real world into the computer, the knowledge-enriched environment targeted by the MIT/ARPA project is embedding the computer into the virtual world.

This is a tall order, far beyond what is available today off the shelf, for instance:

- Voice recognition and signature
- Handies by Nokia, Philips and others, to which the user can talk
- PC software by IBM to which one can dictate (provided terms used are in the thesaurus)
- Speaker recognition devices (not to be confused with voice recognition), which still make mistakes

It takes much more than voice and speaker recognition at the smart machine's side to understand what is said, and difficulty increases exponentially with group talk. At MIT's project, connectivity is provided by reaching in an interactive manner all participants throughout the environment covered by the project. This is done in a way which improves flexibility. It is quite interesting that, in this and in other areas, much of the innovation comes from students working on the project.

Sensors are the intelligent room's business, as stated previously. The aim of room-level sensors is to capture what goes on inside the environment during a session. This may be for command and control reasons, but it might also address a design session, board meeting, or any other event involving action by many participants. Correctly, the researchers saw to it that both events and nonevents were recorded. Such duality permits inference on some critical issues. For instance, why people make certain decisions or choose certain types of things, and why people do not decide, choose, or make something when they are expected to.

Support is provided by the intelligent room's 60 agents, known collectively as the scatterbrain. These knowledge robots are running under different operating systems which have been networked together. The agents have been trained, and continue training, on how to capture and record events and also on how to sense if something happens that should not.

Each of the scatterbrain's knowledge artifacts is responsible for a different intelligent room function. The SpeechIn agent, for example, runs as part of the speech recognition system. Once started, SpeechIn allows other agents to submit context-free grammars corresponding to spoken utterances they are interested in. As the other agents react, SpeechIn updates the speech recognition entity. When a sentence is heard by one of the speech components, SpeechIn notifies those agents who indicated they were interested in it. All knowledge robots handhold with one another. For instance, the Browser agent connects to the Display agent to make sure that, when Web pages are loaded, the browser's functionality is displayed in and used by the intelligent room system.

To explain how this ensemble works, Michael H. Coen, one of the researchers involved in this project and a Ph.D. candidate, designed the video notification scheme presented in Figure 7.3. Notice the nodes involved in this setting, the positioning of the devices, and the Internet link. The user says, "Computer, load the intelligent room home page."

After the Browser agent receives the request from the SpeechIn agent, it loads the Universal Resource Locator (URL) in the browser routine. When the Browser agent loads a new page, it notifies the Web Surfer agent which consults with the Start agent on any new information about the content of the Web page just handled. Note how the knowledge artifacts have been engineered to work in synergy.

In a significant renewal of old input–output routines, the agents talk to their master through human voices and they receive voice commands. If one of them detects something wrong, it will immediately warn its

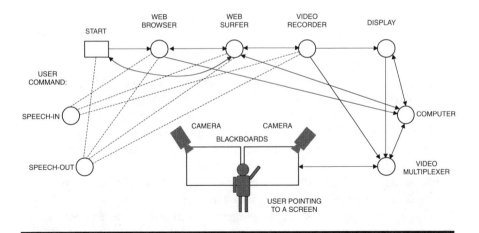

Figure 7.3 The human user says, "Computer, load the intelligent room home page."

master. Through the interactive knowledge artifacts that constitute its scatterbrain, the intelligent environment learns who its users are, and is instrumental in customizing itself to their requirements.

An important systems design characteristic is that this interactive knowledge-enriched environment operates without a central controller. This improves reliability because it makes MIT's intelligent room design more robust. A small startup procedure runs all of the scatterbrain agents, which then autonomously move to the machines on which they are expected to run. Scatterbrain knowledge artifacts work together in parallel with different inputs. Data are processed simultaneously in different places, augmenting the system's flexibility and reach.

A metalayer replaces the classical concept of centralized control. Layered on top of the scatterbrain are higher-level agents that rely on the underlying agents for execution of functions. The overall system is enriched with specific application knowledge artifacts that use facilities supported by the general-purpose agents in the intelligent room.

Not all data collected by the system are stored. Depending on a host of criteria, most of the output of the person-tracking subsystem may be thrown away after it serves its purpose. Few applications need real-time trajectory information for the room's occupants. What is particularly important is to know where someone is at a given moment and when he or she stops moving. Positional information while the person is in motion is less important.

Correctly, researchers reasoned that more rewarding than building a dynamic person tracker is creating a visually-based static person locator that looks for people at rest in places where they are expected to be found. This is a good example of choices which had to be made — choices which usually have to be made in connection with an innovative project.

It is important to emphasize once more this point of choices in engineering design and all other human activities. One of the key questions every manager, as well as every designer, should ask is, "What are my alternatives?" The search for alternatives is needed to stimulate the imagination. In all matters involving uncertainty, therefore in all pioneering efforts, imagination is needed to proceed with creative solutions which lead to new situations. Imagination and the search for all possible alternatives correlate. They also require insight and foresight to promote the perception of events and their understanding.

Though the basics of the Intelligent Room Project are presented in simple terms, this system is fairly sophisticated. Its complexity comes from the novelty it introduces, particularly in the interaction of its agents, though none of the individual knowledge robots is, all by itself, a totally novel concept. This knowledge-enriched solution has been built with the capability to respond to actual events as well as to answer expectations that underlie the operations of a command and control center in real-life situations.

NUTS AND BOLTS OF THE INTELLIGENT ROOM

For performing the functions expected from an intelligent room, the designers incorporated speech recognition and machine vision. Through its sensors, the system which they build can receive and interpret raw data to determine, for instance, the location of a user. This is done through cameras and other devices embedded in the room's ceiling and walls.

The intelligent room's laser pointing system uses a neural network for calculating the projective transformation from wall to image space. Rather than having someone training the neural network through a manual method, the researchers have used the projectors' display of images to simulate a person performing the training. The chosen solution ensures that the neural network can train itself in less than five minutes. The subsystems incorporated into this setting have been designed in a way to complement and reinforce one another. If the multiperson tracker temporarily loses contact with people, then the finger-pointing subsystem provides information useful for tracking.

One of the primary tasks assigned to knowledge artifacts in the intelligent room is to link the speech recognition and video tracking subsystems with database mining. The motivation which led to this solution is that of bringing computation into the real, physical world to support what is traditionally considered a noncomputational procedure or activity.

Special care has been taken to assure that every component of the intelligent environment is embedded into the system and accessed by its users in a seamless way. Concerns regarding availability and reliability have also played a significant role. The chosen solution is multimodal. Aided by agents, users interact with the intelligent environment by means of human-like approaches such as gesture, speech, and context. Traditional media like windows, menus, and the mouse have no place in this solution.

The gesture–speech–context interaction rests on the concept that in the coming years intelligent rooms will have cameras for eyes and microphones for ears, use an ever expanding range of fairly sophisticated sensing technology, and be served by a "golden horde" of agents. Knowledge-enriched sensors help to connect to the real world.

Of course, design choices made by the MIT researchers have their prerequisites. Intelligent environments call for a highly integrated and knowledge-enriched computational infrastructure. They also need multiple connections with the real world in order to participate in it. This constraint does not imply that computational facilities need be everywhere in the environment, nor that people must directly interact with every computational or other device available.

This is tantamount to saying that the project does not use a "computer everywhere" concept where, for instance, chairs have pressure sensors that can register people sitting on them; nor does it have everybody wear infrared emitting badges. Rather, it targets an unencumbered interaction with noncomputational objects without requiring people to attach high-tech gadgetry. This is a example of a good choice made in system design.

Because costs matter, the intelligent room design is based on affordable devices readily available in the market, off the shelf. This, too, is a good example of an optimal choice. Through these gadgets, the system can track up to four people moving in the conference room. The person-tracking subsystem uses two wall-mounted cameras to do this job (see also Figure 7.3).

This tracking subsystem gives the intelligent room the ability to know how many people are inside it and where they are, as well as when people enter or exit. The chosen solution is able to determine what objects people are next to. The system can show data on video display when someone is near a focal point. A person's location in the room provides information about what he or she is doing. Tracking information helps to interpret the output of other room modalities, such as finger pointing. Working interactively, the tracker can supply information to other room vision systems.

Tracking works through background segmentation and performs 3-D reconstruction through a neural network. The output image from each camera is analyzed by a program that labels and identifies a bounding box around each occupant in the room. This information is then sent through a coordination program that synchronizes findings from individual cameras, combining their output.

The intelligent room supports spoken language interactions which are unimodal: they do not tie the user to a video display to verify or correct utterances recognized by the system, nor do they require a keyboard for selecting among possible alternative utterances. The researchers avoided the use of mouse clicking as keyboard replacement. Their aim has been to permit the room's system to engage in dialogues with users to gather information, correct misunderstandings, and enhance recognition accuracy.

To get the intelligent room's attention a user stops speaking for a moment and then says in a loud voice the word computer. The system immediately responds with an audible, quiet signal to indicate it is paying attention. Following this, the user has a 2-second time window in which to begin an utterance directed to the room, generally in the form of a command or a question.

All this is part of the nuts and bolts of the intelligent room design; however, this presentation also helps to identify choices made among alternatives. What are by now old paradigms like the virtual reality hand-glove and the mouse have been dropped in favor of a solution which bets on intelligence embedded in knowledge robots. This choice is wise, because only if there are alternatives to the beaten path can one hope to gain insight into what is truly at stake, and then make choices. Finding the appropriate mixture of concepts and devices entering a design is not a mathematical exercise. It is risk-taking judgment.

To be appreciated from this presentation are the choices made in and the flexibility embedded into the intelligent room system. Also, new departures have been tested, and they work. Prior to discussing the intelligent room's applications, however, it is advisable to take a closer look at the evolution of notions regarding man–machine interaction. For reasons of clarity, this is done in the next section in a somewhat structured sense.

OPTIONS AVAILABLE IN MAN–MACHINE INTERACTION*

The text in this section does not come from the Intelligent Room Project. It has been incorporated into this chapter to present a generic appreciation of what lies beneath the nuts and bolts discussed in the two preceding sections, as well as to explain how difficult is the often heralded (but never realized) ubiquitous or invisible computing solution. Start with the

---

* This section is not part of the Intelligent Room Project; the coverage of the MIT project continues in Chapter 8.

hypothesis that the computer speaks in natural English and so do the six subjects in the room. One of the subjects utters the words, "Start session."

As the session begins, no messages have yet been sent from any one entity to any another. Assuming that one of the subjects wishes to communicate with one or more of his or her colleagues in the control and command environment, this subject says, "Message."

The computer asks, "To whom?"

The subject responds specifying to whom his or her message is addressed, and then says, "Action X." This "X" can specify oral response, interactive visual display (softcopy), hardcopy, information transmitted to databases, or any other activity. It induces the computer to ask for topics.

Suppose the subject is concerned over rumors about an interruption of air transport in Hawaii. If the action choice was display, the computer successively exhibits appropriate frames relaying all available information, including maps. A similar procedure may be followed with oral response.

In Figure 7.4, the sequence of man–machine interaction events which follow one another is in Roman numerals. Superficially, it might be said that one must be crazy to suggest such a structured approach when the most recent trend is toward an unstructured environment. Practically, however, at current state of the art, though it may be invisible to the user, a structured approach must be there for fallback, in case the unstructured solution takes a path beyond the computer's knowledge or reaches a dead end, hence requiring new input.

The way to bet is that, in an unstructured environment (see Chapter 1), there will be a case for which the machine is not trained, or the end user will not yet be accustomed to dealing with the aftermath of infinite choices, albeit a more flexible solution than the one presented.

Returning to the communications procedure, if the message is in softcopy (monitor), the top line of the received display may indicate message ID and timestamp, assignment by computer during the run, and plain or coded name of sender and receiver of the message.

Should the subject sending a message make a mistake or change his or her mind midstream, the procedure must permit stopping for a moment to say message and start anew. A knowledge-enriched structure like that of the intelligent environment will respond with an audible signal.

The spoken language in this man–machine communication is plain English, but, as mapped in Figure 7.4, the metalanguage is a multiple tree with "message," as the root of the tree. If a message is addressed subject-to-subject, composition begins with this root. The selection of any one branch of the first tree leads to another tree representing a subset of requests available to the subject. This process of selection is repeated, until a well-formed message has been completed. All possible routes through the entire collection of displays generate a family of trees. The leaves, or *filials*, are local termination points, therefore, the displays.

Note that by increasing the number of filials the designer can give the user the feeling he or she is dealing with an infinite number of choices. This approach has been successfully used in many cases, including one by Toyota which lets the client "design" his or her car (provided the components the client chooses are in the engineering database).

The actual tree is hidden from the user's view; it is defined to the system in a condensed form supporting alternative courses. Suppose, for example, that a subject in an intelligent environment were to ask for a factual and documented report on the interruption of air transport in Hawaii, rather than merely for status information. Then the entire development of the tree issuing from the "send data" branch would be grafted onto the "report on" branch.

Whether branching or simply browsing, the tree is actually specified to the computer in the form of a flexible network that helps in defining an ultimate sequence which, along the line of our example, will be ad hoc. In the typical case, the net used for the command center simulation has nodes or junctures. The nodes are the rays emanating from circled interventions in Figure 7.4.

The tree structure must be flexible, i.e., perishable hierarchies characteristic of an object-oriented approach. Suppose that this inheritance mechanism serves well the communications needs of half the subjects in an intelligent environment because they are starting to operate in this environment and a step-by-step guidance, like that provided by a tree

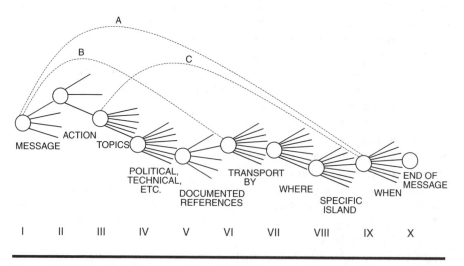

Figure 7.4 Nine selection trees by topic leading to an interactive man–machine communication.

structure, helps in learning how to work with the system. As experience with both interactive videotex and database management systems demonstrates, however, to experienced people this procedure is boring.

In Figure 7.4, the need for seamlessly and directly accessing other subjects is met by a bypass mechanism. A traffic agent is informed, by the end user's own agents, of the skill of the communicators (sender and receiver) providing the possibility to propagate a coded message from node I to node IX – leaving open only the specification of WHEN (arc A). Alternatively, if there is need to specify type of transport, the bypass arc B goes to node VI, or, as arc C indicates, the bypass may concern other intermediate nodes.

A metalayer takes care of the commands necessary to make this approach work. The entire metalanguage is known by the computer. The subjects in the room can independently and simultaneously compose messages or receive them; they can operate very rapidly through direct verbal discourse. Because specific vocabularies can be seen as parameters to basic artificial intelligence programs:

■ Actual language trees, like their biological counterparts, can evolve or devolve.
■ New branches and filials can be grown or, alternatively, eliminated.
■ Obsolescent branches can be chopped off without altering the basic setting.

A number of research projects, as well as practical applications on existing systems, rest on this basis. It is possible to evolve metalanguages that are "natural," or effective for a particular command situation or different levels of command. This can be done by allowing the computer to record what experienced subjects say under specific circumstances. By recording who says what to whom under which circumstances, one can automatically expunge sentences which are rarely used or that, when used, are of minor importance. If a new supply of alternative forms is furnished as these excluded sentences are purged, appropriate metalanguages can be grown in the laboratory as well as in the field.

The described model can also be used to explore intelligent information handling. For example, one might run an experiment contrasting the effectiveness of free language with structured language for command and control reasons. A new structured language can be developed from the one now in operation or it can be an experimental set.

In order to improve overall efficiency, several hundred agents may be included in the system in reference. Live subjects and agents can collaborate in designing nodes and links. A practical application of the described solution has addressed itself primarily not to intrinsic contents of individual messages, but rather to their bulk handling. Its mission has been to process the quantity of messages as they arrive, and to deliver them with full regard to content precision, and minimum delay perceived by the consuming entities.

This is an improvement over traditional message handling services, where this task is not always easily accomplished. Adequate manpower may be available, messages (or parts of them) may arrive in unexpected sequences (e.g., packet switching), serviced entities may impose conflicting demands, or matters of confidentiality may require significant differences in handling procedures.

In conclusion, the organization of the command and control system under review follows the familiar pattern of a conceptual communications model — but with a difference. First, it is an intelligence-enriched structure. Second, it is a pyramid at whose base is a complex technological system in full evolution, while the trees to which reference is made are ephemeral hierarchies based on inheritance. This presents opportunities and constraints.

The leaders and members of projects like those described in the present and following chapters should appreciate that the aftermath of simultaneous changes in both command and control and infrastructural layers is, to paraphrase a BankAmerica saying, like changing the tires in a car running at 100 mph. The challenge is formidable even if policy and supercontrol functions are manned by live managers while all routine activity is delegated to agents.

INTEGRATING THE NOTION OF CONTEXT BY NOKIA

The scenario underpinning the example in the previous section is hardly new; what is novel is that the notion of intelligent agents, ephemeral hierarchies, and metalanguages has found its way into many recent solutions to what is considered pervasive computing. This is also a reminder that no engineering project and no system solution is, or can be, totally "new." Components are always used based on past experience.

The "natural language" label has been around since the 1960s and those who reinvent the wheel in its name favor neither their own carriers nor science and technology. But there are new concepts in many R&D projects. Project Oxygen has several and so does a sister research effort at MIT's department of electrical engineering and computer science on smart materials.[5]

Work done on the notion of context, discussed in this section, can be seen as a bridge between the goals sought by the Oxygen Project and those targeted by MIT's auto-ID center. Will smart materials make it easier for people to compute and communicate? The jury is still out on this issue, but context is one of the elements in a positive answer. Research by Nokia and other leading vendors identifies context as a new frontier in technology, combining information, knowledge, and identification in one envelope.

To better appreciate the three-dimensional frame of reference shown in Figure 7.5, keep in mind that, in a world of smart materials, every device will be able to communicate its identify to everything else, or nearly so. Hence, there is a need to communicate by trillions of objects. But this is only a lower layer solution. Higher up, a major distinction will eventually be made between explicitly guided devices, and adaptive devices which manage their business by themselves.

Both populations can be of a disaggregated type; however, the class of adaptive devices described above will be much more sophisticated. Stand-alone adaptive devices do not necessarily have to be very intelligent. An example of an adaptive device as a stand-alone unit is the thermostat; after one setting, it takes care of managing the temperature because it has a sensor.

Devices which act dynamically require much more. In an increasingly smart world of inanimate objects, the minimum requirement for a device goes beyond having a sensor and therefore being able to tell what goes on in the environment. Smarter devices are contact-sensitive and have a sense of context. Their actions as well as the depth of their response depend on their ability to understand their environment in a contextual sense.

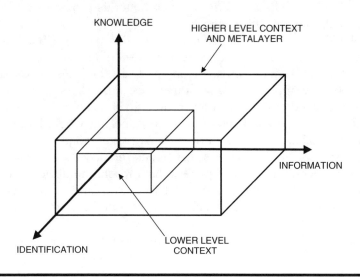

Figure 7.5   A new solution space for man–information communication might be found in this framework.

Context is a complex notion. Its criteria are time, location, status of the intelligent device, presence of other devices; user's explicit and implicit profile, user's history of employing the device, user's emotional state, and other user data. To confront the challenge of context, the device must have a learning mechanism. Developing the user's implicit and explicit profile is a matter of patterning, calling for a significant amount of datamining. Beyond this, the capable handling of context requires a pattern of patterns (metapattern), which characterizes intelligent entities.

Here is an early example: the federal intrusion detection network (Fidnet) is a U.S. Government initiative designed to detect the pattern of patterns of illicit activity across the Internet. The system is based primarily on government computers, but it could also collect user-activity data from privately owned computers and networks in its drive to develop the metapattern of illegal activities.

A metapattern would co-involve algorithms, heuristics, and knowledge engineering artifacts.[6] Transaction histories, site histories, user histories, and all sorts of data series are required; this calls for the existence of large, reliable databases as well as for rigorous datamining. Smart world profiling and patterning will eventually address two populations: human users, who work based on experience, and inanimate but smart devices and systems endowed with the ability of autoidentification.[7]

The concept behind the metapatterning process is that, instead of the user giving instructions, his or her profile and work habits are analyzed. Of particular interest is what he or she has done in similar situations, and whether this can help as reference, even better as prognosticator, for the intelligent device and the system.

Analogical reasoning has been used for this purpose, but it and the case method have some weaknesses, which should be kept in mind when talking of a combination of datamining and case histories. A weakness of the case history approach is that sometimes these cases are rather theoretical, assembled and evaluated through small samples, and influenced by outliers. A more solid reference is to mine the whole bandwidth of corporate or other databases through knowledge artifacts.

For instance, Nokia suggests that agents embedded in an intelligent device can track their master's pattern. As a result, the device in question does not need to be explicitly instructed. Key to this approach is unearthing association rules, episodes, specific patterns, trends, and exceptions and then analyzing them in order to distill a metapattern.

Dynamic patterning is, in principle, the main target and this evidently impacts the role of a system's component parts, including interfaces. The rule used to be that because of consistency one should never change the user interface. Now any user interface can be improved by putting the most frequent choices at the top of the list. Nokia sees this as part and parcel of personalizing the interface. At the same time, patterning and intelligent materials at large pose authentication and privacy problems (see Chapter 16). There is always an exchange between privacy and the patterning of users' actions by smart devices. There are also security issues, some of which are associated with authentication. As Dr. Heinrich Steinmann suggests, the DNA sequence may be the ultimate authentication method.

Apart from encoding for greater security, other lessons exist which can be learned from DNA, for instance, its use as storage of knowledge. DNA's primary function seems to be to store knowledge painstakingly collected through the university of life. This process teaches that species that do not learn do not graduate to the next level of life's sophistication, and chances are that they become extinct.

Finally, everything this chapter has described has an associated testing phase. The earlier a method, devices, or our evolving system is tested, the cheaper the cost of redressing a situation whose weak points have been identified. Because of this, top-tier companies and research laboratories conduct decisive system tests early, while at the same time avoiding a rush to integration before the design process takes shape. Premature system integration usually slows down the parts and subsystems design, and handicaps troubleshooting instead of facilitating it.

Particularly with devices and systems involving sophisticated new software, debugging complexity rises due to interactions between subsystems. This leads to an efficiency penalty. Generally, it is easier to exercise devices near their margins when testing at subsystem level, because one can have direct control over their inputs and outputs. That is what a sound approach often aims to do, particularly one focused within a given context like the intelligent environment.

REFERENCES

1. Chorafas, D.N. and Steinmann, H., *Object-Oriented Databases*, Prentice-Hall, Englewood Cliffs, NJ, 1993.
2. Chorafas, D.N., *Agent Technology Handbook*, McGraw-Hill, New York, 1998.
3. Dertouzos, M.L., *The Unfinished Revolution*, HarperCollins, New York, 2001.
4. Chorafas, D.N. and Steinmann, H., *Virtual Reality – Practical Applications in Business and Industry*, Prentice-Hall, Englewood Cliffs, NJ, 1995.
5. Chorafas, D.N., *Managing Operational Risk. Risk Reduction Strategies for Banks Post-Basle*, Lafferty, London and Dublin, 2000.
6. Chorafas, D.N. and Steinmann, H., *Expert Systems in Banking*, Macmillan, London, 1991.
7. Chorafas, D.N., *Integrating ERP, Supply Chain Management and Smart Material*, Auerbach/CRC Press, New York, 2001.

8

THE USE OF INTELLIGENT ENVIRONMENTS BY THE ENTERPRISE ARCHITECTURE

INTRODUCTION

The topology of an enterprise architecture can be conceived as consisting of horizontal and vertical services. Traditionally, communication networks have focused on the concept of only horizontally layered services, for instance the ISO/OSI model (see Chapter 1), or vertical layering only, primarily due to end-to-end connectivity needs. But, from quality of service (QoS) and level of service perspectives, it is important to understand service interactions and relationships in two dimensions: horizontal and vertical.

Command and control of the enterprise as a whole, as well as monitoring of service interactions, are usually represented as vertical functionality. Related directory and network management support will perform logical-to-physical address mapping, change in configuration, source and destination system profiles, etc. within the functionality supported by the chosen architectural solution.

It is generally expected that knowledge-enriched approaches and smart materials will bring with them a quantum leap in end-to-end identification and authentication, providing added security for application-to-application interactions and transactions. In an intelligent environment, network services that cut across layers of the enterprise architecture help to improve integration by providing seamless end-to-end support to applications. The architectural concept is the glue that binds the system together. This way it may be viewed by each application as a single service provider.

Applications have a corresponding horizontal service function within each service layer. To a large measure, their user-friendliness is defined by their interfaces, to which reference was made in Chapter 7. A basic characteristic of perceptually intelligent interfaces is that they are adaptive to the environment and to the individual user. Therefore, a great deal of current research focuses on learning how to understand user behavior, and defining how such behavior varies in a given situation.

For instance, an automobile's smart subsystems may learn its user's driving behavior, permitting the vehicle to anticipate the driver's actions and reactions and also detecting unusual events to bring to the driver's attention. Another example is audiovisual systems able to learn word meanings from natural audio and video input.

The message here is that, while simple in their current form, such efforts are a first step toward a more sophisticated model of descriptive language, including the ability of habit acquisition. A knowledge-enriched system can automatically acquire some vocabulary, which is then used to understand and generate spoken language (see the fifth section on intelligent interfaces). This is by no means the only challenge faced by an intelligent environment. Another example is that of a global directory service able to provide a consistent management capability for all the distributed resources. Linking function across different levels of directory systems within the information environment supported by the enterprise architecture is also an example (see Chapter 1).

Architecturally, this global directory service must provide integration with and access to external network directory information. The need for this capability is apparent when large corporations wish to interconnect their information network's directory information directly with services supported by the organization. Network intelligence can facilitate global directory service, as Chapter 9 will explain.

Still another challenge faced by an enterprise architecture, as it grows increasingly complex, is how to bill for its services. The following two sections document, through applications examples in banking and other financial institutions, that it is not always clear who the final end user is, or the exact employment of resources which come into design, negotiation, implementation, and maintenance of the system. Yet, these functions may involve higher costs than direct response to end user requests.

APPLYING THE FACILITIES OF AN INTELLIGENT ENVIRONMENT IN BANKING

It is necessary to start with the premise that, according to expert opinion, during the next decade technology will enable routinely sharing some of the fundamental principles upon which most advanced projects are currently based:

- Agent assisted any-to-any networking among communicating entities
- On-line gathering and filtering of inputs at point of origin
- Real-time use of database mining and processing facilities (see Chapter 10)
- Creation of fully interactive animated output

Generated by means of computers and software, virtual environments will make it possible for their users to create entirely new worlds of engineering, business, and other fields of enterprise, and provide ways to augment perception and conception of operating conditions as they evolve.

Increasingly, the first installments of this technology are put to good use in the fields of architecture, engineering, science, education, and finance. New types of applications appear as agent technology and real-time simulation emerge and mature, becoming not only important computer-based tools but also indispensable means to competitiveness and therefore entering the strategic plans of many companies.

What Chapter 7 has discussed in connection to messages between human users and information stored in a machine is largely valid in regard to interactive handling of transactions. In a transaction environment, for instance in banking, agents will reside in network nodes to assure that the flow runs smoothly and that corrective action is taken when necessary for command and control reasons. This can happen, for example, midstream, withholding execution or rolling up the transaction.[1]

As Figure 8.1 suggests, the architectural solution adopted must provide for interoperability and seamless access to underlying resources. Most likely this environment will be served by more than one computer language; some will be oriented to human users, while others will be specifically efficient in regard to the machine components they address (software or hardware). Smart interfaces will also be necessary to safeguard the system's logical boundaries (see the last section in this chapter).

Discussing MIT's concept of an intelligent room and its extension into an intelligent environment with cognizant bankers, the conclusion was reached that robustness and security will be two criteria at the top of their list. An environment becomes so much more attractive to them, and to other business sectors, the more difficult it is to defeat. Therefore, a diagnostic system operating in real-time is an absolutely necessary add-on (currently under development at MIT).

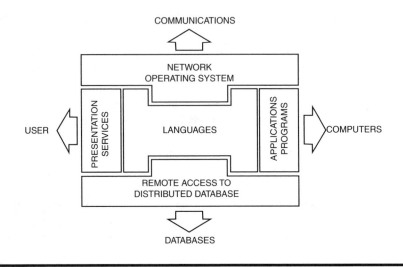

COMMUNICATIONS

NETWORK
OPERATING SYSTEM

USER

PRESENTATION
SERVICES

LANGUAGES

APPLICATIONS
PROGRAMS

COMPUTERS

REMOTE ACCESS TO
DISTRIBUTED DATABASE

DATABASES

Figure 8.1   The architectural solution must provide for interoperability and for seamless access to underlying resources.

Another basic requiement of financial experts is to keep the proprietary day-to-day agents serving the end users under supervision. As Chapter 7 discussed, this calls for metalevel agents to control and audit the activities of proprietary agents and their databases. The best metaphor is what Socrates called his demon, his inner voice that whispers, "Take care."

Mindful of the Orange County debacle that cost Merrill Lynch $400 million in an out-of-court settlement and also cost a rumored $200 million to Credit Suisse First Boston, bankers versatile in advanced technology met to examine use of an intelligent environment close to their hearts. The chosen subject was that of enforcing management control over rogue traders and unreliable salespeople. A snapshot of the sense of that meeting is shown in Figure 8.2.

For starters, the institution's policy levels and command and control entities are theoretically connected any-to-any with the sales force, loan officers, investment advisors, derivatives traders, and other professionals engaging the bank's assets, and its reputation, in transactions. Steady control of inventoried positions is another challenge. In practice, this is a forbidding job if done manually. In the crevices between theory and practice, a significant amount of fraud could exist.[2]

Consider the alternative environment which capitalizes on the advanced technology described in Chapter 7. This solution accounts for the fact that real-time internal control is a job demanding in terms of sophistication and big in information dimensions. It would be a fairly complex mission to bring out whatever strength a computer and communications system may have. Agents are needed to ensure that no deal can be confirmed without

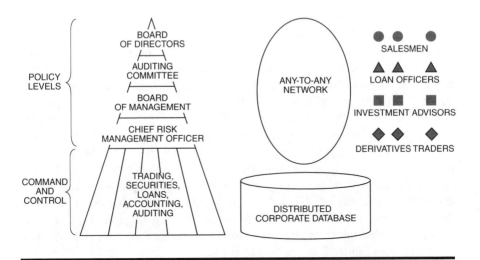

Figure 8.2 Possible use of an intelligent environment to significantly improve the internal control system of a financial organization.

being databased and immediately audited by other agents for legal compliance and limits established by the board. Other agents must track ad hoc communications between front-desk and field operations and the institution's supervisory authorities to keep rogue traders under lock and key without swamping initiative and, therefore, business opportunity.

Since even the best solution will never be static, the orientation and know-how of the bank's technology team should be expected to change as fast as business and technology do, and as the market requires. This was underlined in Chapters 1 and 2 in connection to the choice of the right enterprise architecture. What was not said was that one should plan to develop an enterprise risk management system, which is a tall order.

Not only risk control prerogatives but also cost-effectiveness criteria should characterize the implementation of an intelligent environment of this type. A dynamic technology strategy is required to provide the annual 30 to 40% price and performance improvements that have become the norm in information technology. "Banking technology is all about change," said the chief executive officer of a leading financial institution during a recent meeting.

The goals described in this section, expressed by Figure 8.2 in a nutshell, are doable. Many knowledge engineering projects and associated research areas have achieved sufficient maturity to offer useful, standalone subsystems that can be incorporated into larger, general-purpose interactive projects on an ad hoc basis according to prevailing business requirements. Recall that something similar is done with real-time computer-vision systems, albeit with less breadth of coverage.

The hypothesis that pioneering solutions could evolve in the banking industry out of the deliverables of the Oxygen Project is supported by the work of MIT. To demonstrate the feasibility of the intelligent environment and its potential, MIT has developed a battery of interactions with and applications of the Intelligent Room. Available applications range from an intelligent command post to a smart living room. An extended goal is the on-line integration of the intelligent office and the intelligent home, leading to knowledge-enriched environments or spaces in which computation is seamlessly used to enhance intraday activities. The infrastructure will not be merely user-friendly, but basically invisible to the end user; the interaction with the systems will take place through signs and forms that people are naturally comfortable handling (though not necessarily "invisible" ones). There is always a possibility that the initial implementation of an intelligent environment will not answer all expectations, but even trial and failure can enable learning.

COMMAND AND CONTROL OF LARGER SCALE FINANCIAL OPERATIONS

Experts regard the control of large scale projects and processes, whether in technology or in finance, as stochastic in terms of events associated with real-life operations. Classically, stochasticity concerns probability distributions for times and frequencies of occurrence of expected and unexpected events; an enterprise risk management solution should, however, associate risks and costs with both types of events.

One way to demonstrate the complexity of most business events which necessitate a command and control structure is by rules regarding financial reporting established by regulatory authorities; financial reporting should be homogeneous among supervisors and supervised institutions. Banks usually look at these rules and regulations as unwarranted controls impeding their freedom of action — a misconception on their parts.[3]

A different way of looking at the complexity of business events is through constraints imposed by the market. One of these constraints, looked at most favorably by regulators, is that of market discipline; others, promoted particularly by bank clients, are rapidity and reliability of financial services.

Technology, too, influences the procedures used, and their revamping has organizational aftermath. It used to be that five days were needed to settle a trade (T+5). Now it is T+3, with T+1 the next step, and eventually T+0, which means clearance and settlement done in real-time. Few institutions are able to face this challenge.

Analytics is another important issue faced in an uneven way, in terms of solutions, by financial institutions. In this connection, too, an intelligent environment can provide significant help. As Figure 8.3 suggests, four

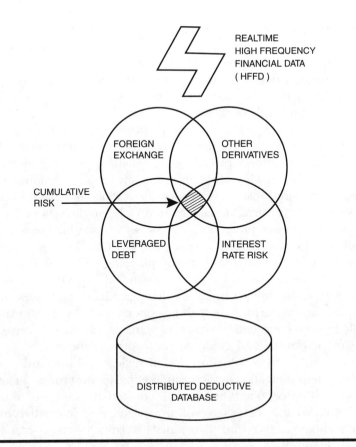

Figure 8.3   Four major areas of banking activity have a common ground of risk and return to be found in databases and tick-by-tick data streams.

major areas of banking activity have a common ground of risk and return, with necessary information elements to be found in databases and tick-by-tick data streams. The enterprise architecture our bank chooses must incorporate the functionality necessary to real-time computation of the details of even exposure and cumulative risk. The functionality provided by the intelligent environment, discussed in Chapter 7, must promote more rigorous analytics than ever before, as well as interpretation and justification functions.

The complexity of the risk control environment, which can be found in 90% of institutions described militates against classical analytical methods and suggests the use of stochastic models, Monte Carlo simulation, chi-square tests, experimental design, expert systems, and agents. In the longer run, even simpler elements grow in terms of complexity and therefore resist attempts to deal with them by concise analytical formulas, let alone by means of classical accounting methods.

Tier-1 financial institutions have long recognized the need the development of quantitative and qualitative techniques for product design in manufacturing firms and risk analysis in finance. Models are essential for making intelligent decisions among alternative approaches to challenges posed by the market, assessing the effect of trading on the bank's exposure, and the aftermath of various constraints.[4]

A financial environment and the enterprise architecture serving it must grow more sophisticated because the advent of derivative financial instruments, and the emphasis placed on global finance, have given rise to projects of a scope greatly exceeding that of any classical banking operation. The market ensures that the pace of innovation in new products and processes must be created virtually *ex nuovo*. These projects evolve rapidly and their milestones of progress cannot be set without high-tech assistance.

Stochastic processes can be modeled, but this does not change the fact that they raise vast problems of planning, management, and risk appraisal. An extensive study of organizational aspects is necessary as well because of the impact of fast evolving products, processes, and risks on the structure of the institution and its operations. Organizational studies typically try to discern critical chains of activity, anticipate adverse events, particularly exposure, and guide action to obviate them.

A recent major project investigated analytical and stochastic means of financial system simulation and concluded that, in most cases, an analytical approach resting on traditional lines is too tedious and too complex to be practical. What is necessary is knowledge-based interactive methods, like the real-time architecture of currency exchange inventory management shown in Figure 8.4.

In the majority of projects, the use of stochastic approaches to simulation utilizing Monte Carlo was found the most promising, followed by the application of operating characteristics curves and levels of confidence. Other projects involved analytical techniques for determining the number of on-line trials necessary to predict risk and return as a function of time and at different levels of confidence.

In one of these projects, a process was elaborated permitting random selection from various distributions simulated by Monte Carlo. This work included probabilistically defined measures of initial and time-dependent performance variables. The drawback was that the institution was somewhat behind in integrating its databases and in mining them in real-time. As this experience documents, an enterprise architecture should pay a great deal of attention to seamless database integration (see Chapter 10). Also, datamining associated with simulation and statistical tests should be done by agents specifically designed for each application served.

Furthermore, because decisions on inventory management of financial instruments and the resulting exposure are often made by committees,

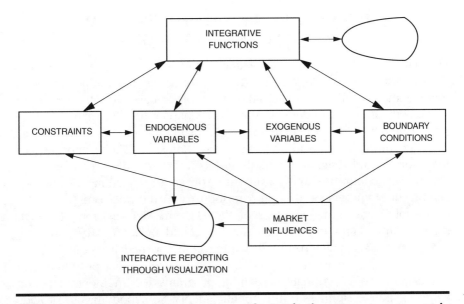

Figure 8.4   A real-time risk and return evaluator for inventory management in currency exchange.

MIT's intelligent room is a good candidate for improvements in systems and methods. Research finds its justification in the fact that, behind the questions classically faced by bank management stand some interesting mathematical problems promoted by derivative financial instruments and globalized banking operations. Bankers do not always appreciate that both sets of problems are represented by irregularly connected three-dimensional networks of the amount of exposure, time, and frequency of different events. Risk and return originate from one or more events whose times of occurrence are stochastic. They terminate at one or more events which are never final but, rather, the roots of new trees.

Seen from a mathematical perspective, this network topology is such that no chain of succeeding events leads back into itself. Complexity is increased by the fact that the duration of intermediate events is not necessarily a known constant, but conforms, in general, to some probability distribution. The problem can be seen as: given the distributions pertaining to isolated activities, what are the probability distributions for the times of occurrence of specific events?

Far from posing an abstract question, this problem has intrinsic interest because closely similar situations arise in the context of modern finance, and they must be addressed by every worthwhile enterprise architecture. Here lies a great deal of the difference between an architectural solution addressing only transactions and one positioning itself to respond to problems encountered by senior management.

SELF-HEALTH CARE, TELEMEDICINE, AND COMPUTATIONAL BIOIMAGING

Dr. Martin Minsky, a computer science professor at MIT, sees a not too distant future in which technology will bring significant advances in genome manipulation, as well as nanotechnology-based robotics that assist the elderly in living independently (see Chapter 6). "We may produce nanoscale devices that circulate in the bloodstream to continuously analyze body chemistry and monitor health," says Minsky. "Those nanodevices may, for example, signal if something has to be added or removed from the body's chemistry, and locate the source of infections or tumors. Nanotechnology will be the ultimate industry in the next century."[5]

Joseph Bonventure, co-chair of the Harvard–MIT division of health sciences and technology, suggests that a child born in 2015 may well have genotypic characterization done before he or she leaves the hospital. That highly personalized tag will allow doctors to predict propensity for disease, define appropriate screening programs for an individual, and examine likely responses to therapeutic agents. Somebody has to provide the information environment within which such applications will take place; this somebody is the enterprise architecture. Smart nanorobots would transmit information to the person's database and agents should mine the datastreams in real-time for limits and outliers. The genotype characterization may help as a unique identification system.[6]

If properly handled in a reliable, secure, and consistent manner, such advances will have a tremendous impact on health care and on society as a whole. "I don't think the answer is extending the current medical system," says one of the medical experts. "The current system attempts to do proactive healthcare but what it, in fact, practices is a kind of centralized crisis management. To be more proactive, it will be increasingly imperative for people to be able to take care of themselves to a greater extent."

This will require a great deal of public education comprising, the ability to give people confidence in taking care of themselves, their illnesses, and their behavioral laws. The bottom line is cultural change and a vast amount of sophisticated technology. Intelligent environments, along the lines discussed in Chapter 7 in connection with the Oxygen Project (and in this chapter in regard to banking), are destined to play a major role in putting into practice the concepts advanced by Minsky, Bonventure, and Pentland.

The enterprise architecture should spell out what it means to provide the right infrastructure. In all likelihood, as the law of the photon suggests (Chapter 3), optical equipment will continue to double the capacity delivered at a given price every 9 months, which is twice as fast as the speed of improvements in semiconductor performance. This has tremendous implications for business, industry, and health care.

Receiving instant medical advice in remote locations is a glimpse of what can be achieved by increasing the capacity of the communications systems tremendously. In Alaska, for example, many communications are isolated in winter months, but with high speed optical communications, x-rays, medical tests, and case files can be transmitted instantly to doctors and the analyses performed practically in real-time.

Experts also suggest that the next decade or two will experience an explosion in the use and scope of medical imaging, with more sophisticated ways and means for computer visualization, visibilization, and visistratction. Already researchers and physicians in advanced medical research centers are using visualization within highly interactive virtual and enhanced-reality systems for diagnosis, treatment, surgical planning, and surgery proper.

Within the foreseeable future, advanced, multimodal imaging techniques, based on more powerful computational methods, will greatly impact medicine and biology, but this cannot be successfully done in a disorganized, heterogeneous manner. Standards are necessary, compatible tests must be developed, and the information has to be appropriately architectured.

For instance, one of the expected breakthroughs is the imaging of anatomical structures linked to functional data, from magnetic fields to metabolism. Researchers project that a properly architectured medical environment will provide comprehensive views of the human body at progressively greater depth and detail than currently possible. But if databases are as disorganized as they are today, it is better to forget about benefits.

The wider use of these technologies will pose many challenges in an architectural sense because currently independent applications must, in the future, share unique standards, multimedia information elements, and interactive reporting requirements. In order for any universal communications-related utility to be successfully implemented in a highly diverse medical culture and technical environment, it must adhere to a rigid set of norms. The utility must be platform-, data-, location- and time-independent. It also must be highly flexible in terms of allowing for changing information requirements, and should provide a consistent, user-friendly interface (see the next section).

The enterprise architecture should make it possible for owners of information to publish via a record broadcast mechanism. It should also allow multiple subscribers to receive it, either real-time, if they are currently listening, or at any point thereafter through the transparent use of the utility's store and forward capability. Furthermore, published data must be differentiated by descriptive tags permitting subscribers to reference any of the information elements through smart tags and a remapping capability.

Subsystems also need to be implemented to maintain and consistently update medical records, address changes, accounting references, and control and movement of funds. The system should provide versatile human interfaces that permit computer illiterate people to communicate with information stored in databases.

All this is doable. The main reason it is not done is that it is alien to current IT culture. As Chapter 7 explained in conjunction with MIT's Oxygen Project, intelligent interfaces are a basic ingredient of intelligent architectural solutions. The case of smart rooms instrumented with sensors that enable the computer to see, hear, and interpret users' actions should find its way into medical applications. Here, as in other domains, the concept is that people in an intelligent room can control programs and share virtual environments without keyboards or special goggles. The room's sensors will provide personalized information about the surroundings, altering, in the process, the notion of communicating with man-made systems. This issue is examined in greater detail next.

DEVELOPING AND IMPLEMENTING PERPETUAL USER INTERFACES

Whether an implementation domain is telemedicine, command and control in finance, the military or any other perceptual user interfaces, it provides an opportunity for revamping and renovating communications between humans and information. A good solution is characterized by interaction techniques that integrate notions of communication, motor, cognitive, and perceptual human capabilities. The aim is to equip the computer's input–output devices with machine perception and reasoning. This makes the user interface friendlier, easier to use, and more compelling by taking advantage of how people typically interact with their environment. It also makes devices and sensors transparent while enabling them to capitalize on strengths and weaknesses of human communication channels, so far as to be easily understood.

Project Oxygen and many other research projects aim to add human-like perceptual capabilities to the computer, making the machine aware of the user and his or her requirements. They emphasize human communication skills, but also require integration at multiple levels of technology such as:

- Speech and sound recognition
- Speech and sound generation
- Language understanding
- Computer vision
- Graphical animation
- Flexible forms of visualization

It has been stated in connection to the Oxygen Project that a basic ingredient of such solutions involves machines' ability to do things on their own, without being told. They should be able to respond to users' needs and wants, as well as to adapt to a changing environment. This is what is meant, at least at the present time, by smart machines.

The attributes that make a man-made device smart ultimately lie with the device and what it has been designed to do. Recall that a conference room outfitted to be smart can identify participants in a meeting and who happens to be speaking at any given time. It can also produce transcripts and an abstract of the discussion because it is able to understand the main topics of conversation.

Architectural characteristics come into full force because computers, software, microphones, cameras, and other tools that go into this smart room must be seamlessly integrated into the system. This may present technical problems. Speech recognition software is usually sensitive to noise, and machine vision can be easily thrown off by changes in lighting. The greater challenge, however, lies in getting the smart room to process and understand complexities of a meeting and uncertainties of the real world. Among other vital components, resolutions of such complexities and uncertainties require good computational models of human activity, plus sophisticated software able to get a computer to perform seemingly straightforward tasks (such as translating spoken words or motion into intent).

As Chapter 7 explained by drawing on experience with the intelligent room, the challenge starts with location and identification of a person. Once the person is located, and visual and auditory attention has been directed to that person, the next step is identification: who is it? Identity is cornerstone to adaptive behavior. Can facial appearance and speech be used as identifiers?

Down to basics, this conceptual approach can be expressed in a block diagram like the one shown in Figure 8.5. This has been used in CALIDA, (California Implementation of an idea database assistant), a knowledge engineering artifact which effected the seamless integration of incompatible databases residing on heterogeneous platforms, in order to improve on-line customer service. (CALIDA was designed and used in the late 1980s by General Telephone and Electronics, now Verizon Communications.)

To serve as perceptual interfaces in a conference setting, person recognition devices need to identify people under nonconstrained conditions. This requires a methodology and a suite of technical design tools to craft a unique, tailored environment for the individual. The solution promoted by the enterprise architecture should permit aggregating the function into a grand design.

Another example where embedded technologies must fit within a broader enterprise architecture is the smart house, which relies on

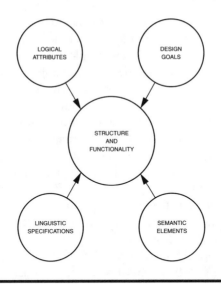

Figure 8.5 Block diagram of the conceptual approach to the design of CALIDA.

radio-frequency tags to integrate electrical subsystems, devices, and groceries into a functional entity. As in the case of smart rooms, advances in smart tags, speech recognition, and machine vision will allow homeowners to speak directly to the house asking it to do important things.

Deliverables are not for tomorrow. What has just been explained is part of a long term goal to develop an adaptive environment that understands what people are doing, predicts what they might want to do, and over time becomes a self-programmable entity. For smart environments to be really functional however, they must, have the ability to understand human behavior and distinguish normal from exceptional activity. This might take a couple of minor miracles to realize.

DESIGN DECISIONS AFFECTING THE GOVERNANCE OF A TECHNOLOGICAL SOLUTION

User-friendly interfaces are far from being the only major challenge with advanced projects. Two additional challenges are tied to the title of this section, i.e., the kinds of policy decisions needed for an intelligent technological system, and what managers responsible for supercontrol will do with facilities provided by the technological system's infrastructure. A linear answer is that live controllers will institute fundamental choices that the agents will interpret and implement while learning from them. For instance, under the knowledge artifacts, acting in conjunction with services intended for policymakers, controllers will:

- Lay down decisions concerning the sorting of messages and their routing over traffic lanes
- Decide the rate at which transactions and messages should be processed over operating channels
- Have the option to reassign priority values as demanded by prevailing operating conditions
- Govern the pattern characterizing message distribution from originators to consumers

In cases of conflict between priorities or shrinkage in channel capacity, live controllers may be asked to assign new and reassign existing channel capacity to cope with production requirements. Eventually, however, intelligent artifacts will do so by themselves. To appreciate the nature of these decisions and the manner in which live managers instruct the agents (or squad leaders of agents), consider the technological organization, which is a step more sophisticated than the one characterizing current systems.

Agents, not people, route, process, and distribute messages in this setting. Because the number of intelligent robots in a system like Project Oxygen will quite likely be big and growing, other knowledge artifacts will act as squad leaders, reallocating lower-level agents that do the legwork in a communications sense. Squad leader agents will also manage knowledge robots acting as traffic controllers, but not those which are personal assistants to end users and are therefore commanded by those individuals.

Even when performed all the way through knowledge artifacts, the intelligent sorting and routing of messages is a demanding job. Only part of the requirements can be structured, for instance, when each message arrives it is classified according to basic categories such as subject, sender, addressee, area, type of expedition, security, finer confidence level, and timestamp.

To avoid channel blocking, the number of arrivals in each defined interval of time can be simulated by experiment. The rate and pace of messages arriving during these intervals will typically be described by probability distributions, or set by experimenters. The classical model with queuing theory is that, when messages arrive they enter a storage queue or waiting line. The first task of a traffic agent is to inspect and sort them, and then decide how to route them over processing lanes. Other agents need to know about security and how to reroute after testing a projected lane's dependability.

Since agents must sort messages in order to route them within the organization, on what basis should they do this? Distinctions need to be made among messages that enter the queue, which means messages must be classified. Hence the need for a methodology which includes the handling of normal cases and also of exceptions.

For instance, designated basic fields by which incoming messages are classified can provide the basis of initial sorting and routing by agents. The downside is that algorithms may be complex. If there are eight fields and up to ten classifications under each, then, multiplying the classification possibilities presented by eight fields, yields 10^8 or 100 million possible combinations.

At current state of the art, sorting into this many possible distinct combinations would be an impossible job when done in real-time, as the agents would have to do something different with each particular sort. The task can be reduced to comprehensible and manageable dimensions, even if still of challenging proportions, by forcing a limited number of policy and control decisions on human managers. (See also the discussion in Chapter 7 on the need for structure to underpin theoretically unlimited free choices.) At the outset, human managers must make two kinds of decisions relating to routing. They have to choose a small number out of, say, eight fields to be the basis on which routing decisions are subsequently made by intelligent artifacts. Within the fields selected, they must decide which sorts of messages should be routed to which of the possible traffic lanes.

The concept behind these last two points leads to the boundary conditions discussed in the next section. Once these routing decisions have been made, reviewed at least on a periodic basis for resetting, and communicated to the agents, the instructions will be carried out and implementation decisions will be made by the knowledge artifacts. The basis for such decisions might need to be changed by the managers on an exception basis, while specific agents are given precise responsibilities for choosing the sorting field and routing within that field.

Depending on the environment served, routing policy might become exceedingly critical. For example, suppose that live managers establish a policy decision for the agents to route according to call expedition. Suppose further that they decide that all flash messages should be routed over lane 1, operational messages of immediate nature over lane 2, second priority messages over lane 3, etc. This looks linear, but in times of stress it might create havoc within the system.

It is conceivable that the route carrying flash messages might become overloaded; consequently, routine and deferred messages might receive attention more quickly than higher priority messages. A similar effect could be observed because of predetermining a geographical distribution served by a wide variety of incompatible channels whose band and functionality vary by two or three orders of magnitude. Other unexpected bottlenecks might develop if one user entity requires priority treatment of messages from specific geographical areas, while another entity calls for special treatment of messages relating to specific classes of subjects, and a third requests minimum delay for all kinds of messages sent by critical outposts.

Sorting and routing decisions are evidently most important in a computer-based distribution system. Therefore, their basis becomes a matter for higher level policy decisions affecting how many times an item is handled (or inspected) before it reaches its destination. This might need to be done at several places throughout the different channels through which it flows, while agents must know which parts of the system have to do what.

Even the most carefully studied situation can turn on its head as the patterns of incoming items change. Hence, the aforementioned considerations and associated change criteria must enter into the design of the intelligent command and control system. We should also not forget that quality of performance is a direct function of the degree of flexibility in organizing the technological infrastructure. The latter must be capable of drastic reorganization during the course of play.

A similar concept to the one outlined in regard to routing applies to other functions. For instance, after routing, the next major duty of a communications system is its processing activity. Typically, for study and experimentation purposes, processing lines are assembled out of unit modules, as shown in Figure 8.6. The basic module consists of a waiting queue and a service station through which messages flow and are processed. Processing is analogous to organizational activities like recording, stamping, data clearance operations, indexing, filing, classifying, and data-mining. In an intelligent system, stations in which tasks such as these are performed will be manned through agents.

Processing modules can be assembled for any specific application or group of applications. Several modules will be arranged to follow one another in a linear series, each constituting a single processing line. The supercontrollers must be able to specify how many processing lines will be available for operation. Flexibility will be maintained if each processing line is completely independent of any other, yet related to it within the specific boundary conditions characterizing the system, this is another mission that the enterprise architecture should perform.

BOUNDARY CONDITIONS CHARACTERIZING SYSTEMS DEFINED BY THE ENTERPRISE ARCHITECTURE

During the course of the mid to late 1980s, tier-1 organizations which pioneered the use of expert systems were successful in generating corporate profits through the development of computer systems in support of a wide range of products and product families.[7] These applications

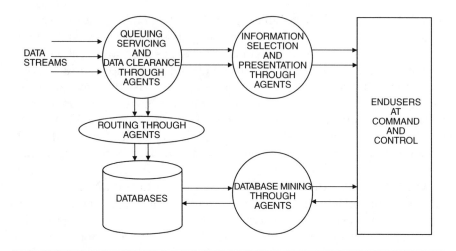

Figure 8.6 Basic modules and processing arrays in a command and control system run by agents.

became critical business partners for their analysts, traders, and sales forces, as they were required to develop novel products, maintain positions, calculate exposure, and determine profit and loss.

From the late 1980s to the late 1990s, decentralized business units were given authority to pursue opportunities, and private networks were established to link these units among themselves and with headquarters. However, it gradually became apparent that, in order to continue the rate of overall success, a much higher level of interbusiness cooperation was needed; somebody had to provide it.

For instance, in banking, exposure resulting from structured deals and derivatives made the real-time control of risk a basic requirement. The problem was that often the hedge instruments used were processed by different business units located on several continents and served by heterogeneous computer systems. At the same time, the corporate credit risk and market risk management functions depended on most timely and accurate information from virtually all business units, making it necessary to identify a flexible common language, one adaptable to the diversity of the businesses and complexity of the transactions involved. There was also a need to establish an information highway between varying technical platforms, providing them with an effective real-time interface, and to elaborate the boundaries of this global information network and its databases (see Chapter 10) in logical or physical terms.

Logical boundaries define a level of end-to-end network service as viewed by applications and end users; these boundaries are followed by service operations managers. Physical boundaries particularly interest network administrators and providers of the network system's components, for instance, the messaging backbone. The interaction of logical and physical boundaries must preserve the integrity of the global network and service interconnectivity that remain transparent to applications.

The proper definition of logical boundaries created by the chosen enterprise architecture should permit viewing the architectural system as a collection of software-based, end-to-end services. The scope of this view depends on the scope of networking, databasing, processing, and other functions accessible to applications and their interfaces. It is instrumental as well in defining system transparency.

For instance, the examples presented in the preceding section are largely associated with the system's logical boundaries, the degree of knowledge embedded into the supported services, and changes in implementation of these services because of steady change in the environment and the presence of outliers. A practical example on boundaries is given by the fact that once a message has been routed to any one line, it cannot leave that line until completely processed. To ease this constraint along each of the parallel processing lines, agents must provide alternative channeling skills.

In a modern enterprise architecture, knowledge artifacts would man the initial routing station and processing lines over which messages are channeled. It is important that these agents process and dispatch messages as expeditiously as available resources allow. For this purpose, the live managers must make further decisions concerning how the knowledge robots are to inspect and evaluate the status of messages at various stations.

Suppose, for instance, that messages endorsed by their senders as meriting a high degree of confidentiality are segregated and routed over a special, high-confidence processing line. At first stage, the agents might elect to expedite "immediate attention" messages with priority 1, command and control messages with priority 2, and so on, according to established policy. The agents would sort messages by subject matter, with further priority treatment given at subsequent stations along criteria relating to the processing line.

Within the confines of established logical boundary conditions, priority control fields and confidentiality criteria leading to subordinate classifications could be changed at the will of live managers. As with changes in routing, changes in assignment of priority and security values can take place during processing as a function of dynamics of the operating environment. Distribution policies will be similarly activated and guided by live managers, but routine execution will be done by agents at all times.

Physical boundary conditions are a different ball game. The enterprise architecture should provide the framework for integration of diverse global, regional, country, local, and building networks into an aggregate of computer-based services. The physical boundaries will be defined by a set of service access points that must be properly set, always keeping quality of service in perspective.

Because of potential disparities among component network types, database supports, processing engines, interfaces, and other devices, a uniform set of services may not be provided to end users across all global physical boundary points. To accommodate such disparities and preserve overall integrity of the global solution, classes of subnetworks, each with its own characteristics, may have to be defined. The way to bet is that these classes would span multiple physical networks.

Whenever this happens, it should be transparent to the users. Since, in a proper architecture solution, applications communicate with each other using a common utility, advancements in systems technology should be applied to a single set of software, rather than requiring each individual component apply the modification separately. This improves the flexibility of design, decreases the cost of long term maintenance, and enables the company to exercise greater control over the implementation of future enhancements.

Nowhere is this solution more important, in terms of networking, than in connection to aggregates involving both fixed and mobile communications links. At the same time, no other solution than the able use of increasingly smarter knowledge artifacts helps the goals an enterprise architecture sets. Chapter 9 explains why.

REFERENCES

1. Chorafas, D.N., *Transaction Management*, Macmillan, London, 1998.
2. Chorafas, D.N., *Reliable Financial Reporting and Internal Control: A Global Implemtion Guide*, John Wiley & Sons, New York, 2000.
3. Chorafas, D.N., *Managing Risk in the New Economy*, New York Institute of Finance, New York, 2001.
4. Chorafas, D.N., *Rocket Scientists in Banking*, Lafferty Publications, London and Dublin, 1995.
5. The MIT Report, Cambridge, MA, February, 2001.
6. Chorafas, D.N., *Managing Operational Risk. Risk Reduction Strategies for Banks Post-Basle*, Lafferty, London and Dublin, 2000.
7. Chorafas, D.N. and Steinmann, H., *Expert Systems in Banking*, Macmillan, London, 1991.

9

LOCATION-INDEPENDENT COMPUTING AND THE ROLE OF AGENTS

INTRODUCTION

The role played by knowledge artifacts, or agents, was explained in Chapter 7, with reference to MIT's Oxygen Project. Knowledge engineering is part of a technological evolution that often comes in waves. In the mid 1980s Dr. Alan Kay predicted a third computer epoch. The first, he said, was the institutionalization of computer usage in the corporate business environment. The second was the personal computer and its windows–icon–mouse interface. Kay correctly foresaw that the late 1990s would see the next wave, which would intimately fuse computers, networks, and knowledge engineering.

This has happened with the Internet, resulting in a powerful user environment very different from previous ones. Instead of using personal computing tools, said Kay, users would be served by agents that behave in a way intimate to their masters, or end user, and their requirements. (See also the discussion on mobile agents in connection with the growing role of intranets and extranets in Chapter 15.)

One of the key differentiators between other computer-based tools and agents is that the latter are proactive knowledge artifacts which prompt and talk to their master. This proactive attitude has never characterized classical computer software and other tools, which the user looks at, individually chooses, and programs or manipulates. To reach the required level of intimacy in order to act as knowledge robots, agents need to learn a great deal about their master's behavior, daily environment, and mission. They must be able to interpret correctly what he or she wants or needs, and then do something about it.

The earliest recorded artificial intelligence (AI) projects started in the late 1950s and early 1960s, but they were largely theoretical. The first knowledge artifacts put into practical use appeared in the mid 1980s in the form of expert systems. Tier-1 banks and manufacturing companies used sophisticated software to enrich their data processing jobs, and get more mileage out of their investments in computers and communications.

One of the first practical applications created through expert systems in banking was that of analyzing a client's investment profile; another was a loan analyzer.[1] Because these artifacts were successful, the late 1980s and early 1990s saw a progression toward smarter, more capable knowledge robots that act autonomously: agents.

It is precisely within this kind of environment that the most imaginative computer applications have emerged during the last ten years. Assisted by experts, a lot of people and companies are putting very sophisticated management-level concepts into practical everyday use. Whether in engineering, manufacturing, merchandising, finance, or other domains of science and the economy, there is now much more emphasis on experimentation, analysis, and optimization at a multidisciplinary level, which requires AI support. The most competitive applications in technology and the globalized Internet market cannot be realized through spent classical tools and obsolete computer languages.

A company's competitive ability is directly related to knowledge-enriched solutions it develops in order to harness the power of the Internet and manage change, using its aftermath as a competitive advantage. This is the best and only strategy able to provide exceptional value and returns for investments made in technology year after year.

As this chapter documents, there is plenty of scope in the development and use of intelligent software agents and personalization technologies. Agents can be effectively used in connection to location-independent computing and to filter important information, automate behavior patterns, recommend products and services, and buy and sell on behalf of consumers and businesses.

Intelligent artifacts have been successfully employed to enhance targeted marketing, sell products with a narrow consumer base or profit margins, provide continuous and detailed user feedback, and perform other active duties which classically were reserved for fairly knowledgeable people. In reviewing, the following practical examples, ask, "What are the kinds of agents the company needs? How will they change its way of doing things?"

A PHASE SHIFT IN THINKING IS NECESSARY TO BENEFIT FROM KNOWLEDGE ENGINEERING

Phase shift means a radical change in the characteristics of a system or in the way this system is used. A simple case is ice melting or water turning into steam. A more complex example is the infrastructural change necessary for a phase shift. For instance, today there is a fundamental phase shift in finance and economics because of change from a regulated to a liberal, globalized economy, where rapid technological innovation makes or breaks a company's future.

One can better appreciate knowledge engineering's contribution to this phase shift when one understands that it has been a revolution in thinking. The story goes that, one day Dr. Herbert Simon announced to a group of his students that he and some of his colleagues had invented a thinking machine. Then he added that the fundamental concept behind such a machine had been around for centuries, but not the practical applications.

René Descartes wondered whether man-made machines would be able to think. In the 18th Century Giambattista Vico wished that he had known what "can now be done by machinery" before he had "wasted 10 years doing it by hand."[2] Nevertheless in the 21st century many important management jobs are still done by hand.

Top-tier companies, however, have derived major benefits from implementing expert systems. One of the best applications in the 1980s was the expert configurer (XCON) by Digital Equipment Corp.[3] As another example, in the mid 1990s, Sollac Atlantique, a subsidiary of one of the largest steelmakers, Usinor, spent $8.1 million on an artificial intelligence system to manage six of its blast furnaces. Called Sachem, this intelligent software alerts workers to minute changes in temperature, water pressure, and thousands of other conditions. Such real-time warnings permit timely and effective process control in furnaces where iron ore and coal are superheated and transformed into pig iron.

Sachem has assisted in making significant improvements in product quality; it has also helped to extend the useful life of the furnaces. One of the ovens that benefited from Sachem, at a mill in Dunkirque, France, was renovated in 2001 after 14 years, well beyond the 9-year industry norm. Also, by optimizing furnace conditions, Sachem helped to cut emissions of greenhouse gasses by conserving fuel.

Usinor estimates that this expert system saves the company $1.55 per ton of steel produced. Multiplied by its annual output of 11.5 million tons, this gives a return of $17.2 million per year for an $8.1 million investment. As Usinor's chairman, Francis Mer, says, "Day after day, we have no other choice than to look at the possibility to save money."[4] (See also Chapter 12 for the role of agents as negotiators on the Internet.)

Competitive markets are instrumental in calling for paradigm shifts. Experts appreciate that the proper study of phase shifts should include information indicating the phenomena to be observed in the foreground, as well as the infrastructural changes needed in the background. The study should also outline how unfolding an ongoing process can help in developing new business opportunities, and which constraints are foreseen, as well as risks conceivably associated with this new business.

In every enterprise and practically all of its activities, a phase shift is necessary for survival reasons. To manage it in an able manner, one needs to appreciate that every new concept and new competitive product of business requires more advanced supports than those used by its predecessors. Companies without these supports will be left in the dust. The solution space shown in Figure 9.1 is valid with practically every product and process. Take any-to-any networking, for example, the physical structure of the new generation Internet provides expanded functional capabilities and broadband channels to everybody. Companies will perform better than their competitors that arm themselves with a flexible infrastructure, use intelligent artifacts, and personalize their products.

A phase shift in computer usage has characterized the widespread acceptance of the Internet as a whole. Another phase shift is in the making because of services provided by agents to the information environment

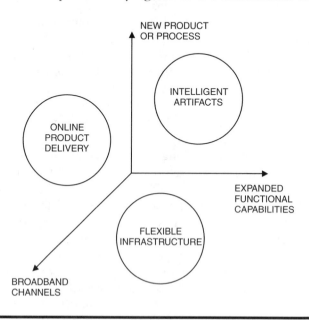

Figure 9.1 Every new business concept requires more advanced supports.

(see Chapter 7). Indeed, there is a parallel between the advent of knowledge artifacts in significant numbers and the population explosion which, over three decades, characterized microprocessors. Within 30 years of the birth of the microprocessor, the world cannot have enough of them. Their population has swollen to about 30 billion — a small but vital subset of the estimated 700 billion integrated circuits (chips) in use. Thirty billion microprocessors means nearly five microprocessors for every person on earth.

It is not difficult to understand such microprocessor inflation. A horde of everyday products is filled with one or more microprocessors: autos, TV sets, radios, watches, cameras, kitchen appliances, vacuum cleaners, and just about everything else made for the consumer. Intel envisions that by 2010 there will be microprocessors with a billion transistors each, featuring 100,000 MIPS. If practical applications are ever realized, molecular computers (see Chapter 6) will make these numbers seem small.

An interesting insight leading to prognosis comes by combining the gains in processing speed with the growth in the number of chips: between 2001 and 2005, chipmakers are expected to produce more number-crunching power than the sum of what currently exists. Much of this computing power will, most likely, propel autonomous intelligent machines specializing in certain jobs. Powered by agents, machines will reinvent themselves and be enriched with capabilities well beyond what they have done so far. Things that think will be a new generation of advanced mechanical, electro-mechanical, and electronic devices and tools, rather than only electronics.

Bill Gates believes that computer systems will eventually understand how one works and learns in an implicit fashion. For instance, workstation software may be adapting to an individual user's needs and requirements, learning automatically from the way its master interacts with computers. Such adaptation can be based on the user's profile mapped into memory by an agent.

Just as important for system reliability reasons are developments in self-healing hardware and software. If a machine has a problem, it should be intelligent enough to automatically request the latest software driver, retrieve it, and upgrade itself across the network, substituting some of its elements with others that are waiting. It should also be able to proceed without the user detecting a component failure. In every application in which it plays a role, the agent performs the assigned task in an intelligent manner. The artifact may be time- or event-driven, but it must be flexible in responding to its master's wishes and the behavior of the process.

There are no standard references for how an agent should best be designed. Neither are there standard protocols and concepts regarding how much intelligence the artifact should have. What really matters is that software is increasingly knowledge-intensive and equipped with autonomous learning capabilities. The constructs undertaken must have the ability to remember past states and adapt themselves using their experience.

Some people look at agents as expert systems endowed with mobility and the maintenance of time. This is a good definition provided one adds to it a fully interactive mode of operations, proactive behavior, and learning characteristics. Closely connected to this issue is the query, "Under which conditions should one call a piece of software an *agent?*" There is no unique technical answer to this question. "Agenthood" is often a matter of what the artifact's functionality and smart behavior appear to be to the user.

ANSWERING THE NEED FOR AGENTS IN NOMADIC COMPUTING

The growth of on-line solutions and any-to-any communications between people and databases gives investors greater access to information, while also providing a new marketplace for products and services. Such operations need to be supported through sophisticated software in order to accelerate innovation, increase accuracy, swamp costs, and produce products with market appeal. Consider the Charles Schwab organization as an example.

Schwab manages over 4 million online brokerage accounts and is adding more at a rate of over 20,000 per week. Some 65% of trades are processed via the Web and more than $250 billion in assets are handled on-line. The Internet has made a substantial difference in Schwab's ability to increase its business, but without sophisticated software brokers would not be able to tap the potential of this market. Schwab knows this, but other brokers do not. One of these brokers asked a customer if he would like to have his asset information on the Internet. The customer said yes, provided that his name never showed up, market price of his holdings was updated intraday, and an agent was able to learn his trading pattern and respond to ad hoc queries. Unfortunately, these were requirements that the broker's mainframes and old style applications software were not able to fulfill.

Ironically, this particular broker with the obsolete computers and inflexible, low-productivity programming languages (mainly different incompatible versions of Cobol) is planning to launch a mobile electronic commerce (me-commerce) service; at the same time, it is failing to prepare for such a strategic move. Management is to blame for not understanding that, without cultural change and a thorough revamping of infrastructure, big plans have no future. Me-commerce is a nomadic computing application requiring intelligent artifacts that know the client and his or her habits. Me-commerce is commerce for *me*, the individual, who, as illustrated above, would not commit without personalization of services.

Clients on the move, in a location-independent computing environment like to be given at least two database access capabilities: fuzzy inquiry and quick inquiry. An inexperienced person can readily retrieve information through fuzzy inquiry, which means that the exact data element is retrievable simply by entering a few items the user easily remembers. However, they are approximate, not exact, for instance, some sort of description or general designation. The system should propose alternatives, helping the user to find what he is after.

Quick inquiry, by contrast, requires exact identification, which permits direct access. This ensures that information can be rapidly retrieved with precision and prioritized. This will not be the typical way of handling customer requests through me-commerce, but for competitive reasons it must be available interactively.

The blocking factor in making the changes necessary for adaptation to the demanding environment of location independent computing is cultural, not technical. Since 1996 knowledge artifacts that specialize in content screening and publishing have been available as commodity software. For instance, one of Autonomy's agents accepts user questions (not just key words) and suggests items relevant to the query, also creating hyperlinks that function in the user's interests. This particular agent works on the Internet, reads the contents of each Web page, and understands the context in which words are used.

A key contribution is user profiling. By means of a matrix of interests to be monitored and evaluated, it is possible to retrieve information on the Internet, as well as to build a dynamic database. One application assisted through this facility is for companies looking for competitors or simply for information about themselves that exists on the Net.

LifestyleFinder is a different agent with similar goals. It develops a profile of its master's interests and exploits a demographics database. This knowledge artifact is able to work out the user's profile by asking multiple-answer questions. For its part, the InfoFinder browses information in databases and indicates relevance or irrelevance of various documents in regard to what its master wants or needs. It searches for required documents and learns from key sentences in those documents.

ContactFinder, a different agent, answers bulletin board questions and finds specialists for specific topics. Another widely available intelligence-enriched artifact is the PowerEditor. This smart software permits the user to have an unlimited number of separate if–then conditions, with various types of orders, e.g., close, stop, market, and limit. In securities trading, for instance, PowerEditor can combine several dozen buy and sell criteria, including complex money management, and apply multiple entry and exit rules connected to client trades and other activities characterizing his or her relationship with the broker.

TradeStation, still another intelligence-enriched software, transforms the computer into a trading assistant that scans the markets tick-by-tick, instantly alerting its master when it finds a profitable trading opportunity. TradeStation also keeps track of all active orders that have been filled, as well as orders that need to be cancelled due to market changes or the prevailing number of open positions. This way, the artifact serves as a smart on-line assistant to intraday market data streams.

Just as smart is a piece of knowledge software known as OptionStation. It targets the best position to be in, based on the user's market assumptions and objectives; searches for the best risk or reward, given specific criteria; and examines the entire database of options for the selected market segment it is investigating. OptionStation uses some 20 built-in strategies, creating combinations of options and futures, or options and stocks for each strategy.

The intelligent software assists the user in analyzing and monitoring different positions, alerting him if market conditions have changed. Once OptionStation has identified some likely option positions, the user can enter the information in a spreadsheet for further analysis, obtaining both tabular and graphical representation of the position's risk and reward.

Still, another commonly available agent targets the market of personal digital assistants (PDA) and nomadic computing. One of the applications it is able to do is broadcasting and narrowcasting. Equally agile in transmitting and receiving, the agent may be instructed by its master to establish a temporary link, such as that provided by a mobile telephone. After the agent accomplishes its work, this link may be dropped. (See more about the work accomplished by agents in Chapter 12.)

Some of the artifacts currently available off the shelf, particularly those of the search-and-optimize type, seem to be so successful in performing their duties that some stores have decided not to let them access *their* databases, even if the majority of electronic commerce stores approve. This is another way of saying that the more advanced the technology used, the finer the grain of transformation the market undergoes, the greater the pain felt by low technology entities, and, eventually, the higher the quality of resulting services and products.

WHEN COMMERCIAL MARKETS ARE ON-LINE, THE DETERMINANT ROLE IS PLAYED BY INTELLIGENT ARTIFACTS

Once commercial markets are operating on-line in a networked form, their products and services are increasingly offered to a global customer base. At the same time, me-commerce customers can afford to become more selective. Because of this bifurcation, high technology offers significant opportunities for leadership. Agents are used not only to advise and support their masters but also to trade on behalf of them. Ingenious new approaches can change the dynamics of the market system, making the interface to the Web intuitive and easy so that people will be more inclined to use it. As the previous section showed, companies and consumers are now employing knowledge artifacts as Web-analyzing programs. These agents not only report information sought, but also advise about organizing work.

A simple example is an application that performs a statistical scan over a large episodic memory (characterized by a flat, object-oriented organization), establishing correlation, elaborating patterns, detecting trends, and analyzing companies' performances. Agents could also help write rules for work that will make teams more effective and results better focused. They assist in watching for thresholds established by senior management or watching over actions of the rank and file.

A timely and accurate response associated to the work performed helps enrich experience and increases attention to detail. This is an issue not taught in school. Many individuals are deprived of the opportunity to gain insight because, as the late Dr. Harold D. Koontz, my professor at UCLA, used to say, "For lots of people 20 years of experience is just 1 year of experience repeated 20 times."

The richness of the work one is doing can be better appreciated through the assistance of personal agents acting on behalf of their master and warning on exceptions or making suggestions as the situation warrants. They may collect, screen, and report information or do other chores. If they are competent and trustworthy, they free the owner from some of the leg work involved in navigating and browsing database contents, interacting with document handling software, status information, and presentation routines.

Cisco is one of the companies that have developed electronic commerce agents. Some of these agents aim to provide customers with greater ease in doing business. The mission of one family of artifacts is to price and order Cisco products; another group is targeting greater operational efficiency of ordering and scheduling, end-to-end. A status agent helps the customer, in real-time, in connection to current status of his order and its delivery schedule. Reporting on scheduling data changes by the minute, the agent gives the client reliable information he can use for his own scheduling and planning.

The pricing agents are polyvalent. They help buy currency, download prices on spreadsheets, and assist the customer in applying discounts to which he or she is entitled. Cisco's configuration agent works in a way similar to that of XCON (see the second section), to assist in configuration of complex systems. It also expedites delivery to customers with much fewer errors than manual methods permit, and it assists the customer in communicating with Cisco by fax or e-mail.

As these examples document, commerce agents can be instrumental in promoting business. They help in normalizing the often challenging process of system configuration, including its costing, and perform their duties end-to-end in a dependable, diligent manner. Such assistance has become necessary because today there is too much of everything: information overloads, alternative choices, tasks to be performed, and complex procedures to be followed. Hence there is a need for intelligent assistants capable of capitalizing on the experience gained with expert systems since the mid-1980s. These solutions, however, are not free of challenges. A key question is: where does intelligent artifact authority start and end? For instance, what if an agent misbehaves, fails to do the job, or delivers lousy results? What if it conflicts or collides with other agents? While technology for the development of knowledge artifacts settles, there are further questions to be answered:

- Should agents or their owner pay a toll for using system resources?
- How are the costs associated with jobs done by agents calculated, and how are they debited?
- Should agents have bank accounts? Should they authorize payments?

Other questions, too, await a factual and documented answer. Should knowledge artifacts act fully autonomously or should they ask for approval? If so, for how long should they wait? What about assets created or liabilities incurred because of initiative taken by agents? A more technical query is: how much storage should agents take? The answer depends on how much functionality their developer or users want out of this agent and how much they are willing to pay for it.

Intermediaries can also be between developers and users of knowledge artifacts. This poses other technical queries. For instance, who teaches the agent? Should the teacher of the intermediaries be the same as the teacher of the frontline agents? For the frontline agents, a simple answer is their master or other agents. But for the intermediaries? Also, how much intelligence and how much complexity does one want the agent to have? This is a functional query, which has a great deal to do with the developer's know-how, the tools he has available, the end user's requirements, and the agent's learning ability.

An agent's ability to learn is always important, and it must be embedded into the artifact from the drafting board. A bank designed an agent whose goal was to improve internal control in trading derivatives' financial instruments. The framework is shown in Figure 9.2. Its implementation

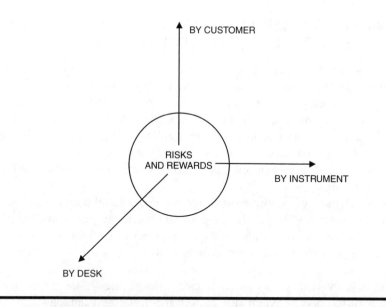

Figure 9.2 A three-dimensional frame of reference integrates information available interactively to the trader.

showed that a single artifact cannot perform well in this three-dimensional space. This led to designing a family of agents, some of which were projected to follow derivatives trading by important clients and report on limits. Others did the same by type of instrument, for instance, assumed forward interest rate risk. Still others compared desk-level limits with the individual limits the desk had established for its traders.

What became known as a risk and return (R&R) agent used the information collected by the specialized artifacts to calculate risk and reward at desk level. This proved to be a good internal control exercise because it brought senior management's attention to results which were thus far hidden. It was also good documentation that appropriate design measures required fundamental understanding of the trade, describing the domain, and defining the necessary boundary conditions.

Among design issues brought forward by this particular project, scalability proved to be important. Scalability is particularly recommended in connection to networked applications which are a major implementation domain for knowledge artifacts. Designers of interactive knowledge robots should take advantage of the network's facilities and characteristics, including existing and projected data flows. Agents can also be instrumental in filtering, as the next section documents.

INFORMATION FILTERING BY KNOWLEDGE ARTIFACTS AND THE CONCEPT OF FEDERATED DATABASES

The application of market data filters can be significantly improved through knowledge artifacts. In real-time profile analysis, for instance, filtering through agents may be dedicated to the requirements of one user or collaborative use. An example of collaborative filtering is the gathering and pooling of customer profiles within a given market segment. Through database mining (see Chapter 10) and filtering, a computer can determine what products or services people like, and how much they may be willing to pay for them.

In the jargon of complexity theory, cross-database access with passthrough involving highly heterogeneous hardware and software platforms can be brittle; one thing goes wrong and everything is a mess. A dozen years ago there was plenty of talk about making widely ranging databases homogeneous. Those companies who tried found this not feasible; it is even more so today because, as Figure 9.3 suggests, there is a great difference between distributed and federated databases. In the 1980s, using distributed information systems, many companies tried to distribute their (nonhomogeneous) databases which, however, remained under central control. Today ephemeral business partnerships on the Internet ensure that the databases of supply chain members work autonomously. They are designed and managed by the firms owning them, independently of one another.

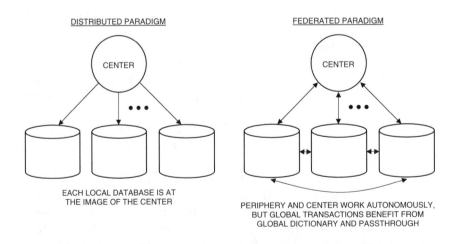

Figure 9.3   There is an essential difference between distributed and federated databases.

Experts believe that a market in steady evolution makes cross-database mining work a never ending challenge, but also gives it the potential to revolutionize electronic commerce. As collaborative filtering moves out of its infancy, on-line shopping could substitute some of the trips to the mall, with agents using profile analysis to gather valuable information on drives and wishes of markets and of individual customers.

The first task of an agent acting as profile analyzer is to know what the end user needs. This is fundamental (though it is rarely enough) and has been repeatedly implemented through expert systems in connection to investment analysis and advice to investors.[1] Activated by the expert analyzer's results, the personalized market data filter would operate on distributed databases to locate pertinent information without taking precious time from the end user.

A heuristic model can easily execute many of the filtering operations the end user wants, supporting a range of alternatives from which to choose. In current status, many of the available market data filters feature a cut-and-paste process used to combine working data in key selection requests. Such a knowledge artifact developed by a credit institution targets currencies. Value-added routines exploit different query types and aim to uncover underlying factors in a volume of elements on currency rates by market makers. Value differentiation software supported by routines providing cross-database access help in choosing the best available foreign exchange rates in a way seamless to the end user.

Market data filtering and database mining correlate between themselves and with other advanced applications of information technology, like modeling, simulation, global risk management, and real-time analysis of business opportunities. This is what Figure 9.4 says in a nutshell. In a modern business environment there exists no lack of market data feeds. The problem is one of filtering incoming data to unearth important information for business opportunity analysis and risk management reasons.

An application of a nature similar to that briefly described in the preceding paragraph was developed in a credit institution. The results were achieved in coordination with a parallel project which addressed problems associated with seamless access of heterogeneous databases. As happens today with supply chain applications on the Internet, every one of the many incompatible databases belonging to the financial institution in the background of this case study was kept operating on a local basis. After careful study it was decided that there would be no global schema because all of the database servers had locality, but were federated through a process of metalevel integration.

This is another type of location-independent computing. All global information requests have access to a global dictionary, with agents ready

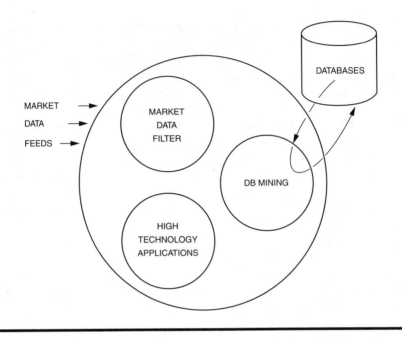

Figure 9.4   Necessary components of an advanced technology financial environment.

to assist in providing passthrough facilities. Active within the overall implementation is a mechanism for decomposition and mapping of running processes. This strategy has been elaborated along four axes of reference made feasible through parallel computing: 1. domain search capabilities, 2. system control responsibilities, 3. object-oriented characteristics, and 4. a flexible layered structure.

In this particular application, domain decomposition focuses on markets and their currencies, as well as different currencies traded within a market. It also includes prices and timestamps. While domain decomposition centers on data hashed across the domain and handled at clerk nodes, control responsibilities divide into two parts:

■ A functional type of decomposition: query, partial query, update, and paste
■ Manager action with query node focus, which was once activated by clerks but is now handled by agents

Systems designers have developed a state transition graph with key branches markets and currencies. This approach permits listing all markets handling a given object (currency, exchange rate, and counterparty). The same is true for different levels of detail characterizing that object. It also makes it feasible to apply timestamps, and list timestamp-price pairs to the details of an object.

The way this knowledge-enriched software operates is that the query node routes requests to target clerk node. In the general case, however, this solution brings up a problem of classification and identification of the information elements that must be handled at real-time.[5] Therefore, a system has been elaborated permitting an unambiguous identification of exchanges, moneys, companies, assets, and other specific key factors per application domain. (Some approaches are discussed in the next section.)

An interesting example of an agent specifically developed for the application discussed is that of one which tracks the execution of foreign exchange deals by customer. For big amounts, exchange rates are negotiated. For example, customer may negotiate changing $5 million into euro dollars, but then does so in small lots. Therefore, the negotiated price no longer applies.

In the past, when the customer would call back to complain about a less favorable exchange rate, the trader would lose an hour to find out why this was the case. Now the agent flashes a message explaining the reason. This helps in handholding with the client and saves precious time for the trader. The agent acts as a productivity tool and a customer relationship assistant.

Applications of this type help in demonstrating the power of modern information technology in a business sense. But there are prerequisites, among them, flexibility. A general schema of a flexible layered structure is shown in Figure 9.5. The atomic business elements of the mid-layer correspond to transaction details. Notice that, through this type of architecturing, products, transactions, atomic units and the resources utilized can be combined in an easily reconfigurable manner.

This specific solution is proprietary, but the concept underpinning it can be generalized. One important aftermath of using such an approach is that it can facilitate the use of middlemen nodes on the Internet in business-to-business applications. Theoretically, the Internet was supposed to do away with middlemen since producers and customers can now connect directly. Yet, as it turned out, buyers needed middlemen on the Net to sort through the vast new choices of suppliers, and suppliers needed to be where many buyers gather, which usually was not on individual company sites but at a certain middle level.

In Internet terms, these middlemen are known as informediaries, vertical portals, or e-markets. They are using the Internet to instantly connect buyers and sellers anywhere; their function is to gather together large numbers of buyers and sellers. According to some estimates, because of their central position, these middlemen might end up by controlling a quarter of the world's on-line business-to-business transactions.

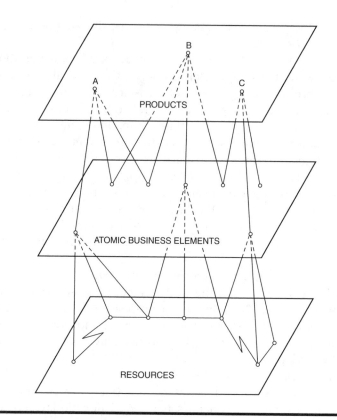

Figure 9.5 A three-layered structure characterizing a financial business and its products, constituent elements, and resources.

A METHODOLOGY FOR OBSERVING TIME-CRITICAL CONSTRAINTS ON ENTERPRISE ARCHITECTURES

One of the promising fields in information technology is that of theoretical research into the mechanisms of the brain. By investigating the subtle mechanics of brain work through bioelectronics, researchers aim to discover new ways of transmitting, receiving, and processing information. This seems to be an ideal means for the study of information handling in life forms and, the second section showed, it can be found at the origin of artificial intelligence.

Some projects in bioelectronics aim to determine which mechanisms of the brain enable one to perceive and recognize objects. Perception is consciousness or awareness of objects. Data act as raw material of this awareness and are collected through the medium of the senses. Knowledge is gained by perceiving, including insight or intuition. Researchers are also seeking clues to human logic processes all the way from ways and means of knowledge acquisition to knowledge representation and usage.

In addition to the immediate use of such know-how in information technology, an aim is to discover the seeds from which knowledge will grow in the 21st century. This is a vast project and nobody can tell when it will bear fruit. Prognostication is very difficult, as Niels Bohr once said, and especially so about the future. It is therefore interesting to speculate on the potential commercial significance of the results of such projects, on the assumption researchers can put their findings to practical use.

The future impact of biomolecular approaches (see Chapter 6) and optoelectronics on enterprise architectures and processes such as image recognition and data filtering remains to be revealed; however, some people in the scientific and business communities have concluded that research in these domains may represent one of the key emerging technologies of the 21st century. Till then, one must do with a growing range of silicon-based artificial intelligence artifacts, some of which are quite successful in their domain-specific jobs.

Knowledge engineering projects have documented that one of the domains where intelligent artifacts can be instrumental is time-critical jobs. But what is the sense of time-critical? Each scientific discipline has its own definition. For example, chemistry takes place in femtoseconds which are quadrillionths, or thousandths of a trillionth, of a second. Measuring such unimaginably short periods of time is the business of femtochemists, who are charged with slowing down chemical time. They do this to a level that current technology allows to be recorded by machines, and in a way that the results obtained are comprehensible to the human brain.

Business processes do not have these stringent time requirements, but they have time-critical characteristics nevertheless. Operators in a financial environment — traders, analysts, investors — were once satisfied with interday data. Stock prices were reported interday with high, low, and closing price; this is no longer satisfactory.

The more competitive a business becomes, the more it needs high frequency financial data (HFFD) available intraday. This poses cultural and technical challenges. Figure 9.6 shows that, between daily and tick-by-tick information (which is often subsecond), a difference of 6 orders of magnitude exists. Analysts require HFFD for their work on prediction of market movement. Day traders, too, need tick-by-tick information to help in making meaningful decisions in real-time.

In the last analysis trading decisions are made by humans, but the process of data capture, filtering, and processing needs to be automated. This is a basic reason for the popularity of using the Internet and its agents as information engines. However, knowledge artifacts also have

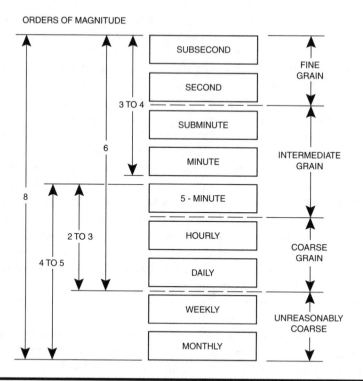

Figure 9.6 The difference between fine-grain and coarse-grain financial data is the orders of magnitude.

prerequisites and, unless the prerequisites are fulfilled, one cannot effectively exploit market dynamics in the best way possible.

Fundamental to cultural change is appreciation that, when one works at the frontiers of available knowledge, missions can be achieved through an evolutionary process which acts on variations affecting the system's internal parameters. Streams of filtered information must be selected and combined into useful clusters, a job which requires a learning algorithm to operate all the time to filter, store, and retrieve information and knowledge.

Knowledge engineering is important to time-critical systems because it is weeding out the human component for a number of reasons: timeliness, cost, and accuracy among them. On the other hand, it is necessary to try to hold on to the human component's associative characteristics through emulation. The model should represent the ability of living organisms to alter the linkage between perceptual experiences and actions. This must be done in a rapid and flexible manner by perceiving, storing, manipulating, and retrieving patterns of activity.

Such a model is applicable in a wide area of activities included in filtering, patterning, and image recognition. Features that can distinguish a more general approach from a more limited one are, in their way, an abstraction of brain structure and function. The goal is inference, that is, reasoning from premises to conclusion, and it can be served through taxonomy and classification.[6] Understanding the sense of approximation helpd to distinguish relevant parts from the irrelevant, segregate significant effects from the insignificant, and translate information and experience in a qualitative form. On the strength of this approach rest the scientific underpinnings of expert system and agents. Knowledge engineering is forcing software developers to be more explicit in their hypotheses, developmental procedures, testing premises, and, generally, their choice of mechanics and dynamics characterizing the constructs which they perform.

This approach to the development and use of technology is a major advantage, especially in time-critical applications, which are the growing domain of computer implementation in the coming years. The outlined approach is a far cry from legacy-type applications, which come from past commitments and the "backward" "electronic data processing" culture of people and companies; it is characteristic of new competitive-type applications.

An example of the latter class is time-critical trade support in a supply-chain seen as a client-oriented solution. The most effective implementations in this field are personalized and quite often require a significant amount of intelligence quotient characteristic of all mission-critical systems and, therefore, location-independent computing as well.

In the years ahead, change in business and industry will accelerate as the computing needs of endusers move well beyond today's PC world. While the personal machine will probably remain for some years in the heart of computing at home, at school, and at work, it will be joined by numerous new intelligent devices and appliances, from hand-held computers and auto microprocessors to Internet-enabled cellular phones. All of them will require a growing intelligence endowment to function properly.

The growing need for speedy action and flexible structures will ensure that more software will be delivered over the Internet, while the boundary between on-line services and off-the-shelf software products will blur. A stream of competitive offerings in a diffused control landscape will continue to change everything by assuring a level of connectivity unimaginable only a few years ago. Every end user will want to participate in this fast evolving environment where fortunes can be made or lost depending on one's ability to face the next challenge.

DESIGN PRINCIPLES FOR PLANNING AND CONTROLLING ARTIFACTS FROM THE LABORATORY FOR INTERNATIONAL FUZZY ENGINEERING

The case of success or failure with advanced computer projects implicitly or explicitly involves the skills of their developers, users, and administrators. In several instances, the physical environment also contributes to successes and failures. Events like power outages, extreme weather, etc. have an impact; the real moving force, however, is the human behind the machine.

More precisely, in a majority of cases the real reason for failure has been near-sightedness. Both senior management and its systems people fail to anticipate possible effects or use an inadequate methodology and worn-out tools for the job. This reference includes obsolete languages such as Cobol and Fortran, and expensive but low MIPS equipment such as mainframes.

A good example of the way challenges of the future have been capably faced in past years and assured the requirements posed by time-critical applications is an artifact developed in the 1990s by the Japanese Laboratory for International Fuzzy Engineering (LIFE). The main goal of this project, known as ROBOT, is to look into the production of a user-friendly, highly intelligent machine which is capable of autonomous action and control and incorporates a macro-decision facility resembling that of humans.

The development of this autonomous vehicle project required research into methods of building high level self-controlled robots, capable of making intelligent decisions by incorporating and using human-type skills and other characteristics. In the case of LIFE, this was approached through the use of fuzzy logic for knowledge acquisition of skills and mapping functional capabilities reflecting human action.

ROBOT had both immediate and future goals. One of its future objectives went beyond making one artifact to confront a limited set of requirements. LIFE looked for a method able to give machines the ability to evaluate macro situations while employing ambiguous situational estimation that resembles that of humans and is based on the interpretation of sense data.

The research project did not take place yesterday, but it was so much ahead of its time that it still constitutes a useful reference. The project started in 1990 with a study of basic systems functions incorporating components necessary to a user-friendly approach. Many system-related problems have been studied in this context, with the aim to learn as much as possible from both successes and failures. Three aspects were particularly important:

- Research on an intelligent human interface with learning capabilities
- Fuzzy algorithms for allowing machines to make behavioral decisions
- Stability evaluations of the fuzzy control mechanism and its components

In terms of learning processes, simulations studies were undertaken by appropriately tuning membership functions of fuzzy rules. The goal was to learn qualitative and quantitative characteristics of behavior in response to instructions from an operator.

Fuzzy algorithms were developed for allowing knowledge-enriched machines to make the necessary behavioral decisions, for example, an action-decision heuristic model for avoiding both moving and nonmoving obstacles. This was written as a group of fuzzy rules approximating human avoidance behavior that ensured that the robot avoided obstacles based on the perceived level of danger during motion.

An important item of the whole project was the ability to take account of the degree of danger during autonomous motion. Methods giving the smart machine the ability to evaluate macro situations based on the fusion of information obtained from multiple sensors were studied, as was making the machine able to order real-life macro decisions in an order-oriented sense.

Stability evaluations attracted particular attention in the case of multi-input approaches, given the difficulty of judging system behavior only by fuzzy labels. Associated with this was development of a reasoning shell based on fuzzy engineering, specifically designed for control purposes. This shell included on-line and off-line rule editors, inference engines installed as libraries, and multiwindow display of a given inference. Particular importance was placed on providing the machine with intelligent behavior characteristics, thus enlarging its capability for decisions. Since this was an open end system, two associated topics were studied by the researchers: a method of switching and a method for danger evaluation.

A method of switching is necessary to give intelligent machines the ability to learn through knowledge acquisition. This method was studied within a framework of smart behavioral decisions enhanced through machine learning. Simulation, testing, and evaluation were indispensable parts of the method and should be included in any project of a certain technological complexity.

The director of LIFE has pressed the point that all situations connected to the implementation of autonomous vehicles are time-critical. Capably facing the many challenges such situations present permits furthering the applications domain by establishing some more generally usable principles to characterize future knowledge-enriched technology.

In conclusion, new design perspectives and knowledge engineering solutions are interrelated because the former need the latter for more accurate response to a control situation. Knowledge-enriched artifacts can be instrumental, whether embedded into physical autonomous vehicles in the new generation of intelligent networks, or in advanced financial products. All involve intelligence-enriched tasks and should therefore benefit from the best tools available in the trade.

REFERENCES

1. Chorafas, D.N. and Steinmann, H., *Expert Systems in Banking*, Macmillan, London, 1991.
2. *Economist*, February 24, 2001.
3. Chorafas, D.N., *Expert Systems in Manufacturing*, Van Nostrand Reinhold, New York, 1998.
4. *BusinessWeek*, February 19, 2001.
5. Chorafas, D.N., *Managing Operational Risk. Risk Reduction Strategies for Banks Post-Basle*, Lafferty, London and Dublin, 2000.
6. Chorafas, D.N., *Integrating ERP, Supply Chain Management and Smart Materials*, Auerbach/CRC Press, New York, 2001.

10

ENTERPRISE DATA STORAGE
AND CORPORATE MEMORY
FACILITY

INTRODUCTION

The concept of enterprise data storage or distributed deductive databases is inseparable from that of analytical studies and experimental approaches which are becoming common among top-tier organizations. The decision to emphasize the enterprise nature of databases is deliberate. "Information about money is just as important as money itself," said Walter Wriston, a former chairman of Citibank.

The challenge to organize and manage databases is not new. One of the problems faced by many organizations, of which top management is not always aware, is that the enterprise architecture is paying less attention to global data storage solutions than it should. Often designed to be heavy on the transaction side, it downplays global database solutions, interactive datamining, and corporate memory facility (CMF) services.

The result is half-baked database approaches sought after without a master plan, and usually negatively affecting vital fields' enterprise activity, such as research on business opportunities, management accounting, portfolio analysis, internal control, and risk management.

The contents of the company's databases are vital organization assets. Quite often, they are competitive weapons which must be used in the most able manner. Even the best qualified people cannot replicate on short notice vital information which was not captured when it should have been.

Each solution to database problems has its pros and cons, but, to start, there should be a thoroughly studied concept for enterprise data storage, including the institution of a corporate memory facility (see the last two sections in this chapter). This is not the general case. A surprisingly large number of companies, particularly those with fat IT budgets, are processing rich and data poor. Because too much money and scanty results correlate, some of the major errors with technology management are:

- Big information systems budgets
- Little attention to enterprise data storage
- Long timetables for applications delivery
- Trivial requirements for return on investment (ROI)

For instance, an institution can be "processing rich" with 30 million Cobol statements, but "data poor" with thin databases, lots of obsolete data, and slow response time to on-line queries. Outdated concepts in IT impact efficiency heavily because they fail to provide operating executives and professionals with real-time updates, the ability to backtrack and analyze past decisions, seamless cross-database capabilities, and database mining assisted by knowledge artifacts.

Many people incorrectly think that datamining is simply some sort of database access; that is wrong. Many competitive advantages come from filtering (see Chapter 9). The ability to do real-time filtering plays a significant role both in companies and in the new economy. Collaborative filtering and recommendation engines on the Web have helped Internet commerce practitioners in improving on-line sales significantly.

A great deal of benefit has been derived from incorporating algorithms and heuristics that create sophisticated customer profiles from analyses of customer buying patterns, price sensitivity, and other databased information. As a recent MIT publication pointed out, algorithms embedded in such applications are used by well-managed firms to adjust prices and focus on their product lines.[1] This is an integral part of the contribution an enterprise architecture can offer.

EVOLVING NOTIONS THAT UNDERPIN ENTERPRISE DATA STORAGE

Consider the fundamentals on what is and is not the sense of databasing. Information is the opposite of uncertainty. The word form appears in the middle of the word information because the latter is conceptually related to formal patterning or complexity of a system. Some of the basic concepts underpinning information theory were developed by Dr. Claude Shannon, while working at Bell Telephone Laboratories. These have been widely used communications engineering, and have been extended to other fields, all the way from organizational theory to management decision processes.

Information has been recorded on stone, clay, paper, magnetics, optical, and electronics media. Usually it is represented through markers or signs. Hammurabi's tablets bore cuneiform writing. Natural systems, too, use markers: nucleotides in a DNA molecule, molecular structure of a hormone, and so on. Advances in man-made information and communication technology have been toward decreasing the matter and energy costs of storing, retrieving, and transmitting information. Cuneiform tablets carried less than 10^2/g; paper improved this by about two orders of magnitude. Magnetic storage provided more than two orders of magnitude improvement over paper, and optical storage makes feasible about 10^{10} bits/g.

Compared to clay as storage devices, optics are more efficient by better than 10^8, or more than 100 million times. Comparing optics to paper, the efficiency of the former is greater than one million times. This is impressive when man–machine media are contrasted to one another, but not when compared to the efficiency of natural systems. The human retina can see more than a matrix of 100×100 spots, which can form 10^{3000} patterns.

Information measures are so vital to every enterprise because, among their other assets, they can be used to evaluate the efficiency of most organizational processes, since organization is based on the pattern of its parts. Disorder and disorganization mean lack of patterning or entropy, which is increasing as orderly information and organization increase. Shannon and Wiener brought attention to the fact that the statistical measure for the negative of entropy (negentropy) is the same as that of information and that a system tends to increase in entropy over time as its level of organization decreases.

The most effective way to look at storage capacity is through a systems approach that includes channel input–output capabilities, as well as the information requirements of the business enterprises served through this input, storage, and output aggregate. This is true of both natural and man-made systems. As Figure 10.1 explains, the more complex an entity is, the lower its saturation point — the blocking factor of its input–output devices. Input, throughput, and output must be balanced in terms of channel capacity. Data storage needs to be managed to increase its efficiency and dependability.

This is generally not difficult to do even if companies fail to pay it attention. The most effective database solutions, however, must be customized, for instance, for new product development reasons. Products and services offered to the market which are too much "me too" should not interest the firm because there is no value-differentiation in them.

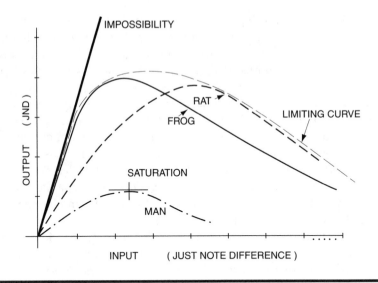

Figure 10.1 The study of the input–output function is very important in information technology for optimization.

Leaders go for imaginative database management solutions; they dislike second class programs that follow the herd.

The knowledge underpinning the foregoing references is not new. What is new is that it finds its way into the design and use of database resources. Indeed, until the late 1970s data storage was managed along concepts developed for accounting machines and their punch-card-type storage. (This reference includes hierarchical and CODASYL database management systems [DBMSs].) Notions connected to database management changed for the better with relational DBMSs and got a major uplift with object-oriented solutions[2] and the use of knowledge engineering artifacts (see Chapter 9).

Object-oriented solutions brought along the notion of instantaneous hierarchies through inheritance of metalevels (higher up) and of metaphors. A metaphor is a paraphrase, or allegory, that both knowledge workers and computers can understand and therefore appreciate. If one changes the metaphor, the meaning communicated between human and machine will also change because one thing is linked to another as if it were that other thing. This sort of procedural linkage makes the process of using data resources much more flexible and adaptable to current needs; it also reduces the level of entropy.

One demonstration of the potential of metalevels concerns the personalization of a reporting scheme designed to convey, for instance, exposure and risk management results. This type of application must integrate knowledge from different sources with the user's viewpoint of looking at information for action to be taken for the control of risk.

This process must be effectively assisted by computers, for instance, agents acting as assistants to the user in establishing the procedure for retrieving information and personalizing the presentation of results. This does away with classical programming which is inflexible, error prone, time-consuming, and dependent on manually performed systems analysis. Basically, a metaphor obeys the principle of resemblance over time through symbolism, and is expressed by repetition despite disparity, which is the sense of recursion in language.

There are other definitions as well. To generate new propositions by recursion means to determine the new term from the old or, more precisely, from a higher up level, the meta. The meta is not a peer level, but provides guidance and control. In this sense it has been used in Chapter 9 in connection to knowledge engineering artifacts.

Anything below the level of metadata is derived data which follow a distribution and behave within conceptual limits — the confidence intervals. This is as true of database structure and utilization as it is of a company's organizational framework. These two notions are brought together in Figure 10.2, which shows three organizational levels; in each case the higher one is the meta of the lower.

The notion of perishable hierarchies outlined is particularly important in handling the evolving classes of long transactions and complex queries as well as their implications in database management.[3] Metalevel concepts

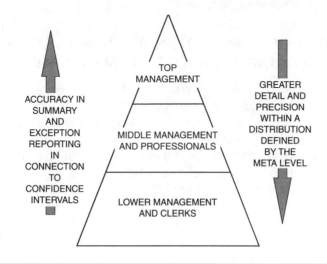

Figure 10.2   Metalevels exist in organization and structure and define the framework of information to be communicated.

also have to do with the definition and exploitation of patterns as well as of behavioral views, which are most important in a fast moving business world where market trends change rapidly.

The transformation of behavioral views by means of metaknowledge is important in engineering and in business. Companies that persist in using low level tools and other obsolete technology at their disposal forego business opportunities and lack needed on-line controls. They find by experience that it is very difficult if not outright impossible to assure that business transformations do indeed take place. As a result, people and companies who concentrate on looking at the past of database management approaches are stumbling backward into the future; the organization is missing the opportunity switch — paying the costs of technology but not reaping the benefits.

People and companies able to face the challenges of this decade and capture its opportunities appreciate the wisdom of interactive solutions that use expanding database bandwidth and permit quick visualization of results. The best strategy is a flexible, focused response, instead of following an old cookbook course of action.

Visualization is greatly assisted by classification[4] and, therefore, the metalevel structure. Whether in finance or manufacturing, knowledge workers often communicate important information by drawing and labeling diagrams that fit certain conceptual classes. Agent technology now makes it possible to communicate by employing graphical metaphors rather than using textual databases and their associated low-performance procedural programming languages.

THE SHIFT OF INFORMATION TECHNOLOGY SPENDING TO DATABASES AND THEIR MANAGEMENT

Today, much of corporate spending on Internet business projects is directed toward upgrading networks and databases to handle the flood of data, voice, and video coming across wired and wireless communications. For instance, spending on optical networking is projected to soar from $35 billion in 2000 to $90 billion or more in the 2003 to 2004 timeframe, while it is projected that Internet investments will go from $119 billion in 2000 to nearly $300 billion in 2003 to 2004.

In other words, in spite of the crisis faced by a number of organizations and, most particularly, by technology outfits in 2001, most companies expect to increase their computer hardware and software budgets. Hardware money, however, no longer favors computing. As Figure 10.3 shows, the emphasis is on storage. Companies used to spend about 25% of their hardware budgets on memory devices; however, that figure has risen to 50% and might hit 75% in 5 years.

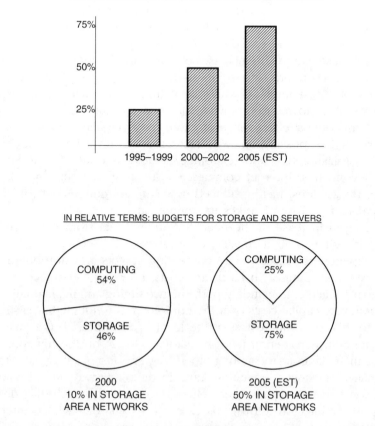

IN ABSOLUTE TERMS AS PERCENT OF BOUGHT HARDWARE

IN RELATIVE TERMS: BUDGETS FOR STORAGE AND SERVERS

Figure 10.3   The rapid growth in spending for computer storage.

This shift of investments from data processing to databases is significant because it identifies the collective wisdom of the markets. Figures from the U.S. Bureau of Labor Statistics (BLS) show that more than half of the productivity gains in 1995 to 1999 came from accelerated technological change. To a very large measure, in that timeframe investments went to computing, but, since 2000 they have moved out of computing and focus on optical networks, wireless communications, and terabyte (eventually petabyte) databases. (A petabyte is 1000 terabytes, or 1 million gigabytes.)

Many factors act together to change the way enterprise data storage is used. Fast growing databasing and datamining requirements, type of media used, database structure chosen, homogeneity and heterogeneity of recording and retrieval processes, and other choices made affect the cost-effectiveness of solutions adopted.

New types of available storage along with new concepts on how to manage our sprawling databases become mandatory. The crucial elements in these solutions, including new tools, form a frame of reference defined by reliability, cost, and speed of access.

As database bandwidth increases by leaps and bounds, speed of access deteriorates. Therefore, our solutions should evolve so that speed and accuracy of access improve while the volume of the database goes from hundreds of gigabytes to terabytes and then to petabytes.

In terms of cost-effectiveness, today's most popular storage media do not give the best possible answers. Here, too, change is important because many organizations are adding storage capacity at a rate of 30 to 80% per year. Beyond this, Internet commerce, with its global customer base of on-line transactions, has introduced new storage requirements, including bursty data streams and spikes in storage capacity.

The rapid increase in the need for on-line data storage ensures that capital investments in hardware for databases are between 50 and 75% of IT expenditures in corporate computing centers and distributed locations. Not everything is in hardware costs, however. Personnel costs for storage management, including performance tuning and maintaining backups, dominate capital costs over the equipment's useful lifetime. Estimates point to this recurring cost as at the level of $300 per Gb per year — a huge amount, considering talk of petabyte storage on the horizon.

The financial industry, among others, requires fast growing data storage capabilities. Financial operations are leading the way in this storage explosion because of the sheer volume of data with which they deal. In enterprise architecture terms, this calls for a backbone with greater reliability than that of storage components at user level platforms. Costs, however, can be staggering: $300 per Gb per year is comparable to and often exceeds the one-time capital cost of data storage; therefore, a new market has emerged for outsourcing data storage requirements to storage service providers. Coupled with continuing decline in the cost of storage capacity per bit of information, this prompted some analysts to predict that, in 5 years, the primary medium for storage backup will be on-line optical disks located on the other side of a scalable enterprise architecture. This will constitute the alter ego of the networked storage infrastructure (see the next section).

Not everybody is convinced that the best way route is to outsource data. Banks, in particular, like to keep confidential data in-house. The United Bank of Switzerland, for example, is establishing a storage-area network based on optical systems from Nortel. This campus network is projected to consolidate the bank's worldwide data centers into two sites in Zürich.[5] The UBS solution will be built around Nortel's OPTera 5200 multiservice platform, which offers 10 GBPS per optical channel and transmits any storage protocols.

In principle, optical interconnection of data centers should allow a system that gives fast provisioning. A crucial role, however, will be played by the architectural solution. The limits established by physical principles are generally not reached because the adopted solution incorporates blocking factors that keep the final result far below the real physical limit. What vendors and some of the user organizations expect is that networked storage will simplify database management by consolidating resources under a homogeneous interface that is increasingly Web-based and easy to use. This contrasts to traditional server solutions that are likely to contain unrelated hardware and software added and configured here and there by employing a variety of incompatible DBMSs.

It will take a few years to prove the soundness of this hypothesis. Based on reliability engineering,[6] the concept of a recentralized enterprise data storage architecture is unattractive because even short-term unavailability due to failure in software, hardware, or operations will be highly destabilizing to the whole company, its operations, and its business partners. No global enterprise can afford such a failure, even if it is short-lived. A key problem with all centralized solutions is that components probably have not been sufficiently tested together; the likely result is crashes or minicrashes. Furthermore the sharing of centralized data storage resources by many users at the same time, is anathema to efficiency.

The point to keep in mind with any system is its potential disadvantages, not only the rosy part of the long-term picture. Networked storage due to increased complexity of systems spread across an applications landscape has its problems, but it is more robust than centralized solutions. Also, while network protocol processing is more expensive than local hardware device access, distributed data integrity and privacy tend to be less vulnerable to unauthorized usage; the worst case is when intruders enter centralized data resources.

RAPID GROWTH IN DATA STORAGE CALLS FOR AN INTELLIGENT ENTERPRISE ARCHITECTURE

In the U.S., data storage needs are now growing at an impressive (and astonishing) annual rate. This 30 to 80% yearly increase snowballs into a problem for IT management at the typical company. Since 1999 a new company, StorageNetworks, has proposed to sell storage capacity to corporations. Is this sort of outsourcing the solution?

Its proponents say, "Why not?" They give as precedent the electric utilities, and explain that energy entrepreneurs convinced people and companies to abandon local electricity production schemes and rely instead on central stations and the power distribution network. From there, the pros suggest that, just like energy, data storage could (if not should) be outsourced to server farms — giant warehouses of information. These server farms would maintain large staffs of specialized data storage engineers, provide petabyte capabilities at a reasonable cost, and have high bandwidth connections to the Internet and other networks.

Some of the hypotheses underpinning this argument are acceptable. For instance, the collapsing cost of bandwidth makes it feasible to store data in offsite computers and to access them as needed. Also, information management is becoming more mission-critical and complex; therefore, it is best left in the hands of data storage specialists. In all likelihood, information utilities will benefit from economies of scale and, the pros say, they will offer economies of skill in a tight-high tech labor market.

Other arguments are shaky, for instance, guaranteed privacy and security, and the virus factor. There is no overriding reason why information utilities will be expert at guarding against viruses and hackers; everybody is exposed to them. Another senseless argument concerns unquestionable cost-effectiveness. It is not always cheaper to maintain and upgrade systems centralized in a huge data center and distribution costs impact the overall cost figure.

With such reservations kept in perspective, consider what a data storage utility might and might not offer. To start, databases have classically been a product that each company buys and manages for its own account, if for no other reason than because, as every manager should appreciate, data is a corporate resource and, to a substantial extent, it is confidential.

As an example, consider StorageNetwork's explanation of its idea of outsourcing part of a company's own databases. A user organization would pay about $50,000 per month for 1 Tb of storage space. This is the digital equivalent of 60,000 file cabinets. The customer's computer data would reside in one of StorageNetworks' 50 data centers in the U.S., each capable of storing 100 Tb. The customer could tap into the information instantaneously over a high-speed fiber-optic line between company offices and the nearest data facility.

The cost figures are not bad, but other key variables still have no quantitative answer. It is too early to say if the practice of storage as outsourced service will be catching up with user organizations. On the suppliers' side, however, established computer companies, such as Hewlett-Packard and IBM, are experimenting with similar offerings because they consider it an area of growth. In 2000, Dell Computers veered away from its dependence on PC sales to include servers in its product line.

Data storage outsourcing is not yet out of the woods; there is a huge issue of accountability. Whether a user organization's fast growing data storage requirements are served in-house or outsourced, its senior management cannot escape assuming direct personal responsibility, for instance, responsibility for privacy protection. There is always personal information in a great number of files.

Another part of the accountability information has to do with costs and performance. Costs matter; performance must be measured. This measurement can be done as accesses per second and response time, or megabytes per second and channel capacity.

Both need to scale with supported storage capacity to accommodate the increasing power and number of database machines, as well as the evolving nature of applications manipulating stored information. Today's complex transactions network information elements and they require more than an order of magnitude greater functionality than that demanded 10 years ago. As an example, Figure 10.4 presents, the key nodes of a transaction involving control of credit risk.

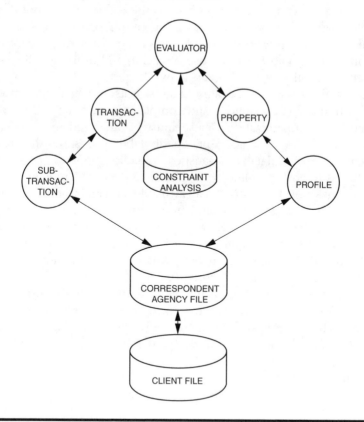

Figure 10.4   The analysis of transactions for credit risk requires access to different databases.

The increasing scale and scope of the use of storage media is largely driven by currently existing storage parameters and implementation mechanisms. These will most likely be stressed beyond their design goals as new, more sophisticated applications are taken on. Database management systems designed to meet evolving requirements will likely be structured around answers they should provide to critical architectural questions:

- What are the limits of projected storage?
- How many network crossings per type and frequency of information element are required?
- What are the bottlenecks and potential bottlenecks of the existing storage solution per application?
- Should control and data travel the same path? What about clustering, redundancies, and other criteria?

Few answers can be given *a priori* to these queries without thorough experimentation and the use of an intelligent infrastructure defined by the architecture. The enterprise architecture can make a major contribution as smart nodes, smart lines, the use of cache, and distributability become basic characteristics of the storage network.

One of the reasons meditating against outsourcing is that more and more ad hoc analytical queries and complex transactions will need to be handled by the organization. These must be analyzed in connection to users' networks. A new concept, distributability, ensures that real-time interactive access to databases satisfies nomadic computing requirements.

Because Internet commerce is global and very competitive, remote access to data must be continuously available, and all information elements must have remote copies updated frequently to protect against regional disasters. Whether in-house or outsourced, database management should benefit from timely, accurate statistics. An intelligent infrastructure will include knowledge banks of agents which operate at links and nodes according to the schema in Figure 10.5.

Within this environment, an integral part of control action is to keep activity statistics which permit dimensioning the network and storage supports. This is crucial for channel capacity and storage availability. Remember that the Internet's infrastructure bandwidth is growing at an estimated 300% per year.

An interesting insight regarding future architectural solutions is that vendors of cashing technology are repositioning themselves to market their products and services directly to Internet commerce companies and corporations hungry for faster delivery of their multimedia information. While caching was once seen primarily as a means to conserve bandwidth

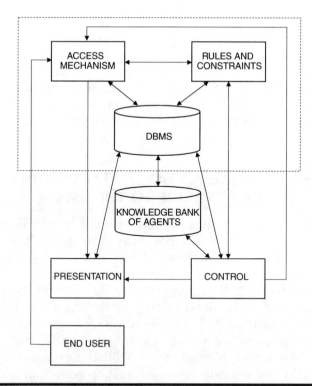

Figure 10.5   An intelligent access and control mechanism must reside at all nodes of the distributed data storage.

in corporate networks, it has now developed into a way to service architectural objectives.

The points raised in this section demonstrate that many of the characteristics assumed by the enterprise architecture, and the grand design of its storage system, are driven by market factors, particularly, the business-to-business market and the implementation and content delivery as a service to business partners and retail clients. To a significant extent, this evolution helps to define the intelligence to be embedded into the system beginning with the drafting board, attributes associated with stored objects and permissions to use these objects, and performance goals, trigger backups, shared access viewpoints, locks, leases, and other administrative chores.

In terms of data storage management, attention must be paid to the number of network crossings, the nature of client-based file systems (including metadata), and the fact that controllers can become a bottleneck because today's disks move data in a way which was not designed for tomorrow's applications. Designers need to parallelize the control component in a coordinated, balanced manner at the enterprise architecture level.

Rethinking the enterprise architecture for data storage reasons means that some of the notions concerning client servers will need to be reexamined. An example is the small local storage (other than caching) that depends on a big regional center for backup and control. Although this solution has served in the past, it is no longer valid because of cost of downloading and uploading, but primarily for security reasons.

WHAT ON-LINE, AD HOC DATABASE MINING CAN PROVIDE TO THE USER

The concept of database mining, and the service to be provided by agents, was discussed in Chapter 9. The possibility of analyzing huge databases and oncoming datastreams with the objective of drawing conclusions is a new opportunity due to the power of computers, heuristic models, algorithms, and knowledge engineering. At the roots of the problem is semantics, as well as the kind of hypothesis which can help in data interpretation, classification, and construction of causal relations.

Tentative statements, or hypotheses, are increasingly used in business and industry. They are particularly needed if data are not sufficiently crisp, which is usually true in a multidimensional event space. Supported through appropriate tools, the mining of large databases can help make entirely new discoveries possible by looking for collections of different observations made at different times and patterns in transactional data or incoming information streams.

This statement is true not only in business but also in age-old branches of science, for instance, astronomy. In a way, it is no longer necessary for an astronomer to actually make observations on the fly. He can collect large amounts of data to be exploited for analytical reasons through a growing array of powerful analytical tools. Through datamining and analytics, the astronomer is able to look at the whole sky over significant time intervals, studying data collected over a period of several years or decades. Rich databases constitute a virtual observatory shared by astronomers, which ensures no duplication of effort and no shortage of raw material from which to reach research results.

The Hubble Space Telescope alone produces 2 billion bytes per day; the European virtual observatory is enriched with 7 trillion bytes of data gathered by the Hubble and several large, ground-based telescopes operated by the European Southern Observatory (ESO) in Chile. The database, stored at ESO's headquarters in Garching, Germany, is growing by 4.5 terabytes a year and is expected to swell to 100 terabytes by 2005 — not far from the petabyte mentioned in the second section.[7]

In finance, too, databases have become virtual repositories of behavioral patterns, in a practice known as service observing. Rich databases are important, but size can be nearly meaningless when considered independently of other crucial factors which permit one to exploit stored information elements. The size of a database, for example, should not obscure the need for data interpretation parameters and their details, and availability of analytical tools, as well as experience in using them.

Security is another crucial implementation parameter. It is a subject bound to become more important with time because of increasing risk of unauthorized access to storage. Security is a critical data storage property which should be at top of database resource consolidation, rapid deployment, real-time management, dependable backup, and effective access mechanisms.

Beyond security, two other implementation parameters help in making the access mechanism more effective. One of them is agents used at the nodes; the other is parallelism. Figure 10.6 comes from a financial application and is a real-life case which used a parallel computer to speed up response time in connection with a large scale database. Parallel search processes helped to reduce access time by more than one order of magnitude.

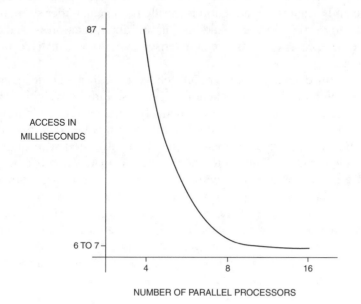

Figure 10.6 Company, market, currency, and share queries over a stable database.

Rapid database access is important for competitive reasons and for personal productivity purposes. Also, the architecture of complex systems has too many layers hiding low-level detail and adding numerous interference effects in database searches. This significantly increases response time visible by end users, and the task of understanding and predicting system behavior.

System performance is not the sole reason for failures in projected database solutions, but it is an issue to be considered as early as possible in the design process. Preoccupation with system performance should be one of the basic aspects of every enterprise architecture. The downside of new advancements is that, as technology grows more complex, prediction of performance is very sparse, with few concrete details available. Yet these details provide a useful insight on what can be expected from database mining and give some architectural guidance on how to obtain the fastest possible response time.

A most critical element in datamining is the algorithms and heuristics used. Abductive reasoning is a good example, starting with hypotheses and estimates regarding chosen characteristics. Mining conducted in large databases also requires a certain level of aggregation, but this raises questions about interaction and interpretation of results connected to database searches. As Dr. Tibor Vamos of the Hungarian Academy of Science aptly suggests, interaction is mostly nonlinear, either strengthening the resulting estimation or weakening it, and interpretation is challenging because the presence of two characteristic symptoms can have different meanings.

Experts in database optimization believe that, in a significant number of cases, the influence of interaction is expressed in the weighing of data, where information elements are alternatively considered to be independent from or dependent on others. Another interaction issue is the hypothetical distribution of the fuzzy estimates very often associated with queries.

The elements to which reference has been made in preceding paragraphs are present not only with ad hoc queries, but also with settled procedures such as daily reconciliations of accounts. According to Dr. Susanne Brandenberger of the Swiss Federal Banking Commission, "The daily reconciliation is difficult because of the heterogeneous information used by the banks. Different machines treat in different ways the various sets of data — and often in terms of management information nobody knows what are the right data. It's a puzzle."

This puzzle, however, does not discourage the use of database mining as a strategic tool. For example, retailers are using their customer base in a proactive way. Marks & Spencer, a merchandiser, mines its databases to sell financial products like life insurance, market funds, and pension funds. By exploiting their databases, insurance companies also come into the banking market opening up deposits facilities. Significant information can be provided through datamining, using data resources to further business aims.

THE ROLE OF A CORPORATE MEMORY FACILITY IN KNOWLEDGE MANAGEMENT

Storage systems are becoming a dominant type of investment in corporate information technology. They are also a critical asset in Internet commerce, thus making the rate of growth of databases a strategic business issue as well as an opportunity for storage vendors. Managing data storage farms, however, is only a small part of the challenge. The modern company needs solutions able to consolidate its information resources and deploy them quickly to help its operations, make these resources dependable and highly available, and develop imaginative database solutions ahead of its competitors. It should be possible to distribute database resources in a dependable manner over global distances and ensure that they are secure against external and internal threats. The company also should provide its managers, professionals, and other employees, with a multiplicity of supports, one of which is traceability.

Traceability is a new term identifying the ability to look back into past management decisions, and perform postmortems. The need to look back into past events, decisions, and commitments, as well as the way decisions were executed, led to the institution of knowledge management. As always, leading organizations have taken the initiative. A 2000 Conference Board survey of 200 executives at 158 large multinationals found that 80% of companies participating in the study had knowledge management projects in the works, and many had already appointed a chief knowledge officer (CKO) or hired knowledge management consultants.

One of the most important knowledge management projects is that of a corporate memory facility (CMF), into which are registered all decisions as well as their reasons and aftermath. Their registration, along with the identification of persons responsible for a decision and its execution, is vital to making any meaningful postmortem. Other CMF residents are expert systems and agents specifically designed for decision support.

This reference points out that top-tier companies are working steadily to improve their tools for knowledge management. Apart from databasing their decisions and their aftermaths, they use stochastic processes, tests of hypotheses, and experimental designs. They also tune their traceability methods and tools to provide interactive support for end user's viewpoint in terms of how technology is employed. In the bottom line, end users want some relatively simple questions to be answered:

- What is available to me?
- Where is it located?
- How can I access it?
- How can I get meaning out of it?

Serving the end user from the triple perspective of information, knowledge, and postmortems is very important because the company's business success, growth, productivity, profitability, and survival depends on shared knowledge. That is one reason why one exchanges information and know-how. Yet, few organizations conduct fundamental studies to establish how they can capitalize on a store of knowledge. Xerox is one of the few and has found that 46% of corporate knowledge is captured by documents in paper form.

The problem is that this knowledge is very difficult to exploit. Typically, it is scattered all over the firm and often time-consuming to find and even outright impossible to use to help make factual and documented decisions by gaining insight over events of the past. In the heads of individual employees, 42% of corporate knowledge resides. This knowledge is inaccessible to their colleagues and will leave organizations as these people change employment or retire. Under current conditions, such knowledge cannot be recovered; precious assets are simply lost unless they have been captured through knowledge engineering and mapped into expert systems. However, only 12% of a company's knowledge is captured in an electronic knowledge base that can be shared.

Today, the majority of this 12% is handled through expert systems and other knowledge artifacts, but only by the best-managed companies. This practice is destined to grow over the coming years at least among those firms who take seriously the issue of safekeeping precious corporate resources in know-how. Furthermore, while the knowledge base of an organization was once thought to represent mainly scientific, engineering, financial, and trading experience, it now increasingly involves interdisciplinary management decisions on a wide variety of topics.

Companies with experience in implementation of a corporate memory facility and traceability suggest that some of the topics stored in the corporate memory facility be recurrent. This ensures that development and use of knowledge artifacts is critical to accessing knowledge when, where, and how it is needed. The able employment of CMF requires agents along the lines discussed in detail in Chapter 9.

Another major change in the corporate landscape is the analysis of stored information. This process becomes increasingly complex as one deals with massive data sets. The point has already been made that effective use of company power requires the ability to exploit terabyte data storage. This brings into the picture the need for powerful algorithms and heuristics able to assist in managing massive data sets and getting meaning out of the information they contain.

For instance, AT&T holds massive data sets that keep track of billing information for 250 million calls each day. This results in 18 petabytes of billing data per year — an unprecedented storage capacity. Such colossal database requirements are not characteristic of all industries, but the trend points that way. After all, only 10 years ago terabyte storage was the reserved area of only some big banks, while today it is becoming fairly common.

Advances in Internet infrastructure, Internet commerce, distributed data storage, datamining, and the implementation of a corporate memory facility are connected. In many cases, careful analysis of information contained in massive data sets becomes an important requirement for business survival. Research now focuses on determining the diameter and the specifics of directed multigraphs, for example, the maximum intermediate acquaintances required to link any two phone numbers, any two business partners, any two traders, or any two credit risk profiles.

Another example is a directed multigraph concerning investment decisions, including diversification in currencies, diversification in market risk, credit risk safeguards, evaluation of alternatives, observance of all necessary investment conditions and constraints, analysis of prices, and other considerations. For instance, investment decisions in a transborder setting will typically involve volatility of currencies and equities and credit risk associated to bonds.

Figure 10.7 presents as an example the framework of holding short and long positions in currency exchange. The block diagram maps the way that the trader's mind works. Traders often act on the basis of their hypotheses on which way the market will move. A corporate memory facility, at trader level, helps in documenting how right or wrong these hypotheses have been, and the frequency of each right or wrong guess. It can also serve most effectively as a training tool.

In conclusion, a directed graph can represent practically any kinds of complex interaction schemes, linking nodes, and algorithms represented by behavioral patterns of trunks and pivot points in the graph. All these may be dynamically changing. Analytical results by tier-1 companies show that complex pattern analysis will replace correlation coefficients in environments rich in nonlinearities and other complex conditions where linear models are no longer useful or even outright misleading.[8]

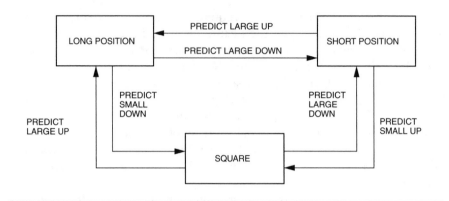

Figure 10.7 A framework of short- and long-trading decisions in currency exchange.

PRACTICAL EXAMPLE OF CMF: A PROJECT REPOSITORY BY XEROX

The previous section used trading in currency exchange as an example in which a corporate memory facility can be of service. Another practical case is that of a project repository, the managed archive of documents vital to a given project. To appreciate this example, consider a document as multimedia information stored for human and machine comprehension. Current and past versions of documents connected to a project are important to the firm; therefore, they should be stored in the repository. This computer-based archiving should be secure, updateable, protected against corruption, easily accessible, and effectively exploitable.

Many different document types make up a project repository, for instance, engineering drawings, specifications, tolerances, and commentaries. There may also be software development references including: functional requirements; project plans; design characteristics; alterations and their reasons; results of design reviews; timetables and their observance; source code; project tracking references, etc. Every repository should be organized so that datamining provides meaningful results. One approach to organization is that each project within, for example, the software development framework has its own repository, while all software development groups hold in a special file common routines to avoid redundancy of effort.

Here is a practical example. Xerox PARC put up a project repositiory initiative in 1997. Originally, the whole software repository effort was organized in a way to make exchange of information possible through e-mail. This worked up to a point, but more was needed in interactivity, so Xerox transited to a Web-based project repository. With this solution, messages reference universal resource locators (URLs) that contain the documents of interest. This approach to identification makes gaining better control over the contents of the project repository possible.

One of the improvements characterizing the Xerox project has been that, while with e-mail notification is "pushed," the content is "pulled" from the Web. This approach also permitted context-setting explanations to be separated from the document, while making it feasible to centralize version control and configuration management at the Web site.

In their article in the *Communications of the ACM*,[9] Rein, McCue, and Slein advised that this project repository application by Xerox also exposed a number of shortcomings of the Web, particularly those inhibiting the ability to support group work as originally intended by the implementers. For instance, the Xerox PARC researchers say that, while current Web facilities do a good job of supporting writers and readers for the project repository, the collection manager's functions are not so well handled. Therefore, they advise that, if Web technology is used to support the collection manager role, it is important to understand and describe the facilities such a role requires by way of support.

Group work applications pose many challenging requirements that go beyond e-mail-type usage. To effectively help in project repositories, Xerox suggests, the Web infrastrucure must be extended to address document management requirements, which are more sophisticated than what is supported today.

In the mid 1970s the University of Michigan advanced and made available to the IT market the concept of a development database, in connection to project PSL/PSA, the functions supported were essentially those that, today, are proper to writers and readers. The collection manager's functions were not then born; today, however, they are seen as vital. These functions include selective viewing, versioning, locks and other security, and administration proper.

Visualization is significantly improved through classification, but not all companies care to do classification studies.[10] Other developments, too, are important. Selective viewing increasingly involves three-dimensional structures, while versioning becomes more and more complex. Locks are necessary to make a document unavailable during editing.

In most applications, the solution given to security can make or break the repository effort. Basically, every solution must account for:

- Allowing universal access by authorized parties (people or machines)
- Making browsing headlines and contents of the repository easy
- Ensuring that adding, editing, and deleting objects is simple and straightforward
- Making it feasible to self-administer the repository.

REFERENCES

1. The MIT Report, February, 2001.
2. Chorafas, D.N. and Steinmann, H., *Object-Oriented Databases*, Prentice-Hall, Englewood Cliffs, NJ, 1993.
3. Chorafas, D.N., *Transaction Management*, Macmillan, London, 1998.
4. Chorafas, D.N., *Managing Operational Risk. Risk Reduction Strategies for Banks Post-Basle*, Lafferty, London and Dublin, 2000.
5. FibreSystems Europe, April, 2001.
6. Chorafas, D.N., *Statistical Processes and Reliability Engineering*, D. Van Nostrand Co., Princeton, NJ, 1960.
1. Economist, June 3, 2000.
8. Chorafas, D.N., *Chaos Theory in the Financial Markets*, Probus, Chicago, 1994.
9. Rein, G.L., McCue, L., and Slein, J.A., *Commn. ACM*, 40, 1997.
10. Chorafas, D.N., *Integrating ERP, Supply Chain Management and Smart Materials*, Auerbach/CRC Press, New York, 2001.

11

ADVANCED TECHNOLOGY AND ENGINEERING DESIGN MUST BE ON A FAST TRACK

INTRODUCTION

Interactive computer aided design (CAD) developed during the 1970s.[1,2] The first practical implementation of the concept underpinning a corporate memory facility (CMF), discussed in Chapter 10, took place with CAD and with computer aided manufacturing (CAM). Another notable application of CMF from about the same timeframe is computer aided software engineering (CASE). While today CMF is closely linked to management decisions and the tracking of transactions, it is important to note that its implementation capitalized on these previous experiences.

Cornerstone to computer aided design is the existence of an on-line engineering database featuring multimedia documentation.[3] This database must contain not only current designs but also past ones, their specifications, tolerances, and drawings. This helps both in terms of reference and in avoiding "reinventing the wheel." In its role as CMF, the engineering database is of major assistance to designers in deciding on the best way to go about their jobs.

CAD, CAM, CASE, and CMF are significant technological innovations, but although very important to competitiveness, technology alone is not enough. It is always necessary to know what one wishes to accomplish and how one is going to effect it. It has been possible to develop alternatives answering in the best possible way the needs of the company and its business partners — alternatives positioning the company ahead of its competitors. A combination of technological and economic conditions often oblige the company to change course, but if it is unsure of its goal, then any road will do.

The core of a best choice in engineering design, as well as in management at large, is the determination of the propriety of proposed action. Three principles must be satisfied. Is the project a logical or necessary one, considered as commercial venture? Has this project been properly developed technically in a satisfactory manner? Is this project the best course of action, considering the interests of the company as a whole? Other questions may also be important:

- What is the relative value of this project compared with other projects under consideration?
- How can it be justified from the standpoint of the return on the capital to be invested?
- How can it support the company and its competitive position in the increasingly global market?

At a time when innovation is king, the success of the enterprise architecture developed and used has a great deal to do with the answer to these queries and, therefore, to the support it provides to product and market innovation by the firm. Companies mistakenly fail to capitalize on high technology in order to maintain and improve their competitiveness. Another major error is that they are so preoccupied with what goes wrong that they let the weak divisions threaten the existence of the strong ones, while the strong ones are operated more for their own sake than the corporation's interest.

The result of no collaboration between divisions is fractal organizational solutions and bad luck. An effective collaboration cannot be assured only at the level of the executive committee, though this, too, is important; it must be established and maintained throughout engineering, manufacturing, and marketing.

To start, the information supported by the enterprise architecture should promote innovation — hence, the work of researchers, engineers, and analysts. It is true that innovation is 80% personal ingenuity and 20% information on competitive conditions and market demands. This 20%, however, is vital in steering the company's efforts. It is also important in suggesting the functionality the enterprise architecture should provide to the engineering design effort. Therefore, the following two sections give an appreciation of research and engineering and the way they can help the company's survival in a competitive market.

THE PACE FROM THEORETICAL DISCOVERY TO PRACTICAL APPLICATION ACCELERATES

It should be self-evident that significant benefits can be derived by developing a competitive technology. Research and development (R&D) teams are in a race to come up with the "new, new thing," and this diminishes the time available for deliverables. As Figure 11.1 suggests, the lead time from theoretical discovery to practical application has been shrinking for more than a century. Still, one cannot always predict which technology will eventually dominate.

This is in an epoch where fast technological evolution is nearly synonymous with growth and survival. The last 40 years have seen extraordinary developments in business and industry. The 18th and 19th centuries, too, were characterized by scientific breakthroughs, but the discovery of a scientific principle was left in the time closet for one or two generations prior to putting it to practical use. In that slow-moving environment, the incubation of an idea was done at a leisurely pace and marketability was no overriding concern. Today, the lead time from scientific discovery to its application has shrunk incredibly. An enterprise architecture worth its salt must bring together different disciplines in real-time.

Companies that attract investors' attention are those known as powerhouses of engineering excellence. When a country has several flagship companies at global scale and features a host of homegrown technology projects, it is at the top of the market's attention. Post World War II, this happened twice in the U.S. in the 1960s and in the 1990s.

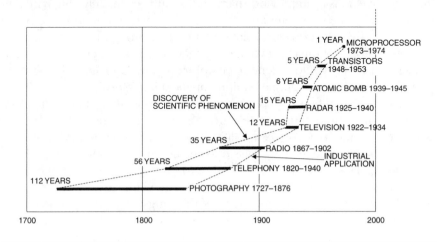

Figure 11.1 **Acceleration of the transition from discovery to practical application.**

Many inventions started with simple ideas and, until the industrialization of R&D, were largely the result of one man's efforts. The story of Thomas Edison is well known but other inventors, too, made contributions which became household items. By the end of the 19th century, Nicola Tesla had figured out how to send alternating current into two sets of coils wound on iron, setting up currents that were 90° out of phase with each other. Tesla's current generated a magnetic field that rotated with each successive burst of current, causing a copper disk to spin. When one put a belt on the disk, he had an electronic motor; the practical application of this invention revolutionized industry.

Many brilliant ideas are based on interdisciplinary observations. A transition occurring in several distinct steps from the ordered crystalline phase to the disordered liquid phase was first noted in a cholesterol-related substance by botanist F. Reinitzer in 1888. Then, the physicist O. Lehmann showed that these steps were thermodynamically distinct phases and named them liquid crystals.

Experimental investigations by Lehmann and mineralogist G. Friedel, together with the theory of liquid crystals presented by the physicist C.-W. Oseen, formed the scientific bases of this new field of research. In the 1950s further progress was made in understanding liquid crystals by F.C. Frank and others. Since mid 1960 the entire theoretical and experimental development has been influenced by Pierre-Gilles de Gennes,[4] who was awarded the Nobel Prize for his work.

Vacuum tubes that served in World War I and World War II also propelled the nascent radio and television broadcasting industries, the recording industry, live music amplifying, ham radio, and, eventually, high fidelity recording. Hundreds of companies sprang up to make tubes and tube-based gear — the first electronics revolution to sweep through the market.

This analog (not digital) revolution flowered in 1911 when Lee DeForest, a scientist in a Palo Alto federal telegraph company laboratory, hooked up a vacuum tube to some phone equipment and a loud-speaker and produced electronically amplified sound. DeForest's invention was dubbed a *triode* because it had three parts: two electrodes, one of them heated, and a tiny grid between them, acting as amplifier but working only in a vacuum.

Other developments were mission-specific. In the 1950s, General Electric research laboratories got the mission to build tiny, powerful lights that could fit within the razorlike wing tips of supersonic aircraft. Researchers first tried increasing the temperature of the tungsten filament to boost its light output, but the tungsten metal quickly evaporated, causing the filament to break. Then somebody got the idea that, rather than filling the bulb with an inert gas, it might be better to use a highly reactive element, iodine. This led to the development of halogen lamps, named after the type of gas that fills the lamp's interior, which is usually iodine or bromine.

The transistor was invented in 1947 at Bell Telephone Laboratories. Triodes, transistors, liquid crystals, halogen lamps, and electric motors have been the new, new things of their time. Were they inevitable developments or was their invention a matter of chance, a sort of lucky strike? This is a tough question, but, most likely their discovery would have eventually happened. What is less sure is the result of their industrialization, particularly their explosive usage.

While silicon physics and chemistry offered many convenient properties that influenced invention somewhat, development of transistor applications might have been much slower and a great deal more expensive if they were not greatly aided by the unique interdisciplinary culture at Bell Labs. This provided a combination of people and resources that could simultaneously tackle physics, chemistry, and engineering.

Business policy, too, played a determinant role. Another key factor to the success of the transistor has been the policy by Bell Labs to openly license its technology on very reasonable terms. This way, companies who wanted to use the new technology avoided the need for their people to work out all challenges from scratch while rising competition drove down the price.

Industry experts now think that, if this far-reaching marketing decision had not been made by Bell Labs, solid-state circuits might still be very expensive, reserved for military products and specialized, high-priced industrial applications. By giving up a potential monopoly on their new technology, the Bell Lab unleashed an evolution that changed the world.

The new, new thing is not free, but companies developing it are free to use their imagination on how to promote it, taking the fruit of their intellectual work and moving it into the hands of competitors to broaden the market. Examples from the 1990s are Netscape and Linus; they put their own software developments on the Net as gifts to the community, betting that what they designed would become a standard. An imaginative marketing strategy pays dividends because, as the pace of practical applications accelerates, companies are in a race to catch the eye of the global market. An aftermath of this policy is that engineering design and marketing skills merge. They must work in synergy or the product will fail.

In conclusion, the time is gone when engineers could design a new product at their leisurely pace, following their standards, and using their experience without paying too much attention to when or how it would be marketed. The first lesson to learn from the cutting edge of technology is that marketing has the high ground and, as the pace from theoretical discovery to practical applications accelerates, the enterprise architecture must efficiently link the company's engineering and marketing skills.

THE PIVOTAL POINT OF CONCURRENT ENGINEERING IS EFFECTIVE COMMUNICATIONS

Looking some years ahead while accounting for the way technology is progressing one could say that concurrent engineering and the Internet have several things in common (see also Chapter 12 to move beyond the communications perspective). Among the larger firms, the evolving fractal structure of manufacturing is one of the reasons for this; smaller businesses are also turning to the Internet to help them grow and compete.

With 200 employees, Sumerset Houseboats is not a big company by present day standards, but it is the world's oldest and largest manufacturer of houseboats sold around the globe. For years, Sumerset relied on periodic mailings and phone calls to keep clients updated on the progress of their orders. This was a slow ineffective method. Often the customer would not see a boat until it was completely finished, at which time he or she might decide it was not what was wanted. Alternatively, customers might visit the company and see the boat late in its development and then try to make changes, which proved to be costly.

The Net has now transformed the way Sumerset Houseboats communicates. The Internet connection allows its customers to view boat concepts on-line and, up to a point, design their boats in collaboration with company engineers. This is a major advancement in client relations and a good example of concurrent engineering. Customers can also watch the progress of their orders by viewing digital photos on the Internet.

Not every company appreciates the need for effective communications early in the product cycle, which is a mistake. Effective communications magnify the impact of technology on products and their marketing, creating the solution space identified in Figure 11.2. Effective communications for engineering and manufacturing purposes through the Internet have saved Sumerset Houseboats and its clients thousands of dollars in travel and other expenses and prevented many costly last-minute changes. Sumerset says that use of the Internet assisted in expanding its business into new markets and increasing the sale of profitable boating accessories. As a result, it has doubled its business activity in just 2 years, while the convenience of the Internet has improved relationships with its customers, thus substantially increasing its repeat business. Never underestimate the effect of the supply chain. As more and more small businesses embrace the Internet, some of their suppliers are ready to help.

The use of metrics is recommended. Cisco, for instance, has developed a qualitative tool for companies of all sizes, called the Internet Quotient. Its goal is to measure an industrial firm's potential to use the Internet in its business. By taking the Internet Quotient test, the management of a

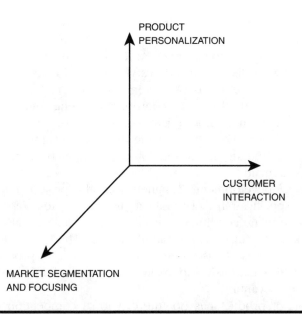

Figure 11.2 The impact of technology on engineering products and their marketing.

company can gauge its readiness and ability to operate in the Internet economy so as to offer its firm competitive advantages.

As these examples demonstrate, the end-to-end solution adopted in concurrent engineering must accommodate heterogeneous software products and tools written in different programming languages. It must also cope with incompatible hardware platforms, while at the same time making technical details that do not directly concern the end user. The idea of concurrent engineering is simple: fundamentally, it is about getting people from different disciplines, different divisions, and different companies to work in tandem to design a new product, develop its manufacturing processes, and promote its appeal and marketability.

The rewards for adopting on-line concurrent solutions go beyond reduced lead times and costs, and increased quality. Concurrent engineering is a frame of mind which should make it natural that people from many disciplines work together to solve a common problem by storing and manipulating original specs as well as subsequent versions of data objects, making multimedia data representations and analyses, and proceeding with very flexible, cost-effective solutions whose market appeal is tested early in the design cycle.

Concurrent engineering can offer wide benefits because every company, every industry and the economy as a whole need advanced engineering, with dependable and efficient deliverables responsive to market needs, and quickly delivered to the market. Advanced engineering results will not come from mediocre minds, however. As Alfred P. Sloan, Jr., stated, "Advanced engineering always, like advanced everything else, brings down upon it the discredit of ridicule of minds who cannot see so far."[5]

For this reason, the Internet's contribution to engineering, manufacturing, and marketing must not be just words but acts demonstrated in such a way that the elements characterizing them are accepted by the market. The market is tough; therefore, consider the facts in the concurrent engineering domain.

In product development, designers typically project a new product, develop its specifications, elaborate its tolerances, test a prototype, and then pass it to manufacturing to construct. The usual case is that designers are not asking for input from manufacturing. This is serial engineering which, as thousands of cases demonstrate, can lead to products too slow to produce, too expensive to make, and of doubtful quality because coordination is wanting.

This sort of product has no future. Global competition ensures that practically no manufacturer can afford to operate in this manner and stay in business. The pressures to be first to market with a product that satisfies customers' requirements on novelty, cost, quality, and reliability are far too great. Precisely for these reasons, concurrent engineering has evolved as the solution — indeed, the means of managing product and process development. At its core is a multidiscipline team with huge multimedia communications requirements to be satisfied by the enterprise architecture.

Several studies have highlighted the main problems associated with adoption of concurrent engineering as the better alternative to the old entrenched company culture and the walls built over the years by departmentalization. These problems are not unique to a certain company, but are general, constituting barriers to change in any walk of life and in any line of business.

In his book Sloan gives a great example of the lessons learned in the 1920s regarding the need for collaboration between different labs for the copper-cooled engine — a project which finally failed. But even a project that does not succeed teaches something. "The significant influence of the copper-cooled engine was in what it taught about the value of organized cooperation in engineering," as Sloan puts it. "It showed the need to make an effective distinction between ... advanced product engineering and long-range research."[5]

The copper-cooled engine proved, more than anything else, that management needed to subscribe to, and live with, firm policies of organization and of cooperative business initiatives. While the copper-cooled car just died out, it left a legacy from which every company will do well to learn in order to avoid repeating the same mistakes.

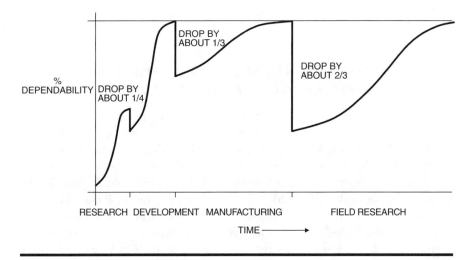

Figure 11.3 The old ways of working in airtight departments of research, development, manufacturing, and field service is detrimental to overall dependability.

The old way of working in closed, airtight departments of research, development, manufacturing, and field service is highly detrimental to the dependability of the product. The result is that quality suffers while costs skyrocket. The graph in Figure 11.3 is based on a transition between labs and the field with three different computer manufacturers: Bull General Electric, Olivetti Electronica, and Univac. This transition concerns research to development, development to manufacturing, and manufacturing to field services.

- When a project passes from research to development, a new team takes over and about one quarter of the project's storage of knowledge is lost or altered.
- This loss increases to one third of the accumulated knowledge in the transition from development to manufacturing. Changes necessary for manufacturing engineering are one of the reasons.
- The greater loss in gained insight and experience happens when the product, for instance a new computer, moves out to the field. Maintenance engineers are widely distributed and must start from scratch gaining expertise with the new product.

The problems come from the fact that coordination between these four major divisions (from research to field service) has been wanting. Yet such coordination should characterize every new project from the very start. Practically every firm has its own way of looking at concurrent engineering, but close collaboration presents advantages because it provides milestone references that make product planning and management so much more effective.

CONCURRENT ENGINEERING AND THE PERFORMANCE OF DESIGN REVIEWS

Modeling is one of the processes which often requires team effort. Because of the need to share files and results, it is important that each member of the research and design team see the models and constructs of the other partners, and do so while working in his or her own domain. To answer this dual requirement, a research team from Keio University, in Yokohama, Japan, designed a three-layered architecture highlighted in Figure 11.4.

In this paradigm, all information elements concerning a cooperative design are distributed and mapped into the common layer. Identification is milestone by milestone, as results become available. Visible to every user of a concurrent engineering team are his own level and the group level. Details existing at each individual level are available to review on a read-only basis. Since the common layer rests on distributed computing and databasing, for navigation purposes, the Yokohama researchers have

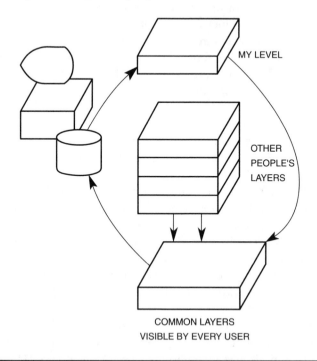

MY LEVEL

OTHER PEOPLE'S LAYERS

COMMON LAYERS
VISIBLE BY EVERY USER

Figure 11.4   A groupware architecture based on three reference layers.

adopted hypermedia. Each user can create his or her navigational views through the network. An asynchronous link is provided by means of e-mail and interpersonal memos using the Web.

Both analytics and optimization routines can be conducted on-line in cooperation between teams. Linear and nonlinear experimental approaches use an on-line library which includes functions for unconstrained and constrained minimization, maximization, multiobject, and semi-infinite manipulation.

Tools are provided for linear programming, quadratic programming, non-negative least squares, and the solution of nonlinear equations. Such tools aid in addressing complex design problems in order to improve cost, experiment on different solutions aimed at improving reliability, increase performance, and execute a range of other operations. Industrial engineering tools are available as well, and aim to promote collaboration between design and manufacturing early in the product cycle.

As this and other examples demonstrate, concurrent engineering solutions have prerequisites. On-line cooperation is necessary, whether for mechanical designs, electrical designs, electronics devices, or programming products. The crux of the matter is that different engineering disciplines must work together on the same project, using more closely knit approaches than those which were satisfactory in the past.

When the Ford Motor Company needed to coordinate design across three countries without driving up its costs, it established the required solution by networking its computer-aided design installations. This made it possible for engineers in the U.S., the U.K., and Germany to work together, through CAD, on products they were developing as if they were in the same location.

Typically, team members come from marketing, design, manufacturing, purchasing, the service department, clients, and suppliers. Once a virtual team is set up and an appropriate level of managerial control has been established, the work of product development is based on a seamless network supported through the enterprise architecture. The function of the teams working in concurrent engineering is two-fold: 1. developing an easy-to-make, reliable, maintainable, low-cost, and commercially viable product, and 2. getting things right, either the first time or through rapid iteration, by allowing everyone involved to make his or her contribution.

Technology allows cooperation among researchers, engineers, marketing people, and other agents, but it is also necessary to build the organizational infrastructure and support systems which make such cooperation possible. Some of the prerequisites posed by concurrent engineering are not always easy to meet. The more difficult part is not technology but an organizational solution able to address all critical issues on priority bases.

According to reliable estimates, at least 85% of a product's life cycle cost is built into the initial product design. Leading companies are therefore addressing this challenge by radically changing the way in which their products are designed and tested. New directives require that research, engineering, manufacturing, marketing, and field service — departments concerned with the life cycle of the product — have their say early in the project. They must get involved from the start rather than when the product is about to go into production.

Because corrections as a new product advances in design lead to changes that are horrendously costly and time-consuming, well-managed companies ensure that every project is subject to regular design reviews. It is not enough that people in a concurrent engineering team are trying to work in parallel to save time. Their work must be supervised, evaluated, and controlled on regular basis and in an interdisciplinary manner, including evaluation from financial and cost-control viewpoints. Based on experience with review and evaluation of engineering projects, Figure 11.5 presents some important statistics on money and time embedded in product development. Typically, the first quarter of the time plan corresponds to about 5 to 10% of the overall cost; a quarter of the cost is invested halfway in the schedule, at about the 55% level in time. Then costs increase exponentially.

Concurrent engineering does not alleviate the need for design reviews; it reinforces it. Top-tier organizations distinguish between major and minor design reviews: the minor are frequent, for instance weekly, or every fortnight; the major are made at the time-and-cost milestone just mentioned; or, alternatively, because the findings of a minor design review are disquieting. Problems might concern slippages in time schedules, lack of quality, or cost overruns. Minor design reviews try to solve problems in an interdisciplinary manner. Major design reviews can kill a project because it is not performing.

If a project is indeed vital to the company, but does not perform well, it may be killed and reinstituted under new leadership. Otherwise, it is eliminated altogether. There are different reasons why a formerly valuable project no longer makes sense. A competitor may have decreamed the market, customer requirements might have changed, embedded costs may not have left enough margin for profits, or the company's strategy may have shifted focus.

In conclusion, design reviews help not only to put a project straight, but also to kill it if it overruns its budget, is behind schedule, or does not meet quality and novelty guidelines. It is much better to do away with a project when it has consumed 10 or 15% of its budget than to let it run without supervision and then kill it at the end, with great loss of time, misuse of human resources, and all or most of the money spent.

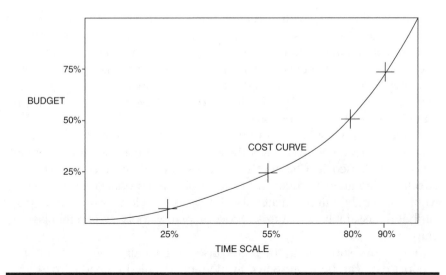

Figure 11.5   The need for design reviews is present in any project. Time and cost are not linearly related.

THE USE OF OBJECTS AND FRAMEWORKS IN ENGINEERING AND MANUFACTURING

Concurrent engineering requires agile and powerful tools. Given the modularity of solutions which it makes feasible, object-oriented approaches help in supporting the entire product life cycle. Because of this as well as efficiency and flexibility, object solutions have gained considerable attention during recent years.[6] Their implementation assists in diverse areas of endeavor:

- Product conception, definition, and modeling
- Product design, evaluation, and testing
- Process and materials planning
- Detailed production schedules
- Follow-up on rapid execution on the factory floor
- Effective internal controls, all the way from quality to costs

Because the able management of the product's life cycle requires group work for parallel product and process integration, the flexibility provided by object-oriented solutions is at a premium. A "must" is access to distributed and often heterogeneous databases, where object-oriented programming can be a major plus. A similar reference is valid in connection to the design and support of the enterprise architecture.

One of the goals with object-oriented approaches is automation of input and export of files, replacing flat files by a solution of cooperating multiuser structures. For instance, General Dynamics has developed an integrated bill of materials (BOM) approach which treats parts attributes, assembly structures, inventoried items, tools, specific references, and planning schedules as objects. The whole is amenable to graphical presentation (see the next section).

Critical to any solution supporting the supply chain in an able manner is seamless access to databases throughout the business partner organizations (discussed in Chapter 10). A consolidated product database can effectively integrate as engineered and as-planned product definition views within a single bill of materials. Information elements include parts attributes, assembly structures, process plans, tools requirements, and graphic designs.

The tools supporting the enterprise architecture must ensure that product data can be represented at the most detailed individual part level with aggregation of components into various assemblies. These assemblies are dynamically specified in verbal or graphical form by the user and often constitute instantaneous but perishable hierarchies. This can be achieved in concurrent engineering environments where design databases are global but information elements have locality.

Figure 11.6 emphasizes that a modern product design process consists of many components whose development must proceed interactively. Typically, this requires multimedia solutions and it also calls for a significant degree of knowledge engineering, as agents already play an important role in design, procurement, production, field maintenance, and other domains. (See also Chapter 9 for the role of agents in a communications environment.)

This is a far cry from the old approach still employed by many manufacturers, where bills of materials are handled off-line in batch mode, and parts are represented only by identification numbers, thus leading to overlaps, duplications, and other confusions. Object-oriented BOM solutions can be compiled on-line using meta and inheritance characteristics for interactive support, as is done with direct-oriented and knowledge engineering approaches.

High performance in the link between engineering, manufacturing, and field service requires going well beyond conventional tools and methods. This further underlines the need for object solutions. The chosen methodology should permit integration of product and process information within a single logical database that may be widely distributed and involve heterogeneous components. Seamless solutions help in improving configuration management, inventory optimization, and the bottom line in financial results.

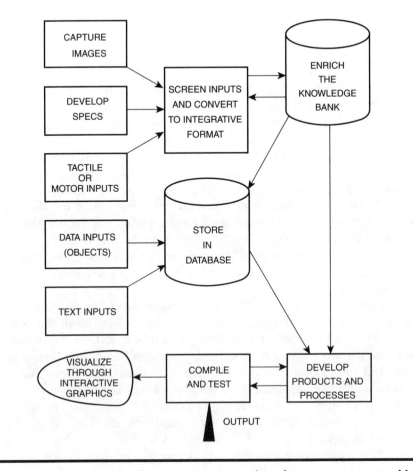

Figure 11.6 A product development process consists of many components which must work interactively.

One of the major problems with the integration of dynamic BOM and computer-aided design at large is that producers and consumers often use different representations for the same information elements. In the absence of a procedural interface standard, the needed integration generally requires development of separate interface software; this can be costly and inefficient.

One of the challenges encountered with Internet commerce and other on-line execution of orders between business partners is that routines are necessary to translate each producer's information elements into a form that can be used by other designers and manufacturing engineers because companies often employ incompatible models and identification numbers.[7] Hence, there is a need for a solution which can capably approach the issues of a common procedural interface, applicable in a cross-vendor sense, and flexible access to distributed databases, supported through object orientation.

Companies aware of this need have collaborated to develop the CAD framework initiative (CFI), which was established in 1988 to answer the requirement for a common procedural interface. As an independent industry effort, CFO promoted the standardization of interfaces between computer-aided design tools and software environments. A common name given to these constructs and their use is frameworks.

By employing the CFI procedural interface, a producer can develop software on time to allow different data representations to be generally accessible. Each business partner elaborates a single set of software to access these information elements, addressing through it the distributed database structure. There is no need for a separate translation step or for separate software to match each vendor's tools. Theoretically, such an initiative can save hundreds of development man-hours in the integration effort. Practically, however, solutions are not that simple for heterogeneous data structures.

Similarly, in regard to the issue of flexible access to distributed databases, an object-based approach is a big step forward from the conventional model of database transactions, which is based on the notions of serializability and atomicity. Legacy applications follow this line of reference and therefore are not appropriate for distributed, interactive engineering systems characterized by parallelism and concurrency.

In conclusion, a necessary ingredient for integrative environments involving several users engaged in concurrent activities is an object-oriented modeler for ease of handling, extensibility, and maintainability. A modular architecture allowing ease of integration among different applications is also necessary. The systems solution chosen for the enterprise architecture should provide superior speed and accuracy, hence the interest in more sophisticated software solutions than those so far available.

A HIGHER-LEVEL TECHNOLOGY FOR AN INTERDISCIPLINARY TEAM

Like computer integrated manufacturing (CIM), concurrent engineering cannot be attained through good will alone. It has to be supported through new tools like high performance computing, intelligent networks, knowledge engineering, distributed databases, and object-oriented solutions. Above all it has to be promoted by means of an appropriate methodology and a new engineering and management culture.

Provisions should be made as well for the migration of existing applications and their integration with the newly developed, more efficient systems. Among other services, this requires intelligent gateways that allow mapping between objects and relations that can capably serve a fully distributed environment characterized by temporal and spatial relationships, and design data involving a large number of data types.

Each of these data types may have a big or small number of instances, but all must be easily and effectively accessible. Schemas should be allowed to evolve constantly, while at the same time effectively handling transactions in design databases that tend to be of long duration. Versioning is crucial. The good news is that design data need not be duplicated at lower levels. This is a tremendous help in databasing and most particularly in datamining (see Chapter 10).

Apart from efficiency, timeliness, and quality of deliverables another reason why solutions fully distributed among business partners are crucial to concurrent engineering is that they promote end user programming. Visual programming and knowledge artifacts help in this direction. Interest in object-orientation comes from the fact that their embedded flexibility permits one to deal effectively with engineering and manufacturing complexity.

Another benefit of a distributed programming environment with professionals taking care of their wares is fast software development and reusability — both a "must" as competition intensifies. Conceiving, designing, manufacturing, and marketing first class products with global appeal requires precise coordination and integration of all resources available. Traditional software and database technology does not adequately deal with relatively short product life cycles, ephemeral partnerships in product development, and manufacturing processes which are farmed out. A distributed database environment and object database management systems are well suited to concurrently addressing: total quality perspectives, just-in-time inventories, flexible manufacturing cells, real-time process monitoring, and statistical quality control.

Object-oriented solutions permit the use of semantic reasoning, which assists many types of engineering work. When it comes to conformance to intended design characteristics, object technology and its methodology make performing means available for group work — a prerequisite to having an interdisciplinary team. The traditional design cycle must be changed to allow product and process development to take place in parallel, in order to exploit marketing opportunity better as well as timing, cost, and quality objectives, and to eliminate, or at least flush out, product and process incompatibilities leading to timing delays, cost overruns, and quality problems.

Companies that master concurrent engineering have developed a whole infrastructure to make it work. One of the means is the adoption of hybrid solutions that permit the use of powerful design shells without discarding old code, as Figure 11.7 suggests. Since the mid 1980s, knowledge

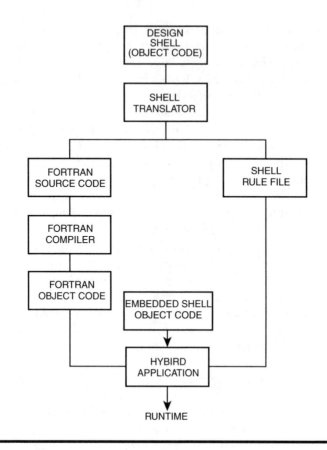

Figure 11.7 Effective use of hybrid systems increases productivity and avoids redundant effort.

engineering has also made a significant contribution.[8] A technology of high-level, editable representations introduced in CAD has become a major extension to solid modeling and feature-based design. Conceptually, this approach is analogous to high-level programming language.

The agent that interprets the editable representation plays the role of a geometry compiler, or an interpreter. It translates the editable shape representation through a sequence of geometric operations, which are carried out by an underlying modeler into a more traditional boundary representation. This increases designer productivity as it does away with the need to write executable machine language. Knowledge-based systems tend to make tough decisions easier, improve product quality and operating efficiency, and make feasible market-driven engineering solutions. Editable representations aim to fulfill design feature definitions extending solid-modeling technology to serve downstream applications in a way fairly independent of the specific modeler employed to create the geometry. Combined with a top-tier classification methodology, a higher level of abstraction provides editable archiving to leverage valuable design assets as families of future designs.[8]

Knowledge artifacts store rules that specify how to construct geometry as a function of parameters and constraints, rather than storing the geometry itself. This captures design intent and fulfills the prerequisites for the creation of design knowledge banks. The method also supports interoperability requirements and helps to optimize the design and manufacturing processes.

One of the advantages of this solution is that it assists in providing a standardized approach to communicate nongeometric attributes. It also helps to capture design intent as well as geometric information from different commercial modelers. In contrast, many proprietary CAD solutions fall short of fully addressing the needs for interoperability and editability even if they are advertised as "open." This handicaps the ability to shrink the time to market (see the next section).

Some engineering organizations that have effectively implemented knowledge-enabled approaches in conjunction with concurrent CAD applications report a reduction of product development time by 40 to 60%. Manufacturing costs are shrinking, the same firms suggest, by 30 to 40%. Furthermore, such reductions go hand-in-hand with improved quality as companies are able to perform model-based experimentation, including products and processes on which they operate, and network with clients and suppliers for real-time coordination of engineering and manufacturing efforts, and in response to new requests. These sort of highly competitive solutions are not the exclusive domain of one industry. Earth-imaging satellites, space probes, real-time simulation in finance, and medical imaging are four different domains where tremendous amounts of data need to be processed extensively to yield useful images, and then communicated through broadband networks for practical use.

Whether a company scans the earth for resources, designs complex machines and large scale systems, analyzes financials flows in the global market, or tracks down deadly tumors, it must have the models, computers, databases and networks available to permit meeting the challenge of the most demanding applications. This can only be achieved in an effective manner with high performance solutions integrated into a knowledge-enriched enterprise architecture.

FAST TIME-TO-MARKET SOLUTIONS FOR GREATER PROFITABILITY

When developing more competitive approaches, high performance computers and communications, as well as sophisticated software, are indivisible from one another, and the same is true of the overriding need for fast time-to-market deliverables. In any modern industry, continuously increasing novelty and complexity are accompanied by the competition for faster time to market. This is the way the global industry goes and it creates formidable challenges.

Many experts think that the driving force behind manufacturing activities is shifting from an emphasis on production to forces unleashed by the marketplace. To stay competitive in this market-driven environment, companies must be uniquely responsive to customer requests, delivering high-quality products at an affordable cost and doing so on time. Otherwise they are not able to maintain market leadership.

Research conducted in the late 1990s in the U.S., U.K., continental Europe, and Japan looked at the world's top manufacturing companies' cross-industry sectors. The senior management of these firms was asked to list its most important competitive priorities for the next 5 years. When the results were compiled, researchers found many similarities in the management thinking of these quite different firms, including product innovation, production costs, dependable delivery schedules, and reliability and quality. There were also two items stipulated only by those companies known to be the best managed among their peers: short development cycles and the ability to make rapid design changes.

Both of these characteristics fall under the fast time-to-market concept and the organizational culture which it involves. Among leading industrial firms, the entire way of operating, from support infrastructure to design, inventory management, and the factory system, is aimed at minimizing time to market. Senior management sets an objective to create an ever-changing stream of new products without upsetting the current production and distribution pattern.

Since the mid to late 1980s, the best managed companies have made time to market one of their most potent competitive weapons. This was one of the last major competitive advantages of Japanese companies prior to their downfall. Today there are impressive examples of firms around the globe that have succeeded in making time the dominant competitive factor. Other things equal, the most successful companies are those that learn to manage fast time to market as a most valuable factor, able to sustain market leadership. The key lies in the ability to use intelligence-enriched software to modify or add on features as defined by each customer, and to do so very quickly, through policies which permit the company to gain a competitive edge in time to market.

To a greater or lesser extent, supply chain management rests on these premises. By implementing its own virtual supply chain, Cisco reduced inventory levels by 45% in the 1995 to 2000 timeframe, and decreased the time to market for its products by as much as 12 weeks. Virtual manufacturing saves Cisco more than $175 million in annual operating costs and makes it possible to provide networking products through a quick reaction strategy.

In the New Economy, implementing an on-line, interactive supply chain system (see also Section III) is a vital element of business success. Therefore, is not surprising that, in the global market, companies are taking advantage of the Internet to create electronic marketplaces where business partners collaborate. In the bottom line, Internet commerce is a proxy for consumer spending. John Chambers, CEO of Cisco Systems, said that the Internet revolution will be over in a decade or two when all corporations become i-companies, completely incorporating the Net in their operations.[10]

The enabling mechanism of real-time handling of customers and suppliers is the culture necessary for rapid development. Once a technology has been brought from the lab, it must be engineered into a product and put into the hands of the sales force. As the preceding sections demonstrated, concurrent engineering improves materials, influences design, puts out an upgraded model, and permits the company to start work immediately on an even better product.

An ideal condition is, therefore, to allow information to flow quickly, easily, and accurately between everyone involved in a development project, regardless of location or the system solution used. Rapid any-to-any communications and data sharing bring people closer together, provided they are working with up-to-date, accurate information supported by the enterprise architecture.

The Internet is an excellent solution for data sharing, as it is for customer focus. Some experts believe that small businesses who use the Internet grow about 50% faster than those who do not. Sumerset Houseboats says that its market share grew by using the Internet and that its sales doubled and profits increased 30% in just 2 years.

Whether through the Internet or otherwise, concurrent marketing upholds the company's promises to deliver, manufacturing automation sees that this can be done at the least cost. Companies unable to work on this fast track find not one obstacle in their path, but many; they leave to competition the market's more lucrative business. Remember this when Chapters 12 to 15 speak of Internet applications.

REFERENCES

1. Chorafas, D.N., *Microprocessors for Management. CAD, CAM and Robotics*, Petrocelli Books, Princeton, NJ, 1982.
2. Chorafas, D.N., *Engineering Productivity Through CAD/CAM*, Butterworths, London and Boston, 1987.
3. Chorafas, D.N. and Legg, S.J., *The Engineering Database*, Butterworths, London and Boston, 1988.

4. de Gennes, P.-G., *The Physics of Liquid Crystals*, Clarendon Press, Oxford, 1974.

5. Sloan, A.P. Jr., *My Years With General Motors*, Pan Books, London, 1963.

6. Chorafas, D.N. and Steinmann, H., *Object-Oriented Databases*, Prentice-Hall, Englewood Cliffs, NJ, 1993.

7. Chorafas, D.N., *Managing Operational Risk. Risk Reduction Strategies for Banks Post-Basle*, Lafferty, London and Dublin, 2000.

8. Chorafas, D.N., *Expert Systems in Manufacturing*, Van Nostrand Reinhold, New York, 1992.

9. Chorafas, D.N., *Integrating ERP, Supply Chain Management and Smart Materials*, Auerbach/CRC Press, New York, 2001.

10. *BusinessWeek*, February 12, 2001.

III

IS THE INTERNET THE 21ST CENTURY'S ANSWER TO AN ENTERPRISE ARCHITECTURE?

12

THE INFORMATION ECONOMY AND THE INTERNET

INTRODUCTION

During the 1990s, the American economy restructured around the information technology industry. Today about 30% of the productivity and roughly one third of economic growth of the U.S. is in information technology and associated sectors of the economy. The Internet is taking an increasingly visible and leading position, particularly because of its potential in on-line commerce.

There are reasons for this development as well as its aftermath. One is the Internet's ability to connect business partners and other users any-to-any, at any time. Another is the effect of very efficient, off-the-shelf Web software. For nearly four decades the computer industry was unable to build software well within a reasonably short timeframe. Both private and commodity software often fail to reach their stated goals; such failures are time-consuming and very expensive.

The anticipated explosive growth of the Internet and its services over the coming decade should provide many benefits. Unfortunately, industry has largely fallen behind in its computing base. There are insufficient staff and trained professionals in the field, particularly so in the design, implementation, and maintenance of an enterprise architecture. Therefore, the Internet is seen by many as a way of breaking this bottleneck.

While the majority of companies using the Internet look primarily at how its contribution materially affects their current business, leaders focus on ways and means through which both the Net and its Web software can promote internal efficiency and market appeal of their organization and improve their capacity to perform and to obtain better results.

The layers of the enterprise architecture, policy formation, command and control, and infrastructural base, are in full evolution and require steady attention and the assignment of appropriate resources. Tier-1 companies actively search for effective solutions permitting them to restructure their information technology policies in a way commensurate with a highly competitive business environment. Their management believes that establishing a position of technology leadership is key to maintaining competitive advantages, and that opportunities for achieving major product and market breakthroughs through the Internet should not be allowed to dwindle.

The most clear-eyed companies do not want just an Internet experience. They want solutions promoting the skills of their people who know how to communicate and have a lot to say about procurement procedures and vendor selection, i.e., Internet commerce; (see Chapter 14).

To be an Internet player, it is not enough simply to have a Web site, but many companies deceive themselves by thinking so. As Figure 12.1 suggests, the worst strategy is "me too," only losses. Serious players choose one of three approaches to an Internet presence:

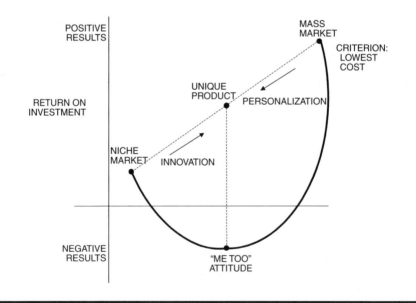

Figure 12.1   Good and bad strategies for being on the internet.

- A *niche*, where return on investment is not high but the solution is not that demanding either
- A *unique product*, which competition encourages as new entrants challenge those already present
- A *mass market*, Amazon.com-style, where competition is cut-throat and the lowest-cost distributor wins

A company may transit from niche to unique product through innovative products appealing to a wider public. It may move from mass market to unique product strategy through personalization of its wares, asking a premium for customization. However, it cannot avoid being proactive, or else it becomes "me too."

Financial analysts and industry surveys no longer ask whether a company uses computers in its daily operations. Instead, they ask about its stream of innovations and their timesaving applications. Increasingly, the answers reveal that a growing number of companies have ambitious blueprints in the works. The Internet, however, is only a catalyst. In every economy on the move, the moving gear is management strategy that looks at the future.

INTERNET ECONOMY AND RESPONSIBILITIES OF THE BOARD

Propelled by the strategy of companies able to read tomorrow's newspaper today, the Internet economy requires entire industries to reinvent themselves and refocus their activities. For instance, the convergence of data and voice networks has been instrumental in providing an industry consolidation, with both startups and leading telecommunications providers of old moving quickly into this lucrative integrated market.

The drive is to partner and acquire a position making it feasible to emerge as a leader in the new markets propelled by the Internet economy. Global markets, however, are tough. The Internet has given corporate America an incentive to fund new ways to save and, at the same time, significantly improve product quality. This can also result in a headache when the company falls behind the New Economy race because of an inappropriate business culture, deficient human resources, retrograde technology, etc.

The key word in this new environment is *change*. Whether smooth or of Herculean proportions, whether predictable or unpredictable, change is an appropriate metaphor for these times. Changes can be salutary and, as Voltaire's Dr. Panglos had it, they may represent the "best of possible worlds." However, one must be prepared for changes in order to reap benefits, because they affect the whole economy, impact many industrial sectors, make or break companies, and revamp personal careers.

Board members, CEOs, and other senior executives would do well to listen to the many experts who say that the transformation happening today in business and industry will usher in a new era in which the playing field will be greatly expanded, but at a different level from that of the existing one. In the course of this transformation, many competing firms will be merged into fewer and bigger ones which will look significantly alike.

An example is Citigroup, the product of the $70 billion merger of Citicorp and Travelers into a financial conglomerate empowering the company to take deposits, make loans, underwrite stocks, sell securities, sell insurance, and engage in a wide variety of other financial services. This is by no means an endpoint because the most important transformation currently taking place is not simply the integration of diverse financial players or other firms under one roof. It is the effect of the virtual industrial firm taking shape through the Internet. Therefore, the Internet has become a critical strategic factor for boardrooms, and directors must be Internet-literate to make meaningful decisions. Some analysts think that 10 years down the line there will be no Internet companies: in order to survive, all companies, whatever their business, will be Internet companies of some type.

A well-designed enterprise architecture enters into this discussion in many ways. Organizationally and structurally, it makes feasible a flat hierarchy that provides the large-group setting of business activities in a complex business entity. Individuals occupy roles that interinvolve one another on the Internet and its broadband successor; each speaks as an officer of an organization located anywhere in the world.

A successful enterprise architecture should rise to the level of policy formation, at the top of the management hierarchy, and introduce a structure of criteria and values kept dynamic at all times. In terms of policy, Internet-propagated information influences policy matters. System performance helps in setting direction, and evaluation of market changes becomes a basic element of operations at any time, for any product.

In a similar vein, the function performed by a modern, intelligence-enriched command and control system like the one in Chapter 7, makes corporate offices and their business or social tasks more efficient. This acts as a sympathetic nervous system and a blood circulation system, with functionality defined by class of actions.

In the background of this scenario lies the fact that fully on-line business represents a strategic inflection point for firms; it is already revolutionizing the way banking and commerce work. A company's survival now depends on how quickly it can adapt to the new culture and how well it can control its risks. Consider operational risk as an example.[1] Contrary to the simplistic approach in many books, this text analyzes operational risk into ten constituent parts:

1. Board (policy formation) risk
2. Command and control risk
3. Professional skill risk
4. Transaction risk
5. Fiduciary or trust risk
6. Payment and settlement risk
7. Back office risk
8. Security risk
9. Technology risk
10. Infrastructural risk

The first, second, and tenth of these risks correspond to the three main layers of the model presented on several occasions in Sections I and II. Five risks, from third to eighth, are details of the interfaces between the top layers of a managerial organization, while security (see Chapter 16) and technology risks interface between command and control and infrastructure.

Each one of these risks is a component of operational exposure and can be detailed with greater precision. Technology risks may be analyzed into risk of falling behind, return on investment, professional obsolescence, project management, slow time to market, vendor failure, network, database, software, quality control, and reliability.[2]

Reliability risk and the mismanagement of IT, which are widely diffused, correlate. Contrary to what mainframe proponents suggest, from an operations viewpoint monolithic centralized approaches are the least reliable. The better solution is a horizontally layered organization like the one shown on the right side of Figure 12.2. The telecommunications network may be theInternet, the entity's own private network, or both.

The board should appreciate that operational risk increases by the fact that business-to-business (B2B) electronic trading has more potential for transforming traditional commerce and bringing it to higher levels of efficiency than business-to-consumer (B2C) closes. According to some U.S. estimates, more than 85% of electronic purchases in 2000 were made by businesses. At the same time; the opportunity to deal with customers in an on-line channel is the most visible aspect of the much larger phenomenon that the Internet forces companies to rethink the way they inform, negotiate, and trade with each other.

Designers of enterprise architectures should appreciate that products and processes are affected by an acceleration in innovation. They are also

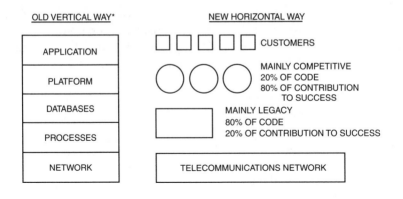

* ALL VERTICAL APPROACHES INVOLVE AN IMMENSE AMOUNT OF DUPLICATION

Figure 12.2   Old and new ways in managing technology as seen by Bankers Trust.

subject to intensified competition across global dimensions. In a nutshell, as the pace of business is fundamentally accelerating, top management must reevaluate how the firm's traditional business chains add value.

In conclusion, the ability to network and communicate much more efficiently with business partners (customers, employees, suppliers, and intermediaries) is changing the basis of competition. Therefore, boards and chief executives must respond with new strategies. Typically, these strategies will leverage Internet technology. Which will, however, require new forms of organization and training because new channels are revolutionizing the practices of management in the New Economy.

COMPANIES MUST REINVENT THEMSELVES TO SURVIVE IN THE INTERNET WORLD

Cognizant analysts on Wall Street say that the future impact of the Internet — and the many business models, organizational solutions, derivative technologies and platforms — will dwarf the comparative reach of the Industrial Revolution. The Net's ability to transform society has gained unheard-of speed and agility, the result will be reflected in thousands of new businesses that should provide partners and investors around the world with access to the greatest opportunities ever.

Other analysts who examine what makes a global market tick suggest that, to survive in the Internet-enabled world, companies must reinvent themselves and their business models every 2 years. This is not the first time "reinventing" has been brought up. In the early 1990s NASDAQ studied Silicon Valley firms and found that a high tech company must reinvent itself every 2.5 to 3 years in order to survive. With the Internet, this pace is accelerating. Reinventing means that companies must rethink their interactions with customers and suppliers as well as their alliances. They must go back to basics on how to capture and leverage knowledge as a strategic asset; the enterprise architecture is a good way of doing so.

A company's survival in a fast changing market is a top management responsibility and can be met only at board and CEO level, though the culture of reinventing the company should filter down through the organization. The problem at the top is that, from the beginning of the computer industry and the business application of data processors, a computer-management gap has existed. Even today, a majority of members of the board and senior managers are not computer-literate; therefore, they cannot think effectively in terms of computer-based restructuring.

Characteristics of on-line technology are change, mobility, and mass distribution. A characteristic of Internet commerce is personalization of the product or service offered. Knowledge of how to exploit this duality and its potential is vital to all firms because it impacts their business know-how. Key to the needed cultural change is to become computer-literate and also to appreciate that a rapidly renewed infrastructural base poses demanding training challenges. Therefore, one of the greatest jobs facing senior management today is to accelerate the ability to learn and to change the way the corporation thinks. How can everybody from chairman to janitor learn new methods, technologies, and processes more efficiently? How can the organization overcome current barriers to fast and effective learning of product and market development practices?

Far from being academic questions, these are at the top of the list of every executive who wants his company to grow and survive. Because the Internet puts unparalleled amounts of information at its users' fingertips, it puts consumers at par with professionals on market news and insights. As a result, it exerts an enormous price pressure on intermediaries everywhere, particularly the most inefficient. It also threatens brokers' margins and other fees.

Here is what top management should know about the Internet economy to avoid falling behind. First and foremost, those businesses ahead of the curve will become more efficient, able to offer the lower prices commensurate with product quality that consumers will increasingly demand. Technical matters that currently limit the application of Internet-related tools and services are apt to be overcome faster than one thinks. Practical issues follow.

Disintermediation through removal of organizational layers and third parties that historically have enabled distribution and increased prices is already occurring. While retail on-line sales still represent only a fraction of total retail sales, the impact of virtual business with virtual inventories could easily drive down product prices in the on-line world. Seeking the best value for their dollar, consumers flock to the Web, getting on-line via PCs, top-boxes, and other network-accessible devices. Consumers are also becoming increasingly choosy, however.

No one should underrate the practical issues associated with this transformation. While retailers are subject to price and margin wars, companies in the value chain of Internet access are striving to provide advertising, marketing, content aggregation, and distribution. A recent Wall Street meeting revealed that approximately 30 to 35% of Amazon.com expenditures are for advertising. Companies that have taken the lead find themselves in the midst of a demand that drives market expansion, massive investment, and unparalleled competition.

Consumers hunting low prices and who benefit from global access will be the engine behind this demand. Other consumers, as well as businesses, will move to adopt the Internet as a primary source of information, knowledge, content, community, and entertainment. As Figure 12.3 suggests, three markets which used to be standalone are now overlapping and the prime reason for their merger is the effect of the Internet.

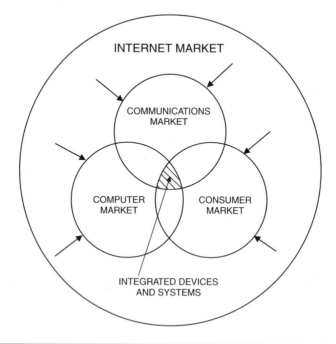

Figure 12.3 The merging of markets accelerates, which is one of the reasons why companies should reinvent themselves.

Indeed, the rapid and unpredictable pace of on-line dynamics has affected strategic planning and product development of many firms, with an impact on creating and scaling up or scaling down new services, competing in fast-paced, unpredictable industries, and innovating for rapidly evolving markets. Microsoft provides a good example of how the fastest growing software company in history has competed on Internet time (see Chapter 13) by reinventing itself and moving rapidly to new products and services, and staying flexible, exploiting leverage, and using the global market as its base.

Few people truly appreciate that the organizational structure necessary to deliver value needs to be different at each stage of product and market evolution. Even fewer people think about designing their organizational strategies at the same time that they project their product strategies. This essentially means steadily restructuring the way of bringing value at the right time to the right people.

Both operational information and advertising and marketing are part of this reference. Control over "eyeballs" and reach has become unprecedentedly important, as people and companies realize the potential of the Internet's information flow for influencing how consumers and corporations spend discretionary time and money. Another contribution of the Internet is that it has knocked down obstacles of place and time. The space is vast, but anyone operating in that space is at par with anybody else. This has an important impact on costs as well as on choices and also makes many experts predict that what has taken place so far is only a preview of things to come. An unprecedented growth in Internet-led business, including new ways of trading, is on the horizon.

The developing consensus says that investments in Internet business would suffer only if venture capitalists lost faith in i-commerce, as opposed to particular firms going bust. While pessimists suggest that a surge of trading among people unskilled in analysis and valuation and unburned by past losses is dangerous, realists say that individual failures are not important. They are the paving stones of the future highway.

THE INTERNET AS A COMMUNICATIONS PHILOSOPHY OF THE NEXT DECADE

The Internet opens so many avenues of marketing potential that it is not always clear what really constitutes i-commerce. The emergence of extranets (see Chapter 15) helps redefine some of the component parts of an enterprise architecture. Technology steers internal and external use of the Net, changing the manner in which people and companies communicate all the way to buying, selling, and distributing goods and services. It also influences how people spend leisure time.

This is not happening for the first time in history. The precedent is the Industrial Revolution and, more specifically, the connectivity infrastructure provided by the railroads in the late 19th century, which required a huge amount of labor and capital. But infrastructures decay. Figure 12.4 shows the rapid decline in U.S. railroad mileage during the last 50 years, counted in miles per 1000 households. Means of communication and transportation are so important because their prevailing facilities reveal the real picture of an economy's strengths and weaknesses. When a reigning solution decays, one is confronted with a major switch — maybe even a U-turn — in the way the infrastructure evolves.

All evidence today suggests that this describes the switch to the Internet; it is a very significant change, creating opportunities for new businesses to grow quickly, but also introducing tough competition into established industries, including media, retailing, health care, energy, financial services, and the now classical mode of transportation: the motor vehicle.

A visit to GM in 1964 resulted in a gift of a book by Alfred P. Sloan, Jr., My Years with General Motors."[3] Some interesting excerpts follow:

> General Motors could hardly be imagined to exist anywhere but in this country, with its very active and enterprising people.

Change "GM" to "Internet start-ups," and this statement, valid in the 1910s, is valid today.

> I cannot fail to note that the automobile presented one of the greatest industrial opportunities in modern times.

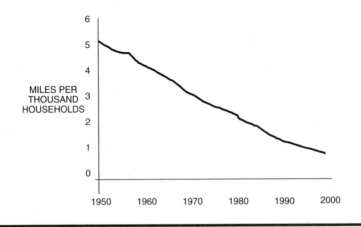

Figure 12.4 Rapidly declining railroad mileage in miles per 1000 households.

Change "automobile" to "Internet companies" and "industrial" to "post-industrial" and Sloan's concept fits hand-in-glove with 2002.

> Survival in the automobile industry … has depended upon winning the favors of buyers of new cars each year.

It would be difficult to explain in better terms the most important factor upon which rests the growth and survival of Internet companies.

> Deliberately to stop growing is to suffocate. Growth and progress are related, for there is no resting place for an enterprise in a competitive economy.

Internet companies are the fastest growing enterprises today. It is therefore not surprising that investment capital, hence market value, massively flowed toward these companies in the late 1990s, prior to the technology earthquake of 2000 to 2001. This is particularly true of firms able to create tools that may alter human behavior or permit study of such behavior in rigorous terms in order to build effective marketing environments.

In the aftermath of the communications philosophy promoted by the Internet, discussions and arguments about ethics and effectiveness of such technologies will probably arise. This sort of debate is necessary to understand more about how rapid innovation and on-line marketing persuade, while inspiring ideas about what should exist in the future. At the same time, new technology creates substantial growth, but the unknowns it engenders involve risks. In business, for example, the Internet creates growth by providing start-ups with the advantage of instantaneous market exposure. Associated with this are two types of risk: 1. some start-ups will not succeed; when the technology market bent, the mortality of Internet companies zoomed, and 2. old economy companies late to capitalize on opportunities provided by any-to-any broadband networks will shrink or disappear altogether.

Few boards look at the aftermath of the Internet economy in this way. Market ethics do not enter into the matter of corporate survival because there are no such things as "good" and "bad" companies. Good for what? For living with its time? For capturing business opportunity as it comes? For not misrepresenting its products and services? Because of the speed with which the Internet is developing, a redistribution of values may occur sooner than many experts think. Clear-eyed investors, therefore, pursue companies positioned to benefit from Internet-related growth, and move away from industries and companies that let themselves be hurt by technology.

Speaking strictly in business terms, enriched with the hindsight of the March 2000 to April 2001 loss of about 65% of the NASDAQ index, some investment advisors believe the overall Internet stock market may well prove to be a bubble. Others are of the opinion that there are good fundamental reasons to own stocks in best positioned technology companies because it is reasonable to guess that at least one Microsoft-sized Internet company will emerge in another 5 to 7 years.

In a discussion of this issue of apparent contradiction in investment advice, one Wall Sreet analyst emphasized that Internet stocks have consistently been expensive because they have the potential to provide unprecedented returns on invested capital. This, the analyst said, should eventually translate into higher P/E multiples; however, the way to profits is paved with the corpses of companies who fell short of cash and customers, which explains the paradox of highly divergent investment opinions.

INTERNET-INTRINSIC BUSINESS MODELS AND NECESSARY SOPHISTICATED SUPPORTS

Since the Industrial Revolution first gained steam, new industries have been born out of bold ideas turned into everyday necessities. Examples are the railroad boom of the 1890s and the automobile's rapid expansion in the 1920s. Just as those events created surging markets, one part of the Internet's appeal stems from the addition of a whole new and rapidly growing industry to the economy. The other part lies in the fact that consumers and companies effectively capitalize on Internet products and services.

A reason other than networking causes established top-tier companies (see Chapter 5 for the example with General Electric) to believe the Internet offers them a good platform: flexibility. Thirty-five years ago, Dr. David Rockefeller, in a Chase-Manhattan-sponsored symposium, discussed why, in all likelihood, the Concorde airplane was not going to "fly" in either a commercial or financial sense. His thesis was that any advanced product which comes in one size condemns itself to failure. It has boxed itself in and cannot recover its costs. Figure 12.5 visualizes this situation which often escapes top management's attention. By and large, what pushes a company toward ineffectiveness is within the organization and the environment in which it operates. The Internet is not boxed in because its software and other products can be of all sizes, anywhere in its universe.

The rush to adapt Internet technology to all sorts of purposes and to create supports which capitalize on Web software is spurring a surge in investments and creation of new businesses, leading to a radical renewal of the industrial base. No doubt, somewhere along the way, there will be

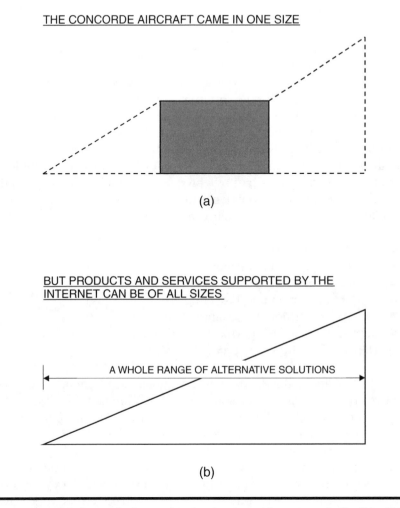

Figure 12.5   **Products of advanced technology must be extremely flexible. If they box themselves in, they are dead.**

brutal sorting of winners and losers as happened in late 2000 and early 2001. The survivors will consolidate, expand, thrive, and redefine their assets and liabilities and reinvent themselves.

Few investors are aware of one of the advantages of Internet companies that contributes to their market valuation: they have little debt. Because of the nature of Internet commerce, they will most likely need rather limited external financing in the future, which tends to keep their gearing relatively low.

Low debt is an asset, but it does not mean zero mortality rate for these companies. As once-promising innovations turn out to be dead ends, many firms that have been leading the boom may disappear. While the stock market value created in a boom evaporates, the risks to each investor can be deadly. At the same time, this sorting process triggers relatively minor disruptions in the economy.

This leads to certain critical questions to be asked with every business model. What does it contribute in terms of creation of wealth? What can it do uncommonly well? What are the prerequisites to a success story? Can it face the challenges of a developing opportunity? Some analysts advise that fairly sophisticated Internet-intrinsic business models are needed to capture the more than $300 billion estimated opportunity in electronic commerce that is part of a broader $500 billion global potential. This presupposes business confidence in i-commerce. However, remember that building up business confidence requires:

- Rapid identification of customer needs
- Merchant-specific information
- Reliable counterparty verification
- Product evaluation and brokering
- On-line negotiation and confirmation
- Improved means for payment and delivery
- Dependable after-sales product service

The first bullet in this list is rapid identification of client needs, with the buyer becoming aware of some unmet requirements he would like to fulfill. Motivation can be propelled through product information, but for a proactive Internet-intrinsic solution, it is necessary to have much more than Old Economy methods. Because a fully networked environment is fiercely competitive, interactive merchant-specific information is necessary to determine from whom to buy. This also includes evaluation of merchant alternatives based on buyer-based criteria like type, price, warranty, delivery time, merchant reputation, brand name, etc.

Product evaluation and brokering include retrieval of information to help determine exactly what to buy, for instance, evaluation of alternatives through buyer criteria applicable to a set of products which focus on the results of merchant brokering. Only then can product evaluation and merchant brokering start negotiation on conditions, followed by confirmation, if there is agreement, and by payment chores — a prerequisite being counterparty verification and secure payments.

Reliable counterparty verification, like security at large, is one of the Internet's weak spots (see Chapter 16). Time and again vendors announce new "reliable" solutions, only to be disproved some time later as hackers break codes, enter supposedly secure databases, and create havoc with vendors and end users. The early September 1999 excuses by Microsoft regarding some security problems are an example of this.

Because the terms of transaction vary, neither negotiation nor payment agreement can have standard duration or follow rigid rules. Neither will they be of the same complexity from one transaction to the other. Much will depend on the negotiators, the market, and the product. For example, in traditional bread-and-butter retail, market prices and other aspects of a transaction are often fixed, leaving little room for negotiation; however, in other markets like homes, cars, etc., the negotiation of price and payment aspects of the deal are crucial to the buying process.

As the use of interactive knowledge artifacts on the Net proliferates, a great deal of negotiation will be done agent-to-agent. Among the better known artifacts designed and sold as i-commerce mediators are Firefly, Personal Logic, and T@T, specializing in product brokering. Bargain Finder and Jango address merchant specific information, while the strength of AuctionBot is negotiation (see also Chapter 9 on the role of agents).

BargainFinder is one of the better known artifacts that has successfully worked on the Internet since its release in 1994; it serves in on-line shopping by comparing prices on the Web. The agent typically takes about 30 seconds to come up with different references and prices relating to electronic commerce. Its activity resembles that of other agents designed and implemented to search and recommend documents, products, or people to their master.

Negotiation, of course, is a crucial component of i-commerce. In an agent-assisted negotiation, intelligent software must find and prepare contracts on behalf of the parties these agents represent. In several cases computational agents are better at finding deals in complex settings without involving delays and human cost. Problems may include payment conditions.

Sometimes payment instruction such as "cash only" limit the flexibility of choices, but as i-commerce expands, payments and delivery options will influence product and merchant brokering. Also, as Internet-commerce grows more complex, after-sales service becomes critical. The same is true of evaluation of satisfaction of the customer's overall buying experience.

In conclusion, the able fulfillment of all seven conditions outlined in this section can help the emergence of new dynamic markets, supply chains, and distribution channels. In an Internet-intrinsic business model, the able solution to each of the seven challenges will be based on intelligent artifacts distributed and operating throughout the network. Only a few of the requirements implied by the framework outlined have been, thus far, capably addressed. The large part of the job is still to be done.

TECHNICAL FACTORS THAT CHARACTERIZE THE NEW ECONOMY

While the Internet is the information turnpike of the New Economy, it is by no means its only important characteristic. The shift in economic output from heavy metal fabricating and smoke-stack industries to advanced information technology and on-line services means that any given increase in gross domestic product (GDP) produces a smaller increase in demand for raw materials. In fairly rapid succession, technological advances have increased the supply of commodities, through higher rates of mineral extraction and crop yields, as well as reduced demand as plastic has replaced metal and optical fibers replaced copper wire.

Another important dimension in economic factors influencing business is that the time necessary to do something has been reduced impressively. Time is the one commodity of which nobody has enough. Vast budgets can buy more computer power, more staff, and more space, but they cannot buy more time, unless ways and means to compress it are found. That is where intranets and extranets come into the picture.

The other pillar of the new economy is sharp reduction in costs while keeping the stream of innovation running and maintaining high quality standards. It takes lots of preparation and foresight to do this, but "chance favors only the mind that is prepared," as Dr. Louis Pasteur once suggested. No product or service can develop satisfactorily if it prices itself out of the market, its mechanism is so complicated that it scares away potential users, or it becomes penalized because it belongs to a dying industry.

Edging into the 21st century, businesses, from the humblest, smallest firm to the most powerful manufacturer or financial institution, are bracing for a revolution the likes of which industry has not witnessed since Henry Ford implemented the first production line. This time around, however, the revolution is as much about business strategies as it is about time to market, just-in-time inventories, and rapid innovation techniques. It is also about size, though "too big" and "too small" are not exactly defined. Money is the driving force behind mergers, acquisitions, and alliances, which aim not only to create a bigger entity but also to slash development costs, drive up quality, bring innovative products quickly to market, and buy time. Or, to put it another way, create time.

While it is impossible to put more than 60 minutes into 1 hour or seven days into a week, it is possible to maximize the potential of how much can be achieved in any one of these periods. Other things equal, the more that can be done in a given time frame, the quicker a product can be finalized, produced, and brought to market. This is another reason why leading companies are accelerating the pace at which products are developed and validated, and using their intranets and the extranets that they establish with business partners to buy time (see Chapter 15). Intranets permit one to take a quick look inside the organization by using off-the-shelf Web software. Extranets do the same outside the organization; they help to see the problem. Simulation is another tool of technology that helps reach management's goals in regard to market leadership.

The old days involving endless hours of pounding a car around a test track waiting for something to fail are long gone. Interactive solutions based on analogical thinking can be found in all laboratories using powerful computer-based simulation programs. Some analysts suggest that, one day in the future, products will be designed, developed, and validated within the computer; the first time that one is actually manufactured will be when full-scale production starts. This, of course, happens already with printed circuit boards and other devices.

The prevailing concept is that virtual testing and validation is possible; cultural change is necessary to take advantage of it. Also necessary is the any-to-any network, which permits instantaneous broadband connectivity between offices or plants and the company as well as business-to-business activity. This is a quantum jump which will differentiate winners from followers and losers, and bring benefits to leaders, but will also require major risks. These risks are both technical and economic. Many people talk of the "bleeding edge" of technology but they fail to see that falling behind can disastrously magnify economic risks. The business of moving ahead and falling behind is by no means one-tantum. There is plenty of evidence it goes on all the time, and Figure 12.6 brings this fact into perspective.

During the first 20 years of computer usage there was slow, steady progression but no quantum jumps; therefore, technical risk was contained. Quantum jumps started in the mid 1970s with distributed information systems and minicomputers. Next were personal computers, 5 years down the line came expert systems, and by 1990 global networks, of which the Internet is one of the best examples, had arrived.

Intensive use of network-based products and services, i-commerce, and supply chain solutions has characterized the leading firms of the last 5 years. In the next 5 years, however, the leadership distinction will go to firms which put emphasis on organizational solutions, produce virtual balance sheets in 5 minutes or less, and operate sophisticated risk models capturing exposure anywhere in the world with any instrument or counterparty.

New, more powerful risk models operating in real-time are necessary because Internet banking (i-banking) is used for forex and for securities. Some institutions offer customers on-line facilities so that they can trade from laptops and there are projects for banking through nomadic computing solutions (see Chapter 9).

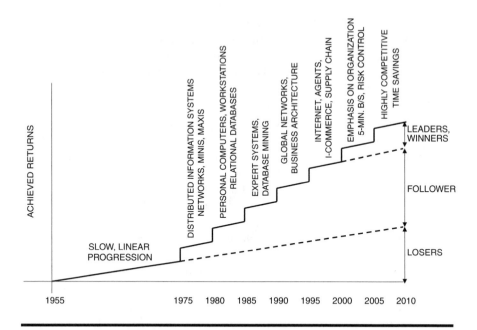

Figure 12.6 Quantum jumps in benefits distinguish winners from followers and losers.

Crossborder i-banking is already happening. Enba, a young technology company, hopes to offer Internet banking services from Dublin in Britain in partnership with established banks, since it does not have a banking license of its own.[4] Citibank, Barclays, and Egg also offer customers free Internet access. Egg is the direct-banking arm of Prudential, England's biggest life insurer.

It is unavoidable that economic risks accompany any new effort. Prudential's Egg was greeted as a breakthrough into retail banking by an insurer; but it is still not profitable. Banc One's Wingspan.com absorbed money like a sponge; it is one of the reasons that the board decided to discharge John McCoy, the CEO.

This does not discourage other credit institutions. In 1997, Barclays offered a proprietary PC-banking service, then decided to become an Internet service provider, looking at the Net as another distribution channel. The problem was that consumer resistance to on-line retail banking has not yet waned. European statistics contrast poorly to the 7.5 million American households that bank on-line. BankBoston says that it has about 375,000 on-line users, more than in England, France, and Spain together.

Banking is not the only business that wants to benefit from Internet as well as extranet solutions. Virtually all sectors of the economy are affected. In the U.S. about 7% of airline tickets are purchased on-line, and this figure is rising. A cool $1 billion of insurance premiums is estimated to be generated over the Net. Considering impressive statistics like these for a new industry as a basis for its judgment, the Organization for Economic Co-Operation and Development (OECD) suggests that cost savings from on-line distribution compared with traditional methods would roughly stand at 89% on banking, 87% on airline tickets, 67 to 71% on bill paying, and 50% on life insurance policies.

For the time being, by far the biggest share of total i-commerce activity, some 80%, is derived through business-to-business (B2B) transactions, though in some products consumer transactions lead. Internet sales now account for 20% of all books sold in the U.S.

CLASSES OF PLAYERS ON THE INTERNET AND BENEFITS THEY EXPECT TO GAIN

The second part of this section title helps give perspective to the first. Experts suggest that, in dollar terms, substantial cost savings from i-commerce and i-banking will be roughly equal to the combined financial impacts of airline and trucking deregulation. Other benefits of any-to-any broadband networks will be improved inventory management, accelerated cycle times for product development, and a wide-ranging marketing effort.

Close on the heels of these benefits will come systematic, industry-wide, supply-chain agreements, additional normalization of products and services, improved just-in-time delivery, and quality improvement programs beyond existing levels. Another likely consequence is outsourcing on a scale that will utterly transform business and industry, giving small startups a chance to become global brand names.

Even if only half the benefits just outlined materialize, there will be a windfall. But who is best positioned to benefit from it? There are two classes of role-players in Internet business that stand a good chance to be among the winners, and one class that most likely will not benefit from the Internet. Figure 12.7 identifies these classes in a snapshot. The role players will be companies that would not exist without the Internet, and companies that have learned to adapt themselves to the Internet.

The former class subdivides into two groups. One includes companies like AOL, Yahoo!, and Doubleclick that, without products produced by and for the Internet, would cease to function. In the other group are entities that came up with the Internet, and are capitalizing on its features even if their lines of business already existed before the Web. Amazon.com, At Home, and e-Bay are examples of these firms; they adapted existing products, making them pace-setting i-commerce services.

The Web seems to be a natural home for both these groups. It is also a natural home for all companies that either perform services electronically

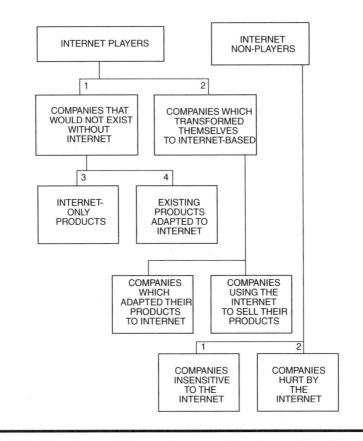

Figure 12.7   Four types of internet players and two types of nonplayers.

or offer their products in digital form. Familiar examples of industries moving quickly to customers through the Internet, intranets, and extranets include news, financial services, software, entertainment, and leisure travel.

The latter class includes entities that transformed themselves to providers of Internet services, at least for part of their business. This class, too, divides into two groups but, contrary to the former class, there is permeability among them. As companies learn to adapt their products to the Internet, they graduate, in terms of using on-line interactive services to sell their products, from group "B" to group "A."

Group A companies learned to adapt quickly to the Internet; they predate the Internet era, but now derive a good part of their income from on-line products, which represent a growing share of their yearly business. Microsoft and Oracle are examples of software firms; Charles Schwab is the best example of a financial firm using the Internet to expand its product line and its reach.

In group B of this same class are companies actively using the Internet to sell their products. Dell is an example. Transport companies like Federal Express and the airlines (see the previous section) use Internet services to cut costs, respond more effectively to customers, obtain more efficient supplies, and better their performance overall. Indeed, FedEx is in the process of moving to the first group as it permits customers to arrange their own pickups and deliveries on-line.

Though distinct in a number of basic characteristics, the four groups mentioned (two relating to the first class and the other two to the second class) share a number of critical factors which transform industries, alter investment opportunities, and change the business landscape. Uppermost in the benefits list are gains that, due to innovation, undergo a multiplier effect as they ripple through the economy. There is evidence to show that the technologies of the Internet are assimilated much faster than the technologies that led to the Industrial Revolution, or any major industrial expansion since then. With globalization and deregulation, labor and capital have become highly mobile with huge consequences for the efficiency of the workplace as well as people's homes.

The other common element underlying the four groups is that, in the knowledge economy, education put on-line to support lifelong learning becomes a major growth sector, greatly changing the face of the university system. College degrees may be earned on-line and, for the U.S. and the U.K., have become one of their most lucrative export industries.

The combination of on-line education and Internet business-to-business and business-to-consumer services will help superstar companies rise quickly, but, then, consolidation and technological convergence will likely unleash waves of global mergers and acquisitions as well as lead to the disappearance of companies that fall behind (see the third section in this chapter).

One should also pay attention to the Internet's non-players. These, too, divide into two groups. In one are those companies insensitive to Internet-based services and global reach. By and large, they see their client base melt and their business evaporate. The more they delay adapting to i-commerce and i-banking, the higher becomes the entry cost — and the more skills and effort needed to carve a piece of the Internet pie, if they ever succeed doing so. The second group of non-players on the Internet stage is not much better off and consists of companies hurt by i-commerce, for instance, mom-and-pop business as well as other entities like real estate investment trusts (REITS). Real estate companies are downgraded by investment advisors for two reasons. First, investors increasingly go for financial assets rather than for real assets. Second, analysts see a slackening in demand for physical retail space.

As consumers move to i-commerce, bookstores, for example, see a notable reduction in visits to their physical business. Think of this when evaluating business perspectives of the firm, and note that the cultural change required to join the New Economy will not come of its own will. One of its basic requirements is to live at Internet time, the theme of Chapter 13.

REFERENCES

1. Chorafas, D.N., *Managing Operational Risk. Risk Reduction Strategies for Investment Banks and Commercial Banks*, Euromoney, London, 2001.
2. Chorafas, D.N., *Statistical Processes and Reliability Engineering*, D. Van Nostrand Co., Princeton, NJ, 1960.
3. Sloan, A.P. Jr., *My Years With General Motors,* Pan Books, London, 1963.
4. *Economist*, April 10, 1999.

13

INTERNET TIME AND SUPPLY CHAIN AS AGENTS OF CHANGE

INTRODUCTION

The Internet has been instrumental in altering many people's attitudes about the desirability of change. People rarely think, "Technology does not affect me." It does affect them, and some of the basic assumptions that people have made about their industries and their professions are no longer dependable. For instance, any-to-any instantaneous telecommunications and multimedia alter the definition of what a product or service is and is not. The ability to design a fairly complex product, manufacture it, and deliver it in $3\frac{1}{2}$ days, as Toyota is doing with customized cars, has a tremendous effect on clients' perception of products and services, and of those from whom they buy them. Notions of space and time are changed by Internet technology.

Collapsing the space frontier has always been a major challenge. In the late 19th century, railroads linked remote places to one another through means other than muscular power. Today, networks link markets and financial centers, altering the meaning of distances and doing away with the notion of faraway places. Networks, which have become more and more commonplace in today's industrial environments, also introduce performance bottlenecks due to their protocols and data structures. The challenge is so much greater because system designers do not "own" the network in the same way that they have control over computers attached to it; in an open network like the Internet nobody can legislate performance regarding security, congestion, or other factors.

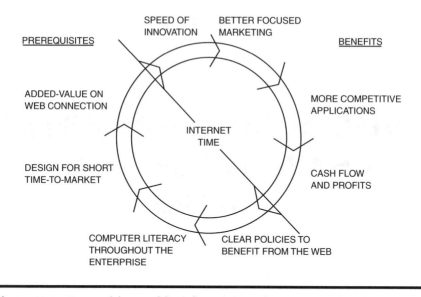

Figure 13.1   Prerequisites and benefits connected to Internet time.

The enterprise architecture chosen and services provided by the Internet have plenty of common ground. One of their characteristics is that space has shrunk tremendously, so that the French saying, "You cannot be at the oven and the mill at the same time," is no longer valid. In fact, not only the concept of distance, and therefore of space, has changed, but also that of time.

Figure 13.1 presents benefits connected to Internet time as well as prerequisites to gaining those benefits. The reason for some of the outlined prerequisites was explained in Chapter 12; this chapter addresses issues closely connected to the restructured supply chain.

Time is a unique resource. It cannot be accumulated, like wealth, yet without it nothing can be accomplished. Shakespeare said that three things do not return in human life: an opportunity lost, a word said, and time passed by. One is forced to spend time, yet, of all resources it appears to be the one least understood, most mismanaged, and in most limited supply. If the steam engine was the prime mover of the industrial age, the clock is central to post-industrial society. The Internet can be seen as technological extension of the clock; its most distinguished aftermath is that it makes time move faster, which is critically important to competitiveness because time has become the strategic factor in enterprise.

At a premium is the ability to identify a market or problem quickly, and then deploy the organizational resources needed to handle it. At the bottom line, it is not always the best technology which wins the day. It

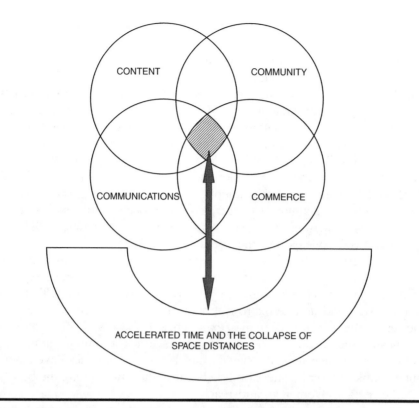

Figure 13.2 Four "Cs" of Internet value and accelerated time infrastructure.

is the most timely approach, the ability to get business partners moving on time, and the timing of products and services in the global market.

Business people who realize this are building 21st Century companies around the Internet, instead of running around trying to fit round pegs into square holes. Analysts talk of the Four Cs of Internet value: *content*, *community*, *communications*, and *commerce*. In reality there is also AT, which stands for accelerated time. All five should be at the kernel of the company's enterprise architecture, as Figure 13.2 suggests.

INTERNET TIME IS A STRATEGIC FACTOR IN MODERN BUSINESS

As the decade of the 1980s came to a close, David Sias, then executive vice president of Bankers Trust, suggested, "For the next 10 years, the bank will continue to make money from paper. The large investments in high technology which we do today aim to change our culture." To take advantage of opportunity, Sias said, one must have a very responsive organization — not just a responsible organization.

This definition of responsiveness as added-value fits hand-in-glove with the notion of Internet time. The responsive organization wins the day. Despite its lack of any proprietary technology, Dell Computer met with business success; this illustrates not only a first-class supply chain design but also responsiveness to market drives in an industry that changes rapidly. Dell's made-to-order strategy proved to be a key asset. Its competitors struggled to avoid the nightmare of unsold inventory, but Dell actually thrived because of the inherent advantages of its fast replenishment policy.

Companies that know how to move at Internet time enable their people to do things that they could not have done in slow moving, highly structured bureaucratic environments. A company's inner core capability lies in gaining maximum advantage of compressed timescales, albeit temporary, in a market where competitive forces may change at lightning speed and old policies become counterproductive.

Associated with Internet IT and propelled by globalization is the rate at which business and industry introduce new products, processes, and organizational structures. Many people associate this process with supply chain design and its aftermath. Although the two correlate, they are not the same thing. The interactive experience is becoming embedded in businesses and consumers every day, and includes communicating, shopping, investing, learning, and having fun. Top-tier companies have already put a chunk of their business on-line because they are seeking the benefits of efficiency, convenience, and reach.

As Figure 13.3 points out, the Internet supply chain is only a part, even if the more efficient part, of supply chain applications. Conversely, this area of activity is a subset of what is feasible through Internet time.[1] It is wrong to think of a modern supply chain as an Internet domain

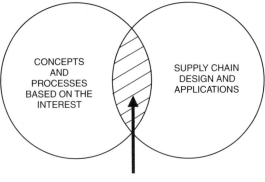

INTERNET SUPPLY CHAIN

Figure 13.3 The Internet and supply chain have many common elements, but they are not synonymous.

exclusively, just as it is wrong to think of the enterprise architecture as a notion and process strictly oriented to the handling of transactions (see Chapter 1).

In this ongoing revolution, the Internet is more than a cost-efficient, shared infrastructure. It is an agent of change, which permits and sometimes forces direct and focused relationships with customers and suppliers. Both big and small companies can benefit from Internet time. Those who gain the most are the more flexible organizations, which understand that modern industry prospers when it can exploit all dimensions of a highly interdependent business world. In this, supply chain is the alter ego of concurrent engineering (see Chapter 11).

Examples from everyday business are a good way to appreciate the reach of Internet time. Auto manufacturing is one such example. Experts believe that Web-based collaboration will pervade every step of manufacturing motor vehicles, from research and engineering design to procurement, assembly, sales, and after-sale services. On-line interactivity helps auto manufacturers chop months from time needed to create a new model, significantly reduces time required to manufacture a car, and permits major cost savings, shrinking the price tag and making the product more competitive.

Starting at research and design, the impact of Internet time is at the heart of this process, which, in the typical case, involves some 20,000 parts provided by about 200 different suppliers, delivered to the factory just in time. It would, of course, be incorrect to credit the Internet with every advance in the motor vehicle industry. The first major breakthrough was the assembly line, which dates back to Henry Ford. This early 20th century development might be called "Ford time;" it made possible manufacturing and selling motor vehicles at an affordable price. Other major developments came in the 1920s with the annual model change, and in the 1950s and 1960s, when auto makers were among the first to use computers and to rethink inventory management.

Other breakthroughs have been of an organizational nature. In the mid 1960s, for example, Ford was the first to feel the need for renumbering all auto parts on a global scale. This would have had an aftermath on engineering, manufacturing, and inventory management and also would have cost $300 million, but the proposal was rejected by Henry Ford II. (At Osram, it was done for 15,000 different types of lamps at a cost of DM 6 million [about $3 million]).[2]

In the 1970s, motor vehicle manufacturers were among the first to adopt computer-aided design (CAD; see Chapter 11). Also, since the 1970s they have been steadily adopting new tools, such as product development management (PDM) software, and new methodologies like computer-aided manufacturing (CAM). Both helped companies slash the time it takes to bring a new model to the market from around 5 years to about 3 years. The telling aftermath is that, in the 1980s, motor vehicle assembly required from 30 to 40 hours; now it takes fewer than 20 hours and is still shrinking. The Internet also facilitates linking on-line internal and external information systems, which is the next big wave in auto manufacturing.

By all evidence, in the coming years the engineering, manufacturing, and sales cycle will start with the customer as codesigner and end with the customer taking delivery of the vehicle in three days. Internet time will capitalize on the virtual integrative business environment, supported by the Web and featuring end user interactivity in real time.

Already the aftermath is felt all the way to the distribution network, in a process which is part and parcel of disintermediation. The underlying concept is shown in Figure 13.4. There are reasons for the consolidation of dealerships — the auto industry's equivalent of disintermediation. The number one reason is to catch up with population shifts by moving stores

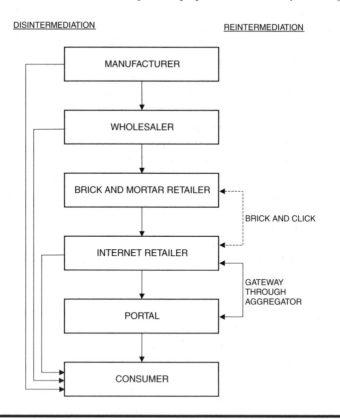

Figure 13.4   Disintermediation through the Internet and partial reintermediation through aggregators.

out of declining cities and small towns into bustling retail zones along suburban highways. This provides a benefit from an effect of mass, hence the elimination of small dealerships.

At the same time, U.S. automakers are pushing dealers to reconfigure their assets. The number two reason is to swamp costly overhead and inventories; the number three reason is to eliminate many expensive body shops, while offering customers better service and a wider selection.

At GM, this reengineering of the dealership chain has been a $1 billion project, and the company says that it is delighted with results. In Bergen County, N.J., for example, sales rose 42% in 1997, after half of the eight dealerships were upgraded or moved.

Examples on disintermediation and reengineering of sales networks are no exclusive domain of motor vehicle vendors. Other industries as diverse as pharmaceuticals and semiconductors also benefit a great deal, with best rewards going to companies that can anticipate which service features are worth investing in and which are worth outsourcing. In the background of this ongoing change is a great deal of concurrent engineering, analytical skills for evaluating "make or buy" alternatives, and knowledge on how to build a true chain of capabilities to keep the company ahead of the curve.

FAR-REACHING POLICIES ARE NECESSARY TO BENEFIT FROM INTERNET TIME

The previous section made the point that, while supply chains play an important role in Internet time, they are not the whole story; neither can they bring wide-ranging benefits all by themselves. Far-reaching management policies are a fundamental prerequisite for capitalizing on modern technology, before and after taking advantage of capabilities provided by Internet commerce.

An example of basic decisions to be made is "make" or "buy," — in-house production or outsourcing, respectively — and the issues of leadership this choice raises. The computer industry provides an example. In the 1950s and 1960s, both IBM and its competitors the so-called BUNCH (**B**urroughs, **U**nivac, **N**CR, **C**ontrol Data, and **H**oneywell), were largely vertical organizations with little cross-fertilization and product innovation across the supported lines of mainframes, peripherals, and software.

Product design was monolithic and processors were designed solely for mainframes; this gave newcomers their chance. First, Digital Equipment came with minis and maxis, then Apple with PCs. At the beginning of the 1980s when the personal computer market gave evidence that it was here to stay, to gain lost time IBM made the decision to build PCs using off-the-shelf components: microprocessors from Intel and operating systems from Microsoft. But IBM's board and CEO failed to change the company's culture to match requirements posed by the shift in market thrust, and major outsourcing agreements which altered the old business perspective.

What happened then and thereafter with IBM and its outsourcers is a good case study with a rich message to companies that, at the present day, contemplate "make" or "buy" decisions while preserving their old ways of doing business. In the 1980s, When "Big Blue" decided to turn its vertically integrated manufacturing philosophy on its head, Intel was not even 10 years old and Microsoft was a fledgling start-up, but 10 years down the line the weak partner had become IBM.

The new landscape in IT was done by Microsoft and Intel because both were companies on the move, while IBM had rested on its laurels. Less than two decades down the line, as the 20th century came to a close, Intel and Microsoft had market capitalization bigger than "Big Blue," even if they trailed the mainframer in turnover. The difference was made up for by the fact that the market usually pays a much higher premium, or profit to earnings ratio (P/E), for market leaders with a clear vision and companies willing and able to change quickly.

Central to a company's policy today is the formation of strategic alliances with international partners, and the provision of efficient access to the global market through a thoroughly studied and cost-effective enterprise architecture. That is where Internet time and Web software play a central role. Business partners now want to access selected contents of their counterparts IT, because this enhances their global services. Companies offer such support through the Internet and the extranets (see Chapter 15).

A basic question is, under which terms? The answer is, those of a universal *de facto* standard. Wintel and Intel inside are examples. Power chip by IBM and Motorola was a great design at its time, but it was difficult to find hundreds of business partners because they looked at it as an outlier with a limited market. Eventually, the power microprocessor, like the Concorde, failed because badly needed business was not to be found.

The lesson from these cases is that companies do not become a symbol of high-tech entrepreneurship by boxing themselves into a market corner. They do so either through the new, new thing, like Netscape's browser, by leading the fast-changing nature of the high-tech industry, or by means of far-reaching strategic decisions which capitalize on Internet time.

Netscape, for example, was started in April 1994 and, in the next two years, it had a market capitalization of $7 billion. Investors rushed to buy the stock because, in just 18 months, the Netscape Navigator browser had

38 million users. This has been one of the fastest-growing start-ups in industrial history, reaching annual sales of $500 million in the short span of 3 years. Microsoft needed 14 years to reach a comparable revenue.

Competitors had to make a U-turn to match Netscape. A couple who knew how to work in Internet time did so through far-reaching strategic decisions. In December 1995, after Microsoft was downgraded by analysts for not being a major player on the Web, Bill Gates declared that his firm was hard-core about the Internet and would integrate it into Windows 95. Within a week of this announcement, Netscape's valuation fell by almost 30%.

Success did not come to Microsoft's Internet policy free of risk. Gates decided to risk billions of dollars to ensure that his company fought its way into the Internet landscape. Between November 1994 and July 1997, there were head-to-head, hard-to-win business battles between Netscape and Microsoft; then Netscape was dethroned from its Internet leadership position. The battle of Netscape vs. Microsoft established one of the cardinal principals of competition on Internet time: be flexible and give way when attacked directly by a superior force, but fight for your turf by all means.

Not everybody is willing and able to do so. When this is the case, the best advice is to take Harry Truman's advice: "If you can't stand the heat, get out of the kitchen." For any practical purpose, this is what Netscape did, after it violated another cardinal principle of competing on Internet time: build external relationships to compensate for limited internal resources, and make sure strategic alliances provide necessary market ammunition and financial staying power.

Ideally, what the second half of this principle suggests should be provided without being swallowed up by the white knight. Netscape failed on that count because it rejected repeated overtures from AOL for a strategic alliance. Finally, it was bought by AOL after weakening in the business battle with Microsoft and losing its leadership position. It is a deadly mistake to delay making strategic decisions. Turning on a dime must be done while there is still time. Delays cost Netscape the opportunity to conquer 12 million users in an AOL alliance and allowed Microsoft to gain ground rapidly by weakening its adversary. In conclusion, Netscape's problems should be laid at the feet of its management, not Microsoft's; Microsoft was a business adversary.

In a similar manner, delays in providing the right enterprise architecture for the company and fuzzy decisions regarding its exact characteristics are mistakes made by the company's management, not that of its competitors or business partners. Top management should understand that while they wait for better times, hopes and illusions cannot become reality, but can turn into destructive forces.

THE INTERNET SUPPLY CHAIN FAVORS
THE PREPARED COMPANY

A couple of examples demonstrate the title above. The first case concerns Cisco and some of its customers. The justification for this choice is that Cisco operates one of the world's largest Internet commerce sites, with an impressive 90% of its orders placed on-line. The company says that, as far as these networked applications are concerned, orders are 99% accurate the first time entered, and that this process represents a contribution of $60 million in operating costs savings for Cisco.

Other companies are impressed and try to learn from a partnership with Cisco. Honeywell, for example, has worked hard to reshape itself in the Internet economy. In July 1999, it launched MyPlant.com, a business-to-business Web site that connected customers and suppliers in the manufacturing industry. Honeywell suggests that, at Internet time through MyPlant.com, approximately 400 software suppliers provide 650 manufacturing applications on the site, for a small transaction fee and with great benefit to users. Large and small companies from around the world share procurement and manufacturing strategies, download software, and participate in industry discussions.

To get such results, however, from this or any other Web-based supply-chain application, business partners must prepare. The whole pyramid of logistics shown in Figure 13.5 must be thoroughly reexamined. This is a demanding task as it involves many layers of management and calls for change, with associated cultural shock going both top-down and bottom-up.

Handled the classical way, the solution of recurring inventory management solutions involving design, manufacturing, and warehousing is always suboptimized. Coordination can take weeks or more. Internet time changes that, as business partners take matters into their own hands in real time, shrinking inventory levels, doing away with delays, saving money, and reducing risk while increasing marketing punch.

MyPlant.com, for instance, has hosted 60,000 user sessions, and the company estimates that one third of the site's users are new Honeywell customers. Collaborating in Internet time results in economies of scale. Because of this, Honeywell implemented MyAircraft.com, a joint venture with United Technologies and i2, to focus on supply-chain management for the aerospace industry. The aim is to match customers and suppliers, providing instant service at low overhead.

Perceived benefits are the reason why a growing number of bricks-and-mortar companies believe that they can become successful bricks-and-clicks. Like Barnes and Noble, Canadian-based book retailer Chapters launched Chapters Online. This company, Canada's largest book retailer operating 70 superstores and 243 smaller stores, designed its site with a focus on books, music, and movies, with reviews by Canadian critics and

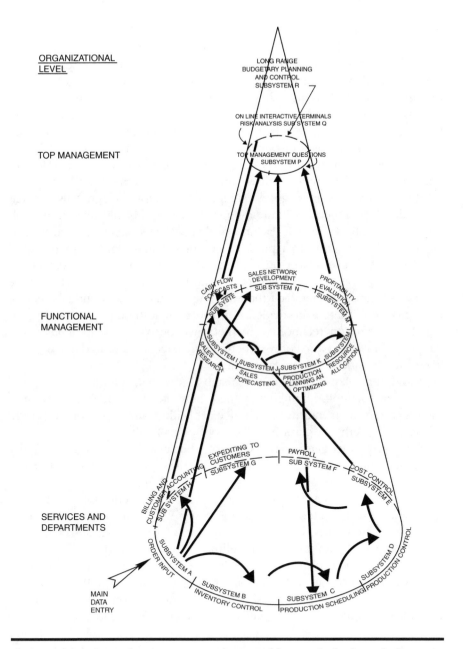

Figure 13.5 Layers of management to be served interactively through the enterprise architecture.

Canadian best-seller lists. It also extended the on-line experience to its retail superstores, which house kiosks that conveniently provide on-line ordering when a book is out of stock.

Chapters' management teamed up with Cisco and AT&T to squash the lead time in launching the site, just as Honeywell had teamed up with Cisco for technology transfer reasons. These two cases are representative of commercial activities known as business-to-consumer (B2C) and business-to-business (B2B). Experts believe that, with two-way television, consumer-to-business (C2B) and consumer-to-consumer (C2C) interactive on-line trades might also gain importance. They think that families have become like small corporations, outsourcing child care and birthday parties.[3] In the bottom line, the responsibility falls upon individuals to make different choices that will be, more or less, influenced by Internet time.

Reverse auctions are a good example of the supply chain activities that might develop in the near future. RequestBid.com sells information technology gear from IBM, Hewlett-Packard, and Sun Microsystems through reverse auction: a buyer requests a piece of equipment and vendors then outbid each other with ever lower prices. GizmoAuctions.com is a different site. It brings together buyers and sellers of used and surplus network and telephone equipment, and also handles the shipping, storage, and refurbishment of used products. There is no evidence, however, that these portals are sweeping the information technology market. Five out of six IT purchases still happen off-line, and a majority of network managers prefer traditional value-added resaler and vendor relationships.

A different way to look at these statistics is that, with a 17% share of information technology purchases, these new sites have been able to carve their niche through Internet commerce. This illustrates a proverbial puzzle of judging whether a glass is half empty or half full.

Sometimes the glass may be empty because the market has been decreased by competitors. Mid-May 2001 brought the news of Bertelsmann's decision to roll BOL, its book and CD Internet retailer, into its more mature book clubs. This signaled the end of Bertelsmann On-Line, the home-grown challenge to Amazon.com's European dominance. Commenting on Bertelsmann's move out of the Internet booksales challenge, Heidi Fitzpatrick, an analyst at Lehman Brothers, said, "It is another indication that the economics of pan-European e-tailing are just not there."[4]

Bertelsmann set up BOL as a stand-alone business in 1999 in hope of spinning it off as a separate public company and a concomitant windfall of profits. Despite being the second largest pan-European on-line bookstore, with 16 countries giving it an impressive geographical foothold, BOL found it hard to achieve widespread brand recognition and failed to catch up with Amazon's head start.

There are other challenges to take into account. For instance, on-line purchases can be more effective if supported through financial services. Here lies the weakness of the Internet's supply chain. The key word is *security* (see Chapter 16) good enough to bring confidence to the triangular

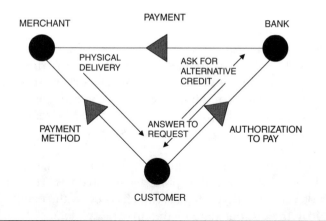

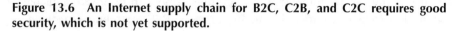

Figure 13.6 An Internet supply chain for B2C, C2B, and C2C requires good security, which is not yet supported.

relation shown in Figure 13.6. This atomic triangle of i-commerce, must be secure everywhere it is applied, for every customer, every merchant, every bank, and every transaction. No one is there yet. Because security costs money, the best option is that of providing a security level on demand. Transactions vary greatly in terms of financial weight. (It is a deliberate choice to keep micropayments out of this text.) Therefore, unequal things should not be treated as equal, but even the lowest level of security must give confidence to the consumer and preserve privacy in an effective way, as will be seen in Chapter 16.

Security in all its ramifications should be integral part of the enterprise architecture. It is necessary to design a secure system to maintain and upgrade it as such. Some banks now provide voice recognition for balance inquiry. However, this is only a small part of a larger problem. All communications connected to the acceptance of an offer, including request for quotes, must be secure. This is not just a matter of the final payment, it is a must for the complete and correct settlement of transactions as explained in the next section.

SUPPLY CHAIN AND THE CHALLENGE OF ON-LINE PAYMENTS

Like so many other companies, financial institutions have joined the Internet revolution. An example is AXP@Work by American Express, whose goal is to make feasible a reduction in servicing costs while improving customer service and accessibility. This dual goal is primarily attempted through on-line program management, which enables a corporate services customer to update card member information, adjust his or her spending level, check transaction status, and obtain on-line access to information and reports.

According to American Express, at the end of the first 6 months of 2000, roughly 13% of its corporate customers were performing maintenance transactions on-line, while approximately 14% were printing management information system (MIS) reports directly from the Internet, rather than requesting that hardcopy documents be faxed or sent via overnight mail. American Express also says that it has been able to develop greater operational efficiencies.

In parallel to this Web site effort at company and consumer level, American Express promotes B2B purchasing initiatives. The results, however, are not yet conclusive; this has much to do with security and what is afforded by the current state of the art worldwide.

If security on the Internet was high, then American Express might have been able to gain more mileage. In America, B2B spending is estimated currently to total well in excess of $1.5 trillion, but less than 5% of purchasing is completed with a credit card. Like other financial companies, American Express tries to put in place the necessary pieces to penetrate the B2B market and maintain a sustainable longer-term growth rate as the industry evolves.

The very low rate of payment through credit cards on the Internet shows that companies and consumers are highly concerned about privacy and security. This is true not only of American Express customers but also of those of any other credit card company, and of financial transactions at large. Among Internet companies, AmericaOnline (AOL) is touting the idea of pushing a range of payments service to its U.S. customers. With a customer base of more than 20 million, AOL might potentially become a major competitor to traditional financial institutions attempting to move into Internet services. The problem is to convince small companies and consumers that the electronic bill presentment and payments (EBPP) service is secure, which is not self-evident.

Companies offering on-line retail banking services think that bill payments to Web customers will spearhead a whole series of open finance offers that could be appealing to an expanding Internet customer base. Financial analysts, however, question the rationale of further moves into financial services by Internet service providers, saying that one could make better profits in other Internet developments without hitting customer resistance head-on because of security.

No matter how one looks at this issue, whether talk is of B2B or B2C, security is most critical, even if it is not the only factor regarding client acceptance. The other side of the equation is that those companies win that have the best logistics. As already discussed in previous sections, delivery time is an integral part of Internet time. It is also a crucial factor in establishing the long-term winner.

Delivery time has two components: physical and financial. For physical goods delivery, delays can happen because items are out of stock, there is a sparse network of factories and warehouses from which to ship, or there is an unreliable delivery service. All three reasons were behind the snafus with Christmas 2000 deliveries of goods ordered over the Internet. Payments also played a major role.

Financial delivery, too, is crucial. At the financial side, Internet time is slowed because on-line payments are not as easy as in the physical world, where consumers use cash, sign checks, or feel at ease to employ their credit cards. There are still many unanswered questions regarding the way a cybermoney system will work, and even more questions about how it can give confidence to those who are supposed to use it.

Precisely because partial solutions are not going to lead anywhere, several companies now take the view that what is needed is a total system addressing all phases of electronic money — not just the financial aspects. The roles, means, and needs of all parties connected to a financial transaction must be accounted for from the drafting phase of the enterprise architecture. Companies trying to do so have found out that a significant difference exists between the current model of the client–merchant–bank relationship and the Internet-oriented three-party model. The merchant needs much more than finality payment. Because such payments may be recurrent over the network, he needs to know the customer.

This brings credit risk and interactive management of exposure into the picture. Figure 13.7 presents the bigger picture. In the old brick-and-mortar world the merchant had locality; while this was a factor limiting

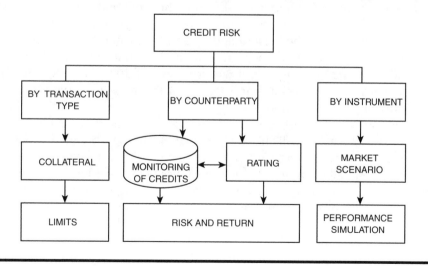

Figure 13.7 The interactive management of exposure to support decisions concerning counterparty risk.

business expansion, it had the advantage that the local merchant knew his clients. Credit was extended on the basis of personal relationships rather than of documentation. All this has changed with cyberspace. The personal relationship is lost, and the merchant's need to have some privacy, which is also a priority for the consumer and the bank. Next to security, privacy is a key reason why the financial industry's commitment to on-line payments is missing today.

For these reasons, no electronic money approach, or product, has achieved critical mass. Furthermore, while some electronic checking standards seem to be emerging, mostly using public keys, they are far from gaining general acceptance. As Chapter 16 will show, there is always a conflict between privacy and, therefore, anonymity and greater security, which brings up the identity argument.

The effects of this dichotomy are compounded by government policies on policing the Net that are, at best, confusing. Reserve banks seem interested in studying the implications, but the responsibility for policing the network belongs to a different government agency, and, so far, initiatives are still wanting. The foundations for a rational approach to the problem of secure payment simply are not there; as long as this persists, it is better to wait and see.

SMALL BUSINESS, INTERNET TIME, AND PERSONAL ACCOUNTABILITY

The cutting edge of today's economy is in high-tech products and services: telecommunications, computers, software, finance, and insurance. New technologies know no frontiers and have been instrumental in opening up the Third World's cheap labor and land to the manufacturing economy. The result is a production boom in Asian and Central American countries similar to the rubber, sugar, and wheat booms of 100 years ago. Then it was opera houses in Manaus and Buenos Aires; now it is skyscrapers in Bangkok and Kuala Lumpur.

With so many investments made abroad, the enterprise architecture must have globality. Will this rush to manufacturing abroad run out of steam like the rush to agriculture in the early 20th century and the rush to mining? Manufacturing is becoming so productive that fewer and fewer people will be needed to make man-made goods. In the U.S., 26% of the work force in 1970 was in manufacturing; however, in 2000 that figure shrank to 15% and, by all evidence, it will become still smaller in the future.

If this rate of decline continues, by 2035 the percentage of Americans working in manufacturing will match the 2.6% now working on farms. Equally interesting is the likelihood that, as some experts predict, much of the output will be from small- and medium-size enterprises. What may the Internet have in store for them?

By definition small businesses are those with fewer than 10 employees and with less than $3 million in annual revenues. Because they have been going on-line in a big way recently, some forecasts suggest that, within 3 years or so, their transactions could constitute more than 10% of U.S. gross domestic product (GDP). Projected growth of their Internet business is shown in Figure 13.8; this figure does not show that the path to Internet time has not been easy for small firms. During the mid- to late 1990s, for many small businesses the prospect of competing on-line with big entities was daunting. By 2001, however, small companies found that they could gang up and pool their resources against their bigger competitors in ways not feasible in the physical world.

Still, small businesses are likely to run into obstacles on the Web that are hard to overcome because of their limited staff and resources. Superior customer service and mastery of Internet technology play a key role, so, unless the small business works along the Silicon Valley model, it finds it difficult to change its culture by leaps and bounds in order to benefit from Internet time.

For a small company that knows about the Internet mainly through newspapers or what the sons and daughters of the boss learn in school, assembling the pieces needed to build a large Internet commerce system, including equipment and network connections, could be a nearly impossible task. There are good reasons to outsource this activity, particularly because systems talent is scarce relative to demand, but few small companies appreciate the need to practice technology transfer.

Because this particular constraint of available skill is well-known, a new company, Loudcloud by Marc Andreesen, is trying to carve a niche

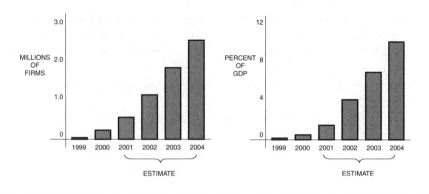

Figure 13.8 American small businesses selling on-line and their share of U.S. gross domestic product (GDP).

as a managed service provider (MSP). Founded in September 1999, Loud-cloud has spent much money to develop technology that helps it to automate the building of Websites for its customers and ensures that those sites are reasonably secure and run well. Notice, however, that outsourcing without technology transfer could turn into a nightmare.

The need for technology transfer is further underlined by the fact that technology is not just part of the future of business and industry, it *is* the future. Despite recent stock market blues, the Internet has proved to be a revolutionary communications technology driving the global business transformation. The change is propelled by a series of self-reinforcing trends as the Web enlarges the marketplace, helps to sharply lower costs, provides a means of pooling resources, and opens up new business opportunities.

Small companies now appreciate that they, too, can move directly into markets bursting with innovative products and services, provided they are able to contribute to the rich applications of today and tomorrow; they can thus capitalize on the fact that people the world over are being enabled to communicate practically without limit (see Chapter 6 on 3G).

This is true whether the new Internet is mobile, letting users on the go tap the power of the Web from net phones and other wireless devices, or the links are broadband optical fibers. Capitalizing on this environment calls for a factual and documented answer to the query: is the small company able to seize the opportunities of the emerging Internet world?

To answer this query in a factual and documented manner, keep in mind that a small company is unlikely to be a global powerhouse in technology or other product lines. Therefore, it may lack resources for participating in the triple play of optical, data, and wireless networking and equipping itself with software and services to support such a feat. Hard choices must be made.

There is something else to which small businesses must pay a great amount of attention. This is the accountability of their chief executive officer and his immediate assistants. Big companies that do not fulfill the trust other businesses and consumers put in them are cut down to size by the market. A small company doing something like that can only expect to be wiped out.

It is therefore surprising that some Internet start-ups think of taking investors and their clients for a ride. A recent prospectus for what was said to be a high-tech company made depressing reading because it was based on smoke and mirrors. This was a firm which employed more than 160 people for a turnover of less than $4 million per year. Its balance sheet showed that the ratio of its "intangible fixed (?) assets" to its "tangible assets" stood at about 10 to 1 in favor of the intangibles.

The world is by no means a better, braver place than it was 50 years ago because of the Internet, or for any other reason. In return for all the standard of living, greater freedom, and civil rights enjoyed today, values which meant so much in 1950 have been downgraded and even, at times, derided. Examples of business principles that have lost much of their original value are:

- A sense of duty
- Self-reliance
- Respect for others
- Reliable financial reporting
- Personal accountability

Sometimes, it looks as if the new key words are lack of market discipline, overleveraging, creative accounting, and overindulgence. For this reason, business leadership ought to take more responsibility for the impact of global operations on quality of product, personal responsibility, and financial transparency. It should also strengthen the rules and institutions for trade, finance, and Internet commerce.

The New Economy requires new thinking but also personal values. When these two basic qualities are absent and people and companies want only the benefits of the New Economy without the corresponding responsibilities, financial fiascoes like that of Long Term Capital Management (LTCM) occur.[5] Other examples are the major defects in Mitsubishi cars and Bridgestone/Firestone tires, which make a mockery of Internet supply-chain solutions. These and many other cases raise serious doubts on the quality of the products that some companies now make and then sell on-line to unaware clients in an effort to cut costs at any price.

DOUBLECLICK: AN EXAMPLE OF WHAT IT TAKES TO MAKE AN INTERNET COMPANY

The NASDAQ and its constellation of high tech companies went into a tailspin at the end of March 2000. That was the first shock, followed by a mild recovery, and then by a second, greater, and longer shock which was in the September 2000 to March 2001 timeframe. Many people lost their faith in technology stocks because of these events, but the Internet is here to stay. It is a great leap forward and it has the ability to change so much of the way one lives and does business that it is not going to disappear.

With the NASDAQ's dive, many Internet companies are gone but, at the same time, the Internet continued to impact the way one communicates, plans, gets information, and buys. It is therefore appropriate, prior to ending this chapter, to take a quick look at how an Internet company operates and what makes it tick. DoubleClick, an Internet ad-placement company, is a good example because of its ups and downs.

DoubleClick would not exist without the Internet. It sells on-line advertising for Web sites and delivers the ads to viewers who fit the profile of prospective customers for its clients, the advertisers. The company's competitive advantage is that it can direct ads to Internet users within milliseconds of their checking into the Web site. When this rapid service first hit the market's eye, it was a first even at Internet time. Because of novelty and efficiency, in 1 year (1998), the company's revenues rose 162% to $80 million. The personnel employed by DoubleClick have interesting CVs. The majority have left more conventional environments such as Time Warner, Andersen Consulting, American Express, Mobil Oil, and Saks Fifth Avenue. But how did they get there? Are they fits or mishires? The company, which obtains 20% of its employees via the Net, believes that referrals sharply reduce mishires.[6]

As with most Internet companies, Doubleclick is a flexible organization; it lacks the bureaucracy's hierarchical syndrome. The structure of the company is flat because top-tier managers now recognize that, to exploit people's bandwidth, they need flat organizational structures. In a global marketplace that moves at Internet speed, large span of control is critical in empowering people to make quick decisions.

What about personnel evaluation, salary, and promotion? The model followed has been successfully used in the past at peer-to-peer level. The difference is that, at DoubleClick, every employee is asked annually to rate his or her manager on 25 criteria. The rating is intended to answer two key questions, both of which are unconventional: did the managers hire good people and did their employees like working for them?

Another interesting cultural perspective is that second guessing by layers of managers who confuse decision-making with political plots has been replaced by teams of people with the autonomy of small-business owners. This is fairly common among Internet companies because they rely on the initiative and imagination of individual employees to foster decisions that are closer to the customer and more responsive to market needs.

This sort of small-business decision environment is in essence what makes an Internet company tick. There is, however, legal risk associated with the way business is often done on the Internet. For instance, after DoubleClick announced it was merging on-line Web profiles with data containing names and addresses, a slew of consumer lawsuits, protests from privacy advocates, and regulatory inquiries sent its stock plummeting. Only by retreating could the company recoup some of its losses.

To understand the sensitivity to public response and the aftermath of looming legal risk, one has to remember that the business model of the Net is based on revenue generated by advertising and is not much different from the traditional business model of broadcast television and radio, as well as that of magazines and newspapers. All over the world, advertisers pay a premium for media that efficiently delivers their target audience. However, off-line media do not usually invade the privacy of their audience to satisfy advertisers, if for no other reason than because they can not do so. Technology enables on-line ad companies to invade privacy; therefore, as the previous section suggested, there should be standards of personal accountability (see also Chapter 16).

In response to public outcry, DoubleClick and other Net companies belonging to the Network Advertising Initiative promised to develop a privacy code. This happened some time ago but experts suggest that they walked away from their responsibilities. Along with security, the invasion of privacy is a much greater risk to the Internet and its outfits than NASDAQ's downturn.

It is wise not to confuse the benefits of the Internet as an interactive, any-to-any communications system with the risk and reward of free-wheeling. Free-wheeling ensures that corrective action inevitably occurs. At the plus side, for instance at Cisco, as many as 70% of 20,000 CVs that the company receives monthly come in digital form, and only one out of four is read by a person. Knowledge-enriched software screens these CVs for key words, a process refined by textually analyzing the résumés of successful hires and then using that knowledge to screen incoming CVs more efficiently.

In these terms, Internet recruiting can be more interactive and personalized than the paper-based way without invading a person's privacy. The Net and knowledge software permit screening and hiring people after they apply, which seems to lead to a more stable employment pattern. Cisco's turnover is very low: 6.7% per year in an industry with typical rates of 18 to 28%. About half of turnover rate is involuntary, the result of the company's policy of annually trimming the bottom 5% of its staff.

An interesting aspect of Cisco's weeding out the bottom 5% of its employment every year is that the decision has nothing to do with the length of service or level of employment. The critical question is, "Is that person adding value?" This brings to mind General Douglas McArthur's famous reply to a member of a U.S. Senate Committee who visited the South Pacific theater of operations. The senator observed that some of McArthur's immediate assistants, the chiefs of the U.S. AirForce and U.S. Army in South Pacific, were too young. The General answered, "Senator, out here we promote them for their brains, not for their age."

REFERENCES

1. Chorafas, D.N., *Internet Supply Chain. Its Impact on Accounting and Logistics*, Macmillan, London, 2001.
2. Chorafas, D.N., *Integrating ERP, Supply Chain Management and Smart Materials*, Auerbach/CRC Press, New York, 2001.
3. Reich, R.B., *The Future of Success*, Knopf, New York, 2001.
4. *Financial Times*, May 16, 2001.
5. Chorafas, D.N., *Managing Risk in the New Economy*, New York Institute of Finance, New York, 2001.
6. *BusinessWeek*, October 4, 1999.

14

WORKING END-TO-END WITH THE INTERNET

INTRODUCTION

Many have hailed the Internet as the ultimate global network, the best example available of what, in the mid 1990s, was called the "information superhighway," designed to be at everybody's service. This is misleading, as millions of networked users have discovered. It takes much more homework than mere access to networked resources to reap benefits, but it is true that one can capitalize on three facts already on hand in order to develop a sound and profitable strategy for individual communications:

1. The Internet is available to everybody at an affordable price. This is true for links and nodes as well as a huge wealth of off-the-shelf Web software. Not everybody capitalizes on such resources, however, because of lack of preparedness, missing technological leadership, and hard-headed attitudes that look to the future through the rearview mirror (mainframes, Cobol, IMS, etc.).

2. The Internet makes it possible for costs to shrink steadily. Therefore, by using resources available within its reach, a company can maintain very competitive pricing. This is a significant advantage to firms that know how to capitalize on their assets. Chapter 12 provided plenty of practical examples to document such a statement in regard to Internet supported services.

3. The Internet answers both globalization and technological requirements. Companies using the Net in an able manner can position themselves in the mainstream of future developments, provided they fulfill the prerequisites of which previous Chapters spoke to a certain detail. This last point is conditional. The time has come

to improve the fabric of the network itself: software protocols on which it is founded, channeling capacity, and other operational aspects.

This said, whether called the Internet, the Web, information superhighway, or cyberspace, the evolving global network has what it takes to alter the business aspects of local, metropolitan, and long-haul communications from the way they have existed for over 100 years. Experts agree that it will prove to be the greatest agent of change since the invention of the telephone, but it will also impact almost everything from operating systems and the development of programming artifacts to the design and use of terminal devices and the entire public telecom infrastructure.

Nearly everyone is getting involved with networking today. Among the most common uses is sending and receiving electronic mail (the largest usage factor), finding information about one's job, providing information about one's company, shopping, selling, recreation, pleasure, or other business. "Other business" includes management and support services by putting together a broad and powerful portfolio of data networking product and utility-type solutions to meet the rapidly growing needs of companies and individuals.

As far as consumers and professional persons are concerned, in all likelihood a major breakthrough will come with direct access to the wireless Web (see Chapter 6). With faster data speeds, workaday mobile applications should start making economic sense one day. Microsoft, for instance, is carrying out pilot programs with European blue chips using personal digital assistant (PDA) phones to link far-flung sales and service staffs.[1]

As for the telecommunications industry, it capitalizes on the fact that a global network helps in the take-off phase of an ogive curve in terms of new products and services. Experts think that, while the path to maturity may take another 20 to 30 or even 40 years, as shown in Figure 14.1 the steep growth will be in the next 10 to 15 years. This is an educated guess, but it is no less true that this is the beginning of a multimedia communications era, and the Internet will play a most important role in it.

END-TO-END CONNECTIVITY MOTIVATES COMPANIES TO BE ON THE INTERNET

The Internet was scarcely even mentioned at Telecom 91. Immediately thereafter, it was widely dismissed as a playground for academics. Yet today, slightly over 10 years down the line, it is appreciated that it may well be the most important public service since voice telephony. The fact that American companies have taken the lead in Internet presence is well known, but what about statistics from other countries? As 2001 came to

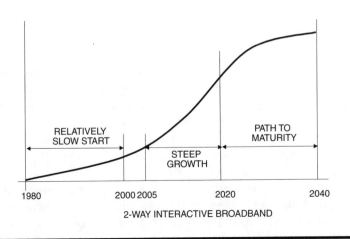

RELATIVELY
SLOW START

STEEP
GROWTH

PATH TO
MATURITY

1980   2000 2005   2020   2040

2-WAY INTERACTIVE BROADBAND

Figure 14.1   The new telecommunications industry will be reaching maturity by 2040.

a close, the latest statistics among industrial companies is that the British, Germans, Italians, and French are 60, 55, 43, and 35% on the Internet, respectively. Not all practice i-commerce, however. Hard data on how many are on the Internet for "me too" reasons are lacking (see Chapter 13), but a guess is that two out of three companies are there for that reason. Three criteria dominate the thinking of firms which are not on the Internet or are there only for cosmetics: lack of skill, imperfect security, and financial costs. The motivation for those who do i-commerce is that the Internet provides a cross-border, easily accessible, level playing field. Their projection of turnover in i-commerce is that it will nearly double every year until 2005. The aftermath of not being there can be loss in market share and inability to grasp new business opportunities.

The risk of losing market share is always in management's mind. After years out of a mainstream development, business may decline and share can be eroded; with this, there is loss of market leadership. Clear-eyed management appreciates that it cannot afford to rest on past laurels. At the end of the 19th century, Lloyds of London controlled 50% of the world's insurance market; in the late 1990s, its share hovered around 2%. Though Lloyds is still present in marine and aviation insurance, in other domains it is no longer a player. The worst fate has been the loss of lucrative business sectors.

Lloyds is a good example of loss of market leadership because it has suffered from an avalanche of badly managed risks.[2] It is important to appreciate that failure to join the new media or introduce lucrative new products can be just as devastating. Whole sectors of the economy die out for this reason. In the late 19th century, the pioneers of the railroads were not the coach companies, autos were not the new product line of rail firms; and aviation had its own beginnings, totally independent from the then-mighty automobile makers.

Therefore, even if the third reason for joining the Internet seems to represent a defensive strategy, overall the reaction can be characterized as a significant change in culture. Companies have their own rationale for joining the Internet bandwagon. Instead of telcos offering services to users, as happens with "vanilla" telephony, it is customer applications that determine: the type of service and the required bandwidth.

This still leaves a big role to carriers, but intermediation by classical telcos — and some of the start-ups — raises some dependability questions. At a debate at the September 1995 Networld+Interop event in Paris, a telecom manager at Paris-based Banque Nationale de Paris (BNP) asked a panel of experts whether Internet service providers today can guarantee quality of service, for example, by assuring that a future BNP Web site would be accessible 24 hours a day, 7 days a week. "On paper, yes. In reality, no," answered the managing director of EUnet France.[3]

Few people and companies really appreciate that service on the Internet is so varied that it creates plenty of opportunities and risks. Only sharply focused newcomers can prosper. There is a very large value gap between merely assuring the communications infrastructure, or *pipes*, and providing the Internet experience, or *content*. The business of providing Internet communications has become a commodity largely because the competition is incredibly intense, and steadily growing, while impediments to increasing bandwidth, which have been largely technological, are fast moving out of the way.

This statement should not be interpreted to mean that improvements would become available automatically, or at low cost. There is no shortage of things that need to be fixed, nor of ideas about how best to go about fixing them, provided one finds the financial means. Experts think two challenges stand out:

1. The growing shortage of addresses needs to be scaled up to cope with faster connections in an efficient manner.
2. The network needs to be scaled up to cope efficiently with fast connections.

These problems are so important because, unless they are addressed, the end-to-end principle on which the power of the Internet rests could be under threat. This is clearly unwanted because end-to-end capability is one of the motivations for companies to be on the Net, bringing more and more of their active business on the Web.

An example from an implementation of Enterprise Resource Planning (ERP) software is given in Figure 14.2.[4] Analytical queries regarding the status of orders are posed by clients to the company. Since delivery of ordered goods is conditioned by the status of orders to suppliers, passthrough routines associated to ERP implementation must look into these requests at suppliers' sites and provide answers in real time. Alternatively, a proactive, just-in-time (JIT), and fast flow replenishment (FFR) system may be instituted, supported by several agents, with the aim to assure automatic status reports.

Whether ad hoc queries or the proactive approach along the aforementioned or a similar frame of reference is chosen, it is important to appreciate that end-to-end is based on a concept which looks at the network as pipes. The Net should be omnipresent, highly capillary but rather dumb.

This may sound surprising, but it is not. What is really expected from an end-to-end solution is to do just one thing but do it well, e.g., send packets from one place to another without fault, with minimal delay, and without any discrimination. All packets must be treated equally and their contents are not to be tampered with. Packets may arrive at their destination in a different order, but computers at each end of the connection do not have to worry about how the packets are delivered. They must have the intelligence to sort them out. Complex assumptions should not be made about such packets as they travel across the communications channels, or the end-to-end simplicity will suffer.

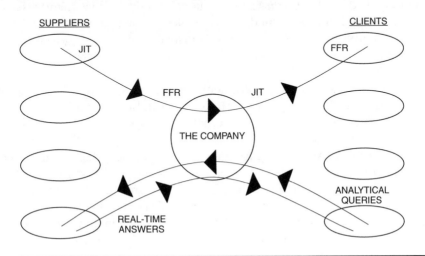

Figure 14.2 Using ERM as passthrough of production planning and control information.

A different way of looking at this issue is that the simpler the network architecture, is the better it can cope with current as well as new types of usage. What was just outlined has been the principle of packet switching from the beginning. Provided one accepts the rules of sending and receiving packets, this system can be used to send and receive anything, from anywhere to anywhere.

Technologically, the challenge is twofold: to maintain the basic simplicity of the Internet's infrastructure, while improving its innovative environment. Every effort should be made to preserve the outlined end-to-end nature of the Net, which means avoiding short-term fixes that disregard the end-to-end principle and hinder future innovative approaches. This is not easy, but it is doable. Now that the Internet has changed from an academic network to an artery of commerce, basic decisions must be made regarding what is best from a purely engineering viewpoint and what is necessary in a global commercial sense.

The challenge posed by the duality of scope just mentioned is exemplified by the divergence and convergence of policies related to the Internet and the funding of information superhighway projects as they made the rounds of government, industry, and community groups. During the 1990s the distribution strategy over the nascent Internet business crossed several milestones (presented in a nutshell in Figure 14.3). There will be many more milestones to cross in the first decade of the 21st century.

The ability to provide a satisfying Internet experience through seamless end-to-end connectivity, innovative content, intuitive software, and a sense of community is a most valued and valuable corporate asset. Almost 100% of the solutions provided were private initiatives even if some governments did pour a big amount of money into projects in new technology during the 1990s.

For example, the U.S. government sponsored the High Performance Computers and Communications (HPCC) project, but nothing practical has resulted. "With the momentum Internet has today, it is very difficult to come up with something really competitive," said one of the leaders of HPCC in a personal meeting. Another lavishly financed high-tech project whose fate was worse than that of HPCC is the RealWorld Computing project with huge financing by the Japanese government.[5] The bureaucrats at Japan's Ministry of International Trade (MITI) had a hit in the 1970s with Project M, which financed IBM-compatible mainframes by Hitachi and Fujitsu. By contrast in the 1980s they incorrectly guessed the direction of technology and misled the Japanese Fifth Generation Computing Project. In the 1990s they poured taxpayers' money into the Real World Computing Project, which became a lame duck in a matter of years.

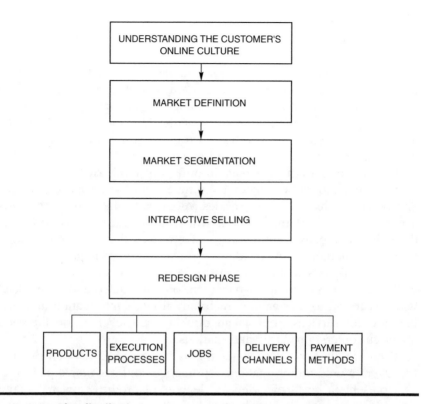

Figure 14.3 **The distribution strategy over the Internet underwent several milestones.**

Looking back into the history of industries which flourished in their time — railroads, telephony, autos, airplanes, computers, etc. — one sees that practically all have been based on private initiatives. Whenever bureaucrats mixed into planning, things went wrong either immediately or in the longer run, as imagination ran dry and routine called the tune. The European Union's Esprit project, which promoted R&D in information technology, is another example. Subsidies, too, are not of any lasting help. It takes imagination and private initiative to succeed in any field, including cyberspace.

THE INTERNET AS ENABLER OF AND CATALYST FOR BETTER INFORMATION TECHNOLOGY SOLUTIONS

People who believe strongly in the revolutionary potential of the Internet and i-commerce tend to keep away from superlatives like *infosphere*, though from time to time they may use the term *cyberspace*. As the growth of i-commerce continues to accelerate in the U.S., many companies now look forward to Europe's reaching the takeoff point that America had attained prior to NASDAQ's downturn, followed soon after by Asia and Latin America.

Over the longer term, a whole new world could unlock multiple investor interests in communications networks, data resources, and new, evolving fields of information technology. Both business and technical challenges would spring from the fact that complex computer systems interact with themselves and their surroundings in products and services whose nature can only be guessed at now.

It is important to think of data, information, and knowledge as inherent in the complexity of both natural and man-made systems, accessible from any point in which the user resides. Along with this concept has arisen a new awareness of the ways in which information should flow freely through a company's entire range of enclaves that have been isolated from one another for many decades. This problem is generic because, today, tiny islands in the information archipelago do not communicate well and are accessible to management only in limited and unpredictable ways. Learning to master the any-to-any flow of information and derive higher-order services from it can offer a huge leverage on knowledge about customers, products, and markets.

Even among tier-1 companies this is not going to happen overnight. Its advent would require patience, prudence, and a strategic plan. Figure 14.4 presents a bird's eye view of degrees of progress toward obtaining a sound information technology policy. The role of the Internet in this policy is that of an enabler and a catalyst.

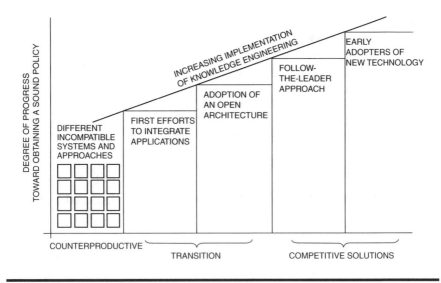

Figure 14.4   Strategy and standards in managing technological change.

As an enabler, the Internet plays the role of a critical infrastructure of a logical and physical system essential to the evolution of marketing operations of the economy. Many industry sectors can benefit from this evolution; among them are telecommunications, computer systems, energy, banking and finance, transportation, power distribution, water systems, and emergency services. In the background are both government and private initiatives.

Many of a nation's critical infrastructures have historically been physically and logically separate, with little interdependence between the two. As a result, advances in information technology and the necessity of increased efficiency have been underrated. The same statement is valid for companies that have not known to take advantage of the latest state of the art. A practical example, albeit in just one domain, is capitalizing on Internet hyperlinks.

The hyperlinking technology of the Web blurs the lines between editorial content and advertising. This makes it easy to lead a consumer from a product review to a vendor ad and then to an on-line store; therefore, it has a significant impact on marketing. Portals do take advantage of hyperlinks. Some companies have a Web site linking all their operations and subsidiaries. For instance, an Internet surfer visiting a production planning board is able to link to another page to learn about a scheduled delivery, then visit an order-handling agent on-line for downloading a new command for goods or services.

As this simple example suggests, using the Internet to integrate one's industrial activities into a globally connected economy can usher in a new economic age for workers, consumers, and investors. But it will also be a world with significant social change as well as with a host of privacy and security issues (see Chapter 16). Many things known or taken for granted today would need to be redefined as the global citizenry starts to adapt their lives to the new virtual community. Experts see a continuation of these technology- and productivity-led developments during the present decade; they judge the current status to be at the foothills of an era of unprecedented opportunities and risks.

Imagine an Internet site that would let anyone in the world log on, type in another party's phone number, and then find out where that party is. This is not science fiction. Nippon Telephone & Telegraph (NTT) has actually developed such a site. Because Japan uses low-powered cell phones on a high-density network, the resulting location can be very precise, down to the specific floor of a building.

It sounds scary and it is. Yet this is a capability that exists with cell phones everywhere. In Switzerland, location data for every cell phone are logged several times per day and archived for a period of months. The Swiss police say that they have found this useful. In the U.S., the

Department of Justice and the FBI successfully insisted that real-time location tracking features be made part of mandatory cellular telephone standards. Not everything is rosy in the global wired world, but it would be silly to suggest that current developments could or would be rolled back and that all future technological progress would disappear.

In fact, quite the opposite is true. As Chapter 6 showed, in the coming 10 years 2.5G and third generation (3G) wireless technology will most likely dominate. Wireless technology is at the core of the mobile Internet, an emerging paradigm for the future in which users access the Web through handheld devices and other kinds of remote networked tools. That is the location-independent environment in Chapter 9, while Chapter 15 elaborates on the role of mobile agents.

Companies will be faced with many challenges on their way toward any-to-any and end-to-end nomadic computing supported by hundreds of thousands of agents. For example, they must accommodate a wide range and diversity of mobile devices, including laptops, cameras, and embedded, wearable, and even implantable devices. At the same time, the mobile Internet must deal with multiple operating systems, and will need to be scalable, from the range of wide-area networks down to the level of personal area networks and beyond.

For security reasons nomadic wireless platforms will need to handle firewalls, feature virus protection, and incorporate other housekeeping functions beyond the operational services to be delivered to the end user. The previous section mentioned change of address as an example of the need to restructure current Internet supports.

The problem with the current specification for Internet Protocol (IP), known as IP version 4 or IPV4, is that it allows for about 4 billion addresses, each consisting of a string of 32 binary digits. When the Internet was originally designed in the late 1960s and early 1970s, this seemed like more addresses than would ever be needed. When the Internet went mainstream in the 1990s, however, it slowly became clear that IPV4's addressing scheme would have to be extended.

This is already happening by means of what is known as network address translation (NAT), which involves putting a computer between a company and the Internet. Its mission is that of relabeling passing packets to enable a large number of machines on the company network to share a smaller number of IPV4 addresses. This solution is seen by many as a violation of the end-to-end principle, since the network is no longer simply passing packets from one end to another but rely on intermediate software and on particular machines having a fixed IP address.

New departures are necessary because, among other things, 4 billion addresses would be eaten up for breakfast by nomadic computing and smart materials.[6] IP version 6 would provide a relief, but the process of developing IPV6 has already sparked a vigorous debate because it would require upgrades to millions of machines; therefore, some experts suggest that it presents a good opportunity to fix other problems besides the shortage of addresses.

Apart from the fact that not everyone is in accord regarding the nature of more advanced features to be added to the Internet's endowment, their incorporation is not in keeping with the end-to-end philosophy discussed in the previous section. More or less everyone accepts the need for low-level encryption and authentication features, as well as support for automatic configuration. However, implementing higher-level features like payment mechanisms and explicit support for media streams would involve second guessing the future development of the Internet. This, opponents say, would constrain the Net unnecessarily. Added to this argument is the fact that IPV6 software is now available, at least in prototype form, and is increasingly supported in routers which direct traffic. Furthermore, 3G mobile telephony is being designed along the aforementioned more limited improvements option in IP software.

The pros themselves are divided. Those who go along with the need for encryption and authentication suggest that a switch to IPV6, as it now stands, is vital if the Internet's ongoing innovation of services is to continue. The use of IPV6 in mobile devices, which will widely outnumber computers connected to the Internet by fixed lines within a few years, will be a factor that encourages adopting the new protocol. Other experts, however, are concerned that IPV6 will become a disruptive technology. Only time will tell.

CONTRIBUTIONS OF THE INTERNET TO INFRASTRUCTURE, GLOBALIZATION, AND NATIVE APPLICATIONS

The best way to think of the Internet is as a nervous system made of glass and microwaves. The network constituting this nervous system spreads to connect the minds of those who wish to be connected to it. The Internet is integrative of people and companies, but it also extracts from those minds values expressed in algorithms, heuristics, and transactions. The modeling is very subtle. Globalization occurs at both the national and international levels within this sprawling network of information streams, episodic memories, and algorithmic or heuristic models.

In terms of cost and benefit derived from end-to-end connections, much depends on:

- How governments, companies, and individuals look at this infrastructure
- How it is regulated nationally and internationally

- How it keeps on developing by recasting itself in new channel capabilities and protocols
- What use is made of available telecommunications capabilities
- How some of the negatives are addressed

The previous section highlighted the fact that, as the Internet expands, new challenges are bound to develop, e.g., the shortage of addresses. Privacy and security concerns will probably increase. New portables leave behind a data trail far more revealing than that left by cell phones today. Users will also tend to keep sensitive information on remote servers not under their direct control. In fact, users will not even know where their data physically reside, just as they do not know the locations of their local telephone switches in the telco network.

Companies and consumers who, for security purposes, rely on strong encryption and other safeguards are in competition with governments who want access to all data everywhere, whether in storage or transit, without a mandatory search warrant. Another big question in end-to-end Internet connectivity is who is really going to control this global infrastructure and its national chunks.

To understand the depth of this last question, recall that the original contributors to the telephone infrastructure were monopolies. During infancy, from the late 19th century to the 1980s, the telephone infrastructure was developed and managed by government agencies or regulated utilities such as AT&T and closely supervised by the government. Deregulation made feasible a greater pace of development and more efficient resource management through the mechanism of free competition. Globalization has opened a new horizon by achieving a balance between efficiency and participatory access, but it has also left some basic questions unanswered.

Some of these questions, indeed the tougher ones in terms of answers, have to do with the fact that networks are part of the social and business fabric. Hence the problem arises of balancing freedom and privacy; this is not easy to solve, if for no other reason than because of lack of experience in establishing and sustaining a balancing act of such proportions.

Some experts believe that public telecommunications have found the right path by themselves. Rather than being financed by governments, the evolving global telecommunications infrastructure is subscribed to by its clients: private individuals and business enterprises. That is an area where the goals of the Internet and electronic commerce meet.

Yes, but … This sort of argument is not based on self-evident truths. In most Group of Ten countries the government is still a major shareholder of the telecommunications utility, as well as its regulator; it also uses this utility as a cash cow, for instance, obliging it to get overleveraged in order to buy new airwave licenses to do its business. As Chapter 6 showed, this is what happened in 2000 and 2001 with British Telecom, France Telecom, Deutsche Telekom, Terra, Sonera, and others.

This sort of background reference is most crucial when talking about the Internet's end-to-end links and nodes because, in the last analysis, the infrastructure is provided by public telecommunications utilities, including those in the above list. It is wise to keep in mind the three-layered structure shown in Figure 14.5 in which Internet commerce is just one of the horizontal layers.

Within this larger aggregate, i-commerce is cast as a major component of the emerging global open marketplace for information, knowledge, goods, and services. This is the background of what has been called the *digital agora*, combining sales, research, and technologies from many fields, as well as expertise from a variety of disciplines developed in different countries by a significant number of companies.

This far greater perspective of the Internet's global impact on the economy as a whole, companies, and consumers is a far cry from statistics

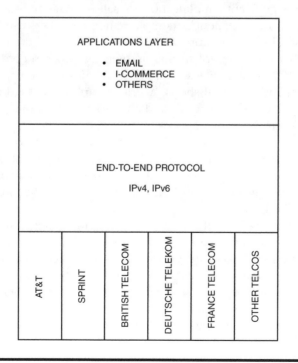

Figure 14.5 **The infrastructure of Internet commerce is still the fractal telecommunications utility of different national telcos.**

revealed by studies just a few years ago. In one of these studies,[7] answers given by companies using the Internet fell into five buckets:

- 15% said that it increases productivity
- 16% said that it increases marketing and sales
- 19% said that it provides better communications
- 26% said that it decreases productivity
- 24% said that the impact is still unclear

Today the emphasis has shifted, and the focus of many experts is not on the aforementioned issues but on the rapid market shift toward Internet-native applications — essentially products and companies which might not exist without Internet-based facilities and services. The way this issue is perceived varies from one party to another. For some, it is a technical advantage of Internet-native applications because of lower deployment and management costs. For others, the most important issue is that internet-native applications can facilitate pervasive use of technological resources. This goes beyond lowering the cost of information technology and brings a significant simplification to data management.

Today, data management is complex and costly because so much of the application logic and information elements are distributed across many heterogeneous computer platforms as well as paper records. It is also because of 1950s-era policies connected to custom-made programming by each company's internal shops. A British bank mentioned in a London meeting that it employs young graduates to maintain programs written before they were born.

Part of the attractiveness of Web software, and therefore of intranets and extranets (see Chapter 15), is that these inefficient and unwise practices are but some problems remain. For instance, software vendors' pricing will need to change radically, from a per-seat license agreement to a total-usage basis.

Some experts believe that the current pricing scheme would be too expensive if continued, and therefore discourage mass adoption by companies. Furthermore, software vendors largely lose control of usage with browser-based approaches, as there is no effective way to restrict or monitor access to applications since each user no longer requires a separate client site installation.

Software firms are preparing to face the Internet-native applications' challenges. The pillars of Microsoft's strategy, for instance, are that Internet-based functionality would result in significant incremental sales of platform and applications software, while in the longer term the company would retain its ability to leverage its dominance of the Internet platform and applications software markets into related business areas such as banking and communications.

This flexibility illustrates that a vendor's commitment to Internet-based businesses is not based upon any loyalty to the structural characteristics of the Internet, or the standards and protocols that define the medium, but on the concepts of nomadic computing, the convergence of computing and communication, and the pull exercised by Web software. Software producers veer toward such strategies because they view the wider deployment of Internet functionality as the most important IT-related event of the coming 5 years.

OPEN NETWORKS, LACK OF CENTRALIZATION, AND THE ESTABLISHMENT OF STANDARDS

What made the Internet so popular in such a few years is that plenty of software was available at very reasonable prices. To a large degree this was the aftermath of so many local university networks attached to the Net, and so many brilliant students contributing the products of their brains.

The U.S. Department of Defense played its part by giving the common platform away for use by universities, which turned the Internet into an American and then globally networked research laboratory. Just as important is the fact that a serious attempt at Internet control and regulation was never made. This was quite different from almost everything else that had existed in the past with telecommunications. For any practical purpose no company or group has a monopoly on services or ideas; therefore, it is widely considered among the user community that lack of central control is the top reason why the Internet works. Nobody needs to go through a central point because the structure is decentralized, and there is no place where one must register a new node or any new attachment to the Net.

Another critical factor in the Internet's success is that its mode of networking benefits from a simple and open architecture to get all the bit streams through. This eases the task of building all applications on top of a transport facility which is proprietary to the vendor. The Net's flexibility and extensibility contrast to closed architectures like IBM's SNA and others by mainframe, maxi, or mini vendors. Even cable television (CATV) can be seen as a closed system.

Designers of enterprise architectures will be well-advised to take notice; their work should benefit a great deal from the Internet concepts and the benefits derived from them. Any architecture is the art of building according to proportion in order to meet functional service goals and face growth requirements. The choices made should help to incorporate change through a system whose completion may exceed the architect's lifetime. An architectural solution assumes a framework for design and makes higher performance feasible at reduced cost per function. In this sense, the enterprise architecture developed is the higher level within which different technologies integrate and handhold with one another.

In contrast to a system architecture bought off the shelf from a computer vendor, the company's enterprise architecture should support an end-to-end wide range of functionality and open standards. What open-eyed companies are after is an open, flexible, horizontal structure that can promote effective solutions regarding current and upcoming business. The best way to look at this issue is that the top-level reference is that of business aims, as shown in Figure 14.6. From these business aims derive functions which require adequacy of support. This support is provided by the bottom line, where the chosen architectural solution resides.

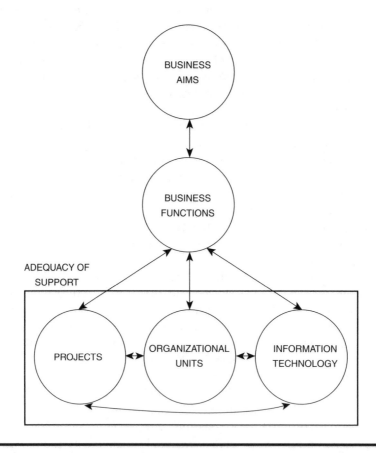

Figure 14.6 A corporate model of business objectives, functions, and support.

Prior to the advent of the Internet, tier-1 companies and their systems specialists actively searched for an open architecture, but their efforts were turned back by the action of vendors who first and foremost wanted to sell their architecture and its income stream. *De facto* standards, and standards bodies like the International Standards Organization (ISO) have played a significant role in this game of cat-and-mouse.

One of the most interesting characteristics of the Internet is that it became a *de facto* standard without any standard body's involvement. It made available a solid set of norms and specifications, and this proved to be one of its greatest assets. The Department of Defense's support of the Internet's norms facilitated their acceptance as *de facto* standards, just as IBM once set *de facto* standards in connection to computers and other vendors aimed to become plug-compatible to them.

Such *de facto* strategy contrasts to that of formal standards organizations that seek a consensus for establishing support for standards. The value of the American National Standards Institute (ANSI) and ISO rests on constituent confidence that the approved standard results from fair considerations and assures more or less life-long support. (ANSI and ISO, as well as all other standards organizations, also serve in coordinating and distributing functions.)

The downside of setting standards on a volunteer contribution basis, like that characterizing the work of standards bodies, is that the product is subject to many pressures and compromises. Furthermore, critics say that ISO, the International Telecommunications Union (ITU, formerly CCITT), and other standards organizations have used the various copyright laws enforced by government to exploit a monopoly on some standards, typically developed by volunteers whose companies paid their participating expenses. Critics also add that the government does not regulate these monopolists of standards and norms.

By contrast, there are government-sponsored or -approved organizations whose authority rests on inverse delegation, from the periphery to the center. An American example is the Financial Accounting Standards Board (FASB), an arm of the Securities and Exchange Commission (SEC), which sets standards for financial reporting. In banking industry standards, the Bank for International Settlements (BIS) is a similar example on a global scale. Both FASB and BIS could serve as models in setting Internet standards.

A suggestion made by cognizant executives is that, no matter how standards originate, the current free character of the Internet must be further exploited to facilitate the widest possible exchange of norms and know-how. The aim should be to increase the accessibility and utility of open standards, creating in the longer run a more responsive and meaningful way for setting them than the setting of standards by formal bodies.

THE NEW ECONOMY ENLARGES THE APPLICATIONS DOMAIN OF THE INTERNET

A few years ago, an article on the fast growth of computer power and the role played by the Web made the statement that "Ford claims it now has more computer power than any other automotive manufacturer in the world, following a 10-year program of IT expansion which has launched its designers into the virtual world. Supercomputer power in the company has grown by over 50 times from 1990 to 1996 and will be over 10 times what it is today by the year 2000."[8] The years that have elapsed since this article was published more or less justified its claims in computer power terms.

This article did not prognosticate that, by September 1999, Ford would team up with Microsoft to sell cars on the Net, but one should appreciate that computer power and interactive use of IT resources tend to correlate. There is also a stronger correlation between interactive IT applications and using the Net to expand one's marketing horizon, at least in the opinions of many experts.

People who disagree with this statement bring into perspective the fact that the majority of current applications on the Net are not of a nature to provide a cutting edge in the movement. Current Internet applications are not at the top of a sophistication scale even if they have universal segmented appeal. They divide into two tiers with approximate levels of popularity shown in order of popularity:

- Tier-1 Applications
  - E-mail
  - Browsing
  - Favored sites
  - Topical searches
  - Visiting URL
  - Supply chain
- Tier-2 Applications
  - Recent news
  - Chat
  - Downloads
  - Games
  - Consumer shopping
  - City guides

This scale of popularity of tier-1 and tier-2 applications is based on different survey results; as can be seen, electronic commerce is near the bottom of both tier 1 and tier 2. Theoretically, consumers use the Internet for purchases, but practically they are much more interested in gathering information, then going to the store and buying.

Yet there are bargains to be found on the Internet. During the Comdex event in Las Vegas, for example, hotels charge those who register by mail about 40% more for exactly the same room than if one searches the Internet to find an accommodation. The top reason why consumer Internet shopping is held back is security. Research among 300 experts at Comdex '98 indicated that:

- 46% fear giving out their credit card numbers on the Net.
- 25% complain about the inability to see and feel products.
- 12% do not know where to find the on-line products that they want.
- 8% prize the human interaction that i-commerce misses.
- 4% think that there is not enough variety in selection.

One of the better ways to bypass credit card fear is to use some other payment medium. Many users pay by check, even if sending a check takes time. Some stores, like Dixon's in the U.K., have surmounted this hurdle: one can walk into the store and pick up a CD for Internet access; his payment will then be debited in the phone bill.

Notice from the above statistics that, if the top drawback with i-commerce is lack of security for payment through credit cards, directly below it is the embedded habit of physical selection. It is not a mere coincidence that electronically delivered products such as hotel rooms and airline reservations are the first to go in Internet sales.

Consumer shopping habits can, however, change as new practices set in and outlets on the Internet increase. The number of ".com" companies is a strong indicator of Web traffic. For example, during the formative years of the late 1990s, there were 250 .com companies in 1997, 475 in 1998, and 880 in 1999.

These numbers have grown to 1580 .com companies in 2000, and 2770 in 2001. The curve which one could draw based on these statistics is not quite exponential, but it does stand a chance to be so in the coming years. A similar statement can be made regarding the potential growth of supply-chain operations.

While today the foremost companies take advantage of the Internet (e.g., Cisco) most firms are still fence-sitting. The fact that, in the 2000 to 2001 timeframe, the New Economy hit an air pocket did not sustain the rapid growth in company supply-chain operations projected a couple of years earlier.[9]

Whether overestimating or underestimating future trends, projections are often prerogative. One should always learn from past events and the failure to prognosticate effects of the wave of change. The two graphs in Figure 14.7 come from Xerox, which in 1970 made an educated guess about its installed capacity in millions of instructions per second (MIPS),

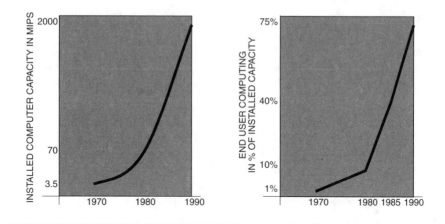

Figure 14.7 Statistics and forecasts in the early 1980s by Xerox regarding millions of instructions per second (MIPS) needed for its operations.

and end user terminals as percent of total installed available MIPS in the enterprise. In both cases the projection was made for 20 years (1970 to 1990) and growth, while impressive, was underestimated. Following these estimates came the mini, maxi, and personal computer revolution, which ensured that, during the following years, the explosion in MIPS and the percent of workstation installations became exponential.

One of the big questions in estimating future growth is whether or not "something" becomes part and parcel of a trend. What we see today with the Net is an increasingly round-the-clock usage. The reason is pull and push between the Internet and the New Economy. From cross-border marketing operations to global design teams, companies are swapping long data streams by satellite and land lines through intranets and extranets (see Chapter 15). Virtual workshops are playing a key role in lowering costs and shortening product lead times. Worldwide design programs see to it that multinationals can operate in the way they call "global".

WING-TO-WING: A VIEW OF BIG FIRMS CAPITALIZING ON THE INTERNET

Intelligent networks permit one to work around the clock without borders. In the past, a company needed significant lead-time to develop and market a new range of products. Now what used to take 4 to 5 years can be turned over in an equal number of months. During the next decade this, too, should shrink to a matter of weeks or days.

In several meetings with financial analysts on Wall Street it was opined that a company's wing-to-wing strategy and its virtuosity in using the Internet to further its goals are becoming a critical element in evaluating its growth potential, survivability, and quality of earnings. One of these discussions focused on GE Capital and its four main themes: globalization, services, Six Sigma, and Internet business (see also Chapter 5 on GE and Six Sigma).

An analyst first highlighted GE Capital's success in Japan, where it has completed two of the largest acquisitions in the country's history: Lake Finance and Japan Leasing Corporation. He then said that GE Capital believes it will achieve a similar foothold in Japan to its European presence through its consumer finance, equipment finance, and insurance divisions, and in roughly half the time due, in part, to currently prevailing weak economic conditions. A goal of GE Capital's initiative is to strengthen the links the company has with its customer base by bundling together a service with a product. Globalization not only refers to acquisitions, but also to the strategic relocation of intellectual assets in order to build a cross-border platform.

But now, the analyst said, General Electric is finding ways to leverage its expertise to generate additional business from its customer base. The wing-to-wing approach means that GE will examine the entire process from the customer's perspective as well as its own, and couple this to Internet-based business services which it sees as a significant $20 billion growth opportunity for its operating technical divisions as well as for GE Capital.

Other analysts, too, offered similar input in terms of strategies followed by major companies to capitalize on what they perceive as Internet synergies. They said GE has recently become a repository of information and expertise; therefore, it is one of the knowledge companies. As a result of this strategic advantage, the company can be leveraged over a huge installed base, itself the product of years of industry leadership, can tie customers to its product lines and marketing channels for decades, and can help to increase asset values, thus making itself more immune to economic vagaries.

In this manner the classical General Electric, more or less a model of consistency, combines with the new growth-oriented and more aggressive GE to form a company that should be valued at least as high as today's growth stocks. This is what is essentially meant by a company's ability to reinvent itself using new technology, and it is not the only example of a firm known to have lifted itself up with the Internet.

At the end of February 2000, about a month before the rising value of the NASDAQ bent, the big auto manufacturers in the U.S. announced that they were matching forces in a supply chain worth approximately $250 billion annually. This is the story of Covisint, the collaborative Internet purchasing agreement of four major players in the motor vehicle industry: General Motors, Ford, Daimler-Chrysler and Renault, and Renault-Nissan.

On the positive side, Covisint illustrates how big companies can put aside their rivalries and work together. The predecessor to this joint supply-chain effort dates back to November 1999, when General Motors and Ford independently started their own Internet autoparts marketplaces and then realized that they could get more mileage by combining forces. Investment bankers acted as catalysts. In January 2000, at separate meetings with GM and Ford in Detroit, Morgan Stanley Dean Witter and J.P. Morgan executives raised the prospect of combining forces by suggesting that this combination could create the world's largest B2B supply chain and it also had the potential to generate up to $10 billion on the stock market within 5 years.

The investment bankers argued that manufacturers of motor vehicles and their suppliers could use Internet power to save billions in costs. The profits of the exchange were not forgotten either. It was calculated that, by charging transactions fees for purchasing orders, the exchange could generate billions of dollars in new revenue.

Insiders, however, say that while, pace-setting, this cooperative i-commerce deal was not without its problems. On the negative side, problems began almost immediately with a lack of responsibility and accountability at the CEO level. For starters, there was not one CEO but several; finally, a "vacancy" sign was hung out for this job. Just as fundamental was the fact that technological conflicts arose almost immediately. Ford settled on Oracle for software to run its exchange, but GM chose upstart Commerce One's marketplace software, and DaimlerChrysler asked why SAP's software should not be employed.

The automakers were not alone in this rush to decision. Several competitors have also been eyeing the leadership in on-line business exchanges for computers and electronics parts. IBM has made agreements with Nortel Networks, Toshiba, and others for a consortium, e2open.com. Its goal is to buy and sell semiconductors and electronic parts over the Internet, with the aim to streamline the purchasing process and bring down costs of semiconductors.

This IBM-led venture was preceded by a similar agreement between Compaq Computer, Gateway, and Hewlett-Packard, who joined forces in creating an on-line marketplace with very similar objectives. Other exchanges with about the same leadership goals have been established or proposed in the chemical and steel sectors.

There are also other challenges. When fierce competitors combine forces to gain advantages of mass, it is unavoidable that their incompatible information technology will stand in the way. This, said, however, the study of metamorphoses of Old Economy firms into New Economy entities makes interesting reading. The careful observer will particularly note the amount of change undertaken in a decade and, associated with it, the rise of some global corporations and the fall of others.

In 1989, the 10 biggest corporations in *BusinessWeek's* Global 1000 list of the largest companies in the world by market capitalization were Japanese, led by Nippon Telegraph & Telephone and the Industrial Bank of Japan (IBJ). In 1999, not a single Japanese company made the Top 10 and IBJ tried to pull out of big troubles in its loans portfolio through a merger with two other large Japanese financial institutions.

What has happened in the interim? The Tokyo stockmarket tanked in 1991 while NASDAQ and the New Your Stock Exchange forged ahead. For the second half of the 1990s, the able use of high technology and the effect of the Internet have been behind both exchanges. Internet-related companies have pushed into the BusinessWeek 1000 list in an amazing way, and though many of them dropped out because of the 2000 to 2001 NASDAQ dive, experts think that some of tomorrow's big firms are among the survivors. It is equally important that many of the elder companies had their businesses transformed by the Net.

REFERENCES

1. *Business Week*, May 14, 2001.
2. Chorafas, D.N., *Managing Credit Risk*, Vol. 2, *The Lessons of VAR Failures and Imprudent Exposure*, Euromoney, London, 2000.
3. *Communnsweek Int.*, October 2, 1995.
4. Chorafas, D.N., *Managing Operational Risk. Risk Reduction Strategies for Banks Post-Basle*, Lafferty, London and Dublin, 2000.
5. Chorafas, D.N., *Network Computers versus High Performance Computers*, Cassell, London, 1997.
6. Chorafas, D.N., *Integrating ERP, Supply Chain Management and Smart Materials*, Auerbach/CRC Press, New York, 2001.
7. *Commn. ACM*, July, 1997.
8. Designer future, *Inf. Strategy*, November, 1997.
9. Chorafas, D.N., *Internet Supply Chain. Its Impact on Accounting and Logistics,* Macmillan, London, 2001.

15

INTRANETS, EXTRANETS, MOBILE AGENTS, AND EFFICIENT OFF-THE-SHELF COMMUNICATIONS SOLUTIONS

INTRODUCTION

As enterprise architectures, intranets have become quite important because they are based on off-the-shelf Web software and are promoted by telecommunications, which hold the upper ground on data processing (DP). In most companies, the telecommunications department is independent from DP and responsible for all voice and data communications, whether local, regional, or long haul. In a growing number of cases, the communications department also has desktop computing under its wing. A major restructuring in IT is in full swing. With industry undergoing rapid change, companies are striving to improve customer service and create new market opportunities while swamping costs. Telecommunication's mission has been rephrased as the responsibility for collapsing the distance between people and processes at a reasonable cost.

This is another way of saying that companies need an enterprise architecture capable of streamlining today's operations while providing capabilities for future expansion in products and services. Intranets enter this picture by assisting in internal company communications, helping to access corporate databases, and providing interactive staff support. They also serve as an information backbone, company publications medium, interactive training framework, and means of communications with business partners.

The latter service is provided by extranets, whose area of activity is to link business partners to one another. Intranets and extranets are very much alike because both use off-the-shelf Web software. This permits rapid deployment, greater dependability, and a significant cost reduction. As Figure 15.1 shows, the Internet, intranets, and extranets are three pillars on which rest a wide range of products and services offered by business and industry today.

To capitalize on benefits presented by the effective use of intranets and extranets, companies are storing internal documents and other data in Web format. They are also using off-the-shelf software like enterprise resource planning (ERP), which allows easy cross-company communications.[1] Employees can call up information elements using Web browser software that runs on any type of desktop machine.

This practice of widespread seamless communications poses questions. Is the PC a computer or a communicator? How many people use a PC to compute? How many use it only to communicate? How much of the installed PC base worldwide does actual computing? To appreciate the impact of the answers to these queries, one must realize that business migrated away from data processing-type computing and made the PC the primary vehicle for gaining access to real-time, widely distributed information. Because of this transition semiconductor manufacturers now

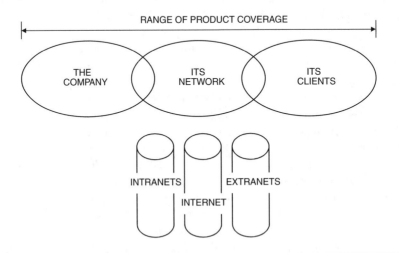

Figure 15.1   Internet interfaces between providers and consumers of products and services.

adopt a system-on-a-chip strategy. These chips feature multimedia presentation and wide communications capabilities; they are the forerunners of sophisticated solutions of the early 21st century, designed to exploit the broadband channel capabilities of earth- and satellite-based communications links (see Chapter 6).

Another trend is to move away from complex application programs to small and simpler software to be created by languages such as Java that can be transferred over corporate networks to any type of computer. Also, use of a growing number of agents (see Chapters 7 and 9) makes man–machine interaction much more sophisticated. This, too, makes the applications more communication-intense than those of classical data processing.

The goal is to simplify programming, ease computer usage, and make intranets handle a broader array of tasks. Instead of simply calling up and reading existing documents, a new generation of programs aims to let workers in separate offices edit documents, keep track of changes, and flash exceptions relying on Internet-style technology that makes it easier to find and share information more effectively.

A BIRD'S EYE VIEW OF WHAT INTRANETS CAN DO: EXAMPLES FROM THE AUTO INDUSTRY

The introduction briefly defined the term intranet as the entire communications structure of a private enterprise network using commodity Internet software. Typically, these are Web-based routines available at very reasonable prices and widely implemented in business and industry on a global basis.

Intranets can run over private local area networks (LANs), metropolitan area networks (MANs), and wide area networks (WANs), or across public networks such as private networks of different types supported by the telephone system or the Internet itself. Although in theory intranets may use any and all networking and communications methodologies, in practice they apply established Internet networking protocols: transmission control protocol (TCP), internet protocol (IP), hypertext transfer protocol (HTTP), and hypertext markup language (HTML), along with its extension XML.

The flexibility of these protocols and their contribution to business activity are illustrated by their easy and efficient support of quite different entrepreneurial characteristics: low- and high-margin, high- and low-volumes transactions, stronger and weaker two-way interactions. Most importantly they assist in:

- Enhancing availability and scalability of IT systems
- Supporting customer relationship management (CRM) applications

- Hooking up to personalized portals
- Facilitating multichannel integration of different product lines

One of the more imaginative applications to be supported by intranets and extranets in the future is that of communications requirements by auto area networks. Today, according to the experts, the value of a motor vehicle's electronic systems averages 22% of the total value of the car. This figure is expected to grow to as much as 35 to 40% by 2010, including everything from smart sensing and fuzzy engineering chips to more mundane applications.

Developers of information technology solutions, specialists working on voice-over data approaches, wireless communication entities, and Internet software firms are living in a world of leap-frogging advances in electronics and telecommunications. It is only reasonable that advances in other fields find their way in auto manufacturing as car companies bet on value differentiation. Current projects include safety networks, chassis electronics, intelligent lightning, control by wire, and new power and signal distribution systems.

Because of fierce competition, auto manufacturers are poised to integrate technology breakthroughs as they occur. The car industry and its suppliers are driving hard to capitalize on new communications systems, which, in turn, pose significant capacity requirements and call for solutions only Internet software can quickly implement.

These and many other examples are not a burden on intranets but an opportunity to provide more and better service. Like any other information network, their functionality rests on state-of-the art hardware and software components, including what is necessary for network management. The layers supporting intranet functionality are shown in Figure 15.2 at the peak of the pyramid where end user functions reside.

One of the differences between intranets and the public Internet is that intranets' access is often controlled by firewalls and other security measures; the same is true of extranets. Employees, customers, suppliers, and other business partners access information stored on intranets and extranets, while unauthorized persons cannot (at least theoretically). Furthermore, corporate intranets tend to be more efficient than the public Internet in terms of available bandwidth and management control.

In principle, companies run on their intranets' Web software. Other programming products are also supported, designed to accomplish some of an enterprise architecture's primary tasks in a way characterized by ease of use, efficiency in resources, and better performance than general-purpose systems. Big iron (read mainframe) products are not favored since they use top-heavy operating systems; the same is true of cycle-consuming DBMSs not designed from the distributed tasks.

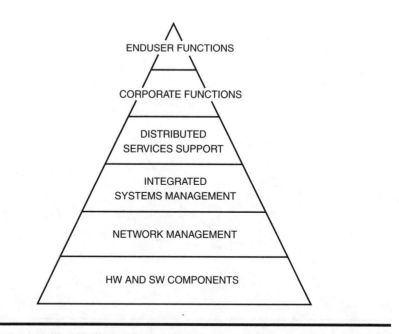

ENDUSER FUNCTIONS

CORPORATE FUNCTIONS

DISTRIBUTED
SERVICES SUPPORT

INTEGRATED
SYSTEMS MANAGEMENT

NETWORK MANAGEMENT

HW AND SW COMPONENTS

Figure 15.2   Intranet functionality permits a more holistic view of network functions than has been possible before.

Because there are so many degrees of freedom in their implementation, the successful use of intranets is by no means a foregone conclusion. When implementation happens, it can have profound long-term implications because the cost-effective, easy use of Web software has the power to transform business processes, as well as to radically change corporate hierarchies, disciplines, and norms. Intranets impact the ways in which people work within the enterprise as individuals and groups, the means through which information is transferred and exchanged, and how corporate communications operate in a crossfunctional, interdisciplinary manner.

A more generic way of looking at intranets is through the viewpoint that what used to be client and server architecture has now been replaced by the Web. A huge market for Web server software is in the intranets, as Figure 15.3 suggests. In the corporate sector, the challenge is to efficiently find and tap into information sources, integrating the points of origin and destination of data streams, and providing flexible transaction capabilities as well as accurate responses to queries from an ever-larger, more demanding user community.

This information must be harnessed in a manner that integrates and enhances the quality of responses through distributed dynamic systems comprising knowledge agents that know the user and his or her requirements (see Chapter 9). Old Cobol software does not lend itself to this

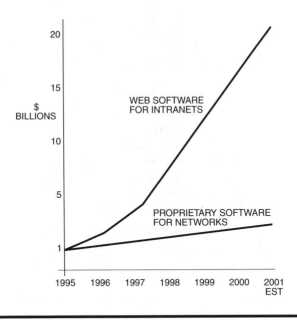

Figure 15.3 The market for web server software is in the intranets while that for closed networking systems stagnates.

sort of usage; this functionality can be provided more effectively by new applications domains, intelligent networks, and sophisticated databases.

A good example of new applications was provided in 1998 with intelligent automobiles. That year, in the SAE Congress in Detroit, Visteon demonstrated voice-activated controls — a key interface to multimedia solutions that include traffic information, turn-by-turn navigation, Internet access, e-mail, voice mail, and cell phone. Navigation Technologies (NavTech) supplied route guidance information, including database mining through a traffic-oriented extranet.

Staff foot patrols mapped, measured, and noted features in every street and alleyway of cities, villages, and towns, as well as connecting roads, motorways, and lanes. NavTech's database could then provide a precise digital representation of the road network with the depth, accuracy, and coverage needed to enable turn-by-turn, door-to-door guidance. The NavTech database includes accurate representation of the road network, detailed information on primary and alternate street names, address ranges and driving rules (one-way, turn, restrictions), and other data of interest to the driver.

Auto networks discussed earlier in this section are good examples of the shift from database and client-server architectures to Web-based communications, storage, and retrieval. This process covers heterogeneous data and, therefore, increases the need for maintaining comprehensive descriptions of metadata reflecting structure, content, and other properties.

Real-life business applications of intranets increase the requirements posed by dynamic manipulation of data and metadata. Distributed knowledge systems provide an agile and flexible interface between information source and interactive presentation, either proactively through agents or in the aftermath of ad hoc queries. Metadata enable the system to decide dynamically how to handle queries from a broad base of end users. They also help the expanding Web environment because exponential possibilities for input and output combinations necessitate possessing intelligent software adaptable to the situation.

In conclusion, Web software is a reliable commodity programming product and also provides facilities to integrate diverse sources of data, allowing complex queries to be made against distributed databases. Used capably, intranets and extranets can become highly competitive, dynamic systems dealing with diverse Web-based information sources.

AN EXPANDING HORIZON OF CORPORATE INTRANETS

With network management moving to embrace mobile users as well as to link new devices, the boundaries of corporate networks are expanding. This enlarged perspective calls for a major cultural change from current practices in IT where the bulk of time is spent managing hardware and basic software, rather than improving information flow in a polyvalent sense. Table 15.1 shows, by order of magnitude, the current use of network management resources.

Table 15.1 Typical Percent Distribution of Staff Time Under the Current Network Management

Percentage	Task
44%	Physical management and troubleshooting
34%	Administration and trivia connected to IT
10%	Network design for new features and solutions
8%	Fairly detailed device management
4%	Other duties within the networking context

A well-known insurance company has provided its thousands of employees worldwide with access to a range of services through an intranet, offering among other goodies training catalogues, travel management, and corporate directories. Then it enhanced the range of supported intranet services by building applications to support a more complex workflow, such as integrative forms repository, biographical data changes and other job-related information, and recruiting, applicant tracking, and individual development planning.

Another global organization used its intranet to correct previously inconsistent platforms, interactive support, and sales processes and tools. This is a fairly complete solution, comprising hardware (including thousands of PCs and laptops software, links to the company's database networks, training, and other activities. Applications developed with the intranet include activity tracking and leads distribution, a marketing materials mall, reference tools for salespeople, management information databases, and a new generation of electronic mail.

Other companies' intranets serve a variety of different uses, for instance, management guidelines, press releases, earnings reports, and other documents. This helps to save the cost of printing and distributing thousands of copies to their factories, sales outlets, and branch offices. A fully integrated system for new Web developments, including seamless database integration, is also on the intranet.

All these system solutions and their applications help to utilize collaborative technologies; they also assist in making the transition to joining the Internet revolution. However, nobody should expect intranet software to produce miracles. Even minor miracles require a high degree of competency and technical expertise. Only the most qualified people can help to reach new markets, create new opportunities, and offer new levels of service.

If the implementation and use of an intranet or extranet is successful, new technical challenges will arise as more applications are taken on board. A top issue is the steady increase in demand for sophisticated services, seamless database accesses, and more bandwidth. In installations worth their salt, demand for resources is so acute that the network may bog down at peak usage times.

One solution is high-speed performance and steadily increasing bandwidth. Another strategy is to assure that the intranet and Internet can collaborate, and that such collaboration provides a seamless access service. According to a 1996 study commissioned by Sun Microsystems and conducted by U.S. Computer, a consulting firm, companies using the Internet for networking can save 23 to 50% over conventional leased-line networks. Savings vary, depending on whether the Net is replacing a high-priority corporate backbone or lower-priority networks that connect branch offices.

The same study also found that major American Internet service providers have successfully merged frame relay technology and Internet backbone network design to guarantee a satisfactory performance record. Effective integrative solutions have always been a topmost requirement and are even more so as multimedia traffic increases.

Science and technology for purely scientific reasons may be good in academic circles, but not in business, where cost-effectiveness reigns. As Figure 15.4 points out, the bottom line is: does it pay to do what has been planned? Steady vigilance and realistic evaluation should characterize all business viewpoints. The Internet, intranets, and extranets serve the interests of the company only as long as they can produce documented results.

Obtaining results may require new departures, including apparently unorthodox solutions. In the early 1980s an unorthodox solution was the PC, particularly so for mainframers. Today, it is the practical use of embedded systems, which represent the art of thinking small by using integrated chips and reducing routines and functions to ever smaller components. This practice fits well with the intranet drive, even if this may not seem to be the case.

Experts expect that, in the coming years, chips will effectively integrate between 50 and 100 million transistors compared to a maximum of 10 to 15 million transistors in the late 1990s. Common performance is projected to reach 2 GIPS for an integrate chip, compared to the more classical 250 to 400 MIPS on a microprocessor. No enterprise architecture designer can leave this concept in a time closet because the net result will be better availability of networking products with greater built-in intelligence. Improved functionality will allow monitoring traffic across an entire implementation landscape, including how different applications use network resources. This sort of monitoring becomes increasingly important as networking changes to application-centric.

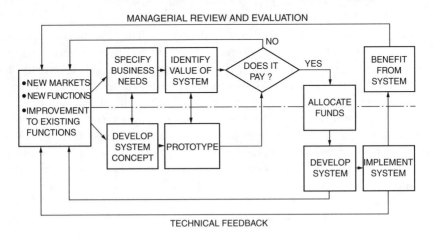

Figure 15.4 Steady vigilance and realistic evaluation should characterize managerial and technological viewpoints.

Experts also believe that intranets will be an even bigger pole of attraction than they currently are because practically every major networking hardware and software vendor is now committed to Web-enabling developments. For instance, with an embedded Web browser and Java management software, network support staff will be enabled to troubleshoot the corporate internetwork using knowledge-enriched artifacts. This will be done in the sense of an extended corporate internetwork and will allow flexible end user access to corporate information, irrespective of location.

The dual goals are to reduce network management expenditures while extending on-line network management facilities to smart phones, portables, workstations, monitors, printers, copiers, voice input and response units, and other devices in and out of the office. On-line solutions may as well include appliance monitoring, energy management services, and the ability to control remotely various subsystems.

Another issue on the table is that the Internet layer of the original TCP/IP protocol will be recast in terms of connectivity to the enterprise backbone. By all evidence, network management based on Hypertext transfer protocol (HTTP) will gain more general acceptance for applications traditionally supported by other protocols, including those proprietary to the various vendors. Today, network hardware manufacturers find it much easier and less expensive to create HTML- and XML-based device management interfaces that plug into a Web browser by writing some sophisticated software. With the expansion of the intranet market, however, device configuration is moving to HTTP while tier-1 vendors use HTTP to extend network management capabilities.[2]

HTTP-based network administration looks so attractive because of its implementation flexibility and potential savings. The overall concept can be assisted by creating Java applets to control the attached devices. Remember that Java, a C+-based development, was originally created to facilitate the design of embedded-system software. Hence, it has a compact runtime approach, a basic interpreter, and library and thread support.

Java applications are portable since the language specifies a machine-independent, intermediate byte-code that can be transferred between network nodes. Also, it is compiled on demand by a local Java runtime environment. The problem is efficiency in execution because downloaded applets need interpretation and the work of the interpreter can be a slow, time-consuming job.

Whether or not applets are used, the more advanced architectural solutions profit from an increasing use of knowledge artifacts. The application in the previous section and the implementation perspectives examined in this section are not conceivable without high technology; agents are an integral part of high tech solutions.

INTRANETS, WEB SOFTWARE, AND THE EFFECTIVENESS OF MOBILE AGENTS

Developed by a myriad of companies as well as people often working from garage outfits, the World Wide Web and its software show enormous promise as an efficient foundation of corporate information infrastructure. Clear-eyed management has many reasons to look favorably to these programming products, because they provide a solution that is ready-made and yet in full evolution, low cost in purchase and implementation, flexible and scalable in its application, and fairly easy for end users to employ.

As the two preceding sections explained, intranets and extranets are a much better alternative than the elder network models that developed sclerotic features leading to the demise of mainframes. For instance, complex, proprietary software lock-in and delays in developing and making that software, high costs and uncertainty regarding timetables, and vendor-specific applications unsuited to the company's needs comprised some of these features. After experiencing public Web sites, many companies seize upon the Web's software as a swift way to transform their organizations. Because Web browsers run on any type of computer, much of this software is portable; all sorts of documents can be converted to electronic form on the Web and handled as well as updated online.

Much is expected from the use of applets, the Java programs that can be loaded automatically onto personal computers or other devices and run at the push of a button. Potentially, applets can do almost anything, including nasty things, such as introducing viruses into the computer. A Java applet is able to reproduce and send itself back out over the network from which it came. The possible use of Java to create and deploy network-based computer viruses should be steadily audited.

On the positive side, applets are a mobile code that migrates from server to client for better interaction with the user. The commercial technology of mobile software programs is improving thanks to faster Java virtual machines with just-in-time compilation. From applets, the next step is proxy sites that accept mobile code sent from a mobile client. Because the main function of proxy sites will be to host mobile code and Internet service providers (ISPs) will receive direct payment for the proxy service, most likely in the form of subscriptions, the ISPs will not be averse to accepting perceived security risks of mobile code. Once mobile-code security is further tested on proxy sites, the services will start to accept *servlets*, i.e., mobile code sent from the client directly to the server or from the proxy to the server.

Nothing is cast in stone in computer terminology; as usage evolves so does the meaning of certain terms. This said, however, a good way to remember the difference between applets and servlets, both of which are mobile and small, is that applets are sent from the server to the client, but servlets are sent from the client to the server.

According to expert opinion, as these servlets become widely used and researchers address the issue of protecting mobile code from malicious usage and accidental failures, a swarm of sites will start to accept mobile agents. This process is expected to give a big boost to nomadic, location-independent computing (see Chapter 9) and to provide useful implementations, each with fast access to information, support for disconnected operation in an integrative way, and killer applications that follow the mobile agent paradigm to new programming solutions. The message embedded in the previous sentence hides many challenges for designers of enterprise architectures and developers of applications to run on them. One of the most important is to provide a clear, visible evolutionary path from current location-dependent approaches to mobile code and mobile agent solutions. Developers must be careful to demonstrate that the switch to a largely mobile environment can be made incrementally without upsetting current operations, and that enough added value exists to justify the cultural change and associated expenses.

Experts also believe that another important evolutionary path is the migration of agent technology from intranets to the new broadband Internet because mobile code technologies will most likely appear first in the safer intranet environment. For instance, a company with a mobile workforce is likely to find mobile agents a convenient way to provide its employees with a wide range of access to its internal databases, where security is of less concern than on the Internet, and wider deployment of agent-supported services can be tested more meaningfully.

End users are expected to play a critical role in both transitions, moving already established Internet connections to the new, more functional level of an intranet, as well as porting intranet-grown mobile agents to the Internet. A reasonable projection is that future tools will add value and improve existing business processes, significantly improving groupware functionality at an affordable cost.

Since the mid 1990s response by business and industry to the Internet, intranets, and extranets has been positive. In 1996, a survey by Forrester Research addressed 50 major companies and documented that 16% already had an intranet in place, while another 50% either planned to install one or were considering doing so.[3] An educated guess is that, in 2002, mobile agents are about where intranets were in the mid 1990s.

Working over a fairly inexpensive but reliable network with acceptable bandwidth and expected to improve steadily in capacity and reliability, presently projected solutions will help to restructure the corporate information flow. They can also be instrumental in assisting system designers in projecting a better enterprise architecture and senior management in changing the company's information technology culture. This statement is in line with the prevailing opinion that one of the most significant impacts of the Internet has been the *de facto* adoption of a new set of standards for cross-platform information access. The past can be a prelude. One of the best examples is the web browser, which emerged as a universal graphical user interface (GUI) supported on every computing platform currently in use.

The generalized acceptance of Web browsing has also fueled the adoption of HTTP, HTML, and XML, which acted as standards for the transport and creation of information elements. They did so by being accepted for the Web on the public Internet, as well as for corporate intranets. In this sense, they have become part of the *de facto* architecture, and they serve a whole new generation of embedded functions.

These examples help in documenting that the promise of future developments like nomadic computing and mobile agents is one of synergy, i.e., tying together information islands within company resources, and therefore cost-effectively assisting in sparking new products and improving productivity. But neither the Internet nor intranets and extranets perform miracles. To get results, senior management must ensure that the implementation of Web standards occurs without manipulation to make them better — and that operating units within the company allow their data to be shared. The larger impact is lost when units refuse to open what they consider proprietary information to other corporate units. Even worse, they build high walls between themselves and competing units, rather than against outside rivals.

Although this is oriented to the company level, some references have a broader impact on the national economy. Gross national product (GNP) and information technology correlate. In the Group of Ten countries, information technology now represents, depending on the country, about 10 to 15% of GNP. After 2020, this share is expected to be closer to 50%.

BENEFITS DERIVED BY COMPANIES THAT APPLY WEB SOFTWARE STANDARDS

No bank, manufacturing company, or merchandising firm can stay out of global networking and still survive. Globability is the number one force behind the Internet. Services provided by Web access today are what the telephone was post-World War II. To be a player, however, a company must fulfill a number of prerequisites, one of which is cost-effectiveness. That is what efficient communications solutions are all about.

Companies that have been quick to appreciate intranets' advantages have gained much. Silicon Graphics began its intranet experience immediately after Mosaic became available. Today, services benefiting web access can be compared to those capitalizing on global telephony post-world war II. The company used the Web to expand the horizon of its employees, and progressed by adding on applications. Today at the company, practically all information elements are on-line; 7200 employees have access to 144,000 Web pages stored on 800 Web sites. Silicon Graphics' story can serve as a precedent to implementing nomadic computing as described in the previous section. At current state of the art, pressing the point of the Internet, intranets, and extranets is like forcing open doors. Consider the following examples.

At Compaq Computer, employees have used a Web server to reallocate investments in their 401(k) plans. At Ford, an intranet links design centers in the U.S., Europe, and Asia; one of its original contributions was to help engineers craft the 1996 Taurus. Other companies started gaining experience with the Internet before implementing an intranet. In November 1994, Federal Express, which moves approximately 2.5 million parcels every day, put a server on the Web that gave customers a direct window into its package-tracking database. This did away with the need for clients to ask a FedEx operator to do the tracking for them. Within a couple of years, 12,000 customers every day will find their way through Web pages to pinpoint their parcels.

A special product, PowerShip, lets FedEx customers order and process their own shipments from their desktop computers. A version of it, FedEx Ship, can be freely downloaded from the company's Web site and used to track packages. Moving along with the success of Internet technology, Federal Express established 60 Web sites inside its organization, largely created for and by employees. It also equipped its 30,000 office employees around the world with Web browsers so they can access intranet sites.

Another early starter, Xerox, has woven an on-line solution that connects all 90,000 of its employees, changing the way the office automation vendor runs its business. In less than a year following day 1 in November 1995, more than 15,000 Xerox employees were given immediate access to the Xerox WebBoard. This internal Web site contains postings of company and market news, a rapidly updated company information area, and phone directories and other common data. The WebBoard also provides links to other Xerox home pages and outside sites of potential interest. Xerox was confident that its intranet would change office automation, particularly in terms of distributing information elements to internal users and business customers.

Xerox is a good example because this company has experience with the persistent strategy required to get results from new technology, not only is it an office automation (OA) vendor but it also conducted a fundamental study with some of its clients which proved that productivity improvements from OA do not come overnight. As Figure 15.5 shows, they need a persistent effort of 2 to 3 years.

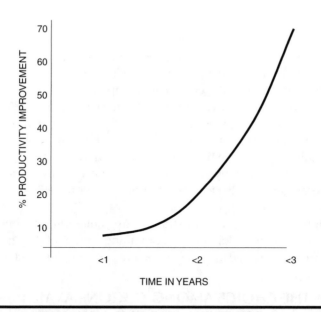

Figure 15.5 Productivity results from office automation do not come overnight. They need a persistent effort.

In their implementation of intranets in the mid 1990s, Xerox technologists built up the WebBoard as an in-house development of Web applications. This was a value-added application after an internal study documented that buying off-the-shelf products was less expensive than developing proprietary software from scratch. Still, for security reasons Xerox decided to keep mission-critical applications off the Web, including videoconferencing, time management, scheduling programs, and accounting routines.

The emphasis has been on value differentiation. To sustain a massive upgrade, Xerox has added Web functionality to its groupware-enabled Xerox network services (XNS), a company TCP/IP-based global document distribution system. It has also followed in parallel a Web strategy because management believed that the Web software could eventually supplant the home-bred XNS. This parallelism in support was quite a feat because, at the time, the company's global corporate network incorporated 1100 LANs with some 80,000 user accounts in 35 countries and 18 time zones, and featured nearly 10,000 servers used to dish out information on demand, in real-time.

Credit card companies offer another good example on relatively early intranet implementation. In preInternet times, to keep its 1200 employees worldwide informed about who was the right contact for each of 19,000 member banks, Visa regularly published two volumes, each nearly four inches think. This very costly publication was out of date almost instantly. Then Visa found a much better solution in extranets, strategy that has been a hit with member banks. Pre-extranet, Visa sent out critical information, such as fraud alerts and marketing updates, on diskettes. By putting that data on-line, the credit card company sped things considerably, cut costs, and got a positive response from member banks. Visa also bet that it would be able to offer more services and let banks tap directly into its databases, for instance, to check the status of a transaction electronically, a process which, before the extranets, was done manually. Other successful company intranets have been established at companies as diverse as General Electric (see the next section), AT&T, 3M, and Levi Strauss.

Examples of intranets and extranets are multitudinous, but this is not yet true of location-independent computing and mobile agents. Hence there is a need for research, development, and implementation.

THE CHOICE AMONG OPTIONS AVAILABLE WITH TECHNOLOGY'S ADVANCES

Corporate decision makers on information technology policy are faced with a multitude of options to evaluate and test before implementing any radical changes in corporate investments. Among other potential advantages which must be studied, tested, and documented, a new implementation should bring improved security and better returns on investment (ROI). To enhance ROI, companies must target innovative services offered over the Internet and as an offshoot of knowledge-enriched applications. With the Internet, intranets, and extranets, ROI goals are served through the potential to create changes more sweeping and beneficial than those in the 1955 to 2000 timeframe.

Time and again, ROI studies show that real benefits are found when efforts are focused on major, not marginal, improvements. Figure 15.6 says as much about gaining a competitive edge by moving out of legacy applications. A competitive edge, however, requires studying different alternatives and options prior to making a definite choice.

Though many people today believe that the famed Year 2000 bug (Y2K) was, in the last analysis, a hoax, few would argue that it contributed a great deal to renewing the programming library of better managed companies. It had a cultural and a technological effect. It gave senior management the message that much can be gained by buying Web and other off-the-shelf software rather than reinventing the wheel. It also pushed companies toward renewing their program libraries, which had been stuck to System 360 programs since the 1960s, with great damage to the companies still using them.

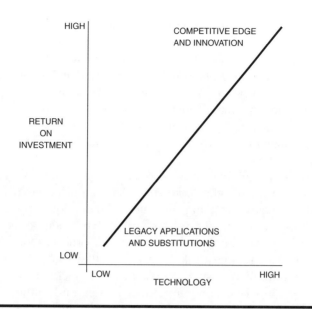

Figure 15.6   The return on investment lies in innovation, not on the beaten path.

Chances are that alternatives in modernizing the company's information system will look at the Internet and intranets as a stepping stone. Using the Internet, for example, General Electric has switched on a global commercial network capable of handling billions of dollars in tender bids electronically. The GE trading process network (TPN) enables qualified subcontractors to receive a wealth of information from current and potential suppliers, submit commercial bids via a fairly secure link, and proactively search for the company's purchase tenders. In the late 1990s, a year after this system went live, General Electric said that its Web site expected to handle more than $1 billion worth of bids and supply contracts per year. The on-line system lets suppliers query and bid for contracts from desktop computers equipped with Internet access and client software developed and freely distributed by GE.

The new design substituted the existing solution whereby GE subcontractors sent bids by fax or post, while using the company's proprietary software and network connection to track tenders and make bids. Using e-mail with 40-bit encryption technology, GE employees send tenders to potential suppliers worldwide. Bidders can then log onto TPN's Web site and download their multimedia tender document.

This is but one example of many. By presenting information in the same way to every computer, intranets and extranets can offer that which computer manufacturers and the majority of software firms have frequently promised but never delivered: cost-effective universal access. This is a key reason why companies and their employees across the business world are creating their own home pages and are sharing details of their projects.

An example comparable to that of GE is provided by National Semiconductor, where engineers use home pages that let their department schedule meetings on-line. Also at National Semiconductor an interactive, Web-based ordering system enables customers to search the company's 30,000-product catalog. Other firms, too, have implemented similar applications capitalizing on the power of Internet tools and their portability to business intranets.

L.M. Ericsson engineers use browsers to query internal and external technical databases. In other companies, communications managers have developed strategies for using the Internet to conduct business. In one such company, the intranet has solved the problem of synchronizing centrally defined sales policies in 350 branch offices. One estimate says that most large companies link at least half their business partners over the Web for transactions such as placing and tracking orders, and that approximately 50% of a company's internal text and traffic is on intranet or the Internet, a fast-growing figure. These statistics would not exist unless companies saw a fairly good return on investment in the Internet connection and the use of off-the-shelf Web software. This is their way of gaining benefit from technology's advances; it amounts to a major change from policies prior to 1990.

The examples in this and the preceding sections show that, given the dynamics of the Web, most successful technology investment models are likely to be replicated by other players, thus ensuring that the market for Web programming products and other tools is much bigger than the Web itself. This has implications for the evolution of a *de facto* Internet standard and its market potential (therefore, its business opportunity).

Many financial analysts are optimistic about the growth possibilities arising from increasingly network-centric solutions. But with so much of what makes up the right approach still undecided, large and highly influential companies are formulating strategies which, at the present time, boil down to this: the only certainty they expect is change.

REACHING FACTUAL DECISIONS REGARDING THE EVOLVING ENTERPRISE ARCHITECTURE AND ITS SERVICES

Born of technology, network innovations command attention among big and small firms who understand that, through these innovations, they can leverage their power and improve support to their research, development, production, and distribution systems. Most of the enterprise architectures in place share a common set of technical design characteristics in the nuts and bolts of networks: transmission, signaling, synchronization, tariffing, provisioning, and regulatory restrictions; however, the grand design of the architecture has its own standards.

Web software is not a steamroller. Even with Web-based normalization much depends on the way an enterprise architecture is designed, maintained, and used. Even so, intranet and extranet solutions find their *raison d'être* in a large class of organizations for whom timely, error-free communications are vital. These communications are provided at an affordable cost and used in a way which simplifies the handshake with business partners.

As preceding examples demonstrated, companies adopting extranets and intranets include multinational manufacturing firms and distribution companies. Other major users are travel related services, brokers, banks, and financial institutions at large.

Customers with growing telecommunications needs want control of the network to assure that timeliness, quality, security, bandwidth, and reliability of networked services are adequate. To achieve these goals, however, companies must go well beyond Internet protocols and commodity software. Absolute authority over the network requires control over design parameters such as:

- Intelligence embedded into the system
- Access to the network and degree of connectivity
- Trunks, switches, and transmission losses
- Quantization distortion for voice
- Bit error ratio for data
- Saturation and restructuring
- Encryption facilities for lines and devices
- On-line diagnostics and maintenance

Organizations that depend on communications for their business require a guarantee that phone calls and data streams will be neither blocked nor tapped. They need some control over routing and to watch for traffic balancing to maintain a uniform grade service, always at reasonable cost. In a highly competitive market, costs matter as much as the service provided.

Enterprise architects must appreciate that this is a study in optimization to be made within the specific operating environment of their company, not in the abstract. When appropriately done, it will most likely lead to a graph dividing the cost-effectiveness space into three parts: 1. low-cost, ineffective solutions; 2. effective, cost-solutions; and 3. effective solutions with reasonable costs.

The third type of solution is the target area of every enterprise architecture. This is precisely what makes the Internet, intranets, and extranets attractive. Described as the next wave of Internet software, enterprise solutions involve opening up parts of an intranet to outside business partners: suppliers and customers. These may range from supply and distribution to finance and marketing services. For most, the goal is to provide all sorts of fully integrated, on-line capabilities. Many companies experienced in enterprise solutions that integrate business partners report that their primary reason for implementing extranets is to maintain business leadership or take the lead from competitors. Along this line of reasoning semiprivate networking is gaining market share as sales orders shift from the phone to the Internet.

Note that extranets for business-to-business commerce are not limited to direct selling. Customers using their bank's extranet can gain access to product information as well as market analysis reports at their discretion. In other applications, customers are provided with a track and trace service to follow the progress of more than just an extension of their own intranet, if they have one.

A participant in a New York meeting once noted that the concept, development, and use of extranets is a different way of saying that a company has entered into network competitions without building its own network. It is doing so by finding ingenious ways to use an infrastructure which also serves other businesses. This solution permits the company to capitalize on the fact that industrial and financial customers like semiprivate networks because they are more confidential than public networks in certain aspects of operation.

If one goes by this hypothesis, then building an extranet is synonymous to developing a more private than public communication solution to link together offices and factories belonging to companies that may be only ephemeral partners, collaborating on a given project. If this provides a common base, then each group of business partners has the option of adding value and therefore gaining the competitive advantage of differentiation.

In conclusion, enterprise architectures present an optimization problem similar to that of other business investments. Therefore, decisions should be made at a higher level in the organization and their execution delegated to the best specialists employed by the company. Information on product offerings, market drives, human resources, and financial staying power converges into these decisions. Every one of these factors impacts advantages to be derived from new technology and return on investment calculations.

REFERENCES

1. Chorafas, D.N., *Managing Operational Risk. Risk Reduction Strategies for Banks Post-Basle*, Lafferty, London and Dublin, 2000.
2. Chorafas, D.N., *Visual Programming Technology*, McGraw-Hill, New York, 1996.
3. *BusinessWeek*, February 26, 1996.

16

WHY SECURITY ASSURANCE SHOULD INFLUENCE THE ENTERPRISE ARCHITECTURE

INTRODUCTION

The preceding chapters have provided plenty of evidence that security in the age of Internet business is not to be taken lightly. Companies are exposed to all sorts of risks; from theft of confidential customer records from their supposedly secure database systems to viruses and the shutdown of revenue-critical applications. People experienced in databases and networks admit that the main contributor to low security and to privacy exposure is the complexity of existing business architectures and systems solutions. Also, enterprises may not have designed their IT systems top-down and bottom-up with security in mind. Network operating systems (OS), for example, have 30 million lines of code or more; they are connected to thousands of other OS just as complex.

Failure to account for security characteristics of the enterprise architecture at the drafting stage, as well as software complexity, create an environment that is very difficult to manage effectively from a security viewpoint. Interconnectivity is what makes the Internet marketplace and networks at large capable of fully exploiting the potential of on-line commerce, but every advance carries risk factors to be understood, measured, and monitored. Any-to-any and end-to-end interconnectivity is not possible without some type of risks.

Not long ago, a survey of 800 British on-line retailers found that 70% consider the Internet more risky for conducting commerce than traditional retail because of fraud and lack of appropriate countermeasures. Of these retailers, 65% said that it takes at least a month for credit card fraud to be detected; approximately 40% had been hit more than once by a single fraudulent customer.

Viruses are another pest. Remember the ease with which the LoveLetter virus swept across the globe, leaving an estimated $15 billion in damages and downtime in its wake. Among other examples of on-line misbehavior, hackers successfully hit Western Union's Web site, resulting in the theft of over 15,000 customers' credit card numbers, and Timothy Lloyd was convicted of causing $12 million in damage to his former employer, Omega Engineering.

Globalization and the networks themselves ensure that news of fraud, viruses, and security breaches travels through the business community very fast. Negative reports on security can seriously undermine a company's reputation, as well as its business and stock price. Security is now considered a major operational risk to be studied very seriously, including insider and outsider breaches.

Insider breaches include malicious code, infection of company machines through viruses, use of company equipment for illegal communications, various abuses concerning computers and communications gear, unauthorized access to databases, managing a personal I-commerce site through company Internet resources, gambling, physical theft, disclosure of proprietary data, and many cases of what has always been considered as plain fraud.

Neither do passwords provide protection. As computer systems became increasingly accessible, storing plaintext passwords is no longer feasible. As a result, many people use password equivalents, created by hashing a plaintext password and storing the hashed version. The concept behind this process is simple: the password one enters at login is hashed and this hash is compared to the stored password equivalent. If the computed hash matches the stored hash, then the system assumes that the user knows the password and permits login.

While exploiting insecure passwords is a gateway to fraud, even more worrisome outsider breaches are viruses and Trojan horses. Others include denial of service, acts related to active program scripting, weak firewalls, encryption codes easy to break, attacks exploiting protocol weaknesses, and attacks on buys in Web servers. Buffer overflows should also be rigorously addressed through the enterprise architecture.

SECURITY CONCERNS AND THE ESTABLISHMENT OF VALID PLANS

The year 2000 Information Security Breaches Survey (IBSC 2000) revealed that almost 75% of British companies that had suffered a serious security breach had no contingency plan in place to deal with such situations. Only 14%, one in seven, had any formally defined information security management system, while the balance were satisfied with half-measures. Statistics in America are not much different.

The introduction to this chapter presented a list of the most frequent security breaches by insiders and outsiders. Contingency plans should account for them and also take care of other reasons specific to the company's operating environment. For instance, power failures, local area network (LAN) time-outs, and server crashes may exacerbate security weaknesses.

Statistics show that, while only about 10% of security failures result directly from malicious external intrusion, even that percentage can have uncontrolled effects on privacy and security. To flush-out weak spots in their security armory, companies increasingly dependent on the Internet are using former hackers to probe weaknesses in their systems. This is done under the euphemism "third-party testing" and is not a bad idea; it is also not a substitute for a rigorous security policy.

Some type of security threat has always been connected to computers, communications, and software. It is only reasonable to expect security risks to increase with the level of system sophistication and the open interconnection basis of the network. Numeric calculation presented fewer opportunities for inside and outside breaches, but, as Figure 16.1 suggests, security threats increased with data processing and private networks. With the Internet, they zoomed.

Some experts compare today's Internet commerce environment to the early days of commercial aviation. If the death rate per passenger-mile today was the same as in 1939, 400 or 500 people a day would be lost, given the current volume of air travel. However, this is not the actual statistic today because air travel is so much safer. The concept behind this argument is that something similar will happen with Internet commerce. But will this occur through mandatory federal regulation for greater security or self-regulation of Internet companies as a whole?

In the second alternative, each entity will be expected to take care of its own security problems. But what if these security problems are connected to those faced by the entity's business partners? This raises a number of other queries, some of which relate to tactical issues and others with strategic issues. Should clients be informed of everything taking place or should security problems and plans be secret?

This chapter will not address all the challenges posed by the preceding queries. Instead, it will emphasize a problem which might permit a valid solution, starting with the premise that on-line privacy and security increase consumer trust, and therefore business confidence.

Personal privacy is the first topic. Internet businesses and Web sites should clearly explain what they do with personal information, how they

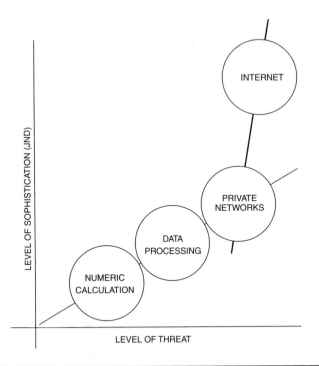

Figure 16.1   When the threat increases, the required level of software sophistication must grow exponentially.

aggregate it with other data, and with whom they share it. This is not done today.

The next fundamental element is choice by the parties to whom such information belongs. People must be given the choice of whether or not to reveal personal data. If they want to opt in, they should be allowed to do so. If not, no data should be collected on them and this process should be audited.[1] In other words, on-line business users, both companies and consumers, must be given the opportunity to opt out, and the mechanics for doing so should not be complex or obscure.

Another fundamental pillar in promoting business and consumer confidence is disclosure. Internet commerce partners, including consumers, must be able to inspect all their on-line files and a mechanism for identifying and correcting errors of omission and commission should be in place.

Enforcement is also very important. If on-line sites invade consumer privacy, there should be penalties high enough to dissuade repetition. This requires legislation. In the U.S., the Federal Trade Commission (FTC) enforces the Fair Credit Reporting Act for credit agencies, the Truth in Lending Act, and the Children's On-line Privacy Protection Act. More is necessary to protect everybody's privacy and enforce sound security standards.

Enforcement of security standards would not be cheap and presupposes a definition of critical issues and rules for their observance. What are the functional requirements of security for Internet commerce? Which key factors identify a sound security system? How can monitoring be done in a dependable manner? Here is the answer in a nutshell:

- Identification and authentication should go beyond simple passwords and obsolete personal ID numbers (PINs). Sophisticated mechanisms are needed to check authorization status.
- Reliable access control: both methodology and tools are necessary to prevent users from accessing material they are not expressly permitted to see or manipulate.
- Protection from attacks: denial of service (DoS) attacks on popular Web sites leave Internet business impaired and create negative publicity. What is the company's solution to prevent DoS from taking down its Web server?
- System scalability: what is the maximum size server farm the on-line site should handle? Has the enterprise architecture incorporated incremental steps from smaller to larger? Is there a migration path?
- Single and multiple users audit trails: does the company maintain audit trails to determine where and when a security breach has occurred? Is every resource that is accessed by multiple users secured? Can each user and his transactions be identified?
- Tracking of multiple locations: if the Web server farm is spread over several locations, is the enterprise architecture incorporating features which effectively help manage a complex Internet commerce environment?
- Reliability and redundancy: what type of redundancy is built into the solution? Which security modules are used? What can the network manager do to maintain reliability in case some components fail? Can the company protect against accidental security breaches? Can it guard against a single user monopolizing resources?

The answer can be found in general and specific security solutions. This involves a list of requirements. At the bottom is encryption to scramble and descramble all communications and database contents and *firewalls* to secure Internet connectivity by providing critical control points, etc. This list progresses to *biometrics*, which provide a reasonable degree of identity validation at the client side (see the sixth section).

There are other technical prerequisites as well, such as *persistence*. Some connections, like the secure sockets layer, require the server that initially handled the connection to take care of the entire transaction for that user. Can the enterprise architecture maintain persistent connection for long transactions executed over a given timeframe?[2]

Performance criteria are also vital. Currently, some Internet sites handle 500 users per second with peaks at three times that number or more. Is the enterprise architecture able to handle such traffic? Can it hold its own as traffic increases? How often would it need to be scaled? What are the thresholds?

Managerial prerequisites, too, must be paid full attention. What is the cost of the security solution? What is the return on investment, given the cost of each threat and breach? What about accountability for performance, for security proper, for business confidence? These are not queries that can be answered on the fly. They need a thorough study, which is often missing from security plans.

SECURITY ON THE INTERNET IS A MOVING TARGET

When in the mid 1990s electronic commerce and the Internet became practically synonymous terms, some security experts expressed the opinion that the Net "was not yet an information superhighway. In terms of security, it is a trail in the wild west." This was an exaggeration, but it also had a grain of truth as far as privacy and security were concerned.

"Perhaps the exploding frontiers of cyberspace are like the western states in the 1800s," suggests Ronald Rivest, associate director of MIT's laboratory for computer science. "Setting up a domain is like claiming a homestead that you surround with barbed wire of cryptography."[3] Rivest adds that the vulnerability of the Internet had recently been exposed by events like the denial of service attack that disabled Yahoo!, eBay, and other major sites.

Nothing less than a carefully developed methodology enriched with powerful tools can provide a comfortable confidence level. Some of the basics of such a methodology were discussed in the previous section, but they were not always successful in helping to fend off vulnerability threats. Sweden has developed a vulnerability detection method that every company would be well advised to study. Computer-based, it is highlighted in the block diagram in Figure 16.2.

Borrowing from the Swedish experience, in security terms foremost attention should be paid to the adopted infrastructure in the context of the company's enterprise architecture. One of the major difficulties in establishing a secure infrastructure is that the adversary against whom the Internet part of the architecture must be defended remains elusive. By contrast, networks belonging to organizations like the Department of Defense have coherency of purpose, and have means to defend it in

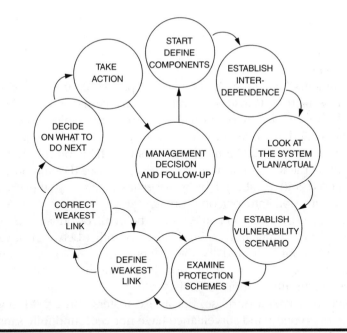

Figure 16.2   Sweden's SBA vulnerability method: keep plans, documentation, and follow-up by computer.

place. Their security characteristics and design choices concerning them are based on a chain of command which can reach immediate decision to close security breaches.

A thoroughly outlined chain of command limits the flow of information to only those cleared to receive it. The problem is that, unlike in military situations, it will be counterproductive to do so in the Internet context. In fact, the strength and weakness of the Internet is that it does not have this coherency of purpose and chain of command which promotes security. It is a large diffuse medium that utilizes many diverse, heterogeneous technologies, has individual, more or less autonomous nodes, and accommodates a large and expanding number of users.

Some experts think that, while users may want to browse in anonymity, the more likely Internet security infrastructure to emerge will, in some way, provide for user identification. One approach to determining how the Internet can work in a more secure way is a set of explicit policy statements about what Internet security means, as explained in the previous section. This would lead to institution of an enforcement policy, but, which agency should be trusted with its supervision?

The creation of an agency to monitor the ID of Internet users is primarily promoted by governments. To the user community at large, it is anathema; yet it is not so far-fetched as it might seem at first sight. In

April 2001 the British government instituted an Internet policing force with a staff of 80. Its mission was to go beyond Internet pornography and child prostitution to include items entering into the broader perspective of on-line security.

Governments look at such agencies as part of their responsibility for computer protection. Consumers and some companies are not in accord. Part of the difference in opinion comes from principles, interests, and means associated with security and protection that sometimes coincide and sometimes diverge. The more rigorous user ID is on the Internet, the higher will be the level of security, but the more user IDs and other details are monitored and databased by a government agency, the greater the amount of intrusion into personal privacy.

In other words, while on some issues the goals of privacy and security tend to coincide significantly, there is also a conflict between privacy and security. This conflict is fed by the relentless expansion of computers, communications, and software functionality, including the ability to acquire and disseminate information globally.

Anonymity serves a purpose, but it also fosters abuses. Privacy issues relating to encryption and surveillance have not yet found fully satisfactory solutions, apart from the fact of a certain amount of identify theft. Network-tapping raises many issues, while digital-certificate infrastructures, which have suddenly become popular (see the fifth section), bring up integrity problems.

Down to its fundamentals, this conflict between privacy and security heightens the tension between the individual's desire for privacy and his or her to have security. Thus, this conflict raises a number of interesting questions:

- How can threats to privacy be best contained while allowing a free economy to function and authorities to pursue criminals?
- What are acceptable limitations on individual privacy, given the responsibility governments have for general welfare and consumer protection?
- If Internet commerce depends on secure communications, when is wiretapping appropriate? Who should be authorized to set the limits? Should it be legalized?
- How would seeking individual transaction records and examination of their content affect businesses and their relentless pursuit of market share?

The very strength of the Internet lies in the fact that it is a large communication system with powerful search engines and any-to-any connectivity. This also enables its abuse by unscrupulous individuals and companies. Because much of modern business greatly depends on databasing and datamining (see Chapter 10), both allowing and not permitting free access intensifies can create problems.

Insider and outsider breaches, briefly described in the introduction, are not the only worries. Even what appears to be legitimate business may degenerate into a security challenge. For instance, by all indications obtrusive advertising is increasing, as are different types of unwanted filtering of information on the Net. Experts also believe the many issues involved in Internet voting are not well understood, even if there is a rush to their implementation. New problems have also arisen from non-proprietary free software; the list of issues out of control keeps growing.

This situation can be faced in an able manner only if the company rethinks the way in which it approaches security problems and the solutions provided. Dr. Heinrich Steinmann says that today, at the defensive side, the large majority of privacy and security solutions are one-dimensional and, for any practical purpose, protect very little. Fraudulent people and companies often use more complex two-dimensional approaches. As Figure 16.3 suggests, to cope with them, three-dimensional solutions able to provide a multichannel shield must be studied and then emplemented.

A two-dimensional approach for example, has been practiced since 1994 by hackers who wrote "sniffers" specifically designed to capture passwords sent by protocols such as FTP, Telnet, and POP, along with software that could hide the sniffers, primarily on Internet Service Providers (ISP) networks. Although rather poorly secured, they carry a high volume of traffic.

Catching this type of intruder calls for a higher level of reference. Say that, in response to this problem, new methods of authentication such as challenge–response are developed. This approach does not send the password across the network; instead, the server transmits a challenge, and the client operates upon it by using some permutation of the user's password. Following this, the client transmits a response to the server. Knowing the user's password equivalent, the server should then determine whether the remote user knows the correct password by repeating the client's operation. Key to this approach is a procedure by which the password, as well as any password-equivalent, never traverses the Internet.

This does not mean that intruders are fended off forever because many are creative individuals who find their way around controls. For instance, a hacker who captures password equivalents stored on a server such as the security accounts manager (SAM) in Windows NT can use them to log into other servers. Hence the need for implementing a higher-up dimension for protection reasons.

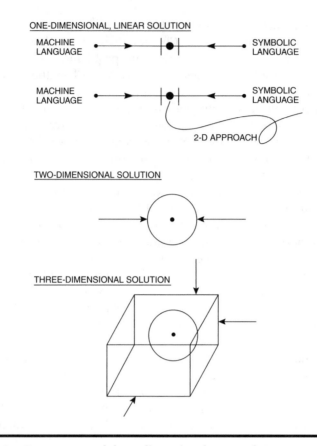

Figure 16.3   One-, two-, and three-dimensional approaches to programming and security protection.

This higher-up dimension is provided by the broader sense of Internet security which is indivisible from auditing an organization's involvement in Web sites, as well as that of its clients. How does the internal auditor fit into this picture? The auditor is an expert in controls and, therefore, control, including security control, should be a major emphasis in his work.

Security auditing will be so much more effective if it is focused, which requires organization. An integral part of developing and implementing the tactical side of a Web site deployment is proper establishment of internal control function. Hence, before such a site can be deployed, the company has to formulate its Internet security strategy and define the severity of security failures that can take place:

■ Catastrophic failures involve severe problems affecting privacy or security and demanding immediate, real-time correction.

- Major failures demand immediate attention but business risk is not catastrophic. Resolution could be within 2 hours, but there should be a limit.
- Average failures have moderate impact. Customer services may not be immediately affected and associated business risk is also moderate.
- Minor failures have minimal impact but they should be identified. Resolution might be deferred and the problem addressed within a more general context.

Every company must do its own analysis of the security risks which it confronts, with particular attention paid to catastrophic and major failures. In these cases, normal business risk is high and vital services may be disrupted. Identifying and solving such problems before they occur amounts to a reengineering process; however, it is also an internal control and program-management responsibility. The auditor can best focus on this activity if the organization realizes the security risks taken.

THE CASE OF INTRUSION DETECTION AND THE BROWSER'S DOUBLE ROLE

Security must be looked at as a system. The solution space searched for protection methods, measures, and tools can be defined as shown in Figure 16.4, which suggests that a rigorous interactive approach to security problems is bound to have semantic, syntactic, and programmatic characteristics. A basic prerequisite is to deploy a family of agents to look for the signatures of known security attacks by steadily inspecting network traffic database violations, manipulation of interfaces, and patterns suggesting possible forthcoming breaches.

It is wise to experiment on new security violations by using analogical reasoning and testing different hypotheses. A security database should be built using all cases of fraud and intrusion from the past, in any industry, in any place, at any time. Hackers and other violators usually repeat each other's patterns. This security database should be mined on-line to suggest possible scenarios the company has not yet experienced and to permit testing different hypotheses about possible future events. It would be better to depend on this proactive approach to security risk analysis than on static approaches like firewalls resembling the infamous Maginot Line.

People who talk of firewalls as the "ultimate" security protection are very much mistaken. Gone is the time when a firewall could provide enough peace of mind for companies and their executives. Today top-tier firms are drafting intricate security policies whose enforcement requires the use of multiple systems, which are characteristically proactive, reactive, multilayered, and very redundant — all in one.

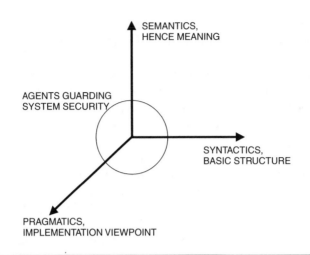

Figure 16.4 A rigorous integrative approach to network security will be found in this frame of reference.

Therefore, it has been a deliberate choice not to include details of subjects like encryption and firewalls here. Rather, the aim is to focus on what lies behind intrusion detection and countermeasures, which should become as commonplace as encryption and authentication. As a field, intrusion detection has matured a great deal during the last couple of years. While present implementations tend to be rather complex, and usually proprietary, the concept behind the process is simple: inspecting all on-line activity, inbound and outbound, registering what moves and what does not move, and identifing suspicious patterns that could be evidence of an attack on any device or the entire system.

Outliers are most valuable indicators for intrusion detection reasons. In fact, there are two fundamental techniques, one based on analysis of likely misuse and the other on anomalies. Misuse detection relies on a predefined set of attack signatures that need to be specified by the enterprise architecture. While looking for specific patterns, the detection system attempts to match every incoming data stream to the signature of a known attack.

Targeting anomalies is another matter. Here the work resembles the analytical skills of the auditor. Consider the case of firewall protection as an example. Companies that disregard anomalies in use patterns because they assume that a firewall is a failsafe security mechanism are in for surprises. Failsafe hypotheses can no longer be validated in most Web environments.

For starters, the common policy is that different types of traffic, or packets, are routed to different specific ports of the firewall router. The latter is a combination of hardware and software designed to filter the traffic that moves from the Internet into the company's internal network. Different Internet security exposures stem from the fact that, when the HTTP protocol was developed, it was projected to use a port of the firewall router, but this led to a dead end. If the firewall filter has not been changed to deny all traffic except HTTP packets, then a computer hacker can coast to this port of the firewall router, access the company's Web server, and modify or delete data at will.

Browsers present a different problem in terms of the origins of insecurity. Some Web site attacks are ingeneously exploiting browser weaknesses. This can happen with all sorts of software, particularly where a program's functionality is extended by the user. For instance, Postscript is employed in some Web environments as a browser, although it was originally designed to provide a printer-independent language for printing complex documents. Because postscript is basically a general purpose programming language that includes input and output functions, any document that has been produced with it acts as a computer program when it is interpreted. This leads to security-type risks; for example, postscript files can contain commands to open, create, copy, delete, or rename other files. Therefore, when a browser that displays Postscript files is used to view another Postscript file, it could overwrite other files in the computer.

This reference includes configuration files that can be used to open the computer to other attacks, such as introducing a Trojan horse or computer virus into the environment in which the browser is used. Trojan horses are an executable code that disguises what it is actually doing. For example, it pretends to log the user into the system while actually coping the user's password to its own file, or altering files, including erasing and destroying records.

The problem with browsers and Internet access at large does not end there. Every time one logs into an Internet site he may be giving away valuable information about himself, his financial status, and his shopping habits. This started some years ago with *cookies*, which in Web jargon, are unique identifiers or codes sent by the server to the browser so that volunteered personal information is remembered and pulled up automatically on the next visit. Theoretically, this appears to be a good idea; it saves the time and trouble of entering the same information again. Practically, however, such an approach has many perils because cookies are also used as tracking devices.

Many Internet users think that they are giving out anonymous information and do not realize that, at least for some Web companies, they have volunteered rather personal data. They did so with their partners by dealing with suppliers and clients on what they buy from or sell to them.

When personal data are linked with information from off-line databases, personal privacy takes leave.

Therefore, it is not surprising that many surveys show that the majority of Internet users have become concerned about on-line privacy and do not want to give up personal information. There have also been abuses by some of the Internet entities. Toysmart, a recently failed dot-com, tried to sell private customer information, including on-line shopping habits, contrary to its announced privacy policy.

True enough, the invasion of privacy is no Internet exclusive; it happens also with so-called "Big Brother" banks. *Bloomberg Markets* carried a story about a bank client who produced her driver's license and a credit card to back her claim on a $200 check written by her sister, a SouthTrust customer. The teller did not think that enough.[4] Increasingly, tellers demand that people who are not customers leave their thumbprints on the faces of checks before the bank hands over any money.

Banks respond to the public's criticism about privacy invasion by saying that they are assuming rising risk. The American Bankers Association (ABA) says that check fraud costs the industry about $1 billion a year. Computers, scanners, and laser printers have made life easier for counterfeiters. Thumbprinting can reduce the number of bad checks passed at a bank by an estimated 60% or more, according to the ABA.[4] The invasion of personal privacy has a price, (see however the sixth section on biometrics).

FRIEND OR FOE? THE CASE OF DIGITAL SIGNATURES

As a growing number of companies do business with each other over the Internet, the issue of identity becomes crucial. How does the company know that the counterparty is who it says it is? How does it know that a document or transaction comes from whom it says it comes from? The answer, one may think, is a digital signature or certificate, a sort of electronic fingerprint. Theoretically, this cannot be duplicated or stolen by an impostor. But what is the reliability of the solution and who is to act as the authority for maintaining and managing electronic fingerprints? Will individual companies track the certificates from all their trusted partners themselves? Will they rely on specialized and periodically verified certification authorities? Will financial institutions that bear ultimate responsibility for electronic funds transfer be responsible for signature validation?

There appear to be no valid answers to these queries. Practically everything rests on the hope that "it will not happen to me." Some governments have been more inclined than others to move ahead with digital signatures. In the U.S., a simple click of a mouse would be enough to make documents legally binding, as the new national digital signature law takes effect. The pros say e-signatures will revolutionize virtually every aspect of consumer transactions. Contrarians warn that such a revolution will take time to settle, flaws will only show up through practice, and many social and technical hurdles stand in the way.

Unlike physical signatures, which remain practically the same over the years, digital signatures change with the transaction or message used and, evidently, with the person. Signatures are created with a private key, an algorithm, and can only be verified by means of a digital identity. After enactment into law, they are legally binding.

A digital ID contains a unique public key sent with each message to verify the signature. This ID is issued by a trusted third party, which typically is a certification authority. For reasons of security management, digital signature systems are going through as many digital IDs as there are electronic merchants registered in an on-line digital ID directory. From a security viewpoint, this is preferable to a single digital identity. Time will tell how reliable this choice is.

Eventually, this technology may save mountains of paperwork and speed up on-line business-to-business transactions. Therefore, many people applauded when, in July 2000, President Bill Clinton signed the Electronic Signatures in Global and National Commerce Act with a swipe of a smart card containing his digital signature held in a chip. Employing digital technology to sign the bill into law made good publicity, but President Clinton also used a pen to sign the paper document — just in case. Even the pros admit that this system is not perfect, but can be reasonably expected to improve over time as experience is gained in digital authentication and hidden weakness in methodology are weeded out. Some major failures may help to find and close loopholes existing in the use of e-signatures.

Merchant and consumer confidence will significantly increase if the system operator provides liability coverage, which some digital signature systems plan to do. Still, a number of challenges remain. One of the most important, even if not generally appreciated, is how to build a secure electronic cash system on an insecure Internet. Several people and companies tried in the 1990s without any great success.

Proponents and opponents of digital signatures agree that giving them the same legal standing as conventional ink-on-paper signatures is essential to further evolution of Internet commerce. Protection provided by laws, however, can only go so far. The most important factor in the use of digital signatures will be their acceptance by companies and consumers; this cannot be legislated.

A systems look at problems associated with digital signatures is important. If the company is or intends to be a major player in Internet commerce, then it should thoroughly analyze digital signatures' weaknesses; its findings should significantly influence the enterprise architecture. Among the elements to be examined is that conducting business-to-business transactions requires a number of documents and associated confirmations. For example, signatures are needed for placing bids, approving purchases, and creating contracts.

Now that there is national legislation backing e-signatures in the U.S., some paperwork can be eliminated, but the risks remain. Technology companies see a bonanza in providing support software that can manage the complex business processes which will eventually replace current paper-based deals. On the other hand, a number of obstacles exists, not the least of which is public confidence in the certification authority (CA).

The digital certificate will involve the certification authority, which acts as a trusted intermediary and whose job is characterized by many layered functions along the "onion skin" principle shown in Figure 16.5. The CA's certification and the government's weight behind it are indispensable in acting as building blocks of Internet commerce in which people and companies have confidence. The principle is fairly simple: when two parties meet for the first time over the Internet to transact, they do not necessarily trust each other; trust can be improved by placing confidence in a mutually appreciated third party who certifies both parties.

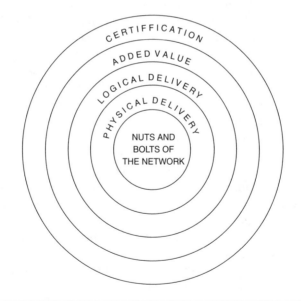

Figure 16.5   A trusted intermediary will be characterized by many-layered functions; the outer layer is security.

There is no fast and dirty way to authenticate identities, including e-signatures, on-line without some authority which guarantees the process of transacting. This is not news; the same principle has existed since the beginning of commerce. Some task-specific CA solutions are already familiar inside some companies. The Federal Reserve Bank, for example, is used to control access to information and certify the sender of a document.

New challenges arise because digital signatures on the Internet must promote widespread usage while always keeping in mind that trust and trustworthiness are the foundations of security. The risk is that, at the same time, trust assumptions may be illusory. Real-life applications seldom handle these assumptions correctly; therefore, the digital ID system should use an operating characteristics curve (OC curves; see the last section in this chapter).

Erroneous trust assumptions can be made at any point. There is a dual risk: one may reject a trusted party or accept an untrusted one. Enterprise architects must constantly deal with trust issues, and not only in connection to the verification of electronic signatures. Proprietary design documents and other data, for instance, are often communicated over channels that should not be trusted.

One of the problems with digital signatures in real-life environments is that many software developers and computer users either misunderstand or completely ignore trust matters. They look at trust in issues along the small trail (and scope) of a single transaction, not as a dynamic process which can hit the system as a whole. It is very dangerous to ignore the fact that, although a given transaction may be secure by itself, the overall system may be untrustworthy. This involves major dangers.

CAN BIOMETRICS HELP IN SOLVING THE SECURITY PROBLEM?

Passwords once provided a reasonable degree of identity validation, but this is no longer the case. Fraudulent acts grow more sophisticated, and millions of people gain entry into and regularly commute in and out of hundreds or thousands of different applications on Web sites.

Recall also that the personal identification number (PIN) paradigm has started to break down. Among alternatives, biometrics offer a way to renew the process of user authorization by substituting a fingerprint, or other biosolution, to password or PIN technology. Once the user is identified by, say, his or her fingerprint, a proxy system can then enter a highly randomized password for that user in the accessed system.

The fourth section noted that the use of fingerprints now enters the banking business at the teller level. Now fingerprints and other biometrics are in Internet business. In the broadest possible definition, the term indicates the scanning of body parts for use in identification. According to the International Biometric Group, there are six major areas of biometric measurement. Four of them have to do with scanning the iris, fingers, hands, face. The other two are based on recognizing someone by signature or voice. Biometrics-based solutions are applied to different processes associated with security, including monitoring and fraud prevention. Certain issues differentiate biometrics from other forms of security, providing a broader or better defined frame of reference.

Password security, for instance, can determine only whether a person knows the proper password. It does not verify that the person entering the password is the individual authorized to do so. By contrast, biometric systems determine whether a given sample, such as voice, comes from a specific individual by comparing that sample with the reference biometric, in this case, a reference voiceprint which is the standard against which the newly input voice sample is evaluated.

Some biometrics are image-based, for example, iris scanning through specialized equipment. Compared to PIN, signature verification, voice recognition or fingerprinting, iris recognition is a different ballgame. For example, a person walks up to a machine and inserts his credit card. A video camera captures an image of either the customer's right or left eye; this image is converted into a digital code and compared with one already stored for that specific individual. With current equipment, this process takes about 5 seconds. If the system perceives a match, the customer can proceed. Otherwise, access, or the transaction, is refused. Recognition is based only on the immutable structures of the iris, which include the trabecular meshwork of connective tissue, collagenous stromal fibers, ciliary processes, contraction furrows, crypts, vasculature, rings, corona, coloration, and freckles.

In a way which resembles individual fingerprints, most of these characteristics are specific to a given person, established by random processes before birth. The iris' pattern is different in each eye and appears to persist virtually unchanged throughout life. Hence, it is a good ID: even identical twins have unique iris morphology. No prosthesis can defeat the system because it detects the minute pulsations and pupil changes that indicate living tissue. This, however, also constitutes the weaknesses of the solution. Some years ago the FBI advised against using the retina for identification because it is conceivable that criminals may extract the eyes of people to use the unique appearance of their retinas to take money from the system.

An interesting comparison from a security viewpoint is between eye-scan, smart card, and GSM. If a card is lost, the finder typically needs to know the card holder's access code (usually a PIN) to use it. Experts suggest that future smart card systems may be able to check the card holder's eye-scan, voice print, fingerprint, or hand print. This, however, may pose more security problems than it solves.

The service smart card might provide for establishing identities and has been central to the adoption of chip-in card modules in mobile phones, particularly for digital systems like GSM. A subscriber identification module (SIM) plugs into the phone and personalizes the phone to the card holder. Theory says this approach is secure; in practice, however, theft of GSM and mobile telephony cards is on the increase. A whole new industry of fraud is based on it.

This is a different way of saying that there are no "ideal" security solutions, including use of biometrics. In principle, a valid approach to the employment of any identification system, its methodology, and its tools must be universal in its implementation, and unique in that it works on the basis of different ID characteristics possessed by each person.

A valid solution should also be permanent, with chosen characteristics neither changing nor being read by different sensors in a different manner. They must also be easily quantifiable, and such quantitative identification should be dependable, expressed at a given level of confidence (see the next section). The system designers working on the enterprise architecture should assure the performance of the chosen solution: its accuracy, speed, resource requirements, and operational factors.

Finally, the solution to be chosen should be socially acceptable. People must be willing to use it in their daily lives without stress or regrets. It should also be robust. Systems easy to fool through fraudulent methods must be rejected outright. All this is a tall order. Only time will tell if biometrics are the answer to security problems outlined in this chapter.

CONCLUSION

There is no doubt that an enterprise architecture needs rigorous, sustainable, and reliable security solutions. Evaluating the performance of identification, authentication, privacy, and security is a challenging research topic. The overall performance of a system must be assessed in terms of its accuracy, precision, speed, and cost. Other factors, like ease-of-use and overall dependability, also affect efficiency.

Presently available security solutions, whether hardware-based, software-based, or hybrid, are not perfect. They will sometimes mistakenly accept an impostor as a valid individual or reject a valid individual. The concept of committing these two types of errors is known from operating characteristics curves, and finds wide applications in quality control and finance.[5] Figure 16.6 shows an OC curve from a recent project in the evaluation of credit risk associated to commercial paper.

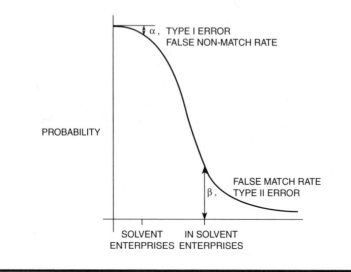

Figure 16.6 Operating characteristics curve and level of confidence.

In the specific case of biometric identification, for instance, type I error (or α) and type II error (or β) are termed false nonmatch rate (FNR) and false match rate (FMR). Their magnitude depends upon how the biometric system operates and the size of the sample on which they are based. As with all technical solutions, there are trade-offs between a system's FMR and FNR at different operating levels. At each level, α and β constitute a comprehensive measure of the solution's accuracy in a given operating environment.

It is high time to quantify a system's reliability in terms of the security which it provides. True security can be an elusive concept because it is kept more or less on qualitative terms and subject to undocumented statements. This permits each vendor or IT manager to succeed in saying whatever he pleases in terms of security assurance.

Internet commerce applications, where concern about security is great, must operate at a small α, which defines the level of confidence. Even $\alpha = 0.01$ gives a confidence level of 99% with 1% probability of error, in the sense of being out of the defined boundary. Designers of enterprise architectures will be well advised to use reliability engineering and quality control standards in connection to their solution, and to study the efficiency of different alternatives through experimental design.

They should always keep in mind that security today is the Achilles heel of electronic transactions. It will remain that way until more rigorous norms are established, along with statistical tests of hypotheses and quality control charts, which permit one to project and then verify the long term reliability of a security system. General Electric's Six Sigma is a good methodology for doing so.[6] It is not enough to acknowledge the weaknesses of current approaches to security, however. It is also necessary to prove the dependability of new solutions in a factual and documented manner.

Experimental design, confidence intervals, and advanced statistical analysis comprise one of the two pillars on which enterprise architecture solutions should be based. The other is the steady improvement of fundamental knowledge representation of rules and regulations for better operability and executability. Provision for the growing role of agents is a basic consideration in a dynamic environment used and managed by non-IT specialists, as are supply chain and other settings involving a growing level of collaboration.

REFERENCES

1. Chorafas, D.N., *Implementing and Auditing the Internal Control System*, Macmillan, London, 2001.
2. Chorafas, D.N., *Transaction Management*, Macmillan, London, 1998.
3. The MIT Report, September, 2000.
4. *Bloomberg Markets*, October, 2000.
5. Chorafas, D.N., *Statistical Processes and Reliability Engineering*, D. Van Nostrand Co., Princeton, NJ, 1960.
6. Chorafas, D.N., *Integrating ERP, Supply Chain Management and Smart Materials*, Auerbach/CRC Press, New York, 2001.

INDEX

A

Advanced statistical analysis, 98
Agents, 21, 161, 181, 182, 184, 185, 187, 188, 259
Ambient computing, 139
Amdahl's Law, 48
American National Standards Institute (ANSI), 305
Analogical reasoning, 154
Any-to-any networking, 159
Applets, 323
Architectural design, 25
Architectural semantics, 44
Atomic unit, 63, 100

B

Benchmarks, 38, 39
Bill of materials (BOM), 234
Biomaterials, 127
Biometrics, 339, 352, 354
Black-Scholes algorithm, 102, 103
Broadband multimedia, 106
Broadband wireless access (BWA), 116
Business oriented architecture, 33
Business process reengineering, 13
Business strategy, 29
Business-to-business (B2B), 249, 278, 310
Business-to-consumer (B2C), 249, 278

C

C++, 88
Certification authority, 349, 350
Chief knowledge officer (CKO), 215
Chorafas postulate, 53
Code division multiple access (CDMA), 117
Coherence, 35

Command and control, 59, 248
Command center simulation, 150
Commodity software, 37
Communications and computers system, 25
Computer aided design (CAD), 86, 221, 238, 271
Computer aided manufacturing (CAM), 221, 271
Computer aided software engineering (CASE), 221
Conceptual specifications, 87
Concurrent engineering, 13, 103, 227, 231–233
Contingency plans, 337
Corporate memory facility (CMF), 199, 215, 221
Cross-database access, 188, 189
Customer relationship management (CRM), 12, 315

D

Database bandwidth, 206
Database management, 207, 210
Database management systems, 135
Database mining, 212, 214
Decision support systems (DSS), 12
Defense Advanced Projects Agency (DARPA), 136, 139
Denial of service (DOS), 339
Dense wave division multiplexing (DWDM), 49
Deregulation, 45, 300
Design reviews, 232, 233
Directed graph, 217
Disintermediation, 251
Distributed information systems, 45
DoCoMo, 117, 118
Dynamic patterning, 154